D1593363

Humanism in the Age of Henry VIII

Maria Dowling

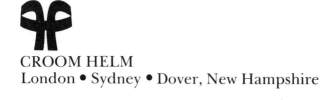

CROOM HELM
London • Sydney • Dover, New Hampshire

© Maria Dowling 1986
Croom Helm Ltd., Provident House, Burrell Row
Beckenham, Kent BR3 1AT
Croom Helm Australia Pty Ltd, Suite 4, 6th Floor,
64–76 Kippax Street, Surry Hills, NSW 2010, Australia

British Library Cataloguing in Publication Data

Dowling, Maria
  Humanism in the age of Henry VIII
  1. Humanism   2. Philosophy—England—History
  I. Title
  144'.0942   B778

ISBN 0-7099-0864-4

Croom Helm, 51 Washington Street, Dover,
New Hampshire 03820, USA

Library of Congress Cataloging in Publication Data applied for

For Margaret and Francis Dowling

Phototypeset by Sunrise Setting, Torquay, Devon
Printed and bound in Great Britain by
Biddles Ltd, Guildford and King's Lynn

Contents

Note and Acknowledgements

In references to and quotations from sixteenth-century documents all spellings and punctuation have been modernised and all contractions expanded. Quotations in foreign languages have been given in English translation in order to preserve the consistency of the narrative. Where possible, published translations have been used and acknowledged, such as the English version of Erasmus's letters published by the University of Toronto. Where these fail I have had recourse to my own translations.

With regard to nomenclature, it would be inaccurate to label the subjects of Henry VIII as 'Catholics' or 'Protestants'; not merely because such terms are anachronistic, but also because very little is known about the specific beliefs of individuals. Consequently, I have adopted Dr Starkey's suggestion of referring to those who opposed doctrinal innovation as 'conservatives', and to those who favoured it as 'evangelicals' or 'upholders of the gospel'. This last is the term used by such people to describe themselves. In addition, the phrase 'new learning' as used in this study stands for humanism rather than radical theology. This was the original meaning of the term, and the sense in which it seems to have been most used by contemporaries.

This book is based on the research for a doctoral thesis supervised by the late Professor W. D. J. Cargill Thompson of King's College, London and by Dr David Starkey of the London School of Economics, and I would like to express my gratitude to them both. I am grateful to the Twenty-Seven Foundation of London University for financial assistance with the production of this book. I would also like to thank the staff of the following institutions for their co-operation and assistance: the British Library, Institute of Historical Research, Public Record Office and Warburg Institute, London; the Bodleian Library, Oxford and Cambridge University Library, and the Bibliothèque Albert I, Brussels. I am grateful to Sandra Tracey and Judith Rowbotham for invaluable practical assistance, and I would like to thank Stephen Baskerville for, among other things, much useful discussion of the subject.

Introduction

The difficulty of defining humanism has never been entirely overcome, while the philosophical connotations of the term have led to confused and often anachronistic speculations as to its nature. Humanists of the fifteenth and sixteenth centuries belonged to no recognisable sect or co-ordinated movement equipped with a universally accepted manifesto of belief, and their enthusiasm for the new learning did not prevent them from indulging in vitriolic controversies with one another. Furthermore, since humanism was nebulous enough to cross doctrinal barriers, scholars like Erasmus, Reuchlin and Lefèvre might receive praise or vilification from conservatives and evangelicals alike. In this study the terms 'humanism' and 'new learning' will not be used as blanket terms for renaissance philosophy, nor will they hold the anachronistic connotation of a 'humane' viewpoint or a preoccupation with the dignity of man.

For present purposes, humanism may be defined as the reappraisal of religious and secular thinking through examination of the literary bases of theology and philosophy: that is, the Christian scriptural and patristic writings and the 'acceptable' pagan classics. Such a return to fundamentals necessitated the establishment of critical and authoritative tests, which in turn called for a developed knowledge of the classical and biblical tongues, Hebrew, Greek and Latin. From these primary concerns arose a number of auxiliary disciplines: concern with linguistic accuracy and the purification of Latin; translation of the texts into the vernacular for the benefit of laymen; and admiration for and imitation of the oratory and literary style of the ancient Greeks and Romans.

The diversity of humanist opinions was immense. Individual scholars differed over such vital points as the relative weight to be accorded Christian and pagan authorities, the utility of the sacred tongues, the place of medieval scholasticism in Christian learning, the value of the vernacular, and the advisability of biblical study for laymen. Interest in Greek and Hebrew did not necessarily preclude an appreciation of scholasticism, and acceptance of non-scholastic biblical exegesis did not guarantee enthusiasm for non-Christian literature. Thus automatic assumptions about a particular humanist's precepts and priorities cannot be made.

Furthermore, in addition, humanist aims and the practicability of their achievement emerged slowly over a long period of time. For example, in England Greek was occasionally taught in a private capacity from the 1470s, but no college statutes provided for its formal study until Fisher's code for St John's, Cambridge in 1516, and no complete Greek text was published in this country until 1543, when Cheke edited two of Chrysostom's sermons.[1] This slow evolution means that it would be unfair to measure the achievements of a figure like Skelton against those of, say, Cheke or Ascham, though all three may be considered humanists. Thus in terms of humanistic progress it is unrealistic and inappropriate to compare the age of Henry VIII with that of Elizabeth. Indeed, the flowering of the renaissance in the latter part of the sixteenth century owed an inestimable debt to the pioneers of the earlier period.

Furthermore, in addition, the religious character of the new learning changed as Henry's reign went on. Humanism was originally non-doctrinal, concerned with reform of devotional practices and ecclesiastical administration rather than with re-evaluation of belief. However, knowledge of the tongues and the existence of authoritative scriptural and patristic texts provided instruments for those who wished to challenge accepted dogma. The new learning was thus affected by the advent of Luther, and humanists were divided between those who were sympathetic to the views of the continental reformers and those who strove to refute them. In the early 1520s the official English response to Luther was unanimously hostile, the King himself leading the literary campaign against him. However, Henry's desire to annul his marriage with Katherine of Aragon and the influence over him of Anne Boleyn — a determined and consistent upholder of the gospel — meant that radical English reformers could be of use to the King and could hope for a hearing at court.

Moreover, as succeeding events made the reinstatement of Katherine and reconciliation with Rome virtually impossible, anti-papalism became the norm rather than a heresy tolerated for its political expediency. Consequently conservative humanists, seeing the danger of vesting authority in the church in a capricious royal 'supreme head', lost the impetus to contribute to public affairs and left the initiative to their more radical brethren. This is not to say that evangelicals walked unscathed in the later years of the reign;

but the English church's independence of Rome, combined with the powerful backing of their court-patrons, ensured that it would be their influence which prevailed.

It is essential, however, not to overestimate the status and therefore the political and cultural importance of scholars under Henry VIII, be they conservative or evangelical. It is all too easily assumed that Henrician England was a humanist paradise in which scholars found glory and financial reward. In fact, the renaissance came late to England, and encountered there not merely uninterest, but active hostility. As late as 1519 Erasmus could be publicly accused of heresy at court, and only the year before the new studies had been attacked at Oxford. Evangelical humanists, who might easily be open to the penalties of the law, were exceptionally vulnerable. In addition, if the effectiveness and influence of humanist scholarship is to be measured, the social and political standing of its proponents must be understood, and thus some remarks on the machinery of patronage are necessary.

Briefly, the patronage system may be considered as a pyramid, with the King — the ultimate source of preferment and protection — at its apex and scholarly suitors at its base. Between these two extremes ran a complex network of intermediaries and lesser sponsors. These figures, though often disposing of little direct preferment, were important as points of contact between the great court-patrons on the one hand, and scholars and academic institutions on the other. Erasmus, for example, constantly relied on agents at court like Ammonio and Pace to remind his English patrons of his scholarly labours and financial troubles, while the humanists of Oxford owed the continuance of Greek studies there to More's and Pace's defence of the new learning at court. The most eminent middleman in scholarly patronage was William Butts, whose unobtrusive services to the evangelical cause played a key part in the course of the Henrician reformation.

Butts occupied a singularly advantageous position. On the one hand he was a royal physician, and it may be imagined that regular attendance on a prince as fascinated by medicine and terrified of disease as Henry VIII would render the appointment an influential one. On the other hand he was a graduate of Cambridge, where he had been a member of Gonville Hall, and he took pains to maintain contact with his *alma mater*. Butts's services to Cambridge and its scholars were praised by his protégé Thomas Smith, who called him 'the refuge of all students, and chief guardian and ornament of this university', and by Ascham, who posthumously commended him as the patron and protector of Cambridge. Butts was also a noted evangelical, characterised by the martyrologist Foxe as 'a singular good man, and a special favourer of good proceedings', and his discreet but important role in the advancement of reform and its adherents is evident from the royal divorce until his death in 1545.[2]

The complexity of the patronage system and the importance of intermediary sponsors can be demonstrated by the early career of one of Butts's evangelical clients. Hugh Latimer was already notorious as an inflammatory preacher at Cambridge when Butts approached him as a potential supporter of the King's case during the university referendum on the Aragon marriage. After serving as one of the delegates appointed by senate to debate the matter in February 1530 he was taken to court by his patron, where he preached before the King on the presentation of the university's verdict and 'remained a certain time in the said Dr Butts's chamber, preaching then in London very often'. The joint intercession of Butts and Cromwell procured him a royal benefice in Wiltshire which adjoined the property of Sir Edward Bainton. The two men corresponded on religious matters, and in 1533 Bainton became Anne Boleyn's vice-chamberlain while Latimer was appointed one of her chaplains. Latimer's elevation to the see of Worcester in 1535 has variously been attributed to Anne, Butts and Cromwell, but it is now impossible to discern the direct influence behind this promotion.[3]

Consciousness of the different levels of the system was expressed in the humanist convention of addressing all patrons except the King as 'Maecenas'. Thus, for example, Robert Whittinton dedicated his *Mirror or Glass of Manners and Wisdom* to Sir Francis Bryan because, he said, the latter was prepared

> . . .not only by your beneficial report to such which be studious to set forth good and virtuous works most necessary to the knowledge of moral wisdom, whereof ensueth the advancement of commonwealths, but also to promote such into the favour of our most redoubted and bountiful prince King Henry VIII; in like manner as Maecenas was wont to do with his sovereign Augustus Caesar, that puissant prince.[4]

Similarly, Thomas Langley called Sir Anthony Denny 'a very Maecenas of all toward wits', while Nicholas Bourbon addressed

Butts as 'Tu mihi Maecenas, tu mihi, Butte, pater'. Mountjoy in his invitation to Erasmus of 1509 declared that the King was 'not *octavus* so much as Octavius', an allusion that hints at his own ability to play Maecenas to Henry's Augustus and Erasmus's Horace.[5]

This literary convention emphasises the dependent position of the scholar. For erudite gentlemen like More, Elyot and Morley, the new learning provided knowledge and accomplishments which might contribute to their private edification or public careers, but which were not essential to their livelihood. For the most part, however, scholars were men of little social standing or useful influence. Though their skills were used and appreciated by ministers and courtiers, they were held in low estimation. Richard Croke's status as a classical scholar of international repute did not prevent his positive ill-treatment by the servants of Henry VIII's bastard son, to whom he had been appointed tutor. Even so eminent a humanist as Juan Luis Vives, another scholar of European renown and a favourite of Katherine of Aragon and Henry, could complain of his living conditions in London and voice his fear of falling ill and thus losing the attention and favour of the court. Hadrianus Junius, a Dutch scholar in the service of the Duke of Norfolk, wrote bitterly of his life at Kenninghall among the uncouth and disrespectful retainers of the Howards. (For Croke's troubles, see Chapter Six, below. For those of Vives and Junius, see Chapter Five.) Thus scholars occupied a lowly position, and both their personal well-being and the adoption of their ideas depended on the goodwill of the great.

Paradoxically, however, their very personal insignificance often meant that scholars could survive the tumultuous events of the reign; as, indeed, could lesser patrons like Butts. The sustained activity of such intermediaries ensured continuity of contact between the lowest level of the patronage pyramid and its mutable higher tiers. While political misfortune and internecine factional strife removed the great patrons of reform — Katherine of Aragon, Wolsey, Anne Boleyn, Cromwell — scholars and their lesser sponsors, protected by their unimportance, could survive and regroup under new leadership. In this way command of patronage changed hands, while the apparently less significant figures, together with the ideology they propounded, could continue.

6   Introduction

Notes

1. *D. Ioanni Chrysostomi homiliae duae* (Reyner Wolfe, London, 1543). For Fisher's statutes, J. E. B. Mayor (ed.), *Early Statutes of the College of St John the Evangelist* (Macmillan & Co., Cambridge, 1859).
2. John Venn, *Biographical History of Gonville and Caius College, 1349–1713* (7 vols., Cambridge University Press, Cambridge, 1897), vol. 1, p. 17; Roger Ascham, *Whole Works*, Rev. Dr Giles (ed.) (3 vols., J. R. Smith, London, 1865, 64), epistle 60 to Thomas Wendy; John Foxe, *Acts and Monuments*, S. R. Cattley (ed.) (8 vols., Seeley & Burnside, London, 1837), vol. 7, p. 454. For Henry VIII's medical interest, A. S. McNalty, *Henry VIII, A Difficult Patient* (Christopher Johnson, London, 1952).
3. Foxe, *Acts and Monuments*, vol. 7, p. 454, from whence the quotation comes Cf. the amplified account in William Gilpin, *Lives of Hugh Latimer and Bernard Gilpin* (R. Blamire, London, 1780).
4. Pseudo-Seneca, *Mirror or Glass of Manners and Wisdom*, Richard Whittinton (trans.) (Middleton, London, 1547), preface to Bryan.
5. Thomas Langley, *Abridgement of the Notable Work of Polydore Vergil* (Grafton, London, 1546), preface to Denny; Bourbon, *Nugae* (Dolet, Lyons, 1538), Book 7, no. 113 to Butts; P. S. and H. M. Allen, H. W. Garrod (eds), *Opus Epistolarum Des. Erasmi Roterodami* (11 vols., Clarendon Press, Oxford, 1906–47), no. 215 from Mountjoy, translated in Wallace K. Ferguson (ed.), *The Epistles of Erasmus*, R. A. B. Mynors and D. F. S. Thomson (trans.) (6 vols., University of Toronto Press, Toronto, Buffalo, London, 1974–82).

1   The Young King and His Court

I

Rapturous euphoria greeted the accession of Henry VIII in the spring of 1509, and humanists were among the most vocal in praising the young King. Indeed, one of the most famous descriptions of the mood of England at that time was sent to Erasmus by the humanist patron Mountjoy:

> Heaven smiles, earth rejoices; all is milk and honey and nectar. Tight-fistedness is well and truly banished. Our King's heart is set not upon gold or jewels or mines of ore, but upon virtue, reputation and eternal renown.[1]

To understand the great hopes entertained by humanists in 1509 one must look back at the limited progress of the new learning in England during the fifteenth century and at the educational and cultural influences on Henry during his father's lifetime.

In the fifteenth century knowledge of the biblical tongues and access to humanistic texts were confined to the small number of Italian visitors to England and of Englishmen who had some contact with the centres of learning in Italy.[2] The former came as papal legates and collectors, scholars in quest of research materials and patrons, and teachers at the universities. As papal officials they found favour and employment under Lancastrians, Yorkists and Tudors, but in other spheres the prospects for foreign scholars resident in England were somewhat limited. Poggio, for example, joined Cardinal Beaufort's household in 1418 but departed in 1422, disappointed at the scarcity of classical texts in English libraries and the dearth of interested English men of letters. On the other hand, there was a market in England for humanist books. The outstanding bibliophile of the century was Duke Humphrey of Gloucester, who commissioned Latin texts and Greek classics in translation from Italian scholars, donated large numbers of books to Oxford during his lifetime, and made bequests to both universities. Other early collectors, among them Robert Fleming, William Grey Bishop of Ely and James Goldwell, Bishop of Norwich, acquired manuscripts on their travels abroad which they bequeathed to Oxford and Cambridge libraries.[3]

Since little humanist scholarship was to be found in England itself before the 1490s, interested scholars went abroad for instruction. A number of Englishmen — Grey, his protégé John Free, Fleming, John Gunthorpe and John Tiptoft, Earl of Worcester — studied rhetoric at Ferrara under Guarino da Verona. A few scholars, among them William Selling, Prior of Christchurch, Canterbury, learned Greek; and Free possibly also acquired some knowledge of Hebrew. These pioneers, who brought back with them the slender beginnings of materials for the new learning, were followed in the last two decades of the century by scholars who were to play a direct part in the establishment of humanism under Henry VIII.

Pride of place belongs to William Grocyn of Magdalen and New College, Oxford, who studied at Florence with Poliziano and Chalcondyles and met Aldo Manuzio in Venice. On his return to Oxford in 1491 he resided and taught Greek at Exeter College. The direct impact of his teaching — the size of the audience, and the number inspired to further study — cannot be known, but an important beginning had been made, in that one of the ancient tongues vital to the new learning had been taught publicly by a native scholar. Grocyn's sphere of influence shifted to London in about 1502. He became intimately acquainted with More and Colet, and Richard Croke joined his household from King's, Cambridge in 1508. His mind, like John Fisher's, could accommodate both the new learning and the schoolmen, and an incomplete catalogue of his books reveals the catholicity of his taste: besides a Greek and Latin new testament and a printed Greek dictionary there are Greek and Latin classics and works by scholastics, the fathers, and more modern authors including Lorenzo Valla, Petrarch, Boccaccio, Erasmus and Gaguin.[4]

John Colet, another traveller in Italy, was as widely read as Grocyn, but he brought back to Oxford a new approach to scripture rather than a knowledge of Greek. His marathon series of lectures on the epistles of Paul, which probably began at Michaelmas 1497, marked a startling departure in biblical exegesis. Colet considered the text as it stood, taking its obvious rather than its allegorical meaning. His literary references were not to Scotus or Aquinas but to neo-platonists like Pico and Ficino; though even here he avoided over-subtleties. This breath of exegetial fresh air was apparently well received, and when Colet was promoted to the Deanery of St

Paul's in 1504 he carried his scriptural exposition into the pulpit.[5]

William Lily, later Colet's first highmaster at St Paul's School and the most influential grammarian of the sixteenth century, probably learned Greek at Rhodes and studied in Italy under Sulpitius and Pomponius Laetus. The fruits of this Greek and Latin learning were employed in London, where he taught from about 1495 and became an intimate friend of More. Another member of the London circle of humanists was Thomas Linacre, who is thought to have spent his early years at Christchurch, Canterbury (where Selling taught Greek) and to have studied at Florence with the children of Lorenzo the Magnificent. Certainly, he studied under Leonicenus at Vicenza, met Ermolao Barbaro in Rome and graduated MD from Padua in 1496. He assisted in the preparation of the Aldine Aristotle between 1495 and 1498, and in the following year Aldo published his translation of Proclus's *De Sphaera*, dedicated to Prince Arthur. It seems unlikely, as is often alleged, that Linacre was tutor to Arthur or royal physician before 1509, but he did teach in London.[6]

The private studies and personal influence of these individuals were echoed in the wider sphere of the revision of academic curricula. The medieval university was dominated by the study of theology, taught according to the dictates and commentaries of the schoolmen without direct reference to the texts expounded; the undergraduate prepared for this by four years of grammar, logic and dialectic. The most important discipline after theology was law, and there was some provision for the study of medicine. Humanists, with their concern for linguistic accuracy, recognised that undergraduate instruction in Latin grammar generally left the student inadequately prepared for more complex studies; indeed, all too often scholars would be plunged into logic and dialectic after a single term of grammar. In addition, an awareness was growing that moral and natural philosophy were more fitting adjuncts to theology than was law. This subtle shift in emphasis found expression in the academic bias of two new foundations at Oxford and Cambridge respectively.

The statues of Magdalen College, Oxford, established in 1455 by Bishop Waynflete of Winchester, show a marked departure from the priorities of early founders. Whereas 20 of the 70 fellows of New College (founded 1379) were to study civil or common law, as were 16 of the 40 fellows of All Souls (founded 1438), Wayflete only provided for two law students on his foundation of 40 fellows. On the other hand, he established public lectures in theology and its auxiliary studies, moral and natural philosophy. More directly important for the progress of humanism in England was Waynflete's provision of a grammar school, integrally a department of the college but open to all members of the university. The under-graduates of Magdalen itself were not to commence logic and dialectic until judged proficient in grammar, and at least two or three of them were to apply themselves 'so long to grammatical and poetical and other humane arts that they could not only profit themselves but be able also to instruct and educate others'. These selected scholars were to be the masters and ushers of Magdalen School, and early teachers there included the grammarians Stanbridge, Anwykyll, Holt and Lily, and Wolsey.[7]

Similarly, Godshouse was founded at Cambridge to redress the long neglect of grammar. In 1439 William Bingham petitioned Henry VI for permission to establish a college for the training of grammar teachers, since he had found 'no further north than Ripon seventy schools void or more that were occupied all at once within fifty years past, because that there is so great scarcity of masters of grammar'.[8] The fellows of Godshouse were bound to become grammarians and to accept a post at any school built within the last 40 years, provided a suitable salary was offered. Besides studying dialectic and logic, they were to apply themselves to the subtler and deeper points of grammar, versification and metrification, and to read poets such as Priscian and Virgil.

The moderate innovations of the founders of Magdalen and Godshouse were repeated and to some extent carried further by Margaret Beaufort, whose benefactions to the universities began after the start of her association with John Fisher, sent to court on Cambridge university business in 1495 and Margaret's chaplain within two years. Fisher's object was to channel his patron's piety into educational endowment, and in this he was successful. In December 1496 and March 1497 Henry VII granted his mother licences to found theology lectures at both universities. The Oxford lecture was not formally inaugurated until the appointment of John Roper in 1500, but from Trinity term 1497 Edmund Wylsford of Oriel College was lecturing in an informal capacity in the schools. Similarly the Cambridge lecture was not properly established until 1502, when Fisher was the reader, but the Grace Book for 1498–9 shows that lectures were being delivered in Margaret's name at a much earlier date. She also founded a preachership at Cambridge in 1504 whose holder was to preach six sermons a year at specified places in Cambridgeshire, London and elsewhere.[9]

A further act of practical piety was Margaret's re-foundation in 1506 of the now decayed Godshouse; possibly the college was chosen in preference to other establishments favoured by Henry VI because of Fisher's longstanding association with its Master, John Syclyng. The statutes of Christ's College (as the new foundation was called) have been applauded for their originality, but in fact they show a marked dependence on those of Godshouse. The readers of both houses were to lecture on logic, dialectic and philosophy (with some additional grammar instruction for the Godshouse men) and from the ancient poets and orators. Christ's also honoured the intentions of the Godshouse founders by stipulating that six of the scholars should devote themselves to grammar so that they could teach anywhere in England at a school which offered a reasonable salary. The important difference between the two foundations — and the point which constitutes any claim that the establishment of Christ's furthered the new learning — is that Lady Margaret's college was designed, not for schoolmasters, but for theologians, who would receive there a more thorough grounding in grammar and rhetoric than was available elsewhere.

Neither Magdalen nor the Godshouse-Christ's establishment were humanist colleges in the sense that St John's, Cambridge and Corpus Christi, Oxford were to be; and the Lady Margaret theology lectures were so far from being devoted exclusively to the new learning that Wylsford expounded at Oxford 'the quodlibets of the subtle doctor', Duns Scotus. Nevertheless these new foundations were important because their provision of public platforms for the exposition of divinity and their emphasis on grammar and literature — the essential preliminaries to the new theological approach — created conditions favourable to the introduction and growth of the new learning in the universities.

If humanism made some small academic advances through the interest of court-patrons, the practical fruits of the new learning — eloquence, language and literary style — were used in government service. Humanists like Grey, Fleming, Gunthorpe and Shirwood were sent on diplomatic missions, while Italian papal officials continued to find favour and began to find literary employment in England. Polydore Vergil came as a sub-collector for Peter's Pence in about 1502; was commissioned by Henry VII to write a history of the kingdom in 1505; and in 1508 became Archdeacon of Wells. Andrea Ammonio was sent to England in about 1504; secured the patronage of Lord Mountjoy; and later became Latin secretary to

Henry VIII. Pietro Carmiliano held a minor administrative post under Edward IV and Richard III; and though dedications to Edward and his son and to a favourite of Richard's failed to secure him promotion, Henry VII made him royal chaplain and Latin secretary. He produced poems for state occasions throughout the reign and well into the following one.

The most crucial area in which scholars could serve at the early Tudor court was the education of Henry VII's children. Once more, the limitations of humanism at this time must be stressed. The princes' tutors were conservative, deficient in and suspicious of Greek, and apprehensive of the effect of some of the new studies on the revered body of medieval knowledge. There also seems to have been some friction between the older court group of Carmiliano, Skelton and André and the younger scholars of the Erasmus–Mountjoy connection. Nevertheless the royal tutors were alive to the importance of grammar and good literature, as the works they prepared for their pupils reveal.

All Henry VII's children learned French with Giles Duwes, later the royal librarian.[10] For the rest, Arthur was principally tutored by Bernard André of Toulouse, royal poet and historiographer and a protégé of Richard Fox, while Henry was taught as Duke of York by John Skelton and as Prince of Wales by William Hone. André prepared a number of grammatical works for Arthur's use, including a Latin vocabulary, treatises on rhetoric and literary composition, and works on orthography, 'the art of memory' and letter-writing. The fruits of the Prince's labours in this last field can be seen in his Latin correspondence with Katherine of Aragon. André also produced expositions and annotations of Pliny, Terence, Statius, Aulus Gelius, Cicero's letters, Virgil's *Eclogues* and *Aeneid* and Augustine's *City of God*, and later claimed that by the age of 15 his pupil 'had either committed to memory or read with his own eyes and leafed with his own fingers' the standard grammatical works, selections from Terence, Homer, Virgil and Ovid, and historians such as Thucydides, Livy, Tacitus and Caesar.[11]

Prince Henry's education is a matter of crucial interest, since his early influences largely determined his attitude to the new learning. Herbert of Cherbury's statement that Henry was chiefly taught theology because he was destined to be archbishop of Canterbury carries little weight, since he was less than ten years old when Arthur's death made him heir to the throne.[12] Skelton, on the other hand, indicates that Henry's early studies were largely grammatical and literary:

I gave him drink of the sugared well
Of Helicon's waters crystalline,
Acquainting him with the Muses nine.[13]

Indeed, the tutor's scholastic bias and his later fulminations against the 'excesses' of the new learning (probably partly aroused by the Wolseyan monopoly of education) should not detract from his literary interests and qualifications. Before becoming Henry's preceptor Skelton had translated Cicero's letters and Diodorus Siculus's *History of the World* into English, the latter from Poggio's Latin version. The works he prepared for Henry included a Latin grammar, treatises on 'royal demeanance', 'sovereignty' and 'honourous estate', and popular tracts from Latin and French with such titles as 'How Men should Flee Sin', 'The Art of Dying' and 'Dialogues of Imagination'.[14] All the same, his *Speculum Principis* (a short collection of moral saws taken chiefly from the Vulgate rather than a renaissance handbook in the style of Erasmus or Budé) is an apt reminder that one cannot expect to find in Henry VIII's education in the 1490s an exact parallel to Cheke's instruction of Prince Edward in the 1540s.[15]

A more significant educational influence on Henry than either Skelton or the shadowy Hone was William Blount, Lord Mountjoy, whom Erasmus reveals as the Prince's companion in studies. It was Mountjoy's closeness to Henry and his efforts to introduce the Prince to humanists that laid the foundations for the establishment of the new learning in England in the following reign. Doubtless it was Mountjoy who arranged Erasmus's and More's visit to the royal nursery at Eltham in 1499, and who secured an autograph reply to Erasmus' letter of condolence to Henry on the death of Philip the Fair of Castile. When Erasmus evinced scepticism about its authorship Mountjoy was able to reassure him by producing discarded drafts of Henry's letters. At a later date, when Henry's anti-Lutheran writings were widely attributed to Erasmus, the scholar told George of Saxony and Cochlaeus that their literary styles were similar because Mountjoy had encouraged the King to read Erasmus' works at an early age.[16]

Some account of Erasmus' reception in England will in fact provide a fitting conclusion to a description of the beginnings of humanism here, since it illustrates both the progress of the new learning and the prospects for scholars. Invited to England by Mountjoy, formerly his pupil in Paris, in 1499, Erasmus significantly chose to remain with his patron, who had access to the court, rather than to proceed to one of the universities. In fact, he only resorted to Oxford when political events prevented his leaving England. Apparently unimpressed with the university, and bravely telling Mountjoy that he would 'put up with all the boredom, and swallow every annoyance, for love of you', he none the less established contact with several congenial scholars, including Colet. He also met Grocyn, Linacre and More, probably in London.

On a subsequent visit in 1506 Erasmus made a determined effort to secure patronage by dedications to benefactors with court connections. Ruthal, Ursewick, Fox and Whitford received Lucian translations, while Archbishop Warham was given Euripides' *Hecuba*. He also procured a brief from Julius II against the possibility of his being offered an English living, and hinted to his superior at Steyn that he hoped for a benefice from Henry VII.[17] The concrete result of all this activity was a commission to accompany the sons of the King's physician to Italy as supervisor of their studies.

From the scholar's point of view, England on the eve of Henry VIII's accession was an attractive proposition. Erasmus's first visit was a financial success, and though the customs at Dover duly relieved him of the money collected from friends and patrons he was sufficiently eager for a second invitation to swallow his bitterness. The universities were not in themselves alluring, but Erasmus professed to be impressed by English scholarship, urging Robert Fisher to return home from Italy because England was so rich in learning 'that I have little longing for Italy, except for the sake of visiting it', and describing to Rogerus five or six men in London so profoundly learned that he doubted whether Italy itself held such scholars.[18] Erasmus sought potential benefactors among high-ranking clerics engaged in government business, but he placed his chief hope in the generosity of a nobleman with influence at court and — most importantly — with the heir to the throne. In 1509 Erasmus was in Italy, where he received invitations to England from Mountjoy and Warham; in view of his previous experiences and of current expectations, it is not surprising that he chose to leave the cradle of humanism and risk his fortune here.

II

Whatever the hopes of Erasmus's patrons and friends, it is notorious that the scholar was disappointed of the fantastic financial vista opened to him in 1509; but nevertheless the complex personality of Henry VIII undoubtedly bulked large in humanist expectations. On the one hand, the King was by no means a reliable or disinterested patron. While he appreciated and employed humanists as government and church servants he was loth to provide Erasmus with a permanent source of income since the latter plainly had no intention of living in England, and his enthusiasm for letters did not prevent his opposition to Fisher's acquisition of Margaret Beaufort's revenues for St John's college. On the other hand, he could be generous on occasion, giving individuals like Erasmus gifts of money and financing the studies of many scholars, including his kinsman Reginald Pole.

Henry's interest in learning and pride in his own accomplishments are attested by the steady stream of panegyric which issued from humanist pens in these early years. Ammonio told Erasmus in 1511, 'As for English news, there is hardly anything worth the hearing except about the King, who every day shows himself in a more godlike guise; but this is old news to you.' Erasmus himself in his dedication to Henry of Plutarch's *De Discrimine adulatoris et amici* expatiated on the King's virtues; Henry was to be applauded because he was not one of those who considered philosophy and kingship incompatible, but himself found time each day for reading and discussion. In 1518 he congratulated Henry on his literary culture, and told Sir Henry Guilford in 1519 that the King by his universal ability refuted those who said that knowledge of letters was a hindrance to a prince. In 1517 Richard Pace, diplomat and royal secretary, attributed the spread of learning largely to Henry himself:

> Englishmen have been given a great opportunity in our own time to apply themselves entirely to the finest of studies. Obviously, since we have a most noble King who far surpasses all other Christian princes in learning as well as in power. He's so disposed to all learned men that he hears nothing more willingly than conversations about learned men and books.[19]

Much of the praise was undoubtedly judicious flattery (which the King obviously appreciated), and the sugared compliments often accompanied hints for more solid remuneration than mere affability.[20] But at the same time correspondents of Erasmus who were unlikely or unable to speak for him at the English court received descriptions of the King's attainments. Writing in 1515 of his material disappointment in England to Cardinal Riario, a Roman patron, Erasmus none the less described Henry as 'a young man divinely gifted and initiated to some degree of elegance in humane studies'. Bombasius was told in 1518 that Henry was the wisest of contemporary princes and a great lover of literature, while Erasmus assured Banisius in 1519 that if the Low Countries had a prince like the King of England humanist learning would triumph there.[21]

Thus the picture of Henry which emerges is of an amateur not merely passively benignant, but personally and actively interested in learning. This interest — intermittent and inconsistent, perhaps, but none the less real — was vital for the establishment of the new learning, which was to be faced with fierce hostility during the first ten years of the reign.

At the same time humanists in England were fortunate that Henry's first Queen was an intelligent and cultured lady with a lively and sustained interest in scholarship. The daughters of Ferdinand and Isabella were destined by their marriages to serve the ends of Aragonese foreign policy and, consequently, since they were to be active advocates of Spain abroad rather than passive queen-consorts, the Infantas were educated beyond the limits conventionally prescribed for princesses.

The renaissance, moreover, had already reached Spain, where it was sedulously fostered by Isabella. Greek and Hebrew lectures were founded at Salamanca and Italian scholars, among them Lucio Marineo Siculo and Pietro Martire d'Anghierra, were invited to court and to the universities. Martire was specifically commissioned by Isabella to reclaim the young nobility from unprofitable pursuits by imbuing them with the culture of Italy. He established an academy at Saragossa and was later to boast, 'I was the literary foster-father of almost all the princes, and of all the princesses of Spain.'[22]

Women shared in the general rebirth of letters, two of them lecturing in rhetoric at the universities of Alcalá and Salamanca. The Infantas themselves were not educated on a par with their brother, Prince Juan, but besides the polite accomplishments usual to ladies they studied the Latin fathers Ambrose, Augustine, Gregory and Jerome, Christian poets such as Prudentius and Juvencus, and classical Latin poets and orators. Their Latinity was later praised by Vives, and their tutors were the Italian poet Antonio Geraldini and his brother Alessandro. The latter accompanied Katherine of Aragon to England.[23]

Katherine herself displayed both interest and accomplishment. Naturally she learned Latin, and corresponded in that language with Arthur from Spain and with Henry VII while in England; it has been said of her letters to Arthur, 'in Ciceronian elegance, Katherine is not inferior to her literary rival'. Later she was to correct her daughter's Latin exercises and, while reproaching Cardinals Wolsey and Campeggio for addressing her in Latin before her household, would proudly declare her knowledge of the tongue. She learned French in Spain (probably with her sister-in-law, Margaret of Austria) at the request of Margaret Beaufort and Elizabeth of York, since neither of the English ladies spoke Latin, let alone Spanish, and in 1529 she interviewed the Cardinals at Bridewell in French. Her literary command of her native tongue has been described as 'remarkably pure and correct' and, though heavy in style, quite clear and decided. Her command of English was such that in 1513 she was able to harangue the troops bound for Flodden in their own language.[24]

Katherine's own interests were not merely linguistic. A story is told that Henry VII, finding her pensive and homesick soon after arriving in England, took the Princess and her ladies to the royal library and 'showed them many goodly pleasant books of works full delightful, sage, merry and also right cunning, both in English and Latin'. In 1506 when requesting a confessor from Spain she specified that he should be an Observant Franciscan and a man of letters. Erasmus in the early years of the reign voiced his admiration of her learning: 'The Queen is astonishingly well read, far beyond what would be surprising in a woman, and as admirable for piety as she is for learning'; 'The Queen loves good literature, which she has studied with success since childhood.'[25]

Katherine's attachment to the new learning was a thing of slow and thoughtful growth. While her husband expressed a vague and general predilection for letters and learned men, the Queen carefully considered each new development of humanism. In 1514 she was anxious to secure Erasmus as her tutor, but in 1519, after doubts raised by her Spanish confessor the Bishop of Llandaff, she bluntly asked a courtier-friend of Erasmus if the scholar thought himself wiser than Jerome, since he had presumed to correct the saint's works. The incident was all the more distressing to Erasmus because he considered the Queen 'a woman of great sense and saintliness and not unlearned', but significantly he blamed the confessor rather than Katherine herself.[26] Her allegiance to the new learning once gained, however, the Queen was to be an asset to its establishment at court and a generous supporter of scholars.

The approval and benevolence of the King and Queen were obviously vital if humanism was to be accepted in intellectual and pietistic circles at court, but it was equally important that these ultimate patrons be surrounded by influential figures sympathetic to the new learning, able to sustain the royal enthusiasm and to forward scholars. Such intermediary patrons were essential, and, fortunately for its survival, humanism found supporters and promoters at every level in court and government. The leading ecclesiastical politicians of these early years, Fox, Warham and their successor Wolsey, were willing to employ humanists and to promote the new learning itself. Wolsey's immense command of patronage and great authority with the King enabled him not only to recruit humanists as officials, but to interfere in Oxford affairs in order to seal the establishment of Greek studies there, while Fox and Warham were able and willing even after their effective retirement from politics to advance the new learning through ecclesiastical and academic influence.

At the less politically exalted level, humanist scholars and patrons filled a variety of positions at court. Mountjoy became the Queen's chamberlain in 1512, a position he retained until her deposition in 1533, and his protégé Ammonio became Latin secretary to the King. Linacre was appointed royal physician in 1509 and in that capacity accompanied the King's sister Mary to France for her marriage. He was generally to be found at or near the court until his death in 1524. More, in receipt of a royal pension of £100 a year from 1516, was made councillor and Master of Requests two years later. Pace was royal secretary; John Stokesley one of the King's chaplains much at court; and Cuthbert Tunstal became Master of the Rolls in 1516.

Besides those actually employed about the King and Queen there were certain figures on the periphery of the court able to exert influence for the new learning there. Fisher preached on occasion before Henry and Katherine, as did Colet; while even before the start of his court career, More's house in the city was a meeting-place for English and foreign scholars. More himself, while disclaiming any desire for advancement at court, was assiduous in his attendance there; Ammonio reported to Erasmus in 1516 that 'he haunts those smoky palace fires in my company. None bids my lord of York [Wolsey] good morrow earlier than he'.[27]

The humanist attitude to courts was an ambiguous one, but few had the audacity of Erasmus, who hoped for a sinecure while eluding the toils of service. Erasmus's opinion of courts in general and England's in particular was notoriously changeable; but while he complained incessantly about the alleged parsimony of patrons he consistently praised the culture of Henry VIII's court. In April 1519 he told the King himself that his court 'is a model of Christian society, so rich in men of the highest attainments that any university might envy it', and a year later he exclaimed:

> What family of citizens offers so clear an example of strict and harmonious wedlock? Where could one find a wife more keen to equal her admirable spouse? What private home, what religious house indeed or university anywhere better supplied with men outstanding for their integrity of life and eminent learning than your court? . . . Time was when from a sort of passion for literature and the delights of learned ease I felt some repugnance to the courts of kings. But now, when I contemplate what a prince and governor rules the English court, its Queen, its nobles, counsellors, officials, I am eager in spirit to betake myself to a court like that.[28]

Pace, high in the King's favour, received an extended panegyric of the court:

> How truly splendid is the court of your native Britain, the seat and citadel of humane studies and of every virtue! I wish you joy, my dear Pace, of such a prince, and I wish your prince joy, whose kingdom is rendered illustrious by so many brilliant minds . . . At this stage I should like to spend my whole life in England, where under the favour of princes the humanities hold sway and the love of honour flourishes, while the painted mask of false piety and the useless and tedious learning of monks are alike exiled and overthrown.[29]

To Mountjoy Erasmus declared himself envious of the English court, 'peopled with so many learned men, while ours [the Burgundian court of the largely absent Charles V] has only Midases'.[30] It is perhaps not surprising that the King's servants should receive such eulogies, but foreigners, too, heard about the cultural superiority of Henry's court. Erasmus told Juan de la Parra, physician and tutor to Prince Ferdinand, of his wish that the Burgundian court would resemble that of England, while he admitted to Bombasius: 'You know . . . how averse I have always been from the courts of princes; it is a life which I can only regard as gilded misery under a mask of splendour; but I would gladly move to a court like that, if only I could grow young again . . . The men who have most influence [with Henry and Katherine] are those who excel in the humanities and in integrity and wisdom.'[31]

This roseate view of the court during the first ten years of the reign should not obscure the very real opposition offered to humanism. Scholasticism and the new learning could exist side by side for scholars like Grocyn and Fisher, but others saw humanism as a threat to the old order which would inevitably breed heresy. Several attempts were made at court to discredit the new learning and its proponents in the eyes of the King and Queen. Colet was the intended victim on one occasion, when two opponents insinuated to Henry that a sermon he had preached against the principle of war was a seditious criticism of current foreign policy. The incident ended happily enough for Colet, though the sermon had no effect on Henry's martial policy.[32]

The test case for humanism in England as elsewhere, however, was Erasmus's publication in 1516 of a new Greek text of the new testament with a Latin translation. Since Erasmus aimed to improve on the Vulgate (traditionally ascribed to Jerome), his version could be construed as heresy, or at the least extraordinary impudence. For humanists, however, the *Novum Instrumentum* was a laudable pioneering attempt to produce a more accurate rendering of the essential textual basis of Christianity. The edition was not simply intended to achieve a theoretical victory for the principle of biblical criticism; Erasmus hoped that a new Latin translation would inspire laymen to read the gospel, and that the Greek text would encourage scholars to learn the language.[33]

Erasmus's edition owed much of its genesis to English scholarship. It was Colet who first persuaded him to apply his talents to sacred literature, and much of the work of collation was done in England using manuscripts from Cambridge colleges and from the cathedral library of St Paul's. Erasmus originally intended the dedication for John Fisher, whom he described as 'A man who to great uprightness of life adds varied and abstruse learning and has a mind above all meanness, and because of these qualities is much esteemed'.[34] Ultimately, however, the preface went to Leo X, a more powerful protector against reactionary criticism, but Fisher accepted the change of plan with his usual good grace.

From its first appearance the *Novum Instrumentum*, concrete symbol of Greek and textual studies, met with acclaim from the more progressive elements in England, and in the crucial years 1516–20 it won the approval of the King, Queen and most men of influence, despite attempts to discredit both edition and editor at court. Scholar-courtiers like Ammonio very naturally welcomed its advent and, more important for its lasting impact on English piety and studies, the more enlightened members of the hierarchy approved it. Warham told Erasmus in June 1516, 'Your publication on the new testament I have shown to several of my brother bishops and some doctors of divinity, and all with one voice declare that you have done something well worth doing.' The following December Fox publicly affirmed his admiration for the work, declaring in a large gathering of people that Erasmus's version was worth more to him than ten commentaries. Colet informed Erasmus that his edition was selling rapidly, and met with disapproval only from the type of theologian ridiculed in the *Praise of Folly*.[35]

The appearance of the text had an immediate effect on private studies. The King himself attempted to learn Greek under Richard Croke's tuition, and Colet and Fisher were both inspired to tackle the language in spite of their advanced age. Fisher persuaded Erasmus himself to give him elementary lessons in August 1516, and by the following summer he was advanced enough to detect printers' errors in the *Novum Instrumentum*, though he still expressed approval for the venture itself. Erasmus tried to persuade William Latimer to continue Fisher's lessons, and though he declined he was full of praise for Erasmus and his pupil:

> You often write to me about the Bishop of Rochester, showing a special degree of affection and good will towards him; and at the same time you show a remarkable desire to promote the study of Greek, in trying so hard to make it familiar to such a leading Bishop who excels in learning of every kind; under his patronage it will be not merely safe from ill-natured persons and detractors, but welcome and popular in almost the whole of England. Who would dare attack it, if the Bishop were on its side? Or who would not be willing to welcome it if he knew it had the blessing of so eminent a prelate?[36]

Efforts were made, however, to wean the court from its approval of Erasmus's new testament. Besides the incident of the Queen's confessor, already recounted, two other episodes occurred. Erasmus sent a malicious account of the first, which took place early in 1519, to Peter Mosellanus. An unnamed theologian preaching before the King attacked Greek studies and translators 'in a style as brazen as it was stupid'. The humanists present were somewhat perturbed, but Henry gave an amused smile and ordered More to defend the study of Greek. This he did so ably and eloquently that the preacher fell on his knees to ask pardon of the king, claiming that during the sermon he had been moved by some sort of spirit. Henry retorted, 'Well, that was not the spirit of Christ; it must have been folly', and asked whether the preacher had read nothing by Erasmus. He replied that he had not, but when the King called him a fool he added that he had read the *Praise of Folly*. Pace interjected that the subject was fitting for the reader, and the unfortunate theologian, perceiving himself beaten, declared that he was not really against Greek because it derived from Hebrew! The King, says Erasmus, was so amazed at the man's stupidity that he dismissed him and ordered him never to preach again at court.[37]

In 1520 a more formidable attempt was made, but fortunately humanist defenders were again at hand. A Scotist Spanish friar challenged Stokesley to defend Erasmus, and attacked the latter for his rendering of the 'Word of God' in John's gospel as *sermo* rather than the traditional *verbum*. The Scotist apparently made himself so ridiculous that the Queen, out of pity, gave him leave to depart. Immediately Henry Standish, Bishop of St Asaph, leapt into the breach. A Franciscan of decidedly reactionary views, Standish had attacked Erasmus on the same point in a sermon in St Paul's Churchyard earlier in the day; now he moved to more dangerous ground. After praising the King's and Queen's ancestors for their defence of the church against heretics and schismatics, he exhorted Henry and Katherine to take notice of the dangerous times and in particular of the pernicious effect of Erasmus's works which, if not firmly opposed, would prove the ruin of Christianity. He then accused Erasmus specifically of heresy against matrimony, resurrection and the Eucharist, and offered to prove his case from the scholar's own works. Fortunately More, taking Stokesley's place, effectively proved the absurdity of the charges, and so embarrassed his opponent that the reassured King changed the course of the discussion out of regard for Standish's feelings.[38]

III

If humanism was securely entrenched in the royal court itself, it became established in the universities through royal and courtly protection and patronage. Victory was by no means complete; reactionary attitudes persisted for decades, and a shortage of funds and of suitable teachers impeded the progress of the new learning. Nevertheless, by the end of the first decade of the reign the new studies had achieved recognition and secured a place in curricula.

Humanism was undoubtedly assisted at Cambridge by the presence of Erasmus, resident there more or less continuously from August 1511 to February 1514. As in the previous reign he only resorted to a university when other sources of preferment seemed unpromising; in this case when his chief patron Mountjoy left England to take up his command at Hammes. Erasmus was by no means enchanted with university life, recognising as he did that financial patronage was to be found at court rather than in the academic world. Many of his letters, especially those to his chief agent at court, Ammonio, are filled with complaints about his poverty, misery and lack of prospects.[39] However, his discontent was not entirely due to monetary considerations. The intellectual atmosphere was scarcely propitious; enthusiasm for the new studies was confined to a comparatively small number of scholars, and Erasmus himself met with derision and hostility from schoolmen. His personal influence, however, contributed to the quiet introduction of humanism into the university.

Tradition holds that Erasmus resided at Queen's college, which he was later to praise for training young men in true learning rather than in barren dialectical subtleties. Fisher commanded a personal influence in the college and Richard Whitford, chaplain successively to Erasmus's patrons Mountjoy and Fox and later to a notable humanist devotional writer, had been a fellow there. Queens' also had a direct link with the court through its President Robert Bekensaw, formerly a servant of Margaret Beaufort and by July 1510 almoner to Katherine of Aragon, and generally in attendance on her. Indeed, the college found in the Queen an active protector of their rights and studies.[40]

Presumably it was at Queens' that Erasmus lectured on Greek grammar, and possibly also on theology. He is generally numbered among the Lady Margaret professors, and himself mentioned to Ammonio that the possibility of divinity lectures was under discussion, adding characteristically, 'The pay is too small to tempt me'.[41] The Greek course attracted a disappointingly small audience, though the lecturer hoped this would improve once he moved from Chrysoloras's grammar to that of Theodore, a more popular work.

If Erasmus's Greek labours went largely unnoticed by the university, his efforts and presence were appreciated by the more open-minded. Among his students were Henry Bullock of Queens', who lectured on Matthew's gospel in 1517 with the aid of Erasmus's annotations, and John Watson of Peterhouse, whom Erasmus later consulted about the *Novum Instrumentum*. Other Cambridge associates included John Bryan of King's college and William Gonnell the schoolmaster of Landbeach, who was later a tutor in More's household. Thomas Lupset, Colet's protégé, was at Pembroke college at this time. He assisted Erasmus in his editorial work, and in return Erasmus helped him resist the blandishments of the schoolmen.[42] Erasmus's sojourn at Cambridge was also important in the more general history of the new learning because of the opportunity of study and research it afforded him. While there he composed works for Colet's school and managed to prepare his new testament and editions of Jerome and Seneca, besides dispatching translations of Lucian and Plutarch to John Yonge, Henry VIII, Warham and Wolsey.[43]

The man who most clearly perceived Erasmus's value to the university and who was most able to help him was its chancellor, John Fisher. Erasmus attempted to win his patronage in 1511 with the dedication of a commentary on Isaiah attributed to Basil of Caesarea, translated from an original in Grocyn's library. He also seems to have hinted at the funds Fisher had reserved for St John's. The Bishop in reply offered to do what he could for the university Greek reader, though not at the expense of his obligations to the new college and promised to urge Mountjoy to help his protégé.[44]

The new learning might have existed at Cambridge for many more years as an advanced but essentially uninfluential intellectual trend had it not been for the early establishment of a college which made serious provision for humanist studies. St John's not only provided such a centre, but also ensured the introduction of humanism with the minimum of controversy by making room for the new studies by the side of the old. Indeed, more potent than any academic hostility to the foundation was the financially-motivated opposition of interested parties. The absence of any specific provision for her intended second college in Margaret Beaufort's will, the unwillingness of Henry VIII, her heir-at-law, to part with any of his inheritance, and the defaulting of other promised benefactors created material difficulties for Fisher and the executors. However the college did have friends at court, and foremost among them was Queen Katherine. Not only did she intercede with the King for the lost Beaufort revenues but herself, as the college records state, 'pardoned us of £50 due unto her for the mortising of the lordship of Riddiswell'. Thus through the determination of Fisher and the active sympathy of well-placed persons the college was established in April 1511 and formally opened in 1516.[45]

That Fisher was eminently qualified to be the effective founder of a humanist college is unquestionable. His experience as a university administrator, knowledge of the academic mind and its prejudices, appreciation of the difficulty of some of the new studies and the value of some of the old, led him to establish a college where innovation blended with tradition. His humanist credentials were impressive enough. Besides his understanding of the importance of Greek, Fisher outstripped many of his contemporaries, including Colet and Erasmus, in his enthusiasm for Hebrew and consistent support for Reuchlin from at least 1514 until the great Hebraist's death in 1522. As with Greek, Fisher's interest in Hebrew went beyond mere theoretical approval. By March 1515 he had studied Reuchlin's Hebrew vocabulary, and in about 1520 he took lessons from Robert Wakefield who later succeeded Reuchlin as reader of Hebrew at Tübingen. (For Fisher's relationship with Reuchlin, see Chapter Five below.)

Fisher's linguistic bias was amply expressed in the statutes he issued to St John's in 1516, 1524 and 1530.[46] As might be expected, the scholars were to understand and speak Latin before admission, while Hebrew and Greek were to be studied by those the master and seniors thought fit; in 1530 Fisher optimistically added Arabic and Chaldee to the list, but these were omitted from the royal code of 1545. Two college lectures in Hebrew and Greek were instituted in 1530. The Greek reader was to lecture to the junior college members on grammar and literature on alternate days, while the Hebrew reader was to expound grammar and the psalter or some other scriptural book to the seniors.

Theology, as the statutes state, was the goal to which all other studies led, but Fisher made it clear that the tongues were not auxiliary concerns but rather the instruments of that study. Nevertheless he allowed the schoolmen their place in the regulations for divinity degrees, and the 1530 chapter establishing a Hebrew lecture permitted the seniors to replace this with a lecture on a schoolman such as Scotus, but with the interesting provisos that the works expounded be first turned into better Latin and, lest the college lose any chance of Hebrew instruction, that the Greek reader apply himself to that language.

Compared with Fox's regulations for Corpus Christi, Oxford, Fisher's statutes make tame reading, but Erasmus attributed the quiet success of humanism at Cambridge to the gradual methods of the founder of St John's. The opening of the college coincided with the appearance of Erasmus's new testament and Jerome; thus, just when official provision was first made for the new learning, the texts essential to such studies became widely available. The stimuli of two such circumstances undoubtedly encouraged much of the humanist interest and activity at Cambridge. For example, it is significant that when John Bryan lectured on Aristotle at King's in 1518 he used the Greek text rather than corrupt medieval translations and commentaries.[47]

By far the most important event, however, was the introduction of a public Greek lecture in 1517. Henry VIII played a leading part in this innovation by recalling Richard Croke from Leipzig and, with Fisher, recommending him to Cambridge as Greek reader. Erasmus told Henry Bullock in February 1518, 'I wish Croke joy, and indeed your whole university, of this new honour added to the other excellent endowments in which he excels already', and congratulated Croke personally on his appointment, no less honourable to the reader than profitable to the whole university. More, reproving the 'Trojans' of Oxford in 1518, cited the example of the rival university 'which you have always outshone; those who are *not* studying Greek are so moved by common interest in their university that they are actually making large individual contributions to the salary of the Greek professor!' In April 1520 Richard Pace, another of Henry VIII's servants, was appointed to the lecture, with an annual stipend of £10. Greek studies at Cambridge thus owed much to the interest of Henry and his court, and the Queen, too, kept an eye on developments there. She planned to visit the university in 1518 and 1519 on her way to Walsingham, and definitely went there in February 1521; she resided at Queens', and the proctors' accounts record her presence in the schools.[48]

Humanism at Cambridge was also assisted by the establishment of Siberch's press in 1521. Among his guarantors to the university were

Bullock and Wakefield, and his publications included a pirate edition of Erasmus's *De Conscribendis Epistolis* (dedicated to Fisher as a safeguard against the wrath of the author), the Lily–Erasmus grammar composed for Colet's school, Linacre's *De Temperamentis*, the pseudonymous *Hermathena* dedicated to Pace, two works of Bullock's and Pace's Latin translation of Fisher's sermon against Luther of 1521.[49]

Meanwhile at Oxford, notwithstanding the much-vaunted 'early flowering of the renaissance', the influence of humanist scholars had largely failed to outlive their actual presence. No continuing tradition of Greek teaching or biblical exegesis had grown out of the labours of Grocyn and Colet, and Scotus and his disciples, with the medieval Aristotle, were the authors prescribed for exposition in the degree regulations.[50] The college of most recent foundation, Brasenose, took no cognisance of the new learning, and its irascible founder, Bishop Smith of Lincoln, is said to have quarrelled with Fox over the latter's predilection for Greek.

The only Oxford college to show any inclination towards humanism was Magdalen. Reginald Pole, the King's most favoured scholar, was a commoner there under the tuition of William Latimer and possibly also of Linacre, and Fox had several connections with the college. Traditionally held to have been educated there himself, and as Bishop of Winchester the college Visitor, he was a close friend of John Claymond, President of Magdalen, 1507–17 and first President of Corpus, 1517–37. Fox also drew many of his first fellows from Magdalen, whence Wolsey was to recruit canons for Cardinal College.

Much therefore depended on Oxford's first humanist founder, who differed greatly in character and career from Fisher, his friend and protégé. Richard Fox was the political prelate *par excellence*, aware of the practical utility of the scholar and impatient with those who clung to academic life rather than employ their talents usefully elsewhere. At the same time he was conscious of the intellectual importance of the new learning, though the press of more mundane business kept him from both his pastoral duties and his learned interests, as Ammonio's court-circulars to Erasmus show. However he maintained official links with both universities; was involved with Fisher as one of Margaret Beaufort's executors in the Foundation of St John's and of a grammar school and chantry at Wimborne; supported poor scholars at Oxford; and received a stream of dedications from scholars.[51]

From about 1512 Fox began to appear less frequently at court, and he finally resigned the privy seal in May 1516. His age and physical disabilities made him increasingly unfit for governmental duties and he retired to his diocese to make reparation, as he said, for many years of neglect. His relative freedom from political obligations enabled him to devote himself to his pastoral duties and to scholarly patronage; Linacre in the dedication to Fox of a presentation copy of his *De Sanitate Tuenda* in 1517 spoke of the Bishop's house as a resort of the learned. His major educational benefaction was originally intended for the good of his diocese. Just as he translated the rule of St Benedict into English for the benefit of the nuns in his see, so the foundation at Oxford was to be a college for the monks of St Swithun's, with some secular scholars. Tradition ascribes his decision to found a secular college instead to a prophetic (and probably apocryphal) remark of Bishop Oldham's on the impending fall of the monasteries, but a more likely influence was the example of St John's and of his associate Fisher.[52]

Fox was granted his licence of foundation in November 1516, and Corpus Christi was opened and given statutes in the following year. Though the college was to be numerically smaller than St John's, the Corpus statutes were much less modest in their bias towards the new studies. The scholars were, naturally, to know Latin grammar before admission, and were also to be learned in approved Latin authors and ready for the study of logic and 'study and advancement in the branches of liberal learning'. Even the two choristers were to study grammar and 'good authors', either in college or at Magdalen school.[53]

So far the Corpus statutes, though certainly humanist in colouring, were no more extreme than Fisher's. Had they merely governed studies within the college they would probably have caused little stir, but Fox, by the establishment of public lectures in rhetoric, Greek and theology, sought to carry the new learning into the university at large; a course of action which threatened the dominance of scholasticism in the schools.

The rhetoric reader was to lecture daily on the pagan classics; for the first time pure, elegant and accurate Latin was to be accessible to the youth of the whole university. On Mondays, Wednesdays and Fridays the Roman orators and historians were to be expounded, while the rest of the week was reserved to the poets and dramatists. The scholars of Corpus were also to have private lectures on more modern authors — Valla, Aulus Gellius or Poliziano — several times a week.

Fox was careful to declare that he had founded a Greek lecture 'because the holy canons have established and commanded, most suitably for good letters, and Christian literature especially, that such an one should never be wanting in this university of Oxford'. This was a reference to the Council of Vienne, which had ordained the establishment of chairs in biblical tongues at the major universities of western Europe. Fox's reader was to expound both grammar and literature and, as with rhetoric, the members of Corpus were to have frequent private lectures.

The most revolutionary of the three lectures, as well as the most important, was that of theology, 'a study which we have ever holden of such importance, as to have constructed this our apiary [that is, the college] for its sake'. The reader was to lecture solely on holy writ, and to cover parts of the old and new testaments in alternate years. This in itself was acceptable; it was Fox's dismissal of the schoolmen as competent authorities for exegesis that struck consternation into the hearts of the orthodox. The theology reader, Fox declared,

> must always in his interpretation, as far as he can, imitate the holy and ancient doctors, both Latin and Greek, and especially Jerome, Augustine, Ambrose, Hilary, Chrysostom, Damascenus, and others of that sort, — not Liranus, not Hugh of Vienne, and the rest, who, as in time, so in learning, are far below them; except where the commentaries of the former doctors fail.

Such irreverent disregard for sacrosanct tradition was bound to provoke a violent reaction. Tyndale described the uproar at Oxford in picturesque terms:

> The old barking curs, Duns' disciples and like draff called Scotists, the children of darkness, raged in every pulpit against Greek, Latin, and Hebrew, and what sorrow the schoolmasters that taught the true Latin tongue had with them, some beating the pulpit with their fists for madness, and roaring out with open and foaming mouth, that if there were but one Terence or Virgil in the world, and that same in their sleeves, and a fire before them, they would burn them therein, though it should cost them their lives.[54]

Rumours of the disquiet Fox's lectures stirred among the teaching body of the university soon reached More in London. The opponents of humanism formed themselves into a body of 'Trojans', the prime object of their hatred being Greek, the gateway to the new exegesis. The climax of the attack came in Lent 1518, when one of their number delivered a sermon which denounced Greek, classical literature and all polite learning. At this time the royal court was at Abingdon; this may have been coincidence, but possibly the 'Trojans' expected royal support for their attitude. If so, they were unfortunate in their miscalculation.

Erasmus gave a concise account of the affair to Mosellanus in the following year:

> at Oxford, where a young man of more than common learning was publicly teaching Greek with some success, some barbarian or other in a public sermon began to inveigh against Greek studies with monstrous great falsehoods. The King, who being quite a scholar himself is a supporter of the humanities, happened to be in the neighbourhood, and hearing about this from More and Pace, he declared that those who wished should be welcome to follow Greek. And so those rascals were put to silence. I only wish we had some such prince or viceroy.[55]

More himself, in attendance on the King as Master of Requests, wrote to the university authorities offering a detailed defence of the new learning against the unnamed preacher.[56] Greek and Latin, he declared, were not prerequisites of salvation, but their study did incline the soul to virtue, while the laws of human nature and conduct, apprehended through philosophy and literature, were essential for the study of theology and for preaching. Linguistic study, moreover, was not detrimental to theology, but an integral part of it. Finally, More warned of repercussions if the attacks on humanists did not cease, and of the displeasure of Warham, Chancellor of Oxford, of Wolsey, and of the King himself; 'His sacred Majesty has cultivated all the liberal arts as much as ever a king did: indeed, he possesses greater erudition and judgement than any previous monarch. Will his wisdom and piety allow the liberal arts to fail?'

Royal intervention thus procured a theoretical victory of Greeks over Trojans. The triumph of principle was sealed by a visit from Katherine of Aragon and Wolsey. The Queen, according to contemporary accounts, was received with as much joy as if she had been Juno or Minerva, while the Cardinal announced his intention of founding public lectures in theology, civil and canon law, Greek, rhetoric, medicine and mathematics.[57]

The fact that these lectures duplicate the three subjects covered by Fox's readers has caused some confusion. The theology lectures are in fact quite distinct, since Wolsey, possibly influenced by Fox's experience, required his reader to expound Scotus as well as scripture, but it seems likely, given the lack of qualified teachers at the time, that the two founders co-operated in filling the Greek and rhetoric chairs. The readers attributed to Wolsey — Clement, Lupset and Vives — all resided at Corpus, though their names do not appear in the *libri magni* which record payments to other college teachers, and it seems likely that Fox provided them with board, lodgings and a lecture hall while Wolsey paid their stipends.[58] Questions of patronage apart, however, the important point is that public lectures in the tongues were both approved and available at this early date.

Both Corpus Christi and the public lectures met with humanist acclaim at home and abroad. More gleefully informed Erasmus:

My Clement lectures in Oxford to a larger audience than anyone has ever had before. It is remarkable how popular he is; he is a general favourite. Even those who almost hate the humanities love him none the less; they attend his lectures and are gradually softening.

Erasmus himself praised Fox's achievement at Oxford to Claymond:

He is an exceptionally wise man, is my lord Richard, Bishop of Winchester, and has always been universally esteemed as such; but let me tell you . . . no act of his has ever proved this more clearly than his consecrating the magnificent college which he has set up at his own expense expressly to the three chief tongues, to humane literature, and to classical studies. What greater service could he have rendered to his fellow men, what monument could more rightly recommend his name to the undying memory of mankind? So should a pillar of the church, so should a bishop act.[59]

The college numbered several luminaries of English and European humanism among its early members, or at least, its residents;

Claymond, Clement, Reginald Pole, Kratzer, Gentian Hervet, Vives and Udall. It was also equipped with a fine library. Fox himself gave many books, including Bishop Shirwood's collection, as did Claymond. Among the early printed books owned by Corpus were Aldine editions of Aristotle, a rare Venetian Tacitus, the Florentine Homer of 1488, and an edition of Cicero's *De Officiis* printed at Mainz in 1466. Books formerly owned by Grocyn were purchased by Claymond from Linacre; they included copies of Proclus, Plotinus, Simplicius and Ptolemy.[60]

Wolsey, meanwhile, received a glowing eulogy from Linacre in 1519 for his work at Oxford:

> Public lectures have been founded at your expense, benefits have been conferred on the learned, and the restoration of the discipline of the schools to its pristine, or at least to a better, condition has been commenced under your auspices.

Erasmus, too, in a general panegyric on English culture sent to Mountjoy singled out events at the university which, he declared, rivalled the most ancient and most famous:

> I have a great devotion to my lord the Bishop of Winchester, who has founded a magnificent college at his own expense expressly for the humanities. Even more do I love the noble and heroic spirit of the most reverend the Cardinal of York, whose wise provision will win fame for the schools of Oxford in the learned tongues and every other field of knowledge, and also for those gifts of character which belong with liberal studies. As for Cambridge university, it has for some time now been adorned with every excellence under the rule of the Bishop of Rochester, a man fit from every point of view to play the part of a distinguished prelate.[61]

Doubtless Erasmus was overestimating the triumph of the new learning, but by 1519 humanism had become firmly established at court and — largely because of the support of the court — in the universities. While it would be over-optimistic to say that an age of gold had begun, England under Henry VIII was justly famed for its scholarship and for its patronage of learning. The following chapters will discuss the contribution of English humanists to national and international theological debates; trace the progress of the new

learning in the universities and schools; examine the relationship
between the English and European renaissance; and describe the
efforts of individual men and women to master the new studies.

Notes

1. P. S. and H. M. Allen, H. W. Garrod (eds), *Opus Epistolarum Des. Erasmi Roterodami* (11 vols., Clarendon Press, Oxford, 1906–47), no. 215. Trans. R. A. B. Mynors and D. F. S. Thomson, in Wallace K. Ferguson (ed.), *The Epistles of Erasmus* (6 vols., University of Toronto Press, Toronto, Buffalo, London, 1974–82). Hereafter cited when used in quotation as 'Toronto translation'.
2. Roberto Weiss, *Humanism in England During the Fifteenth Century*, 3rd edn. (Basil Blackwell, Oxford, 1967), passim.
3. Weiss, *Humanism in England*, pp. 66–7 for gifts from Duke Humphrey, pp. 86–96 from Grey, pp. 103–5 from Fleming, p. 177 from Goldwell.
4. Frederick Seebohm, *The Oxford Reformers*, 3rd edn. (Longmans, Green & Co., London, 1887), passim; Charles Edward Mallet, *A History of the University of Oxford* (3 vols., Methuen & Co., London, 1924, 1927), vol. 1, p. 415; Montagu Burrows, 'Linacre's Catalogue of Grocyn's Books', Oxford Historical Society *Collectanea*, 2nd series (Clarendon Press, Oxford, 1890), pp. 317–80.
5. Samuel Knight, *Life of Dean Colet* (J. Downing, London, 1724), passim; J. H. Lupton, *A Life of Dean Colet* (George Bell & Sons, London, 1909), passim; Allen, *Erasmi Epistolae*, no. 1211 to Justus Jonas, 13 June 1521.
6. John Noble Johnson, *Life of Thomas Linacre*, Robert Graves (ed.) (Edward Lumley, London, 1835), passim; C. D. O'Malley, *English Medical Humanists* (University of Kansas Press, Lawrence, 1965), passim.
7. Joan Simon, *Education and Society in Tudor England* (Cambridge University Press, Cambridge, 1966), pp. 41–3; R. S. Stanier, *Magdalen School* (Basil Blackwell, Oxford, 1940), passim. The Magdalen statutes are printed in E. A. Bond (ed.), *Statutes of the Colleges of Oxford* (3 vols., J. H. Parker and Longman, Brown, Green & Longmans, Oxford and London, 1853), vol. 2.
8. John Peile, *Christ's College* (F. E. Robinson & Co., London, 1900), p. 1; for *Godshouse and Christ's college*, see A. H. Lloyd, *Early History of Christ's, Cambridge* (Cambridge University Press, Cambridge, 1934), passim.
9. C. H. Cooper, *Memoir of Margaret Countess of Richmond and Derby*, J. E. B. Mayor (ed.) (Deighton, Bell & Co., Cambridge, 1874), p. 60; G. C. Richards and H. E. Salter, *The Dean's Register of Oriel* (Clarendon Press, Oxford, 1926), pp. x, 15; *Victoria County History of Cambridgeshire* (8 vols., Oxford University Press, Oxford, 1938–82), vol. 3, pp. 166–7; J. Hymers, *Fisher's Funeral Sermon of Lady Margaret* (Cambridge University Press, Cambridge, 1840), pp. 62–6, 83, 93.
10. Giles Duwes *Introduction for to learn to read, to pronounce, and to speak French truly* (Bourman, London, 1534?), prologue.
11. William Nelson, *John Skelton, Laureate* (Columbia University Press, New York, 1939), pp. 19–20, 75; Albert du Boys, *Catharine of Aragon and the Sources of the English Reformation*, C. M. Yonge (trans.) (2 vols., Hurst & Blackett, London, 1881), vol. 1, pp. 47–8.
12. Edward, Baron Herbert of Cherbury, *Life and Reign of King Henry VIII* (J. Martyn, London, 1672), p. 2. Herbert's source was Paolo Sarpi.
13. 'Poems against Garnesche', quoted in Nelson, *Skelton*, p. 48.
14. William Caxton, *The Book of Eneydos* (Caxton, London, 1489), preface; H. L. R. Edwards, Skelton: *The Life and Times of an early Tudor Poet* (Jonathan Cape, London, 1949), p. 58.

15. The text of the *Speculum Principis* is printed in F. M. Salter, 'Skelton's *Speculum Principis*', *Speculum*, vol. 9, no. 1 (January 1934), pp. 25–37.

16. Allen, *Erasmi Epistolae*, nos. 2435, 204, 206, 2143.

17. Ibid., nos. 187–9, 191–3. The Lucian translations were produced in conjunction with More.

18. Ibid., nos. 118–185 (Toronto translation).

19. Ibid., nos. 221, 272, 657, 834, 966 (Toronto translation); Richard Pace, *De Fructu Qui Ex Doctrina Percipitur*, F. Manley and R. S. Sylvester (eds and trans.) (Ungar, New York, 1967), pp. 139, 141.

20. Cf., for example, Allen *Erasmi Epistolae*, no. 297 to Wolsey, July (1514?).

21. Ibid., nos. 333, 855, 970 (Toronto translation).

22. Du Boys, *Catharine of Aragon*, vol. 1, p. 20. For the Spanish renaissance see W. H. Prescott, *History of the Reign of Ferdinand and Isabella* (3 vols., Richard Bentley, London, 1838), vol. 2, chapter 29; Garrett Mattingly, *Catharine of Aragon* (Jonathan Cape, London, 1944), pp. 14–17.

23. A list of Alessandro Geraldini's works, including a tract on the education of a noble girl (sadly, no longer extant), is printed in his *Itinerarivm ad Regiones sub Aeqvinoctiali Plaga* (G. Facciotti, Rome, 1631).

24. George Cavendish, *Life of Cardinal Wolsey* (G. Routledge & Sons, London, 1885), p. 126; *Calendar of State Papers, Spanish*, G. Bergenroth, P. Gayangos, M. A. S. Hume (eds) (8 vols., HMSO, London, 1862–1904), vol. 1, no. 205 (hereafter cited as *Spanish Calendar*); John Foxe, *Acts and Monuments*, S. R. Cattley (ed.) (8 vols., Seeley & Burnside, London 1837), vol. 5, p. 50; M. A. E. Wood, *Letters of Royal and Illustrious Ladies* (3 vols., Henry Colburn, London, 1846), vol. 1, p. xxxiii; M. A. S. Hume, *The Wives of Henry VIII*, 2nd edn. (E. Nash & Grayson, London, 1927), p. 82. Cf. Pietro Martire's letter in *Letters and Papers, Foreign and Domestic, of the Reign of Henry VIII*, J. S. Brewer, J. Gairdner, R. H. Brodie (eds) (21 vols., HMSO, London, 1862–1932), vol. 1, no. 4464 (hereafter cited as *L&P*).

25. Agnes and Elizabeth Strickland, *Lives of the Queens of England* (6 vols., George Bell & Son, London, 1889), vol. 2, p. 108; Wood, *Royal and Illustrious Ladies*, vol. 1, p. 138; Allen, *Erasmi Epistolae*, nos. 855, 976 (Toronto translation).

26. Allen, *Erasmi Epistolae*, nos. 296, 948 (Toronto translation).

27. Ibid., no. 389 (Toronto translation).

28. Ibid., nos. 834, 964 (Toronto translation).

29. Ibid., no. 821 (Toronto translation).

30. Ibid., no. 1028 (Toronto translation).

31. Ibid., nos. 917, 855 (Toronto translation).

32. Ibid., no. 1211; Lupton, *Life of Colet*, pp. 41ff. Lupton identifies the Franciscans Bricot and Standish as Colet's enemies.

33. Cf. Allen, *Erasmi Epistolae*, no. 413 to Fisher, June (1516).

34. Ibid., no. 253 to Robert Guibé, February 1512 (Toronto translation).

35. Ibid., nos. 425, 502, 423 (Toronto translation).

36. Ibid., nos. 592, 520 (Toronto translation). Cf. no. 481.

37. Ibid., no. 948 (Toronto translation).

38. The incident is recounted, with slight differences of detail, in two of Erasmus's letters; Allen, *Erasmi Epistolae*, no. 1126 to Hermann Busch and no. 1127a to Luther. The account given here (Toronto translation) is a synthesis of the two. No. 1127a does not name Stokesley, but the description is almost identical with that given in no. 855 to Bombasius. Cf. Pace, *De Fructu*, p. 127.

39. Cf. Allen, *Erasmi Epistolae*, no. 238: 'this place really suits me fairly well. Also I see some prospect of earning, if one could act as a man of all work' (Toronto translation).

40. W. G. Searle, *History of the Queens' College* (2 vols., Cambridge University Press, Cambridge, 1867 and 1871), vol. 1, pp. 134–45; 'Particulars Concerning . . . Queens', Cambridge,', British Library Harley MS 7048.

41. Allen, *Erasmi Epistolae*, no. 253 (Toronto translation).
42. For Bullock, ibid., no. 579; C. H. Cooper, *Annals of Cambridge* (5 vols., Warwick & Co. and Cambridge University Press, Cambridge, 1842–1908), vol. 1, p. 303. For Lupset, Allen, *Erasmi Epistolae*, nos. 270–1.
43. Allen, *Erasmi Epistolae*, nos. 245, 270, 281, 325. The dedications are nos. 261, 268, 272, 284.
44. Ibid., nos. 229, 242. Cf. 227.
45. R. F. Scott, *Notes from the Records of St John's College, Cambridge* (3 vols., privately printed, 1889–1913), vol. 1, pp. 5–7, vol. 3, p. 365; J. B. Mullinger, *St John's College* (F. E. Robinson & Co., London, 1901), pp. 18–20; Thomas Baker, *History of the College of St John the Evangelist, Cambridge*, J. E. B. Mayor (ed.) (2 vols., Cambridge University Press, Cambridge, 1869), vol. 1, p. 73; Hymers, *Funeral Sermon*, pp. 183, 195ff; Cooper, *Annals*, vol. 1, pp. 291–2; *Victoria County History, Cambs.*, vol. 3, p. 438.
46. All printed, with the royal code of 1545, in J. E. B. Mayor, *Early Statutes of the College of St John the Evangelist* (Macmillan & Co., Cambridge, 1859).
47. Allen, *Erasmi Epistolae*, no. 948; Simon, *Education and Society*, p. 88; *Victoria County History, Cambs.*, Vol. 3, p. 394.
48. Allen, *Erasmi Epistolae*, nos. 777, 827 (Toronto translation); *St Thomas More: Selected Letters*, E. F. Rogers (ed.) (Yale University Press, New Haven and London, 1961), p. 94; Cooper, *Annals*, vol. 1, p. 304; J. H. Gray, *The Queens' College* (F. E. Robinson & Co., London, 1899), p. 64; Jervis Wegg, *Richard Pace, A Tudor Diplomatist* (Methuen & Co., London, 1932), p. 161. For Croke at Cambridge, Cooper, *Annals*, vol. 1, pp. 305, 310.
49. E. P. Goldschmidt, *The First Cambridge Press in its European Setting* (Cambridge University Press, Cambridge, 1955), passim.
50. Richards and Salter, *Dean's Register of Oriel*, pp. x–xi for Scotism at Cambridge, passim for degree regulations.
51. G. R. M. Ward, *Foundation Statutes of Bishop Fox for Corpus Christi College, with a Life of the Founder* (Longman, Brown, Green & Longmans, London, 1843); Edmund Chisholm Batten, *The Register of Richard Fox while Bishop of Bath and Wells* (Harrison & Sons, London, 1889); *Letters of Richard Fox*, P. S. and H. M. Allen (eds) (Clarendon Press, Oxford, 1929); Thomas Fowler, *History of Corpus Christi College* (Clarendon Press, Oxford, 1893). For Fox's relations with Oxford, Henry Anstey, *Epistolae Academiae Oxon.* (2 vols., Clarendon Press, Oxford, 1898), vol. 2, nos. 363, 525, 527.
52. Allen, *Letters of Fox*, nos. 64, 55; H. C. Maxwell Lyte, *A History of the University of Oxford* (Macmillan, London, 1886), p. 406; A. A. Mumford, *Hugh Oldham* (Faber & Faber, London, 1936), passim. Fox's influence raised Fisher to the episcopate in 1504, and he consulted Fisher's statutes for Christ's in 1506; Allen, *Letters of Fox*, nos. 88, 22. A copy of the Corpus statutes is in St John's Library, apparently corrected by Fisher; E. A. Benians, *John Fisher* (Cambridge University Press, Cambridge, 1935), p. 24.
53. The Corpus statutes are printed in Bond, *Statutes of Oxford*, vol. 2, translated in Ward, *Foundation Statutes of Corpus*, from whence the quotations come.
54. Quoted in Lyte, *History of Oxford*, pp. 435–6.
55. Allen, *Erasmi Epistolae*, no. 948 (Toronto translation). The young Greek teacher was probably John Clement.
56. Rogers, *Thomas More, Selected Letters*, pp. 94ff.
57. For Katherine's reception, H. E. Salter, *Registrum Annalium Collegii Mertonensis, 1483–1521* (Clarendon Press, Oxford, 1921), p. 477, an entry in the Warden's hand; Richard Fiddes, 'Collections' appended to his *Life of Cardinal Wolsey* (J. Knapton, London, 1726), pp. 28–9, Warham to Oxford University, 22 May 1518. For letters concerning the establishment of the lectures, Fiddes, 'Collections', pp. 28–33.

58. Mallet, *History of Oxford*, vol. 2, p. 30; Fowler, *Corpus Christi*, pp. 87–9; J. A. Gee, *Life and Works of Thomas Lupset* (Yale University Press, New Haven, 1928), pp. 94–6.

59. Allen, *Erasmi Epistolae*, nos. 907, 990 (Toronto translation).

60. Mallet, *History of Oxford*, vol. 2, p. 33; Fowler,*Corpus Christi*, p. 89.

61. Johnson, *Life of Linacre*, p. 219; Allen, *Erasmi Epistolae*, no. 965 (Toronto translation).

2 Humanists and Religious Policy

It cannot be emphasised too strongly that the new learning was originally non-doctrinal in character and that the humanist attitude to
religious reform was naive in the extreme. Men like Colet, Erasmus
and More believed that abuses in belief and practice — for example,
over-reliance on externals such as relics, images and pilgrimages —
were the result of man's distance from the original word of God
contained in scripture. Humanists attacked scholasticism, which in
their eyes made theology an arid academic issue concerned with
intellectually clever but ultimately sterile 'questions', and they also
expressed disgust at popular superstition. They believed that if only
the scriptures were placed before the people in their original, unclut-
tered purity, free from scholastic allegory and superstitious distor-
tion, then man would awake to his Christian duties and the church
would be reformed almost automatically.

Consequently the revolt of Luther caused consternation and
perplexity among humanists, raising intellectual questions for the
scholars and practical problems for the politicians and bishops.
Initially it was necessary to evaluate Luther's criticisms and
doctrinal assertions. This was a matter of no little difficulty, as his
denunciation of ecclesiastical and devotional abuse largely
coincided with humanist views and this obscured the revolutionary
implications of his departure from traditional dogma and his asper-
sions on papal authority. While it seemed to conservatives that their
worst fears about humanism had been realised by the German
reformer, there was some initial sympathy for Luther among
English humanists.

This was sedulously fanned by Erasmus, who hoped on the one
hand to avert irrevocable schism and on the other to advance reform
by playing down Luther's heterodoxy and emphasising his concern
with abuses. Despite the publication of the condemnatory bull
Exsurge Domine in 1520 no official action against Luther's teachings
was taken in England, largely because the issue was confused by
Standish and his Fransiscan supporters who identified Luther with
Erasmus and denounced both. A public burning of Luther's books

was apparently contemplated, but the plan was abandoned after Erasmus's mediation with Wolsey, who imposed silence on the theological debate.[1] Erasmus had told Luther in May 1519, that several highly placed people in England thought well of his works and in August 1520 he cautiously told the reformer:

> The King of England is well-disposed, but he listens to people like [Standish] speaking every day. He asked me what I thought of you. I replied that you were too wise a person for someone as unlearned as myself to pass judgment on you. He could have wished that you had written certain things with more prudence and moderation. That is also the wish, my dear Luther, of those who wish you well.[2]

The issue was clarified, however, by the events of 1521, which saw Luther's defiance of imperial and papal authority at Worms, his excommunication by the Pope and the publication of his trenchant attack on the sacramental system, *De Captivitate Babylonica Ecclesiae*. English humanists now saw Luther's doctrinal extremism and refusal to submit to authority as a threat to their own hopes of reform. A literary campaign under the personal leadership of the King was immediately launched against him, together with a policy of internal control designed to prevent the importation and circulation of his ideas.

The true authorship of Henry VIII's *Assertio Septem Sacramentorum*, a direct answer to *De Captivitate Babylonica* which appeared in 1521 and earned the King the long-coveted title of *Fidei Defensor*, has long been a matter of debate. Henry was certainly capable of producing such a work, but it is equally beyond question that he had considerable help, notably from Fisher and More and probably also from more obscure research assistants.[3] The true significance of the King's contribution, however, lies not in his literary or theological abilities, but in the fact that he considered Luther's criticisms important enough to demand a refutation published under his own name. The *Assertio* was not simply a facet of Henry's lust for glory, like his campaigns in France: the King was deliberately putting the prestige of his name and the weight of his authority against a threat to church unity and traditional doctrine. The work provoked a vitriolic reply from Luther in 1522, but the reformer showed his concern with the King's attitude some three years later when, having been misinformed by Christian of Denmark that Henry now 'inclined to the gospel', he sent him an uncharacteristically humble offer of apology. The King was unmoved and after consulting with More and Vives he published a scathing reply.[4] There the matter rested, until the thorny problems of the royal divorce momentarily revived Henry's interest in Luther.

The Queen, too, played an active though less direct part in the literary campaign. As with the new learning, Katherine carefully considered the questions raised by Luther and other reformers and discussed them with her confessor Alphonso de Villa Sancta, a Spanish Observant at Greenwich who was acquainted with More. Villa Sancta produced several works against Luther at her command, besides *De Libero Arbitrio, adversus Melanchthonem.* This treatise and his *Problema Indulgentiarum* were printed by Pynson in 1523 with dedications to the Queen, and Villa Sancta emphasised her role in the controversy by according her the King's title of *Fidei Defensor*.[5]

English humanists were quick to follow the royal lead against Luther. Defences of the King's book were published by More and by Fisher, who also defended the priesthood against Luther and the real presence against Oecolampadius. This last work was dedicated to Richard Fox, partly in gratitude for his early patronage of Fisher, partly because of his devotion to the eucharist which was reflected in the name of his Oxford foundation.[6] In addition Edward Powell sent his *Propugnaculum summi sacerdotii adver. M. Lutherum* to Wolsey for approval and it was published by Pynson in 1523. Thus the first wave of humanist patrons and scholars — Fisher, Fox, More, Katherine of Aragon and Wolsey — were all associated in the defence of orthodoxy.

Not content with marshalling their own literary talent, English humanists encouraged foreign scholars to refute heresy and several Europeans conscious of the English attitude either wrote in defence of the King or dedicated controversial works to Henry and his subjects. The King received Eck's *Enchiridion locorum*, which also contained a letter to More; and Cochlaeus dedicated works to Henry, Fisher, More, Tunstal and Nicholas West. Both Jerome Emser and Thomas Murner of Strasbourg translated Henry's *Assertio* into German and Murner also composed a defence of the work in 1522 and a German treatise entitled *Whether the King of England or Luther Be a Liar* in 1523.[7]

A more illustrious opponent of Luther than these was Erasmus, whose English friends and patrons were foremost among those who urged him to write against the reformer. Reluctant to add to the uproar, Erasmus temporised for as long as possible, exhorting the zealous Turnstal to beware of uprooting wheat with tares and telling Pace of his determination to remain neutral. At the same time, conscious of his vulnerability, he asked Pace to keep him in Wolsey's good graces.[8]

Meanwhile, Mountjoy had warned him that he was suspected of favouring Luther and should exonerate himself by writing against him. Erasmus refuted the charge at some length, stating that Luther was justified in exposing the evils of the times though wrong in his method and denying that he was the author of any Lutheran writings attributed to him. In August 1521 he was compelled to justify himself to Warham and to promise definite action in the future.[9]

At the end of 1521, Henry sent him a copy of his *Assertio* but still Erasmus did nothing and in August 1523 he told Pirckheimer that the King suspected him of being the author of a new Lutheran treatise. The despatch of an agent to England allayed Henry's and Wolsey's fears and also gained the scholar 30 florins by way of gifts from friends. This stick-and-carrot treatment eventually stirred Erasmus to action and in spring 1524 he sent the King a draft version of his *De Libero Arbitrio* which was published in the following September.[10] Vives triumphantly reported its favourable reception at the English court. The King, he said,

> pointed me out a passage with which he says he is greatly delighted, where you dissuade people from prying too curiously into the secret places of the divine majesty. The Queen also rates you highly for the work and bade me at this point add her greetings to you, and thank you for this, that, being the person you are and about to speak on so great a subject, you had humbled yourself and treated the subject with much modesty.[11]

Though he was under pressure from other powerful quarters to come out against Luther (notably, from the Pope and George of Saxony) there is no reason to doubt Erasmus's own assertion that it was chiefly the English who forced him to an open declaration. Besides the threat of Henry's and Wolsey's displeasure, he was subject to the persuasion of friends. Fisher, curiously, seems to have played little part in the matter, but Erasmus himself reveals More and Tunstal as the actual agents of coercion.[12] Erasmus also received a large amount of financial support from England in the form of regular pensions from Warham and Mountjoy and of occasional, generous gifts. All this made it impossible for him to refuse to join the controversy.

From this brief survey of the English literary campaign, it is immediately apparent that Luther's antagonists and those who urged them to write were not the forces of reaction defeated at Oxford in 1518 (who were rendered ineffectual by their inability to distinguish humanism from heresy) but leading proponents of the new learning. With the King so fervently against Luther it would indeed have been impossible to write for him, but no attempt was made after 1521 to keep Henry's mind open on the subject. Moreover, even when combatting Luther English humanists did not relinquish the weapons of the new learning. Vives (admittedly a biased commentator) numbered Fisher among those conservative apologists who were more *Latini* than their evangelical opponents and the Bishop himself, in an anti-Lutheran sermon of 1526, asked pardon for quoting 'after the Greek book', that is Erasmus's new testament, rather than the Vulgate, because the words 'make better against our enemies'.[13]

The literary battle in Europe went hand in hand with a campaign to repress Lutheranism in England itself. Lollardy, the native heresy, had ceased to be a scholarly threat since its expulsion from the universities and its practitioners in early Tudor England were to be found in the artisan and mercantile classes; their literary sources were manuscript tracts and vernacular scriptures derived from the Vulgate. Now, however, Lutheranism was entering England by means of printed books and it was feared that the new European heresy would inject life into the old lollardy and thus turn a lingering tradition into a powerful intellectual movement once more. Consequently, the King and hierarchy made a determined effort to prevent the importation and circulation of Luther's writings.

Cuthbert Tunstal, Henry's ambassador at Worms, was well aware of the inflammatory nature of Luther's writings and of the need to exclude them from England. In January 1521, he sent Wolsey a copy of Luther's condemnation of the papal decretals, urging him to burn it once read and warn the printers and booksellers not to produce or import Luther's works. He also sent a detailed description of *De Captivitate Babylonica*, to which he added piously, 'I pray God keep that book out of England.'[14]

The Cardinal was unsuccessful in his efforts to follow Tunstal's advice and in April 1521 Warham was examining both Lutheran and

Wycliffite writings.[15] Though assiduous in the confiscation of such works, Wolsey was strangely dilatory about destroying them, claiming that his powers from Rome were insufficient to allow him to burn books; one recalls Erasmus's easy suasion of the Cardinal in 1520. Letters from the Pope and Cardinal de'Medici, however, stirred him to action and on 12 May a public ceremony of book-burning took place at Paul's Cross before Wolsey and the Bishops. Fisher preached a sermon in English for the benefit of the people which was immediately turned into elegant Latin by Pace for the enjoyment of the learned. Similar rituals took place at Cambridge and Oxford.[16]

Impressive as the London ceremony must have been, with Wolsey personifying the splendour and outward authority of the universal church and Fisher employing his humanist eloquence in defence of the faith, no halt was called to the importation of forbidden books. In December 1522 Thomas Hannibal sent Wolsey a copy of Luther's answer to the King from Rome and reported his own frantic efforts to prevent the work circulating in that city.[17] Hannibal's anxiety was justified, as Lutheranism had been discovered in both the English universities. (See Chapter Three, below.)

An important move in the government's defensive strategy was Wolsey's promotion of Tunstal to the sensitive see of London in January 1522. Like Fisher, Tunstal was an outstanding humanist, internationally known and admired through his friendship and correspondence with Erasmus, Budé and other scholars. He had seen extensive diplomatic service and, moreover, had observed Luther and his followers at close hand. Therefore, he kept a vigilant eye on the book dealers, summoning them in October 1524 for a lecture against trading in illicit materials and ordaining that the titles of all imported books should be submitted before sale to Warham, Wolsey, Fisher or himself.[18]

The following year there appeared an even more potent threat to Tunstal's peace of mind than Luther's writings. Edward Lee, reporting to Henry VIII from Bordeaux in December, told him that an Englishman had produced a vernacular version of scripture at the solicitation of Luther and intended to send printed copies of it to England. This was a fragment of Tyndale's new testament, printed at Cologne the previous August. The English authorities were sufficiently alarmed to plan a second book-burning ceremony at St Paul's in February 1526. On 5 January Bishop Longland informed Wolsey that he had spoken to the King about his plans for a 'secret search' for books and for a second sermon at St Paul's Cross, for which Henry suggested Fisher as preacher.[19]

Searches for prohibited books were conducted at the London Steelyard and at Cambridge. The first raid resulted in the arrest, examination and abjuration of several German merchants found in possession of illicit material. According to Harpsfield, William Roper, who frequented the Steelyard and was an avid reader of Luther, was also examined by Wolsey, but out of deference to his father-in-law, More, he was released with a friendly warning. Robert Barnes, on the other hand, was arrested at Cambridge and examined in London. He recanted, and appeared with the abjured German merchants at the book-burning ceremony on Quinquagesima Sunday to provide the edifying spectacle of the lost sheep returned to the fold.[20]

This second bonfire had as little effect on the illicit book trade as that of 1521 had done and by the summer Tyndale's completed new testament was circulating in appreciable quantities. Despite his confinement at the London Austin Priory, Barnes was able to sell a copy to one John Tyball.[21] Henry VIII's published *Answer* to Luther of 1526 declared that all 'untrue translations' of scripture would be burned and their readers punished, though significantly the King promised an authorised vernacular version once the realm was rid of religious unrest. In October of that year Tunstal ordered his archdeacons to gather in all copies of Tyndale's work and repeated his warning to the book dealers about forbidden imports, adding specific injunctions about the English new testament. He also attempted to stop Tyndale at source by buying and destroying all copies of his work found abroad, but as George Constantine later revealed to More, Tunstal's money financed future editions. Some time before 1528 a third ceremonial burning took place, with Tyndale's work rather than Luther's providing the fuel and Tunstal preaching in place of Fisher.[22]

In retrospect the campaign against prohibited books seems to have been an unmitigated failure, since it proved impossible to curb the steady flow of such works into England. However, the united front of opposition presented by King, court-patrons and hierarchy had several significant effects on English evangelicalism. No book of dubious orthodoxy could be published in the kingdom; authorship of such works could lead to prosecution and the avenues of preferment were closed to known evangelical scholars.

In these respects the events of Tyndale's early career are instructive. This most influential of English translators hoped to produce his new testament under the auspices of Tunstal, but despite a recommendation from Sir Henry Guildford and the proferred gift of a translation of Isocrates, the Bishop declared that his household was full. Considering Tunstal's record as a humanist and patron of scholars, one can only conclude that Tyndale's reputation as an extremely inflammatory preacher in the west country had already reached his ears. Consequently the translator fell back on the patronage of wealthy London merchants and produced his great work abroad.[23] Official opposition, then, gave English evangelicals the choice of exile or of apparent acquiescence in the *status quo*. Not until political events created more favourable circumstances could radical theological and ecclesiastical tenets be openly proclaimed and their proponents hope to receive patronage from court and hierarchy.

II

This change of circumstance came about through the royal divorce, which shattered the doctrinal unanimity of humanists and drastically altered the nature of the new learning in England. The 'King's Great Matter' posed a dilemma of loyalties, forcing a choice initially between King and Queen and ultimately between King and Pope. The very fact that Henry approached Rome for adverse judgement on a marriage it had originally sanctioned impugned papal authority at a time when it was under attack from a multitude of heresiarchs. Henry either did not or would not see the inconsistency of his action, but as Rome refused to accommodate his conscience he was forced to seek alternative sources of authority to support his case. Inevitably, and despite his distaste for their theology, the King was obliged to use and to afford limited toleration to evangelical humanists because, being opposed to papal authority, they could furnish arguments for the King's ecclesiastical supremacy in his own realm.

The fact that evangelicalism became not merely a tolerated aberration but the dominant strand in English humanism was largely the work of Anne Boleyn. Tradition pictures Anne as a ruthless hoyden who used religion simply as a weapon in politics, but there is abundant evidence that she was herself a devout evangelical, eager to foster reform and shelter reformers. (For Anne Boleyn's personal piety, see Chapter 7, below.) Naturally she was limited by the extent of her influence with Henry and by the King's innate religious conservatism, and blatantly unrepentant radicals could not look to her to save them from the stake; Bilney, Bainham and Frith, for example, were all burned during the period of her ascendancy. None the less, under Anne's aegis the reformers gained such ground at court that they were able to survive her fall and continue under new patronage.

Anne Boleyn, of course, was not wholly responsible for the advancement of the evangelical cause. This depended on the co-operation of sponsors and middlemen somewhat lower down the patronage ladder. Anne worked closely with Cromwell, though he was definitely the junior partner in the alliance; a bureaucrat, no matter how able and knowledgeable, could not compare in influence with the King's Lady.[24] Equally, the ubiquitous Dr Butts can often be discerned as a link in the chain of patronage between Anne and an evangelical suitor. (For Butts, see the Introduction, above.) So, too, can Sir Edward Bainton, who became Anne's vice-chamberlain after her marriage to the King. Thus the existence of a reform faction — a network of well placed and vigilant evangelical patrons — was essential to the success of Anne Boleyn's policy.

However, not all humanist activity after 1527 was evangelical. The attack on papal authority together with the alarming amount of latitude given to evangelicals caused many humanists to side with the Queen. Again, it is traditional to see Katherine of Aragon as pious but reactionary and her followers as fanatical, old-fashioned papalists. In fact, all the Queen's eminent scholarly supporters were proponents of the new learning who were concerned not merely with her defence, but with the continuing battle against heresy. As the momentum of events increased they would be put to death, forced into exile or cowed into acquiescent silence. Thus conservative humanism shared the fate of the discarded Queen, and the field was left to more radical reformers.

Divorce proceedings began officially on 17 May 1527, when Henry had himself cited before Warham and Wolsey in a secret court to answer to the charge of incest. Two factors, however, ensured that the business would not be swiftly and quietly concluded; the resistance of the Queen, who was well aware of her husband's intentions and the sack of Rome by imperial troops, which made a papal judgement against the Emperor's aunt impossible. After much browbeating by English agents Clement VII agreed to allow the case to be tried in London by Wolsey and the

Cardinal — Protector of England, Lorenzo Campeggio. The Italian legate only reached London in October 1528 and the opening of the legatine court was delayed until the following summer.

Immediately, however, the King and Queen began to recruit scholarly support and Erasmus found himself the object of solicitations from both sides. In fact, the great scholar was still smarting from his involvement in the Lutheran question and had no desire to be inveigled into another dispute. Consequently, while politely declining Henry's invitation to England on the grounds of ill-health, he also refused to give the Queen a verdict on the marriage, merely suggesting that it were better for Jove to take two Junos than to put one away. It is a telling comment on the characters of both that, while Henry steadfastly ignored Erasmus thereafter, Katherine sent him gifts of money and continued to read his works.[25]

In contrast to Erasmus's reluctance several English scholars rushed to the aid of their King. Richard Pace, who had suffered a nervous breakdown at Padua in 1525, was apparently judged to be fit for duty. In 1527 he summoned his brother John to him at Syon Monastery: 'And do you set written upon the door "God save the King!" Amen. I know the King's mind. Do you as I command you whatsoever any other man shall say.' He composed at least one book on the marriage and by 1528 was engaged in controversy with Fisher.[26]

At the same time Pace recommended other scholars to the King's service. He sent Henry a Hebrew alphabet to be delivered to Edward Foxe, a protégé of Wolsey, with instructions to learn it by heart; this could be done within a month and would give Foxe (whose learning and fidelity he extolled) enough knowledge to examine the old testament for evidence for Henry's case.[27] Pace also helped Robert Wakefield to transfer his allegiance from Katherine to Henry. This distinguished Hebraist and protégé of Fisher had embarked on the Queen's defence, possibly because of the influence of his old patron. Realising his folly, he helped Pace with his book for the King and persuaded him to write to Henry to suggest that he interview Wakefield so as to note his excellent — and useful — learning in theology and the tongues.

Wakefield himself wrote to Henry proclaiming that he was able and willing to defend the King's case in all the universities of Christendom, 'by good and sufficient authority of the scripture of God and the words of the best learned and most excellent authors of the interpreters of the Hebrews, and the holy doctors both Greeks and Latins in Christ's faith'. He also promised to answer Fisher in such a way 'that I trust he shall be ashamed to wade or meddle any further in the matter'. However, he begged Henry not to tell a living soul that he had switched sides:

> for if the people should know that I, which began to defend the Queen's cause, not knowing that she was carnally known of Prince Arthur, your brother, should now write against it, surely I should be stoned of them to death, or else have such a slander and obloquy raised upon me, that I had rather to die a thousand times or suffer it.[28]

Katherine, of course, always denied that her first marriage had been consummated, but Wakefield's ungallant disingenuity stood him in good stead. The treasurer of the chamber's accounts for 1528–31 show him in receipt of a stipend of £20 a year until March 1529, beside a payment of 66s 8d in the latter month as 'reader of Hebrew'. Significantly, he also came under the patronage of the Boleyns; Anne's father equalled the King's annual salary of £20 and the Lady herself gave him the sum of £100.[29]

A similar case was that of John Oliver, suspected by Cromwell in 1538 of being guilty of 'the mortal, deadly shame of a papist'. In that year he reminded Cromwell of how he had summoned him to his house some years before, 'concerning the Lady Dowager's matter, wherein I plainly declared unto you my opinion to be against her purpose, and how that I never did speak for her, but as I was enforced by the old Bishop of Canterbury'.[30]

Oliver's assertion that he was the unwilling tool of the notoriously timid Warham gained him Cromwell's 'pity and compassion', which in turn procured him the King's favour and the place of royal chaplain, besides 'all the living that I have, which is much better than I am worthy', including his appointment as dean of Henry VIII's college at Oxford. Stubbornness in the Queen's cause would have had far less happy consequences.

One can see Wakefield and his fellows as mere careerists, anxious to serve their King and avoid his displeasure; their function was simply to help him to prepare for the papal court which was to meet in London. However, even before that court met, Anne Boleyn was using literary works to direct the King towards a more radical policy in relation to his marriage and to his ecclesiastical authority in England.

According to John Foxe, a copy of Simon Fish's *Supplication for the Beggars* was sent to Anne, probably in 1528, the year of its publication in Antwerp. It is well known that the book was not so much a radical theological tract as an attack on the rapacity of the clergy, who, in Fish's view, demanded exorbitant ecclesiastical fees and used the cult of purgatory for its own financial ends. Naturally this criticism of clerical privilege and authority interested Anne, whose brother George suggested that she show it to the King, to whom it was dedicated. Henry was so pleased with the book, says Foxe, that he gave his protection to Fish and his wife. They were able to return to England despite the wrath of the chancellor, More, who had replied to the book with his *Supplication of Souls*.[31] At about the same time Anne introduced the King to Tyndale's *Obedience of a Christian Man*, which was equally pleasing to him. Henry declared that this book was 'for me and all kings to read', and doubtless referred to it after the legatine court ended in fiasco.[32]

What, meanwhile, of the Queen's party? Ironically it was Tyndale who most graphically described her position:

> When the Queen was warned, she desired learned counsel to defend her quarrel, that she should have no wrong; and it was granted her, and she chose. But alas, what choice is there among the fox's whelps? All that be shaven are sworn together. And all that be promoted by them must play the Judases with them.[33]

Tyndale blamed Wolsey and his creatures the bishops for engineering Katherine's downfall, but she was the victim, not of clerical conspiracy, but of the fear of the King's anger prevalent among her counsellors. Several distinguished theologians and canonists were appointed for her defence; Warham, Fisher, Clerk, Tunstal, West, Veysey, Standish and Ateca from the episcopal bench, besides Edward Powell, Robert Ridley and Richard Fetherston, Princess Mary's tutor. However, the King's apparent generosity in allowing his wife such advisers does not stand up to close scrutiny.

With the exception of Fisher, who had already prepared at least one book on the case, there was little indication that the Queen's counsellors would offer her much real assistance. Warham had opposed the Aragon marriage from the first and Wolsey told Henry in July 1527, 'I perceive he is not much altered or turned from his first fashion, expressly affirming that, howsoever displeasantly the

Queen took this matter, yet the truth and judgment of the law must have place'.[34] Standish, Erasmus's old enemy, would justify Katherine's mistrust of him by assisting at the consecration of Cranmer in 1533. In time the Queen became openly contemptuous of her advisers. In 1531, when Norfolk told her to be grateful to the King for arranging her defence she retorted that they were fine counsellors: Warham's motto was *'ira principis mors est'*, and he declared that he would not meddle in her affairs; Tunstal said he dared not advise her because he was Henry's subject and vassal: and Fisher merely told her to have courage. Katherine in her bitterness was obviously less than fair on this occasion to Fisher, who not only wrote copiously on her behalf, but sent her books and messages through his chaplain, Dr Addyson, besides making a courageous stand at Blackfriars and taking the risk of conferring with the imperial ambassador.[35]

In truth, the only bishops who acted creditably in the matter were the humanists Fisher, Fox and Tunstal. This last, who owed his advancement to Warham and Wolsey, none the less wrote a book in the Queen's defence; but he was persuaded by the King to absent himself from the legatine court and not to allow the work to be read there. In the next few years he protested against Henry's anti-papal policy, but was forced to submit to the King in 1534.[36] Similarly, Richard Fox was inclined to show courage initially when questioned about Katherine's first marriage. He declared that he 'could not remember' or 'did not recollect' many of the circumstances of her betrothal to Henry and bravely opined that the King loved Katherine for her good qualities. Even so cautious an effort on the Queen's behalf was dangerous, however, and Fox had to send Henry a written assurance that he had obeyed his commands 'as far as my poor wit, my dull memory, and my conscience' had allowed him.[37]

If Katherine was scornful at the timidity of the bishops, she was bitterly disappointed in her protégé Vives, who was in England between October 1527 and April 1528. (For Vives in England, see Chapter Five below.) Vives immediately offered his services and gave her both spoken and written advice and the King responded by placing him under house arrest along with Francisco Felipez, a confidential servant and messenger of the Queen. Both were interrogated by Wolsey, who wanted not only to keep Katherine's advisers away from her, but also to learn her strategy. Vives was forced to confess his communication with her and on his release both she and

Vives thought it expedient for him to leave the country. Thus intimated, Vives departed temporarily from the immediate theatre of war, telling Erasmus of his wish that Jupiter and Juno would seek to propitiate Christ rather than the pagan Venus.[38]

He returned late in 1528, but antagonised the Queen as well as the King. He advised Katherine not to attend the legatine court, as this would force Henry to place himself in an invidious position by having her condemned unheard. The Queen ultimately followed this course, but initially she considered Vives's answer as a treacherous evasion. Like Henry, she stopped the pension she had granted him, and Vives left England forever. His only further connection with the Tudors was a letter of advice he sent Henry in January 1531 which urged him to take Katherine back.[39]

The failure of the legatine court to give Henry the verdict he desired impelled the King to seek further learned authority (orthodox, heretical, judaic, no matter what) for his proceedings. The first plan, that of canvassing the European universities, was first mooted by Cranmer, then an obscure fellow of Jesus, Cambridge, in the late summer of 1529.[40] The suggestion ensured his introduction at court and — significantly — into the household of Thomas Boleyn, where he was employed in writing out his own opinion of the marriage.

The referendum of the universities went hand in hand with the scholarly ransacking of libraries at home and abroad for evidence supporting both the King's view of the validity of his marriage and, later, his claim that jurisdiction in the matter was his own prerogative, not the Pope's. The *Collectanea satis copiosa*, a body of scriptural, patristic, legal and historical material which formed the basis of several later divorce and supremacy publications, was commenced as early as the autumn of 1530. Its principal compiler was Edward Foxe, one of the chief agents sent to the English and foreign universities.[41]

Oxford and Cambridge were approached early in 1530. As might be expected, both returned verdicts favourable to the King, though the matter did not pass without dissension and debate. (See Chapter Three, below.) It proved even more difficult to persuade some of the foreign universities to condemn the King's marriage. European scholars could not be threatened with Henry's displeasure and though they might be bribed the English agents had to compete in this respect with the Emperor's servants. The many difficulties encountered by Henry's men, charged as they were with the double task of canvassing for votes and extracting evidence for the case from suspicious foreign librarians, are illustrated by the adventures in Italy of Richard Croke, eminent classical scholar and former tutor to the King's bastard son.

Croke was chosen to search the libraries of Venice because of his expertise in Greek. He also journeyed to Padua, Bologna and Rome to solicit scholarly opinions on the case. He travelled in great secrecy, and adopted a pseudonym. Like all scholars and government envoys he complained unceasingly of his poverty, alleging that he could scarcely afford to live and to pay his trans- cribers. He managed, however, to pay out sums ranging from one to thirty crowns by way of reward to doctors and authors. His success was greatly hindered by the fact that Charles V apparently paid far more to those who wrote for Katherine than Croke could hope to offer to likely supporters of Henry.[42]

Despite these difficulties the activities of English agents in the law and theology faculties of the universities of France and Northern Italy secured a number of verdicts favourable to the King. Orleans, Paris, Anjou, Bologna, Padua and Toulouse all voted against the marriage between April and October 1530. Events at Paris are particularly interesting, not least because Reginald Pole was the agent employed to sway the university by his humanist eloquence.

In March 1530 an unknown friend wrote to Pole on Norfolk's behalf to congratulate him on acting so loyally for Henry without having been asked to do so, and to report the King's delight at having Pole for his advocate at last. The letter implies that Pole had shown diffidence, but his reports from Paris were full of enthusiasm for the King's cause. However, his attitude to the divorce is something of a problem. Cranmer told Thomas Boleyn that Pole

> hath written a book much contrary to the King's purpose, with such wit that it appeareth that he might be for his wisdom of the council to the King's grace. And of such eloquence that if it [the book] were set forth and known to the common people I suppose it were not possible to persuade them to the contrary.

Unfortunately it is uncertain whether this book preceded or followed Pole's mission to Paris, whether his labours there were the source of his scruples or were undertaken to re-establish his loyalty. He played no further part in the King's affairs, but returned to his studies in Italy still furnished with his generous royal pension.[43]

Although Paris had given Henry the right verdict, the zeal of imperial agents there had reduced the majority to a mere seven or eight votes; a fact which was immediately broadcast by Katherine's supporters. Undaunted by the hollowness of the victory, Foxe, Cranmer and Stokesley compiled a small book of arguments based on the research material of the *Collectanea satis copiosa*, prefaced with the university verdicts against the marriage. This was published as *The Determinations of the most famous and most excellent universities of Italy and France, that it is so unlawful for a man to marry with his brother's wife, that the Pope hath no power to dispense therewith*. It was followed by the publication of *The Glass of Truth*, reputedly the King's own work.[44] Croke, by this time sub-dean of the King's college at Oxford and charged with the distribution of copies there, told Cromwell that many doubted the King's authorship:

> They do confess that his grace's both excellent wit and excellent learning is able to do a thing much better than that, albeit they suppose that his highness lacketh leisure so profoundly to search and butt out a matter of so great difficulty so plainly.[45]

Henry's zeal in his own cause was underestimated by his subjects; in 1528 he had complained to Anne Boleyn of a headache caused by looking for over four hours at 'my book', which 'maketh substantially for my matter', and he annotated a good part of the manuscript of the *Collectanea*.[46] It would seem likely that he at least supervised the new work. Croke reported that many had been persuaded of the justice of Henry's cause by *The Glass of Truth*, and though he was obliged to admit that several refutations had been produced, he loyally asserted that these seemed dull and ineffectual compared to the King's book.

The work was designed for export as well as for home consumption. In October 1532 John Williamson sent Cromwell 'a hundred books entitled *Le Mirroir de Verité* which I have received this present day of Master Palgrave'. This was John Palsgrave, former royal tutor and French grammarian, who was probably the translator; it has been suggested that his presentation by Cranmer to the lucrative living of St Dunstan's-in-the-East in October 1533 was a reward for services rendered.[47] A letter from Nicholas Hawkins, archdeacon of Ely and a member of the embassy sent to Charles V at Bologna, apparently refers to the French translation and to a Latin version of *The Glass of Truth* prepared for the Italian market.[48]

Besides producing general propaganda the King's servants approached theologians on the continent for a public pronouncement against the marriage. They were not always successful; both an official request to Luther late in 1531 and an independent attempt by Stephen Vaughan in 1532 to persuade Tyndale to speak for the King failed miserably. Tyndale had already produced his *Practice of Prelates* which was sympathetic to Katherine, and the Queen must have been astonished to learn that Luther had declared that she must be encouraged and 'must never be allowed to burden herself with an invented evil'. The reformer prayed that God would prevent the divorce:

> Or, if it is not his will to prevent it, then may he grant to the Queen strong faith, sure constancy and a sure conscience so that she may be and forever remain the legal and true Queen of England despite all that may happen and in the face of all the powers of hell and of this world, Amen.[49]

Greater hope was offered by Simon Grynaeus, who came to England in 1531 for purely academic purposes and incidentally, partook freely of the hospitality of More. (See Chapter Five, below.) However on 6 June Chapuys reported that Grynaeus, originally in England on a literary errand, had been consulted by Henry on the marriage and given a sum of money because he promised to send the King the determinations of the doctors of Basle on the question.[50]

While Henry's party canvassed Europe for favourable opinions, a number of the Emperor's subjects produced books on Katherine's behalf.[51] In addition Chapuys tried to enlist the services of his friend Henry Cornelius Agrippa von Nettesheim, who had commented sardonically on Henry's behaviour in his satire *De Incertitudine et Vanitate Scientiarum et Artium*. Unfortunately Agrippa's personal troubles seem to have prevented his serving the Queen effectively, though Robert Wakefield asserted that his *Kotser Codicis* was a refutation of works by Fisher, Vives and Thomas Abell.[52]

Abell was an English chaplain of Katherine; although initially distrusted by her when sent to Spain with her enforced 'request' for the Spanish Brief in 1528, he served her better there than a Spanish servant she had entrusted with a verbal message for Charles V. In addition, in August 1530 Abell told the King's councillors to their faces that those who advised Henry on his marriage were iniquitous and showed them a list of 44 Parisian doctors who had voted for Katherine in the recent referendum. Banished from court, Abell busied himself with a book on the marriage, published in English at Lüneberg in May 1532 as *Invicta Veritas*.[53]

The scholarly — and political — deadlock over the divorce was broken in 1533 by the very human circumstance of Anne Boleyn's pregnancy, which necessitated a swift termination of the King's first marriage and prompt recognition of his second one. The abrupt change in the *status quo* dramatically altered the nature of propaganda; Henry no longer required authority for a projected policy, but justification of a *fait accompli*. In 1533 the King himself, though doubtless with scholarly assistance, produced *De Potestate Christianorum Regum in suis Ecclesiis, contra Pontificis tyrannidem et horribilem impietatem*. In February 1534 the French ambassador told Chapuys that Henry had sent Francis I a book against the papacy written by himself which was more urgent and vehement than any hitherto published. Though the King declared that he was no Lutheran and only wished to correct the vices of the clergy, the Frenchman believed that Anne Boleyn would eventually make him as Lutheran as herself.[54]

In addition, Foxe and Gardiner produced an important work each; the former's *De vera differentia regiae potestatis et ecclesiasticae* was published in 1534, the latter's *De Vera Obedentia* in the following year. Gardiner also composed in Latin a justification of Fisher's death which was translated into English by another scholar. Neither version seems to have been printed, though copies of the work were allegedly in circulation at the French court.[55]

At the same time English policy was justified abroad; Nicholas Olah, Mary of Hungary's secretary, told Erasmus that many 'blasphemous books' were emanating from England. Official publications included a Latin oration by Richard Sampson on the royal supremacy (eventually answered by Cochlaeus), a sermon by Simon Matthew, prebendary of St Paul's and the anonymous *Little treatise against the muttering of some papists in corners*. As a final blast against the Aragon marriage, Wakefield's *Kotser Codicis*, containing a letter to Fisher giving his reasons for finding the union invalid, appeared at some time between 1533 and 1536.[56]

Besides the works sponsored by the government and published by the royal printer Berthelet, a certain amount of independent and indirect propaganda appeared. William Marshall translated Valla's *Donation of Constantine* and Marsiglio's *Defensor Pacis*, but, although the former work was sent to Cromwell for approval and the latter's publication was financed by him, these tracts were not officially commissioned, and so they must be viewed simply as offerings designed to display ability, obedience and willingness to serve.

Indeed, the government's need for propaganda led many scholars to present their own compositions and translations in the hope of preferment and employment. Not all applicants were successful; Elton describes a number of obscure and probably inept suitors who offered verses, prophecies and anti-papal tracts to Cromwell but who apparently received little or no remuneration for their pains.[57]

On the other hand, Richard Morison and Thomas Starkey were eminently successful in their attempts to enter government service by courting Cromwell. Though Morison was retained in Italy as a gatherer of foreign news until spring 1536 (when, perhaps, Cromwell's increased grip on patronage enabled him to offer his client work at home), Starkey found employment soon after his return to England late in 1534. He sent Cromwell an account of his labours in philosophy, the tongues, theology and civil law, which he claimed to have undertaken to equip himself for the service of his country. In 1535 he was engaged on an important piece of propaganda, *An Exhortation to Unity*, and in persuading Pole, his former companion at Padua, to give an opinion on Henry's proceedings. Literary propaganda went hand in hand with the more popular medium of the sermon. The indefatigable Croke preached more than 60 sermons in one year at 37 different places, justifying the royal supremacy by 'evident reason grounded upon scripture; by authority of the ancient doctors; by the saying of More and other papists themselves'.[58]

At the same time, all humanistic opposition to the King was silenced. Fisher and More paid the ultimate penalty for their resistance to royal supremacy in summer 1535, as did two groups of Carthusians and a member of the Bridgettine house at Syon. Abell, Edward Powell and Richard Fetherston languished in prison until 1540, when they were executed at the same time as the evangelicals Barnes, Garrett and Jerome. None the less, resistance to the King continued for a time in the three religious orders which most favoured the new learning; the Carthusians, Bridgettines and Observant Franciscans.[59]

The Observant convent at Greenwich, which had provided Katherine with several confessors, was a particular nucleus of disaffection. Friars Peto and Elston were forced into exile in 1532 after their outspoken preaching angered the King, and Peto published an answer to *The Glass of Truth* and a book attributed to Fisher at Antwerp; he did not return to England until the reign of Mary. Friar Forest, formerly Katherine's confessor, preached inflammatory sermons at Paul's Cross and encouraged his brethren in their resistance. He was removed to a house in the north in 1533 and arrested in 1534. It seems from letters which passed between him and the Queen that his execution was expected, but in fact he was kept alive until 1539. Members of the order visited Katherine, ostensibly to hear confessions from her servants but really to carry messages between the Queen and her daughter. Others, such as Gabriel Peacock, warden of the Southampton convent, preached against the King's policies. The order was deemed so seditious that it was dissolved wholesale in 1534. Some friars fled abroad, some returned to the world, but others were imprisoned, mainly in other convents.[60]

The Bridgettine house at Syon, which had a reputation for piety and humanist learning and a longstanding personal connection with the Queen, refused to accept royal supremacy until 1535. Books by Fisher and Abell, with another attributed to Chapuys, were found there and it took the suasions of humanists sent from court and the arrest of one of the ringleaders, Richard Whitford the devotional writer, to secure the obedience of the community.[61]

It was a similar tale with the Carthusians. In October 1535 imported books — possibly sent by Peto from the Netherlands — were found at the London Charterhouse, where the monks refused to read Marshall's version of *Defensor Pacis* or to accept the supremacy. But like the Bridgettines the Carthusians of this and other houses were eventually reduced to conformity.[62]

Thus by 1536, the year of Queen Katherine's death, humanist opposition to Henry VIII's divorce and breach with Rome had been destroyed or compelled into acquiescence. Henceforth conservative humanists played little part in public debate and their literary spokesmen, Whitford and Sir Thomas Elyot among them, advocated an unquestioning piety and strict abstinence from doctrinal speculation. As far as religious policy went, the defence of orthodoxy was left to men like Norfolk who had no sympathy at all with the new learning. The 'King's Great Matter' therefore swept away the non-doctrinal Erasmian humanism of Henry's earlier years.

1536 was also the year of Anne Boleyn's death, but while her political faction shared her fate, her ideological clients survived to fight another day. In the course of the divorce Anne recruited into her service many evangelical scholars and helped them to ecclesiastical preferment. Among her chaplains were Nicholas Shaxton, Hugh Latimer, John Skip and Matthew Parker. Latimer and Shaxton both caught official attention (or more directly, the eye of Dr Butts) during the divorce referendum at Cambridge and in 1535 they were promoted respectively to the sees of Worcester and Salisbury, both formerly held by absentee Italian bishops. Skip, too, was a Cambridge man, like Shaxton a member of Butts's old college, Gonville Hall, and a frequenter of the White Horse. In 1539 he would become Bishop of Hereford. Anne urgently commanded Parker to court in March 1535 on the death of her chaplain William Betts, another Gonville evangelical. Other reformers advanced by Anne were Edward Crome, whom she nominated to St Mary Aldermary, London (a living in Cranmer's gift) in 1534; and William Barlow, whom she appointed successively prior of Haverfordwest and of Bisham, Berkshire, and who was later Bishop of St Asaph and of St David's. (For other chaplains and clients of Anne Boleyn, see Chapter Seven, below.)[63]

These radical figures managed to survive the fall of their patron because of the skilful machinations of Cromwell. He had been Anne's partner in ecclesiastical and scholarly promotion; he had, for example helped procure Hugh Latimer one of the King's benefices in Wiltshire and William Barlow had asked his assistance when harassed by the conservative officials of the then Bishop of St David's.[64] His relationship to Anne is illustrated by Shaxton's plea to him in May 1536 to continue to uphold the gospel as she had often exhorted him to do, despite her misconduct which had besmirched the cause.[65] Cromwell, by engineering Anne's downfall in an unlikely alliance with Princess Mary's supporters, managed to dissociate both himself and the cause of evangelical reform from the disgraced favourite. In the absence of any intellectual competition, radical humanists were able to influence religious policy considerably during the rest of the reign.

III

Having broken with the universal church and asserted the authority of the crown over the church in England, it was essential for Henry VIII and his advisers to establish a satisfactory formulary of faith. Their attempts to do so must be understood against the mutable background of diplomatic events. From the papal point of view England was heretical, and it was always possible that one of the godly European sons of the church, the Most Christian King of France or the Holy Roman Emperor, might use excommunication as a pretext for war. The government's concern with the repercussions of schism is shown by the propaganda campaign against foreign critics and English malcontents. Morison produced a resounding answer to Cochlaeus, edited the King's own defence of his refusal to attend the Mantuan Council and composed several tracts exhorting English conservatives to obedience, while Pole was rebuked, anathematised and ridiculed by his former patrons and friends once the book the King had urged him to write had shown that he could never accept Henry's reformation.[66]

In England itself conservative unease lingered and the outright apostasy of Pole, the open rebellions and supposed conspiracies of the period illuminated the danger of alienating the King's orthodox subjects by a too rapid reformation. On the other hand, alliance or at least *entente* with foreign schismatic powers was also a perennial possibility, and English evangelicals were eager for further reform on the various continental models. All churchmen agreed that reformation of abuses was needed, but the problem facing those who formulated belief under the watchful gaze of the 'supreme head' was to calm the fears and assuage the desires of all these varieties of opinion; in short, to provide a basis for the unity of the English church.

The first attempt at a definition of faith was the Ten Articles approved by convocation in July 1536. Besides the domestic need for such a declaration, it was hoped that a definite statement of belief would assist negotiations with the German Lutherans, commenced in view of the apparent *rapprochement* between the two Catholic continental powers. The Germans insisted on acceptance of the Confession of Augsburg as a condition of Henry's entry into the Schmalkaldic League and Cromwell clearly hoped to persuade his master to meet this requirement, since he commanded Richard Taverner to translate both the Augsburg declaration and Melanchthon's defence of it. It is wrong, however, to assume that this was printed 'to elaborate the religious settlement'; rather, the project was Cromwell's attempt to influence policy.[67]

In the event the Augsburg Confession was rejected in favour of a formulary which has been described as 'a masterpiece of evasion'.[68] Ostensibly the Ten Articles followed Luther in omitting four of the seven sacraments, but in fact these were passed over in silence rather than decisively rejected, while the remaining three (baptism, penance and eucharist) were defined in an orthodox sense. The article on the eucharist was equivocal as to the nature of Christ's presence in the sacrament and though the efficacy and desirability of prayers for the dead were asserted a definition of purgatory was carefully avoided.

Such an ambiguous statement on doctrine could neither appease conservative fears nor assuage desire for further reform, and consequently the bishops were hard at work on a more satisfactory formulary by the following February. Additional divines were pressed into service, among them Cromwell's clients Starkey and Leighton, who were commanded by the King to consult with the bishops on such matters as priestly celibacy, purgatory and the invocation of saints.[69] Cromwell exercised close supervision over the theologians' deliberations, but he was powerless to force a more radical line on the conservative bishops and there was much dissension. More importantly, the frequent references in the bishops' letters to the King's pleasure and intentions attest his vigilant interest in the matter and this inhibited conservatives and radicals alike from pressing their views too far.

Consequently the *Godly and Pious Institution of a Christian Man* (the 'Bishops' Book') emerged as another cloudy compromise; though transubstantiation was not explicitly asserted and the authority of scripture over Christian tradition was emphasised, all seven sacraments were maintained. Like its predecessor the Bishops' Book failed to make a significant move either backwards to traditional doctrine or forwards to a more radical theology. Henry himself found it unacceptable as the basis of belief for his whole church and though it was published by Berthelet in September 1537, it was never presented to convocation or to parliament, but merely recommended for the private study of the parish clergy. The King undertook to correct the text with a view to a revised edition in 1538, but he met with unexpectedly stiff opposition from his archbishop. Cranmer sent Cromwell Henry's annotations with corrections of his own, which extended to the King's grammar as well as his theology. He explained that 'because the book shall now be set forth by his grace's censure and judgment, I would have nothing therein that

Momus could reprehend: and . . . I refer all mine annotations again to his grace's most exact judgment'.[70] Evidently a religious settlement would be impossible on the basis of this ambiguous formulary.

The uncertainty prevailing among continental reformers as to which way the English cat would jump in both diplomatic and doctrinal terms led to several foreign attempts to influence Henry in favour of the gospel. Münster, Bullinger and Capito all dedicated books to the King, but though these were all accepted Henry did not refrain from criticising the judgements of foreign theologians as thoroughly as he did those of his own churchmen. Nicholas Partridge informed Bullinger that his book — presented to the King through Cranmer and Cromwell — had been well received, since Henry had expressed a wish for an English translation; yet the King's presentation copy of *De Scripturae Sanctae Authoritate*, now in the British Library, bears a marginal note in his hand declaring one argument irrelevant. Similarly, Cranmer told Capito that his *Responsio de Missa, Matrimonio et jure Magistratus in Religionem* dedicated to the King and presented by the archbishop, had pleased him on the whole, though he had taken exception to some of the statements; probably, in Cranmer's opinion, those on the mass.[71]

If doctrine remained undefined in these years, one of the primary aims of humanism was achieved; the production of an authorised vernacular bible. The first complete English bible was Coverdale's edition of 1535, published abroad with an unsolicited dedication to the King. Cromwell secured permission for James Nicholson of Southwark to print three editions of this version in 1536 and 1537 and himself ordered the parish clergy in his injunctions of July 1536 to provide English and Latin bibles in their churches for the use of the laity. A rival version appeared in 1537 in the shape of the 'Matthew' bible, translated by John Rogers and published abroad (probably at Antwerp) by the London printers Grafton and Whitchurch with a dedication to the King. Cromwell at Cranmer's request obtained a royal licence for it to be read freely in England until the bishops should produce a better version; something which, Cranmer observed caustically, would not occur before Doomsday.[72]

The Matthew and Coverdale bibles were independent projects offered for authorisation after completion, but the time seemed propitious for a translation commissioned, supervised and finally approved by authority. The King's readiness to license both independent bibles showed his interest in the matter and in 1538

Cromwell commissioned Coverdale, Grafton and Whitchurch to produce a new authorised version.[73]

Despite technical problems and the hostility of conservatives like Gardiner the Great Bible appeared in April 1539 and ran to seven editions between that date and December 1541. The second edition, of April 1540, contained a prologue by Cranmer and was appointed for use in churches. The Great Bible survived the fall of Cromwell, its principal sponsor and the fourth edition of November 1540 (which excised his arms from its title page) was approved and overseen by two conservative bishops, Tunstal and Heath. A proclamation of May 1541 confirmed the injunction that English bibles should be placed in all parish churches at the expense of priest and congregation and added a penalty of 40s a month for failure to comply. It also stressed that the scriptural text was meant for private reading, not lay preaching and that the laity were not to 'read the said bibles with loud and high voices, in time of the celebration of the holy mass', nor to 'presume to take upon them any common disputation, argument, or exposition of the mysteries therein contained'.[74] Issued as it was with these restrictions, the Great Bible may be considered a humanist rather than a purely Protestant achievement and one that would have been welcomed by humanists in the early years of the reign.

Until 1539 the very vagueness of the 'religious settlement' enabled most churchmen to live with their consciences and within the law and, in the case of harassment from hostile superiors, to secure protection from sympathetic patrons. If future bickering and conflict were to be avoided, however, a clear definition of belief and practice was essential. When parliament met in April 1539 the King himself called for an end to uncertainty and the production of a positive pronouncement on faith. Accordingly a committee was formed consisting of three evangelical and three conservative bishops, with Cromwell presiding as vice-gerent. Naturally enough this evenly balanced body failed to come to grips with the issue and in May Henry went over its head and permitted Norfolk to offer six questions for debate in the Lords. Since these were approved by the King and so worded as to admit of only one answer, they were duly framed as articles and passed into law as the Act for Abolishing Diversity of Opinion. The statute reaffirmed orthodoxy at six crucial points by unequivocal statements on transubstantiation, communion in one kind, private masses, auricular confession, vows of chastity and clerical celibacy.[75]

The 'Act of Six Articles' was directly confirmed by *The Necessary Doctrine and Erudition of a Christian Man*, produced by the bishops in 1543 and generally known as the 'King's Book' because, unlike its unhappy predecessor, it received authorisation from the monarch. Henry's close involvement with the framing of both the statute and the book is attested by his manuscript corrections of the first draft of the Act and of several documents which formed the basis of the printed work. Doctrinal innovation was thus brought to a halt by the direct intervention of the King himself.

Despite the penalties it carried, the Act of Six Articles created few martyrs, though Latimer and Shaxton felt compelled to resign their sees and several lesser lights, including Bale and Coverdale, went into exile. Even so the passage of the Act, coupled with the destruction of Cromwell in 1540, seemed to presage a bleak future for the cause of evangelical reform. John Lassells, who was later burned with Anne Askew, went to court after Cromwell's death and asked two co-religionists how matters stood for the word of God, 'seeing we have lost so noble a man which did love and favour it so well'. Hearing of the temporary pre-eminence and outspokenness of Norfolk, he advised a friend not to be too forward in maintaining scripture but to suffer in silence until the upholders of reaction had betrayed themselves.[76]

That the cause of the gospel did not share the fate of Cromwell was due firstly to the continuing activity of evangelical middlemen like Butts and secondly to another clear transfer of the power of patronage at the highest level. Cromwell's successor was Sir Anthony Denny, member of the King's privy chamber from at least 1532, one of the two chief gentlemen from 1538 and groom of the stool in 1546. The importance of the privy chamber as a centre of patronage has been elucidated by David Starkey, and the continuing existence of a reform faction there in the 1540s explains why evangelicals could still hope for protection.[77]

Denny's credentials as a patron of learning and reform can be quickly established. Himself a product of Colet's humanist school at St Paul's and of Fisher's college of St John's, Denny was active in assisting scholars and their suits at court. In 1539 Thomas Paynell dedicated his *Sermon of Cyprian made on the Lord's Prayer* to him, praising, among other things, 'your sincere affection to God and his holy word'. Thomas Langley in the preface to his *Abridgment of the Notable Work of Polydore Vergil* of 1546 described Denny as 'not only inflamed with desire of knowledge of antiquities, but also a favourable supporter of all good learning and a very Maecenas of all toward wits'. He also spoke of the 'special love and mind that you have to further the knowledge of the truth and abolish ignorance, hypocrisy and all other like painted holiness . . . your alacrity and readiness in preferring the blessed word of God and the sincere setters forth of the same'. In the same year Lady Jane Denny received the dedication of *A Sweet Consolation and the Second Book of the Troubled Man's Medicine* from her servant William Hugh. Lady Denny herself was noted as one of the godly women of the court and Hugh praised her as

> a wife not unworthy of him whom God, the maker of all honest marriages, hath given you for your husband. What commendation is comprised herein judge they that know the goodly and godly qualities, the authority and wisdom, the virtues and singular gifts which God hath moved him withall.

These literary references, though obviously biased by the position of the authors, reveal Denny's reputation with scholars and reformers. So, too, does an anonymous epitaph which bids him

> Farewell, most worthy knight laid up in quiet rest,
> Maecenas to the learned, an author to religion,
> To those an open haven that were for Christ oppressed,
> An enemy to the Pope and his superstition.[78]

Denny is known to have worked with Cromwell on at least one occasion, when they both recommended Elyot and his *Dictionary* to Henry.[79] Given their community of interest, it would be surprising if this were an isolated incident of joint patronage. Thus it would seem that in the highest sphere of patronage a kind of apostolic succession obtained, with the mantle of reform passing from Anne Boleyn working in conjunction with Cromwell, to Cromwell in association with Denny and finally to Denny himself. It may be noted that a lesser figure who co-operated with all three was Butts and both he and Denny figure repeatedly in the stories of conservative attacks on evangelicals in the 1540s.

The first conservative target was, not surprisingly, the Archbishop of Canterbury. Cranmer's absolute loyalty to his 'Supreme Head' could be depended upon, but this did not prevent him criticising religious policy as it developed nor from sheltering evangelicals, and he was vulnerable to attack on another count. Contrary to the popular legend which makes him the only man Henry VIII ever loved or trusted, the evidence of the 1530s shows Cranmer to have been a figure of little personal influence. Whether he was offering his corrections of Henry's annotations to the Bishop's Book, presenting a new translation of the bible or simply asking for passports for scholars going abroad, he was heavily dependent on Cromwell as an intermediary with the King. After Cromwell's removal he was forced to lean on the goodwill and influence of Denny and Butts, both of who figure importantly in the well-known story of the 'Prebendaries' Plot'.[80]

In 1543 the Archbishop's enemies on the council seized on accusations of heresy from his own canons at Canterbury and suggested to Henry that he should be imprisoned so that his accusers would not be afraid to speak against him. The King agreed to have him arrested in the council chamber next morning, but immediately the wheels of protection were set in motion. That night Henry sent Denny to fetch Cranmer to court, warned him with somewhat savage jocularity of his danger and promised him favour. The following day Butts saw Cranmer humiliated by being kept waiting among the lackeys at the council chamber door. He rushed to tell the news to Henry, who roundly berated the conspirators. The story is full of hidden obscurities, since it is not clear whether Henry himself stage-managed the affair assisted by Denny and Butts, or whether Denny persuaded the King to summon Cranmer, and Butts's intervention was quite spontaneous. Whatever the explanation, Cranmer was saved.

Fresh troubles awaited him, however. A commission for Kent was set up to investigate the charges against him, but it was so biased in favour of his accusers that his secretary Morice wrote to Denny and Butts asking them to arrange for Archbishop Lee of York 'or some other stout man' to be sent to Canterbury. His suit was successful and the conspiracy fell to the ground, but not before an attempt was made to discredit Cranmer through the prosecution of one of his diocesan clergy, Richard Turner. Morice again wrote to Denny and Butts, explaining that Cranmer was powerless to help himself because 'it is put into the King's head, that he is the maintainer and supporter of all the heretics within the realm'. This particular plot was foiled by Butts's urbane mediation with Henry 'when the King was in trimming and in washing', and both Turner and Cranmer escaped further persecution.[81]

The reform faction within the privy chamber was itself gravely implicated in a heresy-hunt among the canons of St George's, Windsor in 1543.[82] The prime mover in the affair was Gardiner, whose eagerness to serve Henry during the divorce was ironically at odds with his ultra-conservatism in religious matters. Gardiner's influence was such that, according to John Foxe, 'the gospellers were so quailed, that the best of them looked every hour to be clapped in the neck; for the saying went abroad, that the Bishop had bent his bow to shoot at some of the head deer'. Gardiner secured Wriothesley's co-operation and warned the King 'what sort of heretics his grace had in his realm and how they were not only crept into every corner of his court, but even into his Privy Chamber'.

The organist John Marbeck, who had produced a concordance of the English bible and translated some of Calvin's letters, was interrogated in particular about Sir Philip Hoby and Simon Heynes, dean of Exeter, who Gardiner referred to as 'your captains'. The attempt to incriminate these two was a direct attack on the reformers within the privy chamber. Hoby was a diplomatist and gentleman of the privy chamber of evangelical sympathies, while Heynes, one of those Cambridge radicals who had come to prominence during the royal divorce, was a confidant of Butts and sufficiently intimate with him to write in dangerously unguarded terms ('I shall write unto you as I am wont freely to speak unto you') on the undesirability of the King's reaffirming transubstantiation by statute.[83] Fortunately for the reformers the chief accuser, John London, over-reached himself and was punished for perjury. On 31 August pardons were granted to a number of people who were either members of the privy chamber or associated with it; Hoby, Carwarden, Harman, Welden and their wives, William Snowball, the King's yeoman cook and his wife, and the psalmist Thomas Sternhold.

Butts died in November 1545 and was mourned by John Hooper as one of the 'real favourers of the gospel' who had 'promoted the glory of God to the uttermost of their power'. His importance to the evangelical cause is underlined by a letter from Burgratus of February 1546; a pious letter of consolation in sickness and an epitaph from his protégé Cheke; and another epitaph by Parkhurst.[84] Perhaps it is not entirely coincidence that a number of attempts against radical court figures occurred in the year after his death; certainly a number of them had been assisted by or associated with him. Many of the details of the Crome, Askew and Parr affairs are obscure and it is possible that they were linked, with evidence extracted from each examination being used against future victims.[85]

Edward Crome was a frequent and controversial preacher in the city and at court. He had been compelled to abjure several times in the past, but it was a sermon against the sacrificial nature of the mass given at the Mercers' chapel in Lent 1546 which led to his examination and final recantation at Paul's Cross in June. This proved to be the starting point of a witch-hunt through the court. Latimer was summoned from retirement, charged with encouraging Crome and imprisoned, while the royal physician Huycke was found to have condemned Crome's articles of abjuration; he requested that 'two or three gentlemen of the Privy Chamber may declare his writings to the King's majesty'. Heynes was mentioned, but it was remembered that he had exhorted Crome to make a true recantation. Lassells was also implicated and was put to death the following year with the notorious Anne Askew.[86]

Askew was given a gruelling examination about her supporters at court and asked whether she had received money in prison from Ladies Sussex, Suffolk, Hertford, Fitzwilliam and Denny. She admitted that the last two had sent her 10s and 8s respectively and confessed that a servant of Denny had shown her favour because of her family and friends. Interestingly enough, she chose Crome as one of three acceptable confessors.

Two other evangelicals connected with the court almost shared Askew's fate. Shaxton was arraigned with her for false sacramental doctrine and only escaped the flames by a timely recantation which was published with a preface to the King acknowledging Henry's mercy. He was then sent to reason with Anne Askew and since she proved obdurate he preached a sermon of recantation at her execution. Meanwhile in June John Taylor, Master of St John's and a client of Butts, preached an heretical sermon at Bury St Edmunds for which he was imprisoned, but in September Shaxton persuaded him to sign a recantation identical to his own.

Taylor and Shaxton, though formerly patronised by evangelical courtiers, were comparatively small fry, but the Askew affair was the prelude to a conspiracy against Katherine Parr. Foxe's account of Katherine's 'trouble on account of the gospel' has unfortunately distorted her role in the closing years of the reign and it would be erroneous to consider her the chief advocate of reform at court.[87] Before considering the conspiracy against Katherine Parr, it is necessary to place her in a proper perspective.

The details of Katherine's early life and introduction to Henry VIII are unknown, but it is possible that she was deliberately brought to the King's notice by the radical faction at court, who may have hoped for a sympathetic queen-consort. Certainly some evangelical court figures had played a direct part in the fall of Katherine Howard; notably Lassells, who gave evidence against her to Cranmer, and Sir Edward Bainton, whose wife Isabella was the reckless Queen's half-sister.[88] After Katherine's execution there was some evangelical hope that the King would take back Anne of Cleves and two of the latter's ladies were heard to cry, 'What! is God working his own work to make the lady Anne of Cleves Queen again?'[89]

Katherine Parr herself evidently considered her marriage to Henry as a religious vocation. She later told her suitor Thomas Seymour: 'as truly as God is God, my mind was fully bent, the other time I was at liberty, to marry you before any man I know. Howbeit, God withstood my will . . . [and] made me renounce utterly mine own will, to follow his will most willingly.'[90] There can be little doubt of her personal evangelical piety. She also took reformers like Cope and Parkhurst into her service and she was outspoken in theological debates with her didactic husband. (For Katherine's piety, education and patronage of learning, see Chapter Seven below.)

Pious intent, however, is very different from tangible influence and Katherine seems to have possessed little power over the King. It is significant that of her own literary productions the innocuous *Prayers or Meditations* achieved publication and a measure of popularity during the reign, but the overtly Lutheran *Lamentation of a Sinner* remained in manuscript until after her death. Even Burnet, her devoted admirer, notes that she was unable to intervene in the Windsor heresy-hunt, which took place shortly after her marriage to Henry, though a servant of hers named Fulk did warn the intended victims of their danger.[91]

Thus the attack on Katherine Parr must be read, not as a plot against the head of reform, but as an attempt to undermine the reformers at court through one of the most vulnerable of their number. Ladies Suffolk and Hertford were noted by Foxe as under suspicion and both were mentioned by Chapuys as instigating the Queen to heresy, but the conviction of Katherine would have brought down bigger prey than her own immediate feminine circle; many of the ladies of the Queen's privy chamber were married to gentlemen of the King's, and these would undoubtedly have been affected if their wives had been prosecuted for heresy.

Foxe's familiar story does little to identify the 'godly persons' who warned the Queen of her peril, but it is surely significant that the one figure named is Thomas Wendy, the royal physician lauded by Ascham as Butts's successor in the patronage of learning and like Butts, a former member of Gonville. Since proceedings against Katherine would have had dire consequences for the reformers in the King's privy chamber, it seems likely that their activity in the matter was crucial. Similarly when George Blage, an *habitué* of the privy chamber, was condemned to death for heresy against the sacrament shortly before Anne Askew's execution, members of that institution (notably, Bedford) interceded for him with the King. As in the aftermath of the attempt against the Queen, Henry was 'sore offended' with Wriothesley and his associates 'that they would come so near him, and even into his Privy Chamber' and Blage escaped.[92]

Thus, it seems that evangelicals found a measure of protection against the law and the machinations of Gardiner and Wriothesley because sympathisers were firmly entrenched in that vital institution, the King's privy chamber. Indeed, the sustained activity of the evangelical patronage network, which survived both natural deaths and political disasters, ensured that, though radical theological reform could not be advanced because of the innate conservatism of the King, nascent Protestantism was able to exert considerable influence in the Henrician church. This was certainly the view of Foxe, who declared in his summary of Henry's religious achievements:

> If princes have always their council about them, that is but a common thing. If sometimes they have evil counsel ministered, that I take to be the fault rather of such as are about them, than of princes themselves. So long as Queen Anne [Boleyn], Thomas Cromwell, Archbishop Cranmer, Master Denny, Dr Butts, with such like were about him, and could prevail with him, what organ of Christ's glory did more good in the church than he?[93]

Notes

1. P. S. and H. M. Allen, H. W. Garrod (eds) *Opus Epistolarum Des. Erasmi Roterodami* (11 vols., Clarendon Press, Oxford, 1906–47), no. 1102 to Oecolampadius, no. 1113 to Melanchthon.

2. Ibid., no. 1127a; cf. no. 980.

3. Preserved Smith notes that the *Assertio* is printed in an early edition of Fisher's works, with a note that he assisted Henry; 'Luther and Henry VIII', *English Historical Review*, vol. 25, no. 100 (October 1910), pp. 656–69. For More's contribution, William Roper and Nicholas Harpsfield, *Lives of Saint Thomas More*, E. E. Reynolds (ed.) (Everyman, London, 1963), pp. 33–4. Cf. J. J. Scarisbrick, *Henry VIII* (Pelican, London, 1974), pp. 154–5.

4. Public Record Office SP1/42, fos. 200–1, Vives to Henry VIII, 13 July 1527 (calendared in *Letters and Papers, Foreign and Domestic of the Reign of Henry VIII*, J. S. Brewer, J. Gairdner, R. H. Brodie (eds) [21 vols., HMSO, London, 1862–1932], vol. 4, ii, no. 3261 (hereafter cited as *L&P*); Thomas More, *Correspondence*, E. F. Rogers (ed.) (Princeton University Press, Princeton, 1974), p. 368. The best summary of books is in Erwin Doernberg, *Henry VIII and Luther, An account of Their Personal Relations* (Barrie & Rockliff, London, 1961).

5. Villa Sancta composed other works for Katherine, some of which may have been printed, but these are the only two to have survived. Cf. the preface to *Problema Indulgentiarum*. For his association with More, see the latter's *Apology*, J. B. Trapp (ed.) (Yale University Press, New Haven and London, 1979), pp. 40, 328. Professor Trapp does not positively identify this 'father Alphonse' as Katherine's confessor, though he mentions Stapleton's allusion to More and the Queen's confessor.

6. See More, *Responsio ad Lutherum*, John M. Headley (ed.) (Yale University Press, New Haven and London, 1969). Fisher's works are *Assertionis Lutheranae Confutatio* (Quentell, Cologne, 1523); *Defensio Regie assertionis contra Babylonicam captivitatem* (Quentell, Cologne, 1525); and *De veritate corporis et sanguinis Christi in Eucharistia* (Quentell, Cologne, 1527).

7. Doernberg, *Henry VIII and Luther*, pp. 58, 129, 37–40.

8. Allen, *Erasmi Epistolae*, no. 1369 to Tunstal, no. 1218 to Pace.

9. Ibid., no. 1219 to Mountjoy, no. 1228 to Warham.

10. Ibid., no. 1246 from WIlliam Tate, no. 1383 to Pirckheimer, no. 1430 to Henry VIII.

11. Ibid., no. 1513. Translated in F. M. Nichols, *The Hall of Lawford Hall* (privately printed, London, 1891), pp. 320–1.

12. For pressure on Erasmus from the English, Allen, *Erasmi Epistolae*, no. 1408 to Pirckheimer, no. 1415 to Campeggio, no. 1486 to Wolsey, no. 1493 to Henry VIII, no. 1495 to George of Saxony. For Erasmus's relations with Fisher and More, nos. 1489, 1770, 1804.

13. E. L. Surtz, *Works and Days of John Fisher* (Harvard University Press, Cambridge, Mass., 1967), p. 387.

14. Charles Sturge, *Cuthbert Tunstal* (Longmans, Green & Co, London, 1938), Appendix 10. Not calendared in *L&P*.

15. PRO, SP1/22, fo. 1 (*L&P*, vol. 3, i, no. 1218), Warham to Wolsey, 3 April 1521.

16. British Library, Cotton MS Vitell. B IV 95 (*L&P*, vol. 3, i, no. 1210), Medici to Wolsey; PRO, SC7/64/32 (*L&P*, vol. 3, i, no. 1234), Leo X to Wolsey. For an account of the London ceremony, British Library Cotton MS Vitell. B IV 111 (*L&P*, vol. 3, i, no. 1274). Fisher's sermon was printed in English by Wynkyn de Worde, in Latin by Siberch at Cambridge.

17. Cf. Doernberg, *Henry VIII and Luther*, p. 27.

18. William A. Clebsch, *England's Earliest Protestants*, 1520–35 (Yale University Press, New Haven and London, 1964), p. 13.

19. Sir Henry Ellis (ed.), *Original Letters Illustrative of English History* (11 vols., 3 series, Harding, Triphook & Lepard, London, 1824, 1827, 1846), series 1, vol. 1, pp. 180–4.

20. Harpsfield, *Life of More*, pp. 100–3; Clebsch, *Protestants*, pp. 26, 43–9.

21. John Strype, Ecclesiastical Memorials (3 vols., Clarendon Press, Oxford, 1820–40), vol. 1, ii, pp. 54–5.

22. John Foxe, *Acts and Monuments*, S. R. Cattley (ed.) (8 vols., Seeley & Burnside, London, 1837), vol. 4, p. 671. The third ceremony is mentioned in Barlowe's and Roy's *Burial of the Mass* of 1528. Cf. Clebsch, Protestants, pp. 261–2.

23. For Tyndale, Foxe, *Acts and Monuments*, vol. 5, p. 117; A. G. Dickens, *English Reformation* (Fontana, London, 1973), pp. 105–6.

24. For Cromwell's subordinate position in relation to Anne, Maria Dowling, 'Anne Boleyn and Reform', *Journal of Ecclesiastical History*, vol. 35, no. 1 (January 1984), pp. 31–2.

25. Allen, *Erasmi Epistolae*, no. 1878 from Henry VIII, no. 1998 to Henry VIII, no. 2040 to Vives, no. 2215 to Mountjoy, no. 3090 from Chapuys.

26. PRO, SP1/42, fo. 169 (*L&P*, vol. 4, ii, no. 3236), Pace to his brother; cf. ibid., fo. 168 (*L&P*, vol. 4, ii, no. 3235), Pace to his brother. For Pace's controversy with Fisher, Allen, *Erasmi Epistolae*, no. 1932, from John Crucius, 28 January 1528.

27. Letters from Pace and Wakefield to Henry VIII, dated 1527, printed in Robert Wakefield, *Kotser Codicis* (Berthelet, London, c. 1534), sig. Piii–Piv. Cf. Jervis Wegg, *Richard Pace, a Tudor Diplomatist* (Methuen & Co London, 1932), pp. 273–4.

28. Wakefield, *Kotser Codicis*, sig. Piv.

29. Ibid., sig. Oiv–Pi, Wakefield to Thomas Boleyn.

30. SP1/141, fo. 126–7. Elton tentatively identifies the writer as Oliver; *Reform and Renewal* (Cambridge University Press, Cambridge, 1973), pp. 26–8.

31. Foxe, *Acts and Monuments*, vol. 4, pp. 657–8. More later claimed in his *Apology* (ed. Trapp, pp. 75–6) that Fish repented, 'and came into the church again and forsook and forsware all the whole hill of those heresies'. He died within a few years of his return. His widow, a noted book dealer, married the martyr Bainham, who evidently did not benefit from the royal protection.

32. Strype, *Ecclesiastical Memorials*, vol. 1, ii, pp. 171–3; J. G. Nichols, *Narratives of the Days of the Reformation* (Camden Society, J. B. Nichols & Son, 1859), pp. 52–7; George Wyatt, *Extracts from the Life of the Virtuous, Christian and Renowned Queen Anne Boleigne*, R. Triphook (ed.) (privately printed, London, 1817), pp. 16–17. For a more detailed treatment of this incident, Dowling, 'Anne Boleyn and Reform', p. 36.

33. Tyndale, *Practice of Prelates* ('Marborch', 1530), sig. Hv.

34. *State Papers published Under the Authority of his Majesty's Commission. Volume I, King Henry the Eighth* (HMSO, London, 1830), p. 197.

35. *Calendar of State Papers, Spanish*, G. Bergenroth, P. Gayangos, M. A. S. Hume (eds) (8 vols, HMSO, London, 1962–1904), vol. 4, ii, p. 357, Chapuys to Charles V, 11 January 1532. For Fisher's dealings with Katherine, PRO SP1/142, fos. 201–2 (*L&P*, vol. 14, i, no. 190), deposition of Katherine's servant.

36. Sturge, *Tunstal*, p. 175; Scarisbrick, *Henry VIII, pp. 430–1*.

37. *L&P*, vol. 4, iii, no. 5791, examination of Fox; P. S. and H. M. Allen (eds), *Letters of Richard Fox* (Clarendon Press, Oxford, 1929), no. 89.

38. Vives, *Opera Omnia*, G. Majansius (ed.) (8 vols., In Officina Benedicti Monfort, Valencia, 1782–90), vol. 7, pp. 148–50, letter to Juan Vergara; British Library, Cotton MS Vesp. F III 150 (*L&P*, vol. 4, ii, no. 3943), J. Russell to Wolsey; PRO, SP1/41, fo. 78 (*L&P*, vol. 4, ii, no. 4990), Vives's deposition; Allen, *Erasmi Epistolae*, no. 2061 from Vives.

39. Vives, *Opera Omnia*, vol. 7, p. 134. Vives appears in the treasurer of the chamber's accounts as receiving half-yearly wages of £10 from March 1529 to March 1531, but his letters to Henry and Vergara show that he never received the money.

40. Foxe, *Acts and Monuments*, vol. 7, pp. 6ff. Cf. Scarisbrick, *Henry VIII*, p. 335 for an assertion of the authenticity of the story.

41. G. D. Nicholson, *The Nature and Function of Historical Argument in the*

Henrician Reformation (unpublished PhD thesis, Cambridge, 1977). English agents at Rome were first instructed to assert Henry's immunity from papal jurisdiction in autumn 1530; ibid., pp. 68–70.

42. Gilbert Burnet, *History of the Reformation of the Church of England*. Nicholas Pocock (ed.) (7 vols., Clarendon Press, Oxford, 1865), vol. 1, pp. 148–61. Burnet alleges that two supporters of the Queen received benefices worth 500 and 600 ducats a year respectively. Croke himself was rewarded with the living of Long Buckby, Northants and a canonry at Henry VIII's college in Oxford, both in 1531. For an amusing account of his tribulations in Italy, Scarisbrick, *Henry VIII*, pp. 336–8.

43. British Library, Cotton MS Vitell. B XIV 298; PRO, SP1/57, fos. 99, 248 (*L&P*, vol. 4, iii, nos. 6383, 6505); John Strype, *Memorials of Thomas Cranmer* (2 vols., Oxford University Press, Oxford, 1840), vol. 1, p. 675.

44. Nicholson, *Historical Argument*, pp. 75–117. Steven Haas argues convincingly for a first edition of *The Glass of Truth* in 1531 rather than the traditional date of 1532; 'Henry VIII's *Glasse of Truthe*', *History*, vol. 64, no. 212 (October 1979), pp. 353–62.

45. Ellis, *Original Letters*, series 3, vol. 2, p. 97, Croke to Cromwell.

46. M. St Clare Byrne, *Letters of Henry VIII* (Cassell & Co, London, 1968), p. 82; Nicholson, *Historical Argument*, p. 111.

47. PRO, SP1/71, fo. 146 (*L&P*, vol. 5, no. 1454); *John Palsgrave's Comedy of Acolastus*, P. L. Carver (ed.) (Early English Text Society, Oxford University Press, London, 1937), pp. xlix–l. The living of St Dunstan was worth £60 8 3d and was the richest in London after St Magnus Martyr.

48. PRO, SP1/72, fos. 176–7 (*L&P*, vol. 5, no. 1660), Hawkins to Henry VIII.

49. Luther to Robert Barnes, 5 September 1531; translated and printed in Doernberg, *Henry VIII and Luther*, pp. 86–91. For the approach to Luther, ibid., pp. 83ff.; Clebsch, *Protestants*, pp. 51–4; *L&P*, vol. 5, no. 593, Chapuys to Charles V, 21 December 1531. Elton, *Reform & Renewal*, pp. 39–40, corrects Demaus's view that the approach to Tyndale was an official one originating with Cromwell.

50. Allen, *Erasmi Epistolae*, nos. 2459, 2460, letters of recommendation to Mountjoy and Vulcanius; *L&P* vol. 5, no. 287, Chapuys to Charles V, 6 June 1531.

51. For a list of these treatises, Scarisbrick, *Henry VIII*, pp. 222–3.

52. Letters between Chapuys and Agrippa are calendared in *L&P*, vol. 5, Appendix. Cf. Henry Morley, *Life of Henry Cornelius Agrippa von Nettesheim* (2 vols., Chapman & Hall, London, 1856), vol. 2, pp. 28–4; Maria Dowling, 'Humanist Support for Katherine of Aragon', *Bulletin of the Institute of Historical Research*, vol. 57, no. 135 (May 1984), pp. 47–8.

53. *Spanish Calendar*, vol. 4, ii, no. 396, Chapuys to Charles V, 2 August 1530; John E. Paul, *Catherine of Aragon and her Friends* (Burns & Oates, London, 1966), p. 156. Elton notes that this is the only book written for Katherine to escape the destructive vigilance of the authorities; *Policy & Police* (Cambridge University Press, London, 1972), p. 174.

54. *Spanish Calendar*, vol. 5, i, pp. 59–60, Chapuys to Charles V, 26 February 1534. *De Potestate* is mentioned by Strype, *Ecclesiastical Memorials*, vol. 1, i, pp. 229–30, who states that neither he nor Herbert of Cherbury had seen it.

55. Gardiner's works are all printed and edited by Pierre Janelle, *Obedience in Church and State* (Cambridge University Press, Cambridge, 1930).

56. Allen, *Erasmi Epistolae*, no. 2915 from Olah, 12 March 1534. Official propaganda is listed and described in Elton, *Policy and Police*, pp. 171–98. The only indication of the date of *Kotser Codicis* is a reference to Anne Boleyn as 'Reginam nostram'.

57. *Reform and Renewal*, pp. 20–3.

58. British Library, Harleian MS 283, fo. 129, Starkey to Cromwell, late 1534. For Starkey's and Morison's early careers, W. Gordon Zeeveld, *Foundations of*

Tudor Policy (Harvard University Press, Cambridge, Mass., 1948); Elton, *Reform and Renewal*. For Croke's preaching, Ellis, *Original Letters*, series 3, vol. 2, p. 3.

59. For the humanist learning of the Carthusian martyrs and the Bridgettine Reynolds, Dowling, 'Katherine of Aragon', p. 53.

60. *L&P*, vol. 7, no. 1607, list of Observants; Thomas Bourchier, *Historia Ecclesiastica De Martyrio Fratrum Ordinis Divi Francisci, Dictorum De Observantia, Qui Partim In Anglia Sub Henrico Octavo Rege* (Apud I. Poupy, Paris, 1582), pp. 67ff. (*L&P*, vol. 7, nos. 129–34), letters between Forest and Katherine; PRO, SP1/142, fos. 201–2 (*L&P*, vol. 14, i, no. 190), deposition of Katherine's servant. For the Observants, Paul, *Catherine of Aragon and her Friends*, Chapter 10.

61. G. J. Aungier, *History and Antiquities of Syon Monastery* (London, 1840), pp. 435–8. Cf. Maria Dowling, *Scholarship, Politics and the Court of Henry VIII* (unpublished PhD thesis, London, 1981), pp. 182–5, which corrects the dating of various letters and documents; summarised in Dowling, 'Katherine of Aragon', pp. 53–4.

62. British Library, Cotton MS Cleop. E IV 36 (*L&P*, vol. 9, no. 523), (Jasper Fyllol) to Cromwell, 2 October 1535. For the submission of the Carthusians, ibid. fo. 247, Visitors of Beauvale Charterhouse to the Confessor of Syon; Aungier, *Syon Monastery*, p. 434, Brooke and Burgoyn to the Confessor of Syon.

63. For Latimer's early career, see the Introduction, above. For Shaxton, John Venn, *Biographical History of Gonville and Caius College 1349–1713* (7 vols., Cambridge University Press, Cambridge, 1897), vol. 1, pp. 17–19; for Parker, John Strype, *Life and Acts of Matthew Parker* (3 vols., Clarendon Press, Oxford, 1821).

64. British Library, Cotton MS Cleop. E IV 107, Barlow to Cromwell; *L&P*, vol. 8, no. 466, John Barlow to Bainton.

65. British Library, Cotton MS Otho C X 260b (*L&P*, vol. 10, no. 942), Shaxton to Cromwell, 23 May 1536.

66. Morison's works are *Apomaxis* against Cochlaeus, dedicated to Cromwell (1538); *A Lamentation* and *A Remedy for Sedition* (1536); *An Exhortation to styrre all Englyshe men to the defence of theyr countreye* and *An Invective ayenste . . . treason* (1539). Morison also translated *The Epistle that J. Sturmius . . . sent to Cardynalles and prelates . . . appointed by the Byshop of Rome to serche out the abuses of the Churche* (1538).All works printed by Berthelet. For the King's answer to the Mantuan Council, British Library, Cotton MS Cleop. E VI 311–2 (*L&P*, vol. 12, i, no. 1311).For abuse of Pole, cf. Tunstal's and Stokesley's letter to him, first printed by Reynold Wolfe in 1560 but composed in 1536.

67. For the contrary argument, J. K. McConica, *English Humanists and Reformation Politics Under Henry VIII and Edward VI* (Clarendon Press, Oxford, 1968), p. 170), whence comes the quotation.

68. Doernberg, *Henry VIII and Luther*, p. 110. For the Ten Articles, Elton, *Reform and Reformation, England 1509–58* (Edward Arnold, London, 1979), pp. 256–60; Dickens, *English Reformation*, pp. 243–5. Cf. Scarisbrick, *Henry VIII*, pp. 438, 517, who sees the Articles as 'a blatantly heterodox document'.

69. *L&P*, vol. 12, i, no. 708, Coren to Leighton and Starkey, (24 March) 1537.

70. *Miscellaneous Writings and Letters of Thomas Cranmer*, J. E. Cox (ed.) (Parker Society, Cambridge University Press, Cambridge, 1846), pp. 359–60 (*L&P*, vol. 13, i, no. 141), Cranmer to Cromwell, 25 January 1538. Momus was the God of raillery and mockery.

71. *Epistolae Tigurinae, 1531–58* (Parker Society, Cambridge University Press, Cambridge, 1848), pp. 396–8 (*L&P*, vol. 13, ii, no. 373, Partridge to Bullinger, 17 September 1538; Cranmer, *Letters*, p. 340 (*L&P*, vol. 12, ii, no. 315), Cranmer to Capito.

72. Dickens, *English Reformation*, pp. 184–8; Cranmer, *Letters*, pp. 344, 345 (*L&P*, vol. 12, ii, nos. 434, 512), to Cromwell, 4 and 13 August 1537.

73. For the production of the Great Bible, which was printed in Paris, Dickens,

English Reformation, pp. 189–90. For the earlier difficulties, Dowling, *Scholarship*, pp. 224–6.

74. Paul L. Hughes and James F. Larkin, *Tudor Royal Proclamations* (3 vols., Yale University Press, New Haven and London, 1964–9), vol. 1, pp. 296–8, 6 May 1541.

75. Dickens, *English Reformation*, pp. 246–7; Elton, *Reform and Renewal*, pp. 284, 286–8.

76. PRO, SP1/163, fo. 46 (*L&P*, vol. 16, no. 101), deposition of John Lassells (1540).

77. D. R. Starkey, *The King's Privy Chamber, 1485–1547* (unpublished PhD thesis, Cambridge, 1973), passim.

78. British Library, Harleian MS 78 fos. 25b–26.

79. Sir Thomas Elyot, *Dictionary* (in aed. Berthelet, 1538), preface to Henry VIII.

80. Foxe, *Acts and Monuments*, vol. 8, pp. 24–9. This account follows that of Morice, Cranmer's secretary, which is printed in Nichols, *Narratives of the Reformation*. For a favour Butts had previously done Cranmer, ibid., p. 263. The story of Butts's intervention in 1543 was sufficiently well-known to be included in the later play *Henry VIII* attributed to Shakespeare; though here the incident was anachronisticaly placed in the lifetime of Anne Boleyn.

81. Morice's account, in *Narratives of the Reformation*, p. 253; Foxe, *Acts and Monuments*, vol. 8, pp. 31–4. For this instance of Butts's mediation, see the Introduction, above.

82. Foxe, *Acts and Monuments*, vol. 5, pp. 464–95. Cf. McConica, *English Humanists*, pp. 220–2.

83. British Library, Cotton MS Cleop. E V 60ff. (*L&P*, vol. 14, i, no. 1035), Heynes to Butts, (28 May?) 1539. It is interesting that Butts is buried in Heynes's church of All Saints, Fulham. For Hoby, *Holbein and the Court of Henry VIII* (catalogue of an exhibition at the Queen's Gallery, Buckingham Palace, 1978–9) (Lund Humphries, London and Bradford, 1978), pp. 105–8.

84. Hastings Robinson (ed.), *Original Letters Relative to the English Reformation, 1537–58* (Parker Society, Cambridge University Press, Cambridge, 1846), p. 33, Hooper to Bullinger, 27 January 1546; PRO, SP1/214, fo. 11 (*L&P*, vol. 21, i, no. 176), Burgratus to Butts, 7 February 1546, written in ignorance of his death; John Strype, *Life of the Learned Sir John Cheke* (Clarendon Press, Oxford, 1821), pp. 27–30; John Parkhurst, *Ludicra sive Epigrammata* (apud J. Dayum, London, 1537), p. 100.

85. This was the view of Charles Wriothesley, who declared that Crome 'accused divers persons as well of the court as of the city, with other persons in the country, which put many persons in great trouble, and some suffered death after'. Quoted by McConica, *English Humanists*, p. 223–4.

86. *State Papers of Henry VIII*, pp. 842–51 (*L&P*, vol. 21, i, nos. 790, 810, 823), proceedings against Crome, May 1546; Foxe, *Acts and Monuments*, vol. 5, pp. 537–47. Cf. McConica, *English Humanists*, pp. 223–4.

87. Foxe, *Acts and Monuments*, vol. 5, pp. 553–61. McConica, *English Humanists*, Chapter 7, gives no documentary basis for his exaggerated claims for Katherine. The two most recent biographies by M. A. Gordon (*Life of Queen Katherine Parr*, Titus Wilson & Son, Kendal, 1951) and Anthony Martienssen (*Queen Katherine Parr*, Secker & Warburg, London, 1973) are equally untrustworthy.

88. Cf. Gerald Benan and Edward Phillips Statham, *The House of Howard* (Hutchinson & Co., London, 1907), pp. 284, 299–300.

89. Agnes and Elizabeth Strickland, *Lives of the Queens of England* (6 vols., George Bell & Son, London, 1889), vol. 2, p. 326.

90. Ibid., pp. 445–6, Katherine to Seymour (1547).
91. Burnet, *History of the Reformation*, vol. 1, p. 514. For Fulk, Foxe, *Acts and Monuments*, vol. 5, pp. 494–5.
92. Foxe, *Acts and Monuments*, vol. 5, p. 564.
93. Ibid., p. 605.

3 The Universities: Studies, Controversies and Endowment

I

By 1518, the year of the 'Greeks and Trojans' quarrel at Oxford, the new learning was firmly established in both universities. As has been seen, this was due in large part to the support humanism received from the King and court, and this relationship between the centre of power and the centres of study would continue throughout the reign; the political and religious changes of the period would have a profound effect on studies and endowment at the universities. Scholars at Oxford and Cambridge were involved in a number of problems and issues which called for an intellectual as well as a political response. They were confronted with the appearance of Lutheranism, the royal divorce, separation from Rome and the monastic dissolution, besides the general uncertainty as to what form Henry VIII's 'religious settlement' would take. At the same time they were affected by changing patterns of patronage, as the momentum of change swept away old benefactors and put new ones in their place. Thus developments in the universities were intimately connected with events at court, and the nature of the new studies themselves was directly influenced by political and religious vicissitudes.

In the decade or so preceding the King's divorce the advent of Lutheranism posed serious problems for the authorities of both universities. In 1521 there were bonfires of Lutheran books at Cambridge and Oxford to mark the Pope's condemnation of Luther, but in the following year archbishop Warham, chancellor of Oxford, informed Wolsey 'that divers of that university be infected with the heresies of Luther and of others of that sort, having among them a great number of books of the said perverse doctrine'. Warham pleaded that the matter be handled discreetly in order to avoid scandal:

> For pity it were that through the lewdness [i.e., ignorance] of one or two cankered members, which as I understand have induced no small number of young and uncircumspect fools to give ear unto them, the whole university should run in the infamy of so

heinous a crime, the hearing whereof should be right delectable and pleasant to the open Lutherans beyond the sea and secret be-hither, whereof they would take heart and confidence that their pestilential doctrines should increase and multiply, seeing both the universities of England infected therewith.[1]

He also asked on the university's behalf that either Fisher or Tunstal — both respected humanist bishops — would draw up a table of Lutheran writers and their errors for the information of the students.

At Cambridge, meanwhile, evangelical scholars were meeting regularly at the White Horse Tavern, whose derisory appellation of 'Little Germany' reveals their theological inspiration. The meetings at the White Horse have passed into pious Protestant legend leaving little concrete detail of the activities of those who attended, who were in any case discreet enough to escape persecution. On Christmas Eve 1525, however, Robert Barnes, prior of the Augustinian friars and apparently the leader of the White Horse coterie, preached at St Edward's church on Luther's postil for the day. He was immediately prohibited from preaching by the vice-chancellor, despite his appeal to the judgement of the whole university. Indeed, Barnes's ill-timed display of evangelical zeal had given a hostage to fortune and to the defenders of the faith.

Early in 1526 Wolsey's agents conducted a search for prohibited books at Cambridge. Few, in fact, were found, since Thomas Foreman, President of Queens' and a frequenter of the White Horse, received advance notice of the visitation and managed to warn the owners beforehand. However the investigation did result in the arrest of Barnes, who was brought up to London for examination. On the advice of Gardiner and Edmund Foxe, then in Wolsey's service, he recanted and did public penance, but he fled overseas at the earliest opportunity.[2]

Indications of Lutheranism continued to appear at the universities. William Tyndale, for example, gave bible readings at Magdalen Hall, Oxford which attracted some of the younger fellows of Magdalen college, while Fisher excommunicated a Cambridge student who defaced a bull of indulgence sent by Leo X which had been affixed to the gate of the schools.[3] The vigilance of the authorities of both universities, however, drove the majority of evangelical scholars into discretion and apparent conformity, though a few who were detected were held up as public examples.

Thomas Bilney (the future martyr) and his friend Thomas Arthur, respectively of Trinity Hall and Gonville Hall, Cambridge, were force to recant and carry the faggot at Paul's Cross in September 1527. Skelton, a fervent conservative, gleefully mocked them for having fallen into heresy through lack of learning:

> A little rag of rhetoric,
> A less lump of logic,
> A piece or a patch of philosophy,
> Then followeth it by and by
> They tumble so in theology,
> Drowned in dregs of divinity,
> That they judge themself able to be
> Doctors of the chair in the Vintry
> At the Three Cranes . . .[4]

Skelton's confident derision was, however, seriously misplaced; the new atmosphere engendered by the royal divorce would show that heterodoxy had been silenced rather than rooted out.

It might be assumed that the unequivocal affirmation of traditional doctrine by humanists like Fisher and Warham would automatically preclude further reform of university studies and that the authorities, alarmed that the new learning would open a Pandora's box of heretical biblical study and subversive ecclesiastical criticism, would react strongly against it. Such a supposition would be erroneous. Indeed, far from discouraging the advance of the new learning the Lutheran challenge actually gave a spur to it, since the humanist education of the clergy was both a measure of church reform (and thus an answer to Lutheran criticism) and a means of equipping them to deal with heresy.

Wolsey's public lectures at Oxford, established to consolidate the victory of the new learning there, were only the prelude to a far more grandiose scheme; the foundation of Cardinal college as a seminary of humanism. Half collegiate church and half academic institution, the college was to eclipse in size and financial resources any foundation hitherto contemplated. Papal bulls procured in 1524 allowed Wolsey to dissolve St Frideswide's priory (the projected site of the college) and other monasteries to the value of 3,000 ducats a year, while the royal foundation licence of July 1525 permitted him to endow his establishment with £2,000 in lands and revenues. The statutes provided for a dean and 60 senior canons (graduates), 40 petty canons and 20 pensioners. There were also to be 13 chaplains, 12 lay clerks, 16 choristers, a music teacher, 23 servants and four legal officials besides the four internal and six public readers.[5]

Study at Cardinal college was to follow the example of St John's Cambridge, in its synthesis of scholastic tradition and the new learning. The four college readers, each with a stipend of four marks, were to lecture respectively in logic, dialectic, philosophy and humanity, while the six public readers were to continue to expound theology, humanity, philosophy, civil and canon law, medicine and mathematics. The public theology reader was to lecture on both the old and new testaments and on the *Quaestiones* of Duns Scotus, alternating his subject each quarter. The public humanity reader was to lecture twice daily on both Greek and Roman literature. An interesting devotional point was the provision of masses on the feast days of the four Latin fathers of the Church, Augustine, Ambrose, Gregory and Jerome.

Cardinal college would thus, in theory, bring forth highly educated priests and theologians capable of understanding their own faith and of combatting heresy. Furthermore, Wolsey planned to draw his undergraduates from schools which he intended to found in every diocese in England, and it is unfortunate that a combination of local interest and political disaster prevented him from implementing the scheme fully; in the event, only one school was founded, at Ipswich, his birthplace. Had he succeeded, there would have been a system of humanist education for the clergy extending over the whole country, an apparatus which would have done much towards the reform of the English church. (For Wolsey's scheme of grammar schools, see Chapter Four, below.)

Wolsey's taste for magnificence and addiction to self-advertisement cannot be ruled out entirely as the motives for his educational endowments. Certainly, later critics of the cardinal were to ascribe his munificence to ostentatious pride. Polydore Vergil, for example, observed contemptuously:

> Devoting himself to the execution of grandiose schemes, he decided to found two colleges, that is to say one at Oxford, the other at Ipswich, an unimportant place where he was born; these were intended to enhance his own empty glory rather than serve the interests of religion and scholarship.[6]

The evangelical authors of *The Burial of the Mass* condemned both

Cardinal college and the decayed monasteries Wolsey had suppressed for its foundation, claiming that 'of privy houses of bawdry/He hath made a stews openly'. Though the *Burial* admitted that 'men of great science' were to be found in the college, it added:

> Howbeit, where pride is the beginning
> The devil is commonly the ending,
> As we see by our experience.
> And if thou consider well,
> Even as the Tower of Babel
> Began of a presumption . . .

These, however, were later criticisms by hostile commentators, voiced when Wolsey had fallen from power or when his influence was crumbling. On the other hand, Cardinal college was a valuable addition to the university, and its foundation was welcomed by the chief promoters of learning.

In January 1526, Longland was sent to court to reveal Wolsey's plans in detail to the King and Queen. He showed Henry

> the great good that should ensue of this your noble foundation, as well in bringing up of youth in virtue as . . . to the maintenance of Christ's church and his faith, to the King's honour and of all his realm; and that many should there be brought up which should be able to do his grace honorable service. I assure your grace the King doth consider all this more in the best manner . . . Saying that more good shall come of this your honorable foundation than any man can esteem.

Later he told Katherine 'of the notable lectors that should be there, and of the exercitations of learning, and how the students should be limit by the readers to the same; likewise in the exposition of the bible'. The Queen, displaying her usual enthusiasm for learning, 'was marvellous glad and joyous to hear of this your notable foundation and college, speaking great honour of the same'.[7]

Wolsey went to great pains to equip the college library, asking the Doge of Venice for transcripts of Greek manuscripts formerly owned by cardinals Bessarion and Grimani and planning the transcription of all the manuscripts in the Vatican library. In October 1525 he took the bishop of Chichester on a tour of the college buildings, and his visitor was so impressed that on his return home he looked through his library for books to donate to Cardinal college.[8] Wolsey also went to considerable trouble to recruit the best available scholars, employing Robert Shorton, the Queen's almoner, to persuade the brightest minds of Cambridge to migrate to the other university.[9]

The foundation of Cardinal college completed the trio of academies first established in England to further the new learning. The battle against Lutheranism thus resulted, not in a conservative backlash, but in the cultivation of the new linguistic and literary studies as a means of fighting heresy. Humanists like the founders Fisher, Fox and Wolsey saw no incompatibility between reassessment of the textual bases of Christianity and maintenance of traditional orthodoxy.

Humanism also continued to flourish at Cambridge, which Erasmus compared favourably with Louvain because the English university did not treat the new learning as an enemy.[10] Between his return from his studies abroad and his arrest in 1526 Barnes brought Roman literature into the Augustinian Priory there. John Foxe comments,

> what with his industry, pains and labour, and with the help of Thomas Parnell his scholar, whom he brought from Louvain with him, reading *'copia verborum ac rerum'*, he caused the house shortly to flourish with good letters, and made a great part of the house learned (who before were drowned in barbarous rudeness) as Master . . . Coverdale, with divers others of the university, that sojourned there for learning's sake. After these foundations laid, then did he read openly in the house Paul's epistles, and put by Duns and Dorbel.[11]

It is noteworthy that Barnes's humanist practices attracted no hostile comment; it was his open espousal of Lutheranism, not his predilection for the new learning, which earned him condemnation.

In 1524 Fisher issued St John's with a new code of statutes, and according to one of his earliest biographers 'He also minded to have erected yet a third college in Cambridge of his proper charges, and therein consulted with Erasmus by sundry epistles of his advice; but . . . he was prevented by the iniquity of time that shortly after followed'.[12] A symptom of the iniquitous times ahead for orthodox humanists appeared in 1527. While Henry VIII opened his divorce proceedings in London a heresy scandal erupted in Oxford which displayed both the hidden persistence of Lutheranism there and the degree of protection its adherents might expect in the changing political circumstances. A relatively minor incident in itself, the Oxford scandal was a harbinger of future change.

The story is familiar from John Foxe's account. Among the Cambridge scholars who migrated to Cardinal college were, ironically, a number of evangelicals, including John Clerke, John Frith, Richard Coxe and William Betts. Clerke lectured on Paul's epistles in his rooms and gave sermons in the summer at Poghley, where the students retreated to escape the plague. Lutheranism was alive and well in the college, and forbidden books were kept and read there. The most notable supplier of such provender was Thomas Garrett, formerly of Magdalen college. He was later burned with Barnes and Jerome, but at this time he was curate of All Hallows in Honey Lane, London. Besides Greek and Hebrew books and humanist authors like Erasmus, Garrett provided more inflammatory material including the works of Luther and Lambertus and Tyndale's new testament. When his activities came to the attention of the authorities Garrett took to his heels (the forces of orthodoxy pursuing him with the aid of an astrologer), but the investigations resulted in several arrests, including most of the evangelicals at Cardinal and scholars of Magdalen, Corpus Christi, Gloucester and the Augustinian college. Some of the suspects died through being imprisoned in the fish cellar at Cardinal in hot weather, though others managed to escape. There was a number of recantations and the customary bonfire of books, while Garrett was captured and made to do public penance at Oxford.[13]

The different fates of two of the Cardinal college 'heretics' illustrate the two faces of the Henrician reformation. Frith went into exile to produce theological writings, was captured on a visit to England in 1532 and was burned in the following year. Coxe, on the other hand, later won the favour of Goodrich and Cranmer and rose to be dean of Oxford, the King's almoner and tutor to Prince Edward. While blatant and unrepentant heretics like Frith would always face the flames, the more discreet gospellers could find protection and even preferment.

A sure sign of the future which emerged during the Cardinal college scandal was the role of Anne Boleyn. In 1528 she interceded with Wolsey himself for one of the chief culprits; 'I beseech your grace with all my heart to remember the parson of Honey Lane for my sake shortly.' It is uncertain whether she was referring to Garrett or to his rector Thomas Forman, who was that president of Queens' who had warned Cambridge evangelicals of the raid by Wolsey's agents in February 1526. Certainly Forman had been implicated in Garrett's book dealing, and is mentioned by Foxe among those 'troubled and abjured' in 1527 and 1528, in which latter year he died. Garrett, on the other hand, flourished for a time, and may have been that chaplain of Hugh Latimer whose preaching upset Bishop Longland in 1536.[14]

Two other offenders in the Oxford affair later received favour from Anne Boleyn. William Betts, formerly of Gonville Hall, returned to Cambridge and became Anne's chaplain in about 1533. Nicholas Udall of Corpus Christi recanted and remained in Oxford, but it seems that his unorthodox opinions prevented him from taking his MA until 1534. However in 1533 he and his friend John Leland were commissioned to write verses for Anne's coronation pageants, and perhaps it was her favour which enabled him to take his degree. In 1534 he also became headmaster of Eton, and had a selection from Terence published by the royal printer. The advent of the King's Lady obviously augured well for evangelical scholars.

II

The King's divorce and breach with Rome affected the universities and their members in three ways. Firstly, with Wolsey disgraced and Warham and Fisher — respectively chancellors of Oxford and Cambridge — in increasing bad odour with the King, they were constrained to find new patrons and protectors. Secondly, the universities were expected to participate in Henry's proceedings by giving a judgement against his first marriage and by formally accepting the oaths of succession and supremacy. Finally, separation from Rome rendered canon law inapplicable in England, and the removal of this discipline from the curriculum provided an opportunity for a general reform of university studies.

An inevitable result of Wolsey's fall was the dissolution of Cardinal college. Besides the financial gain which would come to the King, it was well known that the college and the school at Ipswich were objects dear to Wolsey's heart, and thus malice may be discerned in the measures taken against them. In July 1528 when Henry was impatient at the slowness of the divorce proceedings he accused Wolsey of taking money corruptly for the establishment and support of his colleges. This was a hint to the Cardinal to be more zealous in his master's cause, but the charge was undoubtedly true. John Chaffcombe, Abbot of Bruerne, purchased his election with a gift of 250 marks and 280 of the best oaks from the abbey woods for the building of Cardinal college; and on the very day that Wolsey wrote to the King exonerating himself from the suspicion of corruption Longland asked him to favour his nephew George Heneage in a matter of church preferment in exchange for a gift of £200 towards 'the building of your honorable college'.[15] Wolsey's susceptibility to bribery — albeit in a good cause — thus gave a handle to his enemies.

In the summer of 1530 Wolsey wrote to a number of men of influence asking their intercession with the King for his colleges, among them his former protégés Gardiner, Sampson and Cromwell. He told this last that he could not eat or sleep for anxiety over his colleges, and he begged Henry himself, 'prostrate at your majesty's feet with weeping tears', to spare them.[16] In the event Henry promised the dean and canons of Cardinal college that he would not destroy it but re-establish it as 'the King's College in Oxford'. However he warned them that the new foundation would not be as magnificent as Wolsey's, 'for it is not thought meet for the common weal of our realm'. Moreover, and although theology lectures were to be given there, it would no longer be an academy but simply a collegiate church, and the canons would be royal chaplains and scholars like Croke, Wakefield and De Burgo who had proved useful on divorce business. Thus Wolsey's stupendous scheme for the humanist education of the clergy came to nothing, and his great foundation dwindled to a mere sinecure for state servants.[17]

The disgrace of Wolsey also left a vacuum in university patronage which was filled by Cromwell and Anne Boleyn. Cromwell was useful because, as a bureaucrat, his knowledge of the workings of patronage was invaluable, while Anne as the King's Lady was in a position to influence Henry directly and to dispose of preferment herself. Cromwell had kept scholars of his own at Oxford and Cambridge before the fall of Wolsey, and after that event he was very active in the affairs of both universities.[18]

At Oxford Longland was elected Chancellor by the King's command on the death of Warham in 1532. A conservative in religion, the bishop was apparently more concerned with the detection and punishment of heresy at Oxford than with the suits of scholars. Like his predecessor, Longland had been a patron of

Erasmus, but his fears seem to have diverted his energies from scholarly matters to religious ones. Thus the university and its members were more inclined to turn to Cromwell for assistance.

The canons of the new King's college used Cromwell as an intermediary with their founder. In December 1532 they sent Croke (their sub-dean) to court to inform Henry of the death of the dean and receive his instructions. Croke also carried a letter to Cromwell from the canons, who assured their 'sole Maecenas' that their spokesman would do nothing before consulting him. They wished the new dean to be one of themselves, and reminded Cromwell of their poverty.[19]

Cromwell was also approached in 1534 by 'the King's scholars' at Oxford. These seem to have been miscellaneous students supported by Henry, and certainly both the treasurer of the chamber's accounts and the privy purse expenses show that the King was accustomed to maintain scholars at university. In March 1529 the treasurer of the chamber paid out 33s 4d for John Bryan's exhibition at Oxford and 50s for Sir John Hurt's, while in August 1530 Roger Smith received £6 13 4d as an annuity towards his charges at Oxford. The privy purse expenses also show various payments for scholars at Oxford. In December 1529 Master Heneage received £20 for three scholars and the sub-dean of the King's chapel £4 for four. These last also had payments of £8 in May and October 1530, April and September 1531, and September 1532. In addition Heneage received £2 for two Oxford scholars at Buckingham in August 1531, and in August 1532 Dr Chamber received the large sum of £56 13 4d for the scholars of Oxford.[20]

Henry's munificence, however, tended to be an inconstant thing. In January 1534 'the scholars of the King's exhibition' at Oxford sent two representatives to court with a letter for Cromwell, whose 'angel's wit' they praised. The previous year they had begged the King to pity them, but as Cromwell had been away they had been discouraged; the minister had often offered to help them all to honest livings. Henry had promised them yearly exhibitions, but so far the money — £28 7 2d in all — had not been forthcoming. As the scholars pointed out, this was 'to his majesty a small sum, and to us all a maintenance of good study'.

By April the scholars were desperate. Cromwell had been busy when their spokesmen approached him, so he had sent them back to their studies promising to secure them their exhibition. The scholars were now deeply in debt and feared that they would be forced to sell

their books. It is to be hoped that Cromwell found time to intercede
with the King for them.[21]

Cromwell was also involved in the affairs of individual Oxford
colleges and students. Sir Anthony Fitzherbert, for example, asked
him to help a kinsman who was a scholar of Oxford to a prebend in
the King's gift worth 33s 4d; while in 1536 John Man, Greek reader
in New College, asked him to get an exhibition from Henry for five
years' study abroad. In addition Richard Myll approached him by
way of Hilsey, bishop of Rochester, who wanted him to be a scholar
in Oxford. It is not known whether these suitors gained their desire,
but in the last two cases it seems unlikely; there is no trace of Myll as
a student at Oxford, while Man, MA in 1538, senior university
proctor in 1540–1 and fellow of his college until 1553, seems to have
remained at the university.[22] Thus while scholars and patrons were
quick to appeal to Cromwell there was no guarantee that his
influence or interest would be sufficient to work for them.

The same may be said of Cromwell's efforts to promote his own
protégés at Oxford. An instance of his success was his intervention
in the affairs of All Souls. In July 1533 Robert Woodward, the
warden, promised to try to get Cromwell's scholar Richard Biscley
elected fellow. The election, however, depended on a majority of
the fellows, not on the warden, but Woodward was glad of a chance
to do Cromwell a service. He advised him to write to the Archbishop
of Canterbury to ensure that he supported Cromwell's man rather
than put forward a candidate of his own, since Cromwell could be
sure of the right choice if Cranmer recommended Biscley. In the
event Biscley was elected, and held the place until 1535. In that year
he received a benefice in Kent through Cromwell's influence, and in
1537 he became the King's scholar with an exhibition of £6 a year.[23]

On the other hand Cromwell was unsuccessful in trying to secure
the presidency of Magdalen for Thomas Marshall, son of his literary
client William. In May 1535 he wrote to Dr London (warden of New
College) and Claymond (president of Corpus) informing them that
the president of Magdalen was very willing to resign in favour of
Thomas Marshall but that the fellows were opposed to it. Cromwell
wanted Claymond and London to persuade them to admit Marshall,
or at least to inform him who the most stubborn of his opponents
were. In fact, Cromwell was unable to secure the place for Marshall,
and in January 1536 the college signified to him their willingness to
accept Owen Oglethorpe, the King's candidate, as president.
Cromwell may have been superseded by Henry in this matter, but

equally, he may have realised the impossibility of Marshall's being elected peacefully and have withdrawn from the contest.[24]

It may be mentioned here that Marshall's brother Richard was an apparently unsuccessful suitor to Cromwell. In 1539 he asked him for assistance in taking his bachelor's degree, claiming that his father had kept him at Oxford since his earliest years, and sent him a Latin poem on the theme of suffering and forebearance as a sample of his talents. Possibly Cromwell helped him with a gift of money, but Richard's first piece of church preferment came as late as 1554.[25]

Thus Cromwell's grip on university patronage was by no means absolute, and it would be inappropriate to consider him the equal of his late master the Cardinal; Wolsey's immense pluralism, enormous influence with Henry VIII and extraordinary authority in the church gave him a command of patronage which no one under the King could hope to rival. An example of Wolsey's power is his dealings with Magdalen college in 1525. On 8 November the vice-president and fellows wrote to thank Wolsey for their new president, regretting, however, that since their statutes bound them to consult the Holy Spirit on the day of the election they were unable to promise beforehand to favour his candidate. A later letter, however, was more fulsome. The members of the college gladly granted Wolsey's request for the use of their stone quarries for materials to build his asylum of the Muses, which they would be pleased to offer even if they were gold mines. They also thanked him for appointing a very judicious president, a wise choice which had quenched all their heartburnings.[26] As has been seen in the case of Thomas Marshall, the Cardinal's high-handedness in over-riding the wishes of the college was something Cromwell could not hope to emulate. The important point about Cromwell is not that he was all-powerful but that he was a court-figure likely to be able to advance the suits of scholars.

His influence in Cambridge affairs is much more marked than in those of Oxford. Certainly Cambridge was the more evangelical of the two universities; it was Dr Butts's *alma mater*, and Anne Boleyn both kept students there and drew many of her chaplains from Cambridge. Cromwell's interest was also personal, as his son and nephew studied there. Thus a considerable number of other scholars was anxious to sue for his favour.

Gregory Cromwell, though most likely not a member of the college, was taught at Christ's by Henry Lockwood, master from 1531. It seems highly probable that Lockwood owed his place to

Thomas Cromwell, whose help he begged in material patronage. The minister assisted him in a forced exchange of land with the King in 1532, and later in that year Lockwood asked him to help the college to a parsonage in Kent and to secure promotion for some of the fellows. Two years later he reminded Cromwell of his longstanding fidelity: 'For God's sake, Sir, remember that I was one of the first suitors to you after you were put in authority under the King's grace, and hath continued a suitor to you ever since that time.' Evidently Lockwood feared to be swamped in the increasing number of petitioners who courted Cromwell's favour.[27]

Cromwell's nephew Christopher Wellefed was also at Cambridge, apparently with Gregory, and he received a regular exhibition from his uncle up to 1539. In March 1533 he asked Cromwell to send him books which were required urgently and asked him to favour the bearer, who had taught Gregory to write. In January 1535 Wellefed told Cromwell that the letters from the King which his uncle had procured had gained him board and lodging at King's Hall; would he now get him a privy seal so that he could have the first vacant place there?[28] In April 1535 Edward Plancknay, Wellefed's companion, told Cromwell that his nephew was advancing in his studies. He lectured three times a day in his hall on Horace and the Latin authors as well as on Aesop's fables from the Greek. Sometimes, said Plancknay, they kept company with Alexander Alesius, a man no less pious than learned and upright who lectured on the psalms in the schools.

Plancknay himself, a former fellow of Corpus Christi, Oxford, was to some extent a dependant of Cromwell. In an undated letter he complained at length of a lawsuit he was engaged in and begged to be allowed to live in Cromwell's house. He also offered to teach Gregory, 'in which labour neither he by the grace of God shall delight in idleness neither I take loss of time'. By April 1535 Plancknay was plainly established at Cambridge and was able to thank his Maecenas for collating him to a benefice.[29]

Other scholars and their relations sought Cromwell's interest. In February 1533 Sir Richard Bulkeley wrote to him on behalf of his brother John, a scholar at Cambridge. John had no exhibition apart from what Sir Richard could spare him, and so he asked Cromwell to procure him the living of Danam, Cheshire by interceding with the patrons. The benefice was worth £20 a year, but Sir Richard offered Cromwell for his pains £20 to buy a saddle and promised that John would give him one-third of the yearly profits of Danam.

Presumably Sir Richard's gift to Cromwell cost less than maintaining his brother at university for several years, and the benefice was certainly a valuable one. John Bulkeley cannot be traced definitely at Cambridge, though a John Buckley was BD in 1534 and DD in 1539; the two may be identical.[30]

A rather different client was Richard Lyst, that former lay-brother of the Observant house at Greenwich who sent Cromwell and Anne Boleyn reports of disaffection in the convent. By October 1533 he was a scholar at Clare Hall. He hoped to become a priest and to have Cromwell's favour in business he would have in London at Christmas. He sent the minister a small token, and asked him to forward his letters to Anne.[31]

Martin Tyndall, a fellow of King's college, found himself in straightened circumstances in 1533 on the death of his patron, Henry Denton, dean of Lichfield. He needed books and clothing and sought Cromwell's goodwill with a rather rough translation of Erasmus's biography of Colet (that is, his epistle to Justus Jonas) and two letters singing his praises as a benefactor of scholars. Tyndall is worth quoting at length as an example of the rather fulsome eloquence which scholars habitually employed to win the good offices of patrons;

> to whom might I better sue than to your mastership? Whose charity is so highly commended that it need not be doubted of your good will, if the party be not thought indigne and not worthy the benefit, and again (thanks be to God) if you be in that case and degree of honour that you may aid and succour the penury of many such poor suitors, and yet it little seen in your yearly revenues. Wherefore I desire your mastership with your most gracious eye to look upon me, a poor orphan, and with your helping hands to sustain the charges of my study, and I shall (seeing I am not able to acquit your goodness otherwise) pray unto the Lord above, which registers they benefits done to his little ones in the court-rolls of his remembrance, that he will (according to his promises) treasure up the hundrethfold of your goodness against your coming thither, and here to direct your walking in the pathways of his word.

This mixture of piety and flattery — with the description of God as a bureaucrat, like his servant on earth — may have had effect, since Tyndall remained at Cambridge for another six years or so.[32]

The university authorities, meanwhile, were undoubtedly anxious in view of their chancellor Fisher's dangerous resistance to the King. In January 1529 they showed their gratitude to the Bishop by passing a decree for the observation of his anniversary and sending him a letter of compliments, but as Fisher became increasingly vocal in opposition they looked elsewhere for protection. Recognising Cromwell's influence at court, they voted him an annual stipend in 1533 and elected him high steward of the university. In August 1535, after Fisher's attainder and death, the vice-chancellor John Crayforde wrote to Cromwell with a remarkable lack of flattery to inform him that he had been elected chancellor for life.[33]

A patron so occupied with affairs of state, however, might not always have time for the requests of scholars, and so Cromwell's will might be flouted or ignored by those who thought he was too busy to notice. Thus Thomas Aleyn complained to him that the Master and fellows of Corpus Christi, Cambridge would not obey his letters and grant Aleyn a fellowship. When Aleyn remonstrated with the Master he was told, 'Master Secretary doth send many letters in a year and regardeth as much the trip of a man's finger as the speeding or performing of his letters.' Aleyn took this 'for no little rebuke, although', he added piously, 'I thought it was neither true nor comely'. In the event Aleyn got his fellowship at Corpus in 1536 and retained it until at least 1541.[34]

Anne Boleyn also proved to be a friend and benefactor to the universities. Her chaplain and biographer William Latymer states that she persuaded the King to exempt Cambridge and Oxford from the payment of tenths and subsidies, and this is confirmed by a letter of thanks for her efforts from Cambridge. Latymer also claims that she gave both universities £40 in the first year of her marriage and £80 a year thereafter for the maintenance of poor students.[35] Certainly William Barker shows that she did support scholars at Cambridge. Dedicating his *Nobility of Women* to Elizabeth I in 1559 he recalled that Anne, 'earnestly minding the advancement of learning, employed her bountiful benevolence upon sundry students that were placed at Cambridge, among the which it pleased her highness to appoint me (most unworthy) for one that should enjoy the fruit thereof.' Barker remembered Anne's generosity again in 1571 when, having been implicated in the Ridolfi Plot with his master Norfolk, he had to throw himself upon Elizabeth's mercy:

The Queen's majesty her mother gave me exhibition at my first coming to Cambridge, as she did to many more, whereof I think there be but few alive, the which was to me an encouragement to continue, which I did a long time . . . Therefore I desire her highness to pardon me, and as by her majesty's noble mother I first began at Cambridge, tasting of her munificence, so by her majesty's clemency I may end the rest of my sorrowful days there.[36]

Anne also appears as the patron of John Eldmer, a monk of St Mary's York and a candidate for the vacant abbacy there in 1530. Anne intervened in the election to ensure that Eldmer, if not elected, would be allowed to continue his studies at Cambridge. Some years later she wrote indignantly to the Abbot because she had learned that Eldmer, 'a man . . . of good leaning, sad demeanour and virtuous governance', had been recalled from the university and loaded with administrative duties which prevented him from studying. Accordingly she demanded his return to Cambridge with sufficient exhibition. Her will seems to have been accomplished, as the university records show that Eldmer, who took his BD in 1530, became DD in 1536.[37]

Anne Boleyn was most noticeably active as a patron to university scholars — and a protector of the more radical spirits among them — after both Cambridge and Oxford were obliged to participate in the divorce proceedings. The idea of asking the English and European universities for a judgement on the Aragon marriage was first proposed in the late summer of 1529 by Cranmer, then an unknown fellow of Jesus, Cambridge. Significantly, Cranmer entered the household of Anne Boleyn's father, and the divorce referendum was to prove useful to the careers of a number of evangelical university scholars.

However, the fact that both Oxford and Cambridge eventually obliged Henry with the required verdict should not obscure the resistance offered to the King's proceedings. The divorce debate was a crucial issue which bitterly divided the bodies of both universities. While fortune obviously favoured those who favoured the King, a number of humanists found it difficult or downright impossible to tailor their consciences to Henry's. Before following the successful careers grounded on the royal divorce, it is important to consider the opposition, vain though it was.

Resistance at Cambridge was almost certainly encouraged by

Fisher; it is remarkable that all those who opposed the King were members at one time or another of either Christ's or St John's. Nicholas Wilson, formerly of Christ's, Henry's chaplain and sometime almoner to Queen Katherine, was Master of Michaelhouse (where Fisher himself had studied) from 1533. He wrote against the divorce and supported Powell and Hubberdine in their controversy with Hugh Latimer. He refused the oaths of succession and supremacy with More, was imprisoned in the Tower until 1537 and was replaced at Michaelhouse by Cranmer's chaplain Mallet, who was promoted there by Cromwell. John Watson, Master of Christ's and friend of Erasmus, was one of the university delegates appointed to debate the marriage, but his name is not marked as one of those favourable to the King. He was replaced as head of Christ's by Lockwood, Cromwell's client. Nicholas Metcalfe, Master of St John's, was praised by Ascham in *The Schoolmaster* and mentioned by Robert Wakefield as the 'mutual friend' who carried letters between himself and Fisher. He sided with the Queen initially but was driven to conformity, and in 1536 was one of the university proctors for the new oaths of succession and supremacy. Similarly Robert Shorton, former Master of St John's, Master of Pembroke and Katherine's last almoner, was the Queen's steadfast supporter at first; in 1531 he told a furious Norfolk that it would be against his duty, honour and conscience to advise her to accept the judgement of Paris university. He must have submitted in time, however, as he was still dean of Stoke-by-Clare (a benefice in the queen consort's gift) at his death in 1535.[38]

There is also evidence of resistance at Oxford. The King warned the scholars explicitly to comply with his will: 'In case you do not uprightly according to divine learning hand yourselves herein, ye may be assured that we, not without great cause, shall so quickly and sharply look to your unnatural misdemeanour herein that it shall not be to your quietness and ease hereafter.' None the less there were dissension and agitation among the MAs between February and March 1530 and Henry had to send another letter. The King was amazed at the contentiousness of the youth of the university but trusted that the seniors would impose conformity, and he hinted darkly at the dangers of stirring up a hornet's nest. Even so, the desired verdict was not reached until 8 April, after a third royal letter had been despatched.[39]

Indications of opposition at Oxford continued. In 1531 Greek and Latin books which defended the Queen's case were found at New college, where the scholars strenuously denied reading or owning them. One Goldwell of Canterbury college was relieved of two books which were apparently on the same subject. He later denied on oath that he had read them and said that he would have destroyed them if the warden had not ordered the scholars to keep any writings that might be the work of John Deryng, an accomplice of the Nun of Kent. In late 1532 or early 1533 John London, warden of New college, had to clear himself of the suspicion of having opposed Henry's proceedings at Oxford. He cited Henry Norris and Anne Boleyn's servants Barlow and Taylor as witnesses that he had done his duty and promised to perform any service for the King and Anne.[40]

If resistance to Henry was dangerous, zeal in his cause could reap rewards. Thus in April 1534, when four candidates for the two university proctorships were causing unrest at Oxford, the chancellor Longland gave his recommendation to Howell of All Souls, who was the King's scholar, and to Cary of Lincoln college, who had distinguished himself in 'the King's great cause'.[41]

It was Cambridge scholars, however, who were the more spectacularly successful in gaining advancement through the royal divorce. Here a word must be said about the machinery of patronage as it related to the universities. Some suitors approached Cromwell and Anne Boleyn directly, but as these powerful patrons were busy with high politics and affairs of state it was more usual to use a middleman as intermediary. The most notable sponsor of this sort was Dr William Butts, and his singular position as both royal physician and protector of Cambridge has already been described. (See the Introduction, above.) At the same time, it is likely that scholars who had gained a foothold at court would recommend each other for promotion or protection. Whoever the initial patron in each individual case, it is noteworthy that among the Cambridge men advanced by the reform faction at court there was a preponderance of scholars from Gonville — Butts's own college — and a number of friends and associates of the evangelical martyr Bilney. Gonville's reputation for heterodoxy is graphically illustrated by a comment which Bishop Nix of Norwich made to Warham in May 1531: 'I hear no clerk hath comen out lately of that college but savoureth of the frying pan, though he speak never so holily.'[42]

The rise of Hugh Latimer after attracting Butts's attention during the divorce referendum has already been rehearsed. (See the Introduction, above.) It seems probable that Nicholas Shaxton had a similar early career. Certainly it is interesting that he graduated BA from Gonville in 1507, the same year as Butts. Like Latimer he was known as a radical, and in 1531 he was forced to recant after carrying heretical books into the diocese of Norwich; Bishop Nix, referring to Bilney and Shaxton, is said to have exclaimed, 'Christ's mother! I have burnt Abel, and let Cain go.' Despite his heretical history Shaxton received a large amount of preferment. In 1533 he became Anne Boleyn's chaplain and almoner, received a benefice from the King and became treasurer of Salisbury cathedral. In 1534 he received a prebend at Westminster, and in 1535 he became Bishop of Salisbury while Latimer was made bishop of Worcester. Their elevation to the episcopal bench caused them both some financial anxiety as neither could afford to pay first-fruits to the King. Luckily Anne Boleyn lent her protégés £200 each, debts which were still owing two months after her death.[43]

John Skip was another fellow of Gonville and a frequenter of the White Horse, as was Simon Heynes, president of Queens'. Both were sent to Cambridge to preach the royal supremacy in 1534. Skip became Anne Boleyn's chaplain and her almoner in succession to Shaxton. Heynes, a *confidant* of Butts, voted for the King in the university referendum. He received the wealthy livings of Stepney and Fulham, was sent to Germany with Christopher Mont to persuade Melanchthon to come to England, became a canon of Windsor and was made dean of Exeter.[44]

Two other Gonville men who benefited from the new *status quo* were Thomas Patmore and Edward Crome. Patmore, who was parson of Hadham, Herts was accused of heresy by Stokesley in 1530 and confined for two years in the Lollards' Tower. His supporters claimed that he was persecuted because the Bishop wanted the living for a client of his own, but in fact Patmore was specifically charged with keeping and reading heretical books, uttering heresy at Cambridge, and consenting to the marriage of his curate Simon Smith, who was also a former member of Gonville. His release was finally secured by petitions addressed to the King through Anne Boleyn, and in 1535 Henry ordered a commission of nine (including Cranmer, Cromwell, Audley and Hugh Latimer) to investigate Patmore's charges of mistreatment against Stokesley and his vicar-general Foxford.[45]

Crome led a somewhat chequered career. In February 1530 he was proposed to the university committee which was to debate the divorce but was rejected (along with William Reps, another former

Gonville man) because he had already approved Cranmer's book against the Aragon marriage. He preached before the King twice in Lent 1530, receiving a reward of 20s on each occasion. Though appointed one of the university commissioners for the examination of heretical books in May 1530 he was himself examined by Stokesley in the King's presence because of his preaching, and was forced to recant. None the less Anne Boleyn nominated him to the living of St Mary Aldermary, London, and he was later a frequent — though controversial — preacher at court and in the city.[46]

Anne Boleyn recruited several of her chaplains from among the Cambridge evangelicals. Her employment of Latimer, Shaxton, Skip and William Betts has already been mentioned. On Betts's death in March 1535 she was eager to replace him with Matthew Parker, and Skip wrote to him on her behalf twice in one day. He urged Parker: 'I pray you resist not your calling, but come in any wise to know of her pleasure. Bring with you a long gown, and that shall be enough until you shall return to Cambridge.' Anne promoted him to the deanery of Stoke-by-Clare, where he founded a notable humanist school, and shortly before her death gave him some sort of charge over her daughter Elizabeth. Parker managed to survive all the vicissitudes of the reign, including the execution of Anne and of Cromwell and the passage of the Act of Six Articles. In November 1544 Henry VIII recommended him as Master of Corpus Christi, Cambridge as 'a man as well for his approved learning, wisdom and honesty, as for his singular grace and industry in bringing up youth in virtue and learning, so apt for the exercise of the said room, as it is thought very hard to find the like for all respects and purposes.'[47]

Another of Anne's Cambridge chaplains was William Latymer — like Parker and Betts a member of Corpus — whose 'Brief Treatise or Chronicle of the Most Virtuous Lady Anne Boleyn' is a valuable biographical source for the period. Anne's chaplains formed an important link between their mistress and penurious scholars. For example, in September 1535 John Cheke of St John's asked Parker to approach Anne on behalf of William Bill, an able scholar of his college who was too poor to take up a fellowship. It was well known, said Cheke, that people like Bill only had to be recommended by Parker, Skip or one of the other chaplains, and Anne would be generous. It is pleasant to note that she was so in this case.[48]

III

Thus for some university scholars there was much to be gained from the King's divorce and the attendant political changes. At the same time, the nature of study in the universities was drastically altered by political events. In academic terms the repudiation of papal authority in England rendered the study of canon law obsolete. Cromwell, however, was not merely content to abolish this one discipline, but took the opportunity to review studies in general.

William Marshall, doubtless acting on Cromwell's behalf, made inquiries about conditions at Oxford. He was answered by his friend Michael Drome, a fellow of Canterbury college. As a fervent evangelical Drome complained of those who worked quietly against the King's ordinances and railed against the gospel and the new English books, and hoped that someone like John Hilsey could be sent to Oxford to teach justification by faith. His chief academic objection was that the heads of study were themselves unlearned; they should be sent to their parishes to make room for those whose learning made them necessary to the commonwealth. He also suggested the institution of Greek and rhetoric lectures in the colleges and, recalling Vives's residence in the 1520s, the importation of foreign professors.[49]

Some of Drome's recommendations (though not those concerning doctrine) were directly embodied in the injunctions Cromwell issued to both universities in 1535. The chief reforms were the abolition of canon law, the establishment of Greek and Latin lectures in the larger colleges, and the total eradication of the schoolmen from the studies of philosophy and divinity. To ensure the enforcement of these directives visitors were despatched to both universities.

Thomas Leigh reported the joyful reception of the injunctions by the whole university of Cambridge, 'saving three or four of the pharasaical Pharisees, from whom that blindness that is rooted in them is impossible, or else very hard, to eradicate and pluck away.'[50] Leigh gave additional injunctions of his own, which included the establishment of a public Greek or Hebrew lecture at the university's expense. (No public reader of Greek seems to have been appointed after Pace, who was promoted to the place in April 1520.) A Greek lecture was established at Gonville by order of the visitors, and one in rhetoric was founded there by a private donor within three years. Ralph Standish, of an unnamed and unknown college, wrote to warn Anthony Burcher to make provision for his brother, as the visitors had ordained that all scholars whose Latin was insufficient for philosophy and the arts were to be sent back to grammar school; only those who mastered the language within three years would be re-admitted to college.[51]

More is known of the visitation and its consequences at Oxford. Richard Leighton told Cromwell that the visitors had 'set Duns in Bocardo' (the town gaol) and established Greek and Latin lectures in the larger colleges which members of the less affluent houses were bound to attend. He reported that the lectures at Magdalen college in theology, philosophy and rhetoric were 'well kept and diligently frequented', so that it was only necessary to add one in Greek, while Fox's public lectures at Corpus were evidently functioning efficiently.[52]

Theoretically, separation from Rome and the consequent Cromwellian injunctions were distinctly advantageous to the standing of humanism in the universities, but the triumph of the new learning should not be overestimated. In practice, shortage of funds coupled with a recrudescence of the old Trojan hostility often limited the effectiveness of the innovations at Oxford. There seems to have been a disturbance at New College which concerned the new learning. In October 1534 22 of the members wrote to Cromwell begging him to redress an injury done to two of their number which affected them all. They praised Cromwell's services to humanism in warm terms:

> While we consider the great wisdom and high judgment of your mastership . . . we know ourself much bound to God, which hath in our time sent such a favourable defender of the truth of God, that whereas of long time unlearned learning and rude barbarousness hath reigned, to the great hindrance of good learning and the true knowledge of God, yet now by your high wisdom is clean abolished and put to silence, and good learning brought in their place.

They implored Cromwell to favour them and see justice done, for 'if it should chance these men not to return by your pitiful goodness showed to them, we all shall be discouraged to this good learning brought in by your mastership'. Since both the injured scholars, William Holmes and John Man, retained their places for a number of years it may be assumed that their colleagues' intercession was successful.[53]

Besides actual opposition to humanism there was often very little effort to implement the visitors' instructions in the colleges. As late as 1538 the only members of Brasenose to receive humanist instruction were those holding the scholarships founded by Claymond's will, who were bound to attend the public lectures at Corpus; no Greek lecture existed at Brasenose itself until at least 1572.[54] At Magdalen some of the fellows objected that the new Greek lecture was prohibited by their statutes. The more enlightened members begged Cromwell not to listen to such 'sinistral information' and lamented that

> before time our youth hath been brought up very corruptly and led in ignorance for lack of the Greek tongue, and have had, moreover, their principles of logic so blindly and in such confusion taught them that neither they could tell whereabout they went when they learned it nor what profit they had gotten by it.

They rejoiced, however, that the injunctions now made it possible for the university to bring forth 'those that shall be able to do that service to the uttermost, both in private matters of their prince and in common affairs of the commonalty, besides as shall be required of any men of their degree and profession'. Unfortunately there is no record of payment for a Greek lecture at Magdalen before 1540, though after that date regular payments occur.[55] Despite these obstacles it would seem that the political events of the early 1530s broadly assisted the progress of the new learning in the academic sphere.

At the same time, however, the lack of any clear national religious settlement after the breach with Rome led to a considerable amount of dissension and controversy in both universities. Conservative and evangelical humanists quarrelled bitterly and accused each other loudly of heresy and popery, while both sides still had to contend with the old Trojan spirit of reaction. Thus in September 1535 the members of St Alban's Hall, Oxford petitioned Cromwell for the reinstatement of their principal, Robert Huycke, deprived by the commissary of Oxford

> only because he hath been a man of right judgment and of clean

and substantial learning, and hath nothing favoured barbarous-
ness, but laboured with all his endeavour to restore to us the old
eloquence and commendable learning, inveighing when he had
opportunity against Duns . . . and such other barbarous authors,
calling them the destruction of good wits.[56]

Huycke's humanism was probably not the sole reason for his
dismissal, since in his later career as a royal physician he was to be
noted as an active evangelical at court, but he was obviously under
attack on this occasion for the new learning. The Trojans were
fighting a losing battle, however, and the quarrels which disturbed
the universities were usually between humanists of different
doctrinal views.

Conservative disaffection lingered at St John's, Cambridge even
after Fisher's demise, despite the large number of eminent
evangelical scholars there. When electing a Master in 1537 the
fellows steadfastly ignored Cromwell's letters nominating George
Day as his own and the King's candidate and chose instead Nicholas
Wilson, newly pardoned and released from imprisonment for
resistance to the royal supremacy. Wilson, however, was a broken
man, and was probably genuine when he told Wriothesley that he
had no foreknowledge of his election and that the fellows' decision
had caused him 'no small grief and heaviness'. He hoped that
the King would overlook their youthful lack of consideration
of their duty. As by this time they had in fact repented of their
rashness and wisely chosen the royal nominee after all, there were
no repercussions.[57]

The fellows of St John's had learned to be circumspect, and when
Day was elected provost of King's college the following summer at
Henry's command they dutifully replaced him with another royal
candidate, John Taylor. He was a protégé of Butts and, according to
John Foxe, 'a man in those days not far disagreeing from the gospel,
and who afterwards, in the time of King Edward, was made Bishop
of Lincoln, and at last, in the time of Queen Mary, was deprived
from the same; and so ended his life among the confessors of Jesus
Christ.' Such a master was bound to provoke discord, and the
college was rent with dissension after his election because of opposition from the conservative fellows. As a result a formal visitation by
Goodrich, the evangelical Bishop of Ely, increased the powers of
the Master and reduced the number of fellows who were to be drawn
from the more conservative northern counties. These changes were

confirmed in 1544 by a new code of status drawn up by Cheke and issued by the King.[58]

The reminiscences of Roger Ascham provide a less negative view of the religious differences at St John's. Ascham recalled that Nicholas Metcalfe, who was Master before Day

> was a papist indeed, but would to God, amongst all us protestants I might once see but one that would win like praise in doing like good for the advancement of learning and virtue. And yet, though he were a papist, if any young man given to new learning (as they termed it) [Here, 'new learning' means evangelical religion rather than humanism.] went beyond his fellows in wit, labour and towardness, even the same neither lacked open praise to encourage him nor private exhibition to maintain him.

Metcalfe demonstrated this concern with academic excellence somewhat curiously in 1534, when Ascham was a candidate for a fellowship but almost ruined his chances by speaking against the pope:

> I was called before him and the seniors; and after grievous rebuke, and some punishment, open warning was given to all the fellows, none to be so hardy to give me his voice at that election. And yet for all those open threats, the good father himself privily procured that I should even then be chosen fellow. But, the election being done, he made countenance of great discontentation thereat. This good man's goodness and fatherly discretion used towards me that one day shall never out of my remembrance all the days of my life.[59]

Ascham's recollections after so long a period are undoubtedly rose-tinted, but even so it seems that love of learning could, on occasion, triumph over doctrinal antagonism.

At Oxford, meanwhile, mutual accusations of heresy and popery flew about. Robert Huycke, the former principal of St Alban's Hall, approached Richard Morison as a means to Cromwell in January 1537 and spoke of his troubles at Oxford. He declared that the veil of Moses had been lifted from his eyes some five years previously when he had perceived that justification did not come from the law. His efforts to propagate this view had met with hostility at Oxford, where Pelagius still reigned, but he expressed his confidence in

Cromwell, the servant of the earthly King Henry and the heavenly King Christ. Oddly enough Huycke's successor as principal of St Alban's Hall, Richard Smith, was accused of asserting papal supremacy in September 1538.[60]

The warden of New college was also constrained to defend himself against the suspicion of popery. Though formerly in the habit of addressing Cromwell directly John London was so far out of favour in August 1537 that he was forced to court the minister through, not one, but two intermediaries. He wrote to Bedyll of the distress Cromwell's accusation had caused him; lamented that since the schoolmen had been prohibited the youth of the college would not read good authors like Lefèvre, Melanchthon and the Greek text of Aristotle; declared that he wanted to enforce the order of study Cromwell had personally recommended to him; and reminded Bedyll that he had made Thomas Knight, a client of Wriothesley, dean of arts in the college and had engineered his election as university proctor.

Bedyll took the hint and obligingly passed the letter to Wriothesley, defending London as a great reformer of clerical superstition and ignorance and begging him to ask Cromwell to send the wretched warden a few words of comfort. Since London retained his position and survived to harass evangelicals after the passage of the Act of Six Articles, his timely subservience was evidently effective. In June 1538 he affirmed his loyalty by bringing before the Mayor of Oxford two members of his college accused of discussing the papal supremacy.[61]

At Corpus Christi, too, the fellows were busy accusing each other of popery; their complaints were sent to Cranmer, who forwarded them to Cromwell. It is noteworthy that conservative resistance to religious change was most vigorous in the oldest established humanist colleges, Corpus, Oxford and St John's, Cambridge; another indication that the defence of orthodoxy was not the preserve of reactionaries.[62] On the other side Longland's wrath was provoked by evangelicals at Oxford who ate meat in Lent 1530. He wrote to Cromwell demanding the punishment of the miscreants, who themselves sent the minister a petition from 'the whole number of your scholars in Oxford, those only which are favourers of God's word'. They confessed their offence but claimed to have eaten meat solely for their health, and to have done it secretly in order to avoid scandal. They had, however, been betrayed by one of their number whom they thought might have been bribed by Longland. It seems unlikely that any retribution followed, since Longland was indignantly demanding punishment for the same offence in August 1539.[63]

In 1542, after Cromwell's fall, a controversy occurred at Cambridge which, though at first sight purely academic, undoubtedly reflected the religious divisions within the university. Some seven years previously Cheke, Thomas Smith and John Ponet had introduced a new and theoretically more accurate pronunciation of Greek. Gardiner, Cromwell's successor as chancellor, took exception to this, reproved Cheke — now Regius Professor of Greek — for the innovation, and issued an edict forbidding any alteration in the pronunciation of Greek and Latin. Both Cheke and Smith produced treatises defending the new pronunciation but Gardiner was unmoved, and he gently warned Smith that he had talent which would come to great things if not hindered by trifles of this kind.

The Bishop was far from being a humanist himself; anxious to impose discipline in the university, he told Cheke that it would be better to do away with Greek altogether than allow the youth of Cambridge to learn arrogance, vanity and rashness from him. Moreover, as a conservative Gardiner was uneasy about the turn religious affairs were taking after the breach with Rome. Besides his instinctive opposition to innovation of any kind, it is reasonable to suppose that the fact that Cheke and Smith were evangelical clients of Butts played a large part in determining his conduct. His hostility to the new learning was ineffective, however, and he was still trying to enforce the prohibition in 1554.[64]

IV

A major ecclesiastical change which humanists hoped would benefit the universities was the dissolution of the monasteries. Though undoubtedly a financial measure primarily intended to enrich the crown, the dissolution was quite compatible with humanist ecclesiastical and economic criticism. Erasmus had attacked monks and monasticism in private correspondence and published works such as the *Praise of Folly* and *Colloquia*, and indeed, one of the latter was translated and published anonymously as *The Pilgrimage of Pure Devotion* as propaganda for the new policy. Starkey's *Dialogue of Lupset and Pole*, composed in the early 1530s, complained of the aggravation of population decline through deliberate celibacy and castigated religious who withdrew from society as sailors afraid to leave the harbour in case of storms.[65] In practical terms, Fisher and Wolsey had suppressed small and decayed monasteries in order to re-apply their lands and revenues to the endowment of St John's and Cardinal college.

In view of all this it was natural to hope that money and property released by the general dissolution would be used at least in part for educational purposes. Starkey told Cromwell that the conversion of the existing great monasteries into small universities would help re-establish English religious credibility abroad,[66] while a variety of institutions and individuals was quick to petition Cromwell and the King for church lands to be applied to specific educational uses. In the event, of course, most of the revenues and possessions of the religious houses came directly to the crown, but a certain limited success was achieved by those who hoped to divert monastic property to the endowment of learning.

Cambridge university was prompt to remind the King of its poverty and to request one of the dissolved monasteries, praying that the houses formerly given over to superstition might become colleges for the propagation of learning and the true doctrine of Christ.[67] Again, this comment should not be interpreted as mere lip-service to the official reasons for the dissolution; it was also a continuation of the attitude of early reformers like Colet and Erasmus. The visitors to the university granted it the site of the Franciscan friary, but since custody of the property had been given to a hostile serjeant-at-law the scholars were forced in 1538 to ask Cromwell's aid in retaining it, declaring:

> When we consider the King's highness' most gracious and ardent desire to the increase of virtue and learning . . . we cannot doubt; and when we look on your lordship's continual and propense furtherance of the same; we must needs have great hope that by turning the houses dedicate to vain religion into colleges of true and sincere doctrine, learning and virtue should greatly be augmented.[68]

King's college petitioned successfully for the restoration of the two pensions formerly paid by them to the London Charterhouse (£33 6 8d) and to Wilton abbey (£13 6 8d). The members gave cogent reasons for the request: their yearly expenses for the past nine or ten years had exceeded their revenues by at least £100, so that the scholars were obliged to forgo a third part of the stipends allotted to them by the founder; the scholars were compelled to pay for the college lectures out of their own allowances because the college itself was too poor to give stipends to the deans and readers; and (most topically) lands worth 800 marks a year had been given to certain monasteries because 'it was then thought to be a deed more meritorious and acceptable to God to give such lands to religious persons than to students in the university'. In addition to the release of its pensions an Act of 33 Henry VIII safeguarded the college's revenues due from alien priories.[69]

Cambridge gained in other ways from the dissolution. In 1542 the court of augmentations paid the stipends of the Lady Margaret reader and preacher, formerly due from Westminster abbey, and in 1544 paid the university £10 for an anniversary for Henry VII, due from the same house. In addition Thomas Audley founded Magdalene, Cambridge on the site of the Benedictine house known as Buckingham college in 1542, establishing eight fellowships and endowing it to the value of £100. In the same year an Act of Parliament authorised the heirs of Hugh Denys to transfer £20 originally granted to the Charterhouse of Sheen to Magdalene, 20 marks of which were to be used to establish two 'King's fellowships'.[70]

Against these unsystematic material endowments must be set the loss of monastic houses of study and individual scholars to the universities. Oxford complained to Cromwell in 1539 that the number of its students had been halved by the dissolution, and indeed, the university registers for 1505 to 1538 record the names of 357 religious. A number of former monks did take advantage of the dissolution to return to academic studies. Thus, for example, Thomas Coventree, a monk of Evesham acquainted with Morison, requested and received a pension at the dissolution in order to continue his studies in the tongues, undertaken, he claimed, to 'wipe away the colours of all those which have painted a papistical and sophistical divinity and mired the clean vein of God's word with man's dreams and fantasies'. Such individuals, however, were comparatively few, and the loss of monastic colleges and students was palpably felt by Oxford and Cambridge.[71]

The King's plan of creating new bishoprics from old monasteries was meant to compensate for this and to eclipse the benefits the religious houses had bestowed on learning. The Act of Parliament concerning this new policy, drawn up by the King himself, declared

Henry's intention of replacing the slothful and ungodly religious houses with new sees and cathedral churches, 'whereby God's word might the better be set forth, children brought up in learning, clerks nourished in the universities . . . readers of Greek, Hebrew and Latin to have good stipend'.[72] The new bishopric of Westminster, erected in 1540, was obliged to support five Regius professors at both Cambridge and Oxford, besides 20 students of divinity at the two universities and a grammar school of its own. The Regius chairs were the most significant attempt by the court to utilise monastic wealth for educational purposes.

The choice of the Regius professors is interesting from a religious point of view. Richard Smith, the former principal of St Alban's Hall, was appointed to the divinity chair at Oxford; his own theological bias can be gauged by two treatises he dedicated to the King, *The Assertion and Defence of the Sacrament of the Altar* and *A Defence of the Sacrifice of the Mass*, both printed in 1546. At Cambridge, on the other hand, the Hebrew chair went to Thomas Wakefield, brother of the celebrated hebraist and divorce propagandist, Robert, while the chairs of civil law and Greek went respectively to Thomas Smith and Cheke, clients of Butts. It is possibly significant that the first dean (and last abbot) of Westminster was William Boston, an acquaintance of Denny and Butts who had previously shown kindness to the latter's protégé Nicholas Bourbon.[73]

The Regius chairs were undoubtedly an important addition to educational endowment, but otherwise the benefits which came to the universities through the monastic dissolution were unsystematic, limited and dependent on individual initiative. (This also holds true for the endowment and foundation of the schools in the wake of the dissolution; see Chapter 4, below.) If comparatively little was gained for learning in the earlier stages of the dissolution, its ultimate phase threatened to destroy the universities altogether. In 1545 was passed the Chantries Act which authorised the suppression of all colleges and the transference of their possessions to the crown. The motive for this proceeding was undoubtedly financial; a modern historian notes that the Act was an expedient to recoup the enormous outlay for the war with France and Scotland and to pay the King's servants for debts owing to them and services rendered.[74] Matthew Parker alleged that Henry was influenced by 'certain officers in the court and others then in authority under the King, importunately sueing to him to have the lands and possessions of both universities surveyed, they meaning afterwards to enjoy the best of their lands and possessions by exchange of impropred benefices and such other improved lands'. Certainly Parker's accusation recalls Ralph Morice's tale of Sir Thomas Seymour's attempt to discredit Cranmer in order to persuade the King to resume the lands of the church.[75]

Between March and November 1545 three Oxford colleges — Durham, Canterbury and Henry VIII's establishment — surrendered to the crown, while New college yielded up Peckwater's Inn, one of its hostels. Commissioners were appointed to survey the university colleges in January 1546, and both universities hastened to throw themselves on the King's mercy and to solicit the interest of influential sympathisers at court. Oxford assured Henry of its confidence in his goodwill, of which they had been informed by his commissioner Richard Coxe, dean of Oxford, while Cambridge approached Sir William Paget and Katherine Parr.[76]

It seems difficult to believe that Henry seriously intended to dissolve the universities as thoroughly as he had suppressed the monasteries.[77] Indeed, the surrender of the see of Oxford and of the King's college there on the same day in May seems to indicate that he already contemplated the foundation of Christ Church, while Katherine Parr's reply to Cambridge (in the main a pious and somewhat anti-intellectual warning to the humanists there not to imitate the pagan Athenian philosophers) hinted that the King intended to establish a new college:

> notwithstanding his majesty's property and interest through the consent of the high court of parliament, his highness, being such a patron to good learning, he will rather advance and erect new occasion therefore, than confound those your colleges; so that learning may hereafter ascribe her very original, whole conservation and sure stay to our sovereign lord, his only defence and worldly ornament.[78]

It is also noteworthy that the commissioners appointed by the King were the university vice-chancellors and other academics rather than hostile courtiers. According to Parker, Henry was persuaded to use the former (on the grounds that it would be cheaper) by 'certain friends of the university'. These would undoubtedly have been humanists and patrons of learning who were influential at court and had been approached by the universities:

Coxe himself; Cheke, like the former, a tutor to Prince Edward; Thomas Wendy, whom Ascham called the successor of Butts as protector of Cambridge as well as royal physician; and Denny, who, besides his usual interest in his *alma mater*, interceded with Henry at this time to save Parker's school at Stoke-by-Clare.[79]

The result of the visitation is well known. The King accorded a favourable reception to the Cambridge commissioners (Parker, vice-chancellor and Master of Corpus, William May, president of Queens', and John Redman, warden of King's Hall), and on 29 October Michaelhouse and the King's Hall surrendered to the crown, while Gonville ceded Physwick Hostel.[80] These properties were to be the basis of Trinity college, founded by letters patent on 19 December for a Master and 60 fellows. Redman, the first Master, received £2,000 from the court of augmentations in December for the establishment and building of the college, and sums of £300 and £290 for the scholars' exhibitions in early January 1547.

Similarly, at Oxford a new college was established on the site and with the revenues of the King's college, Canterbury college, Edward's Hall and Peckwater's Inn. Like its prototype Cardinal college, Christ Church combined a collegiate church (in this case the cathedral of Oxford) with an academy. The college was established by letters patent on 4 November 1546 for a dean, eight canons and 100 students, and was endowed with the prodigious sum of £2,200 a year, while dean Coxe was granted £2,400 in December towards the building costs.[81]

In the event, then, the property crisis of 1546–7 proved a blessing rather than a curse to the universities. Moreover, Trinity and Christ Church followed directly in the tradition of earlier experiments in the establishment of humanist academies. Both were obliged to pay the stipends of the Regius professors of Hebrew, Greek and theology, thus, like Fox's and Wolsey's colleges, providing public lectures in the humanities. Ascham later claimed that Trinity, 'that princely house now, at the first erection was but *colonia deducta* out of St John's, not only for their Master, fellows and scholars but also, which is more, for their whole both order of learning and discipline of manners'.[82]

The pioneering work of the early humanist founders, developed by the Cromwellian injunctions of 1535 and the establishment of the Regius chairs, thus reached its logical conclusion with the founding of richly endowed royal colleges for the education of the clergy in the new learning. The Henrician achievement in the endowment of learning was not as spectacular as humanists might have wished, but by the end of the reign the new learning, consistently promoted by the court, was firmly established in both the old and the new colleges.

Notes

1. Sir Henry Ellis (ed.) *Original Letters Illustrative of English History* (11 vols., 3 series, Harding, Triphook & Lepard, London, 1824, 1827, 1846), series 3, vol. 1, pp. 239–42. Misdated 1521 here and in *Letters and Papers, Foreign and Domestic, of the Reign of Henry VIII*, J. S. Brewer, J. Gairdner, R. H. Brodie (eds) (21 vols., HMSO, London, 1862–1932), vol. 3, ii, no. 1193 (hereafter cited as *L&P*).

2. William A. Clebsch, *England's Earliest Protestants, 1520–1535* (Yale University Press, Newhaven and London, 1964), pp. 26, 43–9.

3. H. A. Wilson, *Magdalen College* (F. E. Robinson & Co., London, 1899), p. 73; Richard Hall (ascr.), *Life of Fisher*, Ronald Bayne (ed.) (Early English Text Society, Oxford University Press, London, 1921), pp. 21–5.

4. 'A Replication Against Certain Young Scholars Abjured of Late', printed in Ian A. Gordon, *John Skelton, Poet Laureate* (Melbourne University Press, Melbourne and London, 1943), p. 112.

5. The Cardinal statutes are printed in E. A. Bond (ed.), *Statutes of the Colleges of Oxford* (3 vols., J. H. Parker and Longman, Brown, Green & Longmans, Oxford and London, 1853), vol. 2; summarised in Henry L. Thompson, *Christ Church* (F. E. Robinson & Co., London, 1900), pp. 3–4.

6. *The Anglica Historia of Polydore Vergil*, Denys Hay (ed.) (Camden Society, Offices of the Royal Historical Society, London, 1950), pp. 315, 317.

7. Ellis, *Original Letters*, series 1, vol. 1, pp. 180–4.

8. C. W. Ferguson, *Naked to Mine Enemies: The Life of Cardinal Wolsey* (Longmans, Green & Co., London, 1958), p. 214; Richard Fiddes, *Life of Cardinal Wolsey* (J. Knapton, London, 1726), p. 288; Chichester to Wolsey, Public Record Office SP1/36, fo. 111 (*L&P*, vol. 4, i, no. 1708).

9. For Shorton's relations with Wolsey, Charles Henry and Thompson Cooper, *Athenae Cantabrigienses* (2 vols., Deighton Bell & Co. and Macmillan & Co., 1858, 1861), vol. 1, pp. 55–6; Fiddes, 'Collections', appended to his *Life of Wolsey*, pp. 170–2.

10. P. S. and H. M. Allen, H. W. Garrod (eds), *Opus Epistolarum Des. Erasmi Roterodami* (11 vols., Clarendon Press, Oxford, 1906–47), no. 1238 to Nicholas Everard, c. October 1521; cf. no. 1111 to Vives (June 1520).

11. John Foxe, *Acts and Monuments*, S. R. Cattley (ed.) (8 vols., Seeley & Burnside, London, 1837), vol. 5, pp. 414–15. Cf. Clebsch, *England's Earliest Protestants*, pp. 43–6, who denies that Barnes was a humanist.

12. Richard Hall, *Life of Fisher*, p. 32.

13. Foxe, *Acts and Monuments*, vol. 5, pp. 421–8; H. C. Maxwell Lyte, *A History of the University of Oxford* (Macmillan, London, 1886), pp. 459–69. Garrett's flight and capture can be followed in *L&P*, vol. 4, nos. 3962, 3968, 3999, 4004, 4017, 4073, 4075.

14. Anne Boleyn to (Wolsey), British Library, Cotton MS Vesp. F III art. 32 (*L&P*, vol. 4, app. 197): Foxe, *Acts and Monuments*, vol. 5, p. 42. The chaplain is identified as Garrett by G. R. Elton, *Policy and Police* (Cambridge University Press, London, 1972), p. 37. Cf. PRO SP1/103, fo. 304; 104, fo. 157 (*L&P*, vol. 10, nos. 891, 1099).

15. Wolsey to Henry, 15 July 1528, printed in *State Papers Published Under the Authority of His Majesty's Commission* (HMSO, London, 1830), p. 317 (*L&P*, vol. 4, no. 4513); Stanford E. Lehmberg, *Sir Thomas Elyot, Tudor Humanist* (University of Texas Press, Austin, 1960), p. 33; Longland to Wolsey, PRO SP1/49, fo. 129 (*L&P*, vol. 4, no. 4527).

16. Ellis, *Original Letters*, series 2, vol. 2, pp. 32, 35–8 (*L&P*, vol. 4, nos. 6524, 6529, 6574–8) for letters from Wolsey to Henry, Cromwell and others.

17. Lyte, *History of Oxford*, p. 481; Henry VIII to his college at Oxford, PRO, SP2/M, no. 8 (*L&P*, vol. 4, no. 1181). Cf. the King's college at Oxford to Henry, 11 April 1531; British Library, Cotton MS Faust. C VII 99 (*L&P*, vol. 5, no. 185).

18. For Cromwell's scholars, R. B. Merriman (ed.), *Life and Letters of Thomas Cromwell* (2 vols., Clarendon Press, Oxford, 1902), vol. 1, pp. 326, 334; *L&P*, vol. 4, no. 5069.

19. The canons to Cromwell, British Library, Cotton MS Faust. C VII 100 (*L&P*, vol. 5, no. 1647). Cf. Croke to Cromwell, 15 December 1532, *L&P*, vol. 5, no. 1632.

20. Treasurer of the chamber's accounts, in *L&P*, vol. 5, pp. 305, 309, 321; Sir N. H. Nicholas (ed.), *Privy Purse Expences of Henry VIII* (William Pickering, London, 1827), pp. 8, 13, 46, 82, 125, 165, 260, 148, 243; A. B. Emden, *A Biographical Register of the University of Oxford, 1501–1540* (Clarendon Press, Oxford, 1974), pp. 79, 306, 526.

21. The King's scholars to Cromwell, 24 January and 5 April 1534, PRO SP1/82, fo. 118; 83, fo. 70 (*L&P*, vol. 7, nos. 98, 439).

22. Fitzherbert to Cromwell, PRO SP1/70, fo. 160 (*L&P*, vol. 5, no. 1141); Myll to Cromwell, SP1/100, fos. 84, 85–6 (*L&P*, vol. 9, nos. 1128–9); Emden, *Register of Oxford, p. 375; G. R. Elton, Reform and Renewal* (Cambridge University Press, Cambridge, 1973), p. 30.

23. Woodward to Cromwell, 29 July 1533, PRO SP1/78, fos. 55–6 (*L&P* vol. 7, no. 916); Emden, *Register of Oxford*, pp. 49–50.

24. Cromwell to Claymond and London, PRO SP1/101, fos. 104–5 (*L&P*, vol. 8, no. 790); the Fellows of Magdalen to Cromwell, 16 January 1536, *L&P*, vol. 10, no. 109; Emden, *Register of Oxford*, pp. 381–2.

25. Richard Marshall to Cromwell, PRO SP1/156, fos. 5, 6 (*L&P*, vol., 14, ii, no. 758); Emden, *Register of Oxford*, pp. 380–1.

26. Magdalen to Wolsey, PRO SP1/36, fos. 143–4; and British Library, Cotton MS Faust. C VII 187 (*L&P*, vol. 4, nos. 1754–5).

27. Letters from Lockwood to Cromwell, PRO SR1/70, fo. 156; 71, fos. 30–1; 78, fo. 10; 82, fo. 14 (*L&P*, vol. 5, nos. 1136, 1309; 6, no. 848; 7, no. 16).

28. Wellefed to Cromwell, PRO SP1/75, fo. 1; 89, fo. 75 (*L&P*, vol. 6, no. 221; 8, no. 107).

29. Plancknay to Cromwell, PRO SP1/91, fos. 203, 205 (*L&P*, vol. 8, nos. 506, 507); Emden, *Register of Oxford*, pp. 450–1.

30. Sir Richard Bulkeley to Cromwell, 22 February 1533, *L&P*, vol. 6, no. 179.

31. Lyst to Cromwell, 12 October 1533, PRO SP1/79, fo. 186 (*L&P*, vol. 6, no. 1264).

32. Tyndall to Cromwell, PRO SP1/77, fos. 148–9; and British Library, Harleian MS 6989 fo. 45 (*L&P*, vol. 6, nos. 751, 752).

33. *L&P*, vol. 4, no. 5226, Fisher's anniversary; E. A. Benians, *John Fisher* (Cambridge University Press, Cambridge, 1935), p. 38; Crayforde to Cromwell, 30 August, 1535, PRO SP1/96, fos. 9, 10 (*L&P*, vol. 9, no. 208).

34. Aleyn to Cromwell, PRO SP1/105, fo. 207 (*L&P*, vol. 9, no. 192); John and J. A. Venn, *Alumni Cantabrigienses, Part One, From the Earliest Times to 1751* (4 vols., Cambridge University Press, Cambridge, 1922–7), vol. 1, p. 19.

35. William Latymer, 'A Brief Treatise or Chronicle of the Most Virtuous Lady Anne Boleyn', Bodleian Library, Oxford, MS C Don, 42, fo. 28b (hereafter cited as

Brief Treatise); Cambridge to Anne Boleyn, British Library, Cotton MS Faust. C III 456.

36. William Barker, *The Nobility of Women*, R. Warwick Bond (ed.) (2 vols., Roxburgh Club, privately printed, London, 1904–5), pp. 87, 33.

37. M. A. E. Wood (ed.), *Letters of Royal and Illustrious Ladies* (3 vols., Henry Colburn, London, 1846), vol. 2, p. 191; Venn, *Alumni Cantabrigienses* vol. 2, p. 99.

38. John Peile, *Biographical Register of Christ's College* (2 vols., Cambridge University Press, Cambridge, 1910, 1913), vol. 1, p. 7 for Watson, p. 8 for Wilson; Cranmer to Cromwell about Mallet's promotion, British Library, Cotton MS Vesp. F XIII 97b (*L&P*, vol. 10, no. 120); Thomas Baker, *History of the College of St John the Evangelist, Cambridge*, J. E. B. Mayor (ed.) (2 vols., Cambridge University Press, Cambridge, 1869), vol. 1, pp. 78–9.

39. Henry's three letters to Oxford, all undated, are printed in Fiddes, 'Collections', appended to his *Life of Wolsey*, pp. 144–7. Wood's account of the unrest at Oxford, though derided by Burnet, is evidently confirmed by these missives.

40. Warden of New college to Cromwell, PRO SP1/68, fo. 124 (*L&P*, vol. 6, no. 630); warden of Canterbury to Cromwell, SP1/69, fo. 86 (*L&P*, vol. 6, no. 757); Dr London to Cromwell, SP1/71, fos. 75–6 (*L&P*, vol. 5, no. 1366). The date of this last is fixed by a reference to Anne Boleyn as 'Lady Marquess'.

41. Longland to Cromwell, 21 April 1534, PRO SP1/83, fo. 154 (*L&P*, vol. 7, no. 524).

42. Quoted in John Venn, *Caius College* (F. E. Robinson & Co., London, 1901), p. 34.

43. Foxe, *Acts and Monuments*, vol. 4, p. 650; Allan G. Chester, *Hugh Latimer, Apostle to the English* (University of Pennsylvania Press, Philadelphia, 1954), pp. 104, 230. Cf. *L&P*, vol. 9, nos. 203, 252, 272–3; vol. 10, no. 1257 (ix); vol. 11, no. 117.

44. W. G. Searle, *History of the Queens' College* (2 vols., Cambridge University Press, Cambridge, 1867, 1871), pp. 178–82. Dr Butts is buried in Fulham Church.

45. Foxe, *Acts and Monuments*, vol. 5, pp. 35–7; John Strype, *Memorials of Thomas Cranmer* (2 vols., Oxford University Press, Oxford, 1840), vol. 1, pp. 643–4. For Hugh Latimer's mention of Patmore and Smith in a sermon against Hubberdine, John Strype, *Ecclesiastical Memorials* (3 vols., Clarendon Press, Oxford, 1820–40), vol. 1, ii, p. 179.

46. Wood, *Letters of Ladies*, vol. 2, p. 188; John Venn, *Biographical History of Gonville and Caius College, 1349–1713* (7 vols., Cambridge University Press, Cambridge, 1897), vol. 1, p. 28.

47. Skip to Parker, 23 March 1535, in *Correspondence of Matthew Parker*, John Bruce and Thomas Perowne (eds) (Parker Society, Cambridge University Press, Cambridge, 1853), nos. 1, 2. John Strype, *Life and Acts of Matthew Parker* (3 vols., Clarendon Press, Oxford, 1821), vol. 1, pp. 16–18; Henry VIII to Corpus Christi, 30 November 1544; British Library, Additional MS 5, 853 fo. 124b (*L&P*, vol. 19, ii, no. 680).

48. Parker, *Correspondence*, no. 3; John Strype, *Life of the Learned Sir John Cheke* (Clarendon Press, Oxford, 1821), p. 8.

49. Drome to Marshall, 9 March 1534, PRO SP1/82, fos. 273–4 (*L&P*, vol. 7, no. 308).

50. Leigh to Cromwell, 27 October 1535, in Ellis, *Original Letters*, series 2, vol. 2, p. 362. For the injunctions to Cambridge, C. H. Cooper, *Annals of Cambridge* (5 vols., Warwick & Co. and Cambridge University Press, Cambridge, 1842–1908), vol. 1, pp. 374–6.

51. Venn, *Caius College*, p. 37; Standish to Burcher, 4 July 1535, PRO SP1/93, fo. 234 (*L&P*, vol. 8, no. 983).

52. Ellis, *Original Letters*, series 2, vol. 2, pp. 60–1.

53. Certain scholars of Oxford to Cromwell, 24 October (1534), PRO SP1/86, fo.

82 (*L&P*, vol. 7, no. 1300). All the signatories who can be traced were New college men.

54. The Brasenose statutes are printed in Bond, *Statutes of Oxford*, vol. 2.

55. Twenty fellows of Magdalen to Cromwell, 9 September 1535, PRO SP1/96, fos. 118–9 (*L&P*, vol. 9, no. 312). Wilson, *Magdalen College*, p. 77.

56. St Alban's Hall to Cromwell, 13 September 1535, PRO SP1/96, fo. 160 (*L&P*, vol. 9, no. 361).

57. Wilson to Wriothesley, 3 August 1537, PRO SP7/80 (*L&P*, vol. 12, ii, 425).

58. Foxe, *Acts and Monuments*, vol. 5, p. 227; J. B. Mullinger, *St John's College* (F. E. Robinson & Co., London, 1901), pp. 32–3.

59. *The Schoolmaster*, in *Roger Ascham, English Works*, William Aldis Wright (ed.) (Cambridge University Press, Cambridge, 1904), pp. 279, 280.

60. Huycke to Morison, 24 January 1537, *L&P*, vol. 12, i, no. 212; interrogations of Thomas Bewciam, 8 September 1538, *L&P*, vol. 13, ii, no. 308.

61. London to Bedyll, 3 August 1537, PRO SP1/123, fos. 189–90 (*L&P*, vol. 12, ii, no. 329); Bedyll to Wriothesley, 5 August 1537, SP1/123, fos. 223–4 (*L&P*, vol. 12, ii, no. 448); Mayor of Oxford and others to Cromwell, 25 June 1538, SP1/133, fos. 203–4 (*L&P*, vol. 13, i, 1257).

62. *Miscellaneous Writings and Letters of Thomas Cranmer*, J. E. Cox (ed.) (Parker Society, Cambridge University Press, Cambridge, 1846), pp. 381–4.

63. Longland to Cromwell, (20 April) 1538, PRO SP1/131, fo. 176 (*L&P*, vol. 13, i, 811); scholars of Oxford to Cromwell, (April) 1538), SP1/141, fo. 232 (*L&P*, vol. 13, ii, App. 19); Longland to Cromwell, 21 August 1539, SP1/153, fos. 46–7 (*L&P*, vol. 14, ii, no. 71).

64. Winthrop S. Hudson, *The Cambridge Connection and the Elizabethan Settlement* (Duke University Press, Durham, North Carolina, 1980), p. 44n. The controversy is summarised in *L&P*, vol. 17, nos. 327, 482, 483, 611, 742, 803, 891, 892.

65. Henry de Vocht, 'The Earliest English Translations of Erasmus' *Colloquia, Monumenta Humanistica Lovaniensa* (Louvain University Press, Louvain, 1928), pp. xxxvj–lviij; Thomas Starkey, *A Dialogue Between Reginald Pole and Thomas Lupset*, Kathleen M. Burton (ed.) (Chatto & Windus, London, 1948), p. 53.

66. Starkey to Cromwell, 1536, *L&P*, vol. 11, no. 73.

67. Cambridge to Henry VIII, British Library, Additional MS 5873, fo. 95b and Cotton MS Cleop. E VI 242 (*L&P*, vol. 13, ii, nos. 496, 593).

68. Cambridge to Cromwell, PRO SP1/137, fo. 265 (*L&P*, vol. 13, ii, 677).

69. King's college to Henry VIII, PRO SP1/156, fos. 62–4 (*L&P*, vol. 14, ii, 788); *L&P*, vol. 14, ii, 264 (1), grants in September 1539; L. L. Shadwell, *Enactments in Parliament Concerning Oxford and Cambridge* (4 vols., Clarendon Press, Oxford, 1912), vol. 1, p. 128.

70. Cooper, *Annals*, vol. 1, pp. 403–4, 416; *L&P*, vol. 17, no. 382 (9), grants in April 1542; Shadwell, *Enactments*, vol. 1, p. 132.

71. Joan Simon, *Education and Society in Tudor England* (Cambridge University Press, Cambridge, 1966), p. 203; Aston, Duncan and Evans, 'The Medieval Alumni of Cambridge', *Past and Present*, 86 (February 1980), pp. 9–86; Coventree to Cromwell (1539), PRO SP1/154, fo. 99 (*L&P*, vol. 14, ii, 437).

72. Shadwell, *Enactments*, vol. 1, p. 124.

73. Nicholas Bourbon, *Nugae* (Etienne Dolet, Lyons, 1538), p. 82, letter to Boston. For Wakefield's appointment, *L&P*, vol. 16, no. 305 (20), grants in November 1540.

74. Jane E. A. Dawson, 'The Foundation of Christ Church, Oxford and Trinity College, Cambridge in 1546', *BIHR*, vol. 57, no. 136 (November 1984), pp. 209–16. I am grateful to Dr Dawson for allowing me to read this paper before its publication.

75. Parker, *Correspondence*, p. 34, minute of an interview with Henry VIII,

1546; J. G. Nichols, *Narratives of the Days of the Reformation* (Camden Society, J. B. Nichols & Son, London, 1859), pp. 260–3.

76. Oxford to Henry VIII, 19 February 1546, *L&P*, vol. 21, i, no. 244; Cambridge to Paget, 13 February 1545, ibid., no. 204.

77. Cf. Dawson, 'Foundation of Christ Church and Trinity', passim.

78. Katherine Parr to Cambridge, in Strype, *Ecclesiastical Memorials*, vol. 2, ii, p. 337 (*L&P*, vol. 21, i, no. 279).

79. Cf. Dawson, 'Foundation of Christ Church and Trinity'. For Denny and the school at Stoke, see Chapter Four, below.

80. *L&P*, vol. 21, ii, no. 320, surrenders at Cambridge, 29 October 1546.

81. Thompson, *Christ Church*, pp. 11–12, App. B.

82. *The Schoolmaster*, p. 280.

4   The New Learning in the Schools

As every humanist knew, the basis of sound learning in the university was a thorough grounding in the humanities. Facility in accurate, pure Latin was essential before the complexities of university study could be attempted and the would-be under-graduate should also have some knowledge of 'good literature', Christian and pagan. Thus provision in the schools for the new learning was of paramount importance.

In addition, there was a small but significant increase in the number of laymen who received grammar instruction at school. Though most men, clerical and lay, were tutored privately at home, the schools in Henry VIII's reign catered for the sons of courtiers, lawyers and merchants who would pursue secular careers as well as for boys destined for the priesthood. The former, it was felt, though unlikely to study theology to any depth (if at all) would benefit from learning correct and elegant Latin and from having some acquaintance with Christian and classical literature.

Before the reign, schools were founded by a variety of institutions and individuals for a number of purposes. There were elementary schools, which taught the rudiments of reading and writing with other basic skills; town schools, where boys of the merchant and artisan classes were taught practical subjects, including accountancy; and ecclesiastical schools.[1] These last would be attached to cathedrals, monasteries, collegiate churches and chantries. They normally concentrated on liturgical music and provided the minimum of Latin necessary for purposes of church ritual; though in some monastic houses there were theology lectures for the monks and grammar lessons for the novices and almonry boys, while founders of chantries sometimes stipulated that the mass priest should teach grammar to the children of the locality. In the fifteenth century a few exceptional schools, such as Magdalen school and Banbury school, which benefited from the teaching of John Stanbridge, were more directly concerned with Latin grammar.[2]

The reigns of the first two Tudors saw a large increase in new foundations; in the south west alone, seven grammar schools were fully endowed between 1499 and 1524, a larger number than the whole of the preceding century.[3] This chapter will be concerned with grammar schools under Henry VIII and will consider the extent and sources of educational endowment; how far the schools specifically provided tuition in the new learning; and the extent to which school education was affected by patronage from the court and by political circumstances.

The most famous humanist school founded in the Henrician period was Colet's school at St Paul's, dedicated to the boy Jesus and his mother. It is not known whether this was a re-foundation of the old cathedral school or an independent establishment, but Colet's contempt for ecclesiastical song schools (an emotion he shared with Erasmus) ensured that his foundation would be more than a mere boarding school for choristers.[4] His statutes, traditionally held to be based on the lost statutes of Banbury school, show a refreshing attitude to grammar study. Colet had dispensed with the schoolmen in his Pauline lectures at Oxford and now he attempted by the humanist bias of his school curriculum to prepare his scholars for their encounters with scholasticism at the universities. The statutes declared:

> I would they were taught alway in good literature both Latin and Greek and good authors such as have the very Roman eloquence joined with wisdom, specially Christian authors that wrote their wisdom with clean and chaste Latin . . . all barbary, all corruption, all Latin adulterate with ignorant blind fools brought into this world . . . that filthiness and all such abusion which the later blind world brought in, which more rather may be called bloterature than literature, I utterly abanish and exclude out of this school.[5]

The Latin authors Colet prescribed were post-classical Christians: Proba, Lactantius, Sedulius, Juvencus and Baptista Mantuanus. The omission of the pagan classics is not surprising, in view of both the pupil's age and Colet's own extreme Christocentricity; in 1517 he told Erasmus:

> Nothing can be better, in view of this brief life of ours, than that we should live a holy and pure life and use our best endeavours every day to become pure and enlightened and perfected. These things are promised us by Reuchlin's Pythagorical and Cabalistic

philosophy; but in my opinion we shall achieve them in no way but this, by the fervent love and imitation of Jesus. Let us therefore leave all these complications behind us and take the short road to the truth.[6]

Colet's scholars were provided with an accidence and a catechism, a short Latin syntax prepared by William Lily and the same scholar's *Carmen de Moribus*. Lily and Erasmus also compiled a Latin grammar for the school; the work was originally entrusted to Linacre, but Colet considered his grammar too complex for schoolboys.[7] In addition Erasmus produced at Colet's request the *Carmina scholaria* and *Concio de Puero Jesu in schola Coletica pronuncianda*, a small collection of devotional pieces printed in one volume in 1512 and later translated and published in English as *A Sermon on the Child Jesus . . . to be pronounced and preached of a child unto children*. He also sent Colet a copy of his *De Ratione Studii*, and at his request gave the school his *De Copia*, a work originally intended for Prince Charles of Castile.[8] In the dedication to Colet he declared:

you founded a school that far excels the rest in beauty and splendour, so that the youth of England, under carefully chosen and highly reputed teachers, might there absorb Christian principles together with an excellent literary education from their earliest years. For you are profoundly aware both that the hope of the country lies in its youth — the crop in the blade, as it were — and also how important it is for one's whole life that one should be initiated into excellence from the very cradle onwards.

The school statutes recommended no particular Greek texts for study, a lack of detail due not simply to Colet's own ignorance of the language, but also to the dearth of Greek teachers. The statutes required that the highmaster be 'learned in the good and clean Latin literature and also in Greek if such may be gotten' and Colet was singularly fortunate to secure William Lily as the first holder of the office. Richard Pace in his educational tract *De Fructu Qui Ex Doctrina Percipitur* praised Colet both for founding the school and for appointing Lily:

you've chosen a virtuous and at the same time a skillful man to teach the boys and young men. In this you've imitated Isocrates, who wisely thought (as usual) that boys should be educated only by someone whose virtuous way of life went hand in hand with a sufficient amount of learning. That way, when they give themselves over to the imitation of their teachers, they'll absorb not only a certain amount of learning, but also good character. And now, because of what you've done, they can easily do both. For they have a teacher whose life and character are impeccable. Besides that, his learning is so great that he has driven out almost all the barbarism our boys once spent their youth on, working long to learn nothing and as a result he seems to have introduced into our Britain a more polished use of Latin, in fact, the Roman tongue itself.[9]

Lily's immediate successors were his son-in-law John Ritwyse, educated at Eton and King's college, Cambridge and first surmaster (undermaster) of Colet's school from 1517 to 1522; and Ritwyse's son-in-law Richard Jones, who had been surmaster from 1522 to 1532.[10] According to the statutes the surmaster should be 'some man virtuous in living and well-lettered', while the chaplain, who taught the catechism, creed and commandments, was to 'pray for the children to prosper in good life and in good literature'. Colet, like all humanist educators, perceived the link between virtue and learning and accorded equal emphasis to both.

Colet's school was not meant to be a charitable institution, but a training ground for the sons of gentlemen and courtiers. All but one of the 153 pupils were to pay a fee of four pence, which was to be given to the one poor scholar as payment for sweeping out the school. Nor were the boys to come unprepared for the rigours of humanist study; before admission they must be able to read and write English and Latin and they ought to know the catechism. Among pupils at various points in the reign were the humanist scholars John Clement and Thomas Lupset; the antiquary John Leland; Elyot's friend Sir Edward North; William Paget and Sir Anthony Denny. The King's privy purse expenses for 1531 and 1532 record payment of various sums to the schoolmaster for George and Nicholas Fraunces, pupils at the school, while Katherine of Aragon in about 1518 granted an exhibition there to John Ainsworth. Ainsworth, like Denny, followed the humanistic progression from Colet's school to Fisher's college of St John's and repaid the Queen's benevolence some 20 years later by preaching in her favour.[11] Another pupil was John Constable, whose *Epigrammata*, published by the royal printer in 1520, contains verses to Lily, William Latimer, More, Queen Katherine and Henry VIII.

Another link with the court was the practice of performing plays and masques there; these were meant to be part of the boys' training in eloquence but they also provided courtly entertainment. In a later petition to Henry VIII when he had become ill and unfit to teach, John Ritwyse recalled that by the command of the King and his council his pupils had played comedies before ambassadors and other foreign visitors. Ritwyse's play *Dido* was performed before Wolsey, an anti-Lutheran masque was staged at Greenwich in November 1527, and one of Terence's plays was performed at an official banquet in 1528.[12]

Naturally, not all young gentlemen took happily to humanist instruction, as the early life of Sir Peter Carew shows. Carew was sent to Colet's school by his father Sir William after frequently playing truant from school in Exeter. He was committed to the charge of the highmaster, but his school career was far from successful:

> he being more desirous of liberty than of learning, was desirous of the one and careless of the other; and do what the schoolmaster could, he in no wise could frame this young Peter to smell to a book, or to like of any schooling.[13]

In the end Carew went abroad for adventure and on his return seems to have been happier as one of the King's henchmen than as a scholar.

Colet's establishment of such an explicitly humanist academy, richly endowed and strategically close to the court, aroused conservative hostility in the earlier years of the reign. Erasmus's quest for an undermaster at Cambridge drew sneers from the Scotists there and Colet himself mentioned a bishop who called the school a 'home of idolatry' because the poets were taught there.[14] Once more, however, defenders of the new learning came forward. Pace's treatise *De Fructu Qui Ex Doctrina Percipitur*, with its triple dedication to professors of knowledge, good students and John Colet, was a manifesto for the type of instruction offered at St Paul's, while More told Colet:

> I am not surprised that the school of Jesus excites the envy and anger of dissolutes and obdurates. These perverse people can

only contemplate with fear this crowd of Christians who, like the Greeks from the Trojan horse, spring from that academy to destroy their ignorance and disorder.[15]

Reactionary ill-will failed to affect adversely the fortunes of the school, which flourished under the guardianship of the Mercers' Company (of which More was a member) and the eye of a benevolent court.

Colet's school of the boy Jesus was not merely an isolated phenomenon; rather, it was an inspiration to school founders in the ten or so years following its establishment. An impressive number of grammar schools was founded in the earlier years of Henry VIII's reign, and though the curricula of the majority are unknown several looked directly to Colet's foundation as a model, or at least reflected his preoccupation with accurate grammar and good literature.[16]

Richard Fox, the humanist founder of Corpus Christ, Oxford, was also active in the sphere of school education. As executors of Lady Margaret Beaufort Fox and Fisher were involved in the foundation of the grammar school attached to the chantry she established for her parents at Wimborne Minster. The school was formally founded on 12 March 1511, but was evidently functioning by Easter of the previous year. It was a free school and grammar was to be taught after the manner of Eton or Winchester college.[17] Fox himself founded grammar schools at Taunton in his diocese of Winchester in 1523 and at Grantham, near his birthplace, in 1528. Taunton school cost him the considerable sum of £226 5s 10d and later benefited from the generosity of Roger Hill, a local merchant. Fox also joined with Lord Sandys in re-founding the guild and free chapel of the Holy Ghost near Basingstoke, with a school.[18]

Fox's friend and associate Hugh Oldham, bishop of Exeter, was not only effective co-founder of Corpus and a generous benefactor to Brasenose, but also the founder of a grammar school in Manchester in 1515. Oldham himself was no humanist scholar and was characterised by Francis Godwin as 'A man of more devotion than learning, somewhat rough in speech, but in deed and action friendly . . . Albeit he was not very well learned, yet a great favourer and a further of learning he was'. Oldham's aim was to equip his scholars for service in the community; according to his biographer, 'He did not create or desire to create any love of learning for its own sake in Manchester but he fostered such study as would lead to enlightened service.'[19] None the less Oldham's school statutes were based on Colet's, the appointment of the Master was vested in Corpus Christi and that Master was to teach grammar after the manner of Banbury school (that is, from Stanbridge's grammar) 'or after any future manner'.[20]

Bruton School was founded in 1520 by Richard Fitzjames, bishop of London; his nephew John, later chief baron of the exchequer and chief justice of the king's bench; and John Edmunds, like the Fitzjameses, a local man. The three had probably maintained a free school at Bruton during the preceding decade. The new school was also to be free and open to all, poor as well as rich, and the teaching was to be specifically humanistic.

The pupils of Bruton were not to learn song, reading in English or reading from the matins book or psalter. Instead they were to learn Latin grammar 'after the good new form used in Magdalen College in Oxford, or in the school at Paul's in London, or after such good form as for the time shall be used'. It was the intention of the founders, 'with Our Lord's mercy, only to have the grammar of Latin tongue so sufficiently taught that the scholars of the same, profiting and proving, shall in times to come, forever be, after their capacities, perfect Latin men'. As at Colet's school, great emphasis was laid on prayer. Each morning the boys were to pray for the founders and benefactors of the school and for their own increase in virtue and learning and at the end of the day they were to say the *De Profundis* (the psalm used for souls in purgatory) with another general prayer for the founders. Like Wolsey, Ascham and Cranmer the founders perceived the harm done by excessive corporal punishment; the master of Bruton was to be discreet in correcting his charges and was not to strike them on the face or head.[21]

There are other glimpses of humanist education in the west country during this period. John Jewel was educated at a number of schools in the region. In 1529 at the age of seven he received instruction at Heanton Puncharden, Devon from the rector, John Bellamy. However, as with Richard Hooker, taught by John Moreman, DD, vicar of Menheniot, Cornwall, it is not clear whether he was a private pupil or a member of a school. In the early 1530s Jewel studied at Braunton school for a short time and also attended schools at South Molton and Barnstaple. Another pupil at Barnstaple was Thomas Harding, later a Catholic professor at Louvain and Jewel's opponent in religious controversy.[22]

In 1519 a school was founded at Winchcombe by the executors of Lady Joan Huddleston. She had intended to establish almshouses, but as there were insufficient funds for this, a free grammar school was founded instead. One of the executors was Christopher Ursewick, Erasmus's friend and it is possible that the school reflected his concern with the new learning. In 1524 the school at Great Torrington, Devon, benefited briefly from the teaching of the protestant martyr Thomas Bennett after his withdrawal from Cambridge.[23]

However, there is also negative evidence about schooling in the south west which is probably symptomatic of events and circumstances in the country as a whole. Bishop Oldham conducted a visitation of the Benedictine priory at Tywardreath, Cornwall in December 1513, where he had to order the provision of grammar instruction for the novices and other members of the house. Similarly in July 1526 it found that the four novices of Keynsham monastery, Somerset, were receiving no grammar teaching. Bishop Ruthal, who died in 1523, apparently intended to found a grammar school at Cirencester, but according to John Leland 'he promised much, but prevented by death gave nothing'.[24]

Meanwhile in other regions the new learning was gaining ground in school education. A sign of the times and of the humanist emphasis on practical piety was the conversion of his chantry at Sedburgh into a grammar school by Roger Lupton, provost of Eton. The school was under the direction of St John's and provided the college with many scholars; when it ran into difficulties later in the reign its affairs were settled by a student of both St John's and Colet's school, Sir Anthony Denny.

The most ambitious scheme of school education propounded in the 1520s was the idea of Cardinal Wolsey, himself a former teacher at Magdalen school. His magnificent college at Oxford was not meant to be an isolated seminary of the new learning but rather, the keystone of an educational system planned to extend over the entire kingdom. According to the statutes of Cardinal college, Oxford, drawn up in 1527, the 40 petty canons (that is, scholars) were to be drawn from schools Wolsey intended to found in the dioceses of York, Durham, Lincoln, Bath and Wells, Norwich, London, Ely, Rochester, Canterbury, Chichester, Coventry and Lichfield, Exeter, Salisbury, Winchester and Worcester.[25] If this comprehensive scheme had materialised humanist instruction would have been available to potential clergy — and to laymen — in almost every corner of the realm.

It was fortunate that Wolsey provided in the Cardinal statutes for the possibility that there would be insufficient candidates from his schools for the canonries at Oxford. Sadly, his plan foundered, apparently through local jealousy and suspicion of the Cardinal. The details of his attempt to establish a school at Tunbridge are known. He intended to suppress the priory there and found a school in its place, but though Archbishop Warham, acting on Wolsey's behalf, showed the townspeople that 'it should be more for the advantage and commodity of them and their children perpetually to have forty children of that country to be brought up in learning and afterward to be promoted to Oxford . . . than to have six or seven canons', the vast majority (with the exception of certain individuals with a score to settle against the priory) preferred the old monastery to the new learning.[26]

It seems likely that resentment at Wolsey's interference in local affairs was mingled with suspicion as to the motive behind his educational endowments. Later critics of the Cardinal such as Polydore Vergil and the authors of *The Burial of the Mass* certainly ascribed his munificence to ostentatious pride rather than to love of learning. (See Chapter Three, above.) There was in some quarters a marked reluctance to assist Wolsey and one member of the nobility tried to snub him while he was building Cardinal college, Ipswich. The Dowager Countess of Oxford was pointedly unenthusiastic about granting him Harwich stone for the school, stipulating that no hurt or prejudice be done to her town there; though later she was obliged to give him a free hand, as his reply to her letter had 'discomforted' her.[27] Certainly the school at Ipswich, founded in 1528, was in its own way as richly endowed with material goods as the Oxford college and Wolsey took great care over such non-academic externals as chapel vestments and furniture and the provision of boys for the choir. To ascribe his work of foundation merely to the desire to show off, however, is to belittle the vision behind his regrettably short-lived achievement.

Cardinal college, Ipswich, like the Oxford foundation, was to be a collegiate church as well as an academy. The licence of foundation of 29 June 1528 provided for a dean or master, twelve priests, eight clerks, eight singing-boys and poor scholars and thirteen poor men who were to pray for the King, the Cardinal and others. An under-teacher was also to be appointed to teach grammar both to the poor scholars and to any others from any part of the realm who wished to study at the college.[28]

Wolsey took a direct interest in studies at Ipswich, and in the

following September he sent the masters a grammar for the scholars'
use compiled by himself and based on Lily's work, along with a
detailed plan of instruction for the eight forms in the school. (It may
be noted that Colet's school of Jesus was also divided into eight
classes.) This plan of studies reflects the humanist concern that
children should not be frightened away from learning; after the fifth
form the mode of instruction was to be left to the teacher's discretion
and severity — even in looks — was to be avoided, since it was apt to
discourage the learner.[29] Wolsey's injunction recalls both the
precepts of Roger Ascham and the opinion of Archbishop Cranmer,
himself a school founder, on the intellectual damage done to him by
his own brutal schoolmaster. According to Cranmer's secretary and
biographer, Ralph Morice:

> his father did set him to school with a marvellous severe and cruel
> schoolmaster. Whose tyranny towards youth was such, that, as he
> thought, the said schoolmaster so appalled, dulled, and daunted
> the tender and fine wits of his scholars, that they commonly
> [more] hated and abhorred good literature than favoured or
> embraced the same, w[hose] memories were also thereby so
> mutilated and wounded, that for his p[art] he lost much of that
> benefit of memory and audacity in his youth that by nature was
> given unto him, which he could never recover, as he divers times
> reported.[30]

The pupils in the lower classes of Wolsey's school were to acquire
a basic knowledge of grammar and literature. The first form was to
learn the rudiments of grammar, the second might study Cato's
precepts and Lily's *Carmen Monitorium*. The third form could read
Aesop, Terence and Lily's *De Nominum Generibus*, and the fourth
might study Terence and Virgil. The authors Wolsey recommended
for study in his four higher classes also make an impressive list of
ancient and modern humanistic texts. The fifth form was to study
some of Cicero's epistles; the sixth form, Sallust or Caesar's
commentaries, with Lily's syntax; the seventh form could read
Horace's epistles and Ovid's *Metamorphosis*; and the eighth form
studied Valla's *Elegantiae* and other higher studies.[31]

The academic life of the college seems to have got off to an auspi-
cious start. In January 1529 William Goldwin, the schoolmaster,
sent the Cardinal some samples of the boys' handwriting,
presumably the Italian hand prized by humanists and employed by

Goldwin himself. The master also voiced his hope that the scholars would soon be able to speak Italian, and told Wolsey that the number of pupils was increasing at such a rate that the schoolhouse was already becoming too small.[32]

Unfortunately these signs of promise were doomed not to come to fruition, since Cardinal college, Ipswich, shared the fate of the Oxford foundation when Wolsey fell from power. Unlike the Oxford college, however, it was not re-founded in any shape or form by the King. Wolsey's notorious affection for his college, which undoubtedly made them an especial object of his enemies' vindictiveness, is reflected even in Erasmus's mocking and punning description of the fallen Cardinal as fortune's play-thing, who had risen from a schoolmaster to be master of a kingdom. (*'Hic est fortunae ludus, ex lugimagistro subvectus est ad regnum.'*)[33] Had Wolsey not incurred the King's displeasure it is possible that he might have founded other schools like the one at Ipswich. As it was, one of the consequences of his fall from grace was that the cause of humanist education in the schools suffered a grave setback.

In the years between the fall of Wolsey and the dissolution of the monasteries — a period which corresponds roughly to the era of the royal divorce — no scheme for the foundation of new schools similar in magnitude to the Cardinal's was drawn up and the matter was left to local and personal initiative. Between 1530 and 1533 grammar schools were established at Stamford, Newark-on-Trent, Horsham, Bristol and Newcastle, but there is no way of knowing how far — if at all — their statutes and curricula could be termed humanistic.[34] However, one school was founded in this period which was outstanding for its explicit bias towards the new learning. In November 1535 Anne Boleyn promoted her chaplain Matthew Parker to be dean of the collegiate church of Stoke-by-Clare, Suffolk. In that same year he founded a grammar and song school there. Parker was a friend of the Cambridge humanists Cheke and Haddon, and his statutes, which constituted Anne Boleyn founder of the school, amply express the educational priorities of the new learning.[35]

Besides learning music and singing for the church services the scholars were to be taught 'not only grammar, but brought up in all other studies of humanity'. In contrast to the social bias of Colet's foundation the school was to be open to all, though the poorer sort were to be taught free, and the grammar master was to have a stipend of £10 a year. The most apt of the choristers were to receive exhibitions of 40 shillings, four marks or £3 for study at some college in Cambridge. Parker further stipulated that if any money was left over after the expenses of the college had been met it was to be used as a reasonable stipend for a scripture lecture. This was to be read in the college at least four times a week, either by one of the members of the foundation or by a scholar of Cambridge or Oxford, and it was to be read in English for the first half hour and in Latin for the second.

The school at Stoke met with the approval of Parker's humanist friends. Cheke translated the statutes into elegant Latin, and Haddon commented: 'that place seemed in a manner to be made on purpose for scholars, both to learn themselves, and to teach others . . . its situation was such, that above all others it best suited for honest and ingenious pleasures.' None the less Stoke, like all such institutions, was threatened by the Chantries Act of 1545 which authorised the suppression of all colleges, chantries and hospitals and the transference of their property to the crown. (For the Chantries Act and the universities, see Chapter Three, above.) As Stoke lay in the queen consort's gift Parker hastened to approach both Katherine Parr and her council for mediation with the King, alleging the many benefits the college had brought to the locality:

> The house standeth so that her grace's tenants be round about it, as well to be refreshed with alms and daily hospitality as is there kept, as to be instructed with God's word of certain of her grace's orators doing the same; beside the commodity that the childer of her grace's tenants and farmers fully enjoy by their teaching and bringing up, as well in grammar as in singing and playing, with other exercises and nurtures meet for their ages and capacities; being there sundry teachers attending upon their instructions in the same.

It is not recorded whether either Katherine or her council acted on Parker's request, but in the event it was the intervention of Denny which moved Henry to spare the college dissolution.[36]

II

It has already been observed that the dissolution of the religious houses in the years 1536–9 led humanists to hope that monastic property would be used to finance educational endowment. (See Chapter Three, above.) As with the universities, however, there was no systematic attempt to use the new revenues for the establishment and improvement of schools. Six new bishoprics were created (Oxford, Gloucester, Bristol, Chester, Peterborough and Westminster) and it was expected that the incumbents of both the new sees and the old would provide grammar schools; but in the absence of any clear mandate from above the initiative devolved upon individual bishops and clergy and private donors, with predictably variable results. For example Simon Heynes, the evangelical dean of Exeter, proposed a number of humanistic reforms at the cathedral there, including the establishment of two schools, one for grammar and one for song. The 40 children of the song school would learn Latin, Greek and Hebrew as well as singing and playing. The grammar school was to be free and open to all comers (the master receiving the generous stipend of £20 and the usher £10, both paid by the cathedral) and 60 poor scholars would have an exhibition of one shilling a week to buy food in the city. Heynes also suggested twelve scholarships at both Oxford and Cambridge for those who had mastered grammar. This excellent scheme would have made Exeter an important centre of humanist education, but it was never implemented.[37]

Cranmer, though more successful than Heynes, did not entirely get his own way at Canterbury. He would have preferred to abolish prebendaries at the cathedral altogether and characterised such clergy as slothful gluttons. He told Cromwell that it would be better to have 20 divines at Canterbury with stipends of £10 each than to maintain twelve useless prebendaries at £40 each.[38] The humanist improvement was not adopted, however, and the canons remained to plague their archbishop with accusations of heresy in 1543.

On the other hand Cranmer did ensure that his cathedral school was oriented towards the new learning. He stipulated that the headmaster should be 'learned in Latin and Greek, of good character and pious life, endowed with the faculty of teaching' and secured as first incumbent of the post the antiquary John Twine, a former pupil of Vives at Oxford. The scholars were to know their pater noster, creed and decalogue before admittance, and Cranmer's scheme of studies for his six forms is worthy of comparison with the provisions of Colet and Wolsey for their schools. The first form was to learn the rudiments of Latin grammar in English and to practise translating short phrases from Latin to

English. The second form was to study Cato and Aesop with some 'familiar colloquies', while the third was to read Terence and Mantuanus and translate sentences into Latin. The fourth form was to read stories from the poets and the letters of famous men, the fifth was to tackle 'the chastest poets and best historians', and the sixth form was to read Horace, Cicero and similar authors along with Erasmus's *De Copia*.[39]

The most striking aspect of Cranmer's work as a school founder was his insistence that poor boys had as much right to humanist study as the sons of gentlemen. Indeed, the Archbishop gave a spirited and quite radical oration on the right of the lower classes to education. 'Poor men's children,' he declared, 'are many times endued with more singular gifts of nature, which are also the gifts of God, as with eloquence, memory, apt pronunciation, sobriety, with suchlike, and also commonly more given to apply their study, than is the gentleman's son delicately educated.' This view aroused the opposition of several courtiers appointed to assist him in establishing the school, and Ralph Morice has left a very full account of the debate which followed:

> Whereunto it was on the other part replied, that it was meet for the ploughman's son to go to plough, and the artificer's son to apply the trade of his parent's vocation, and the gentlemen's children are meet to have the knowledge of government and rule in the commonwealth; for we have as much need of ploughmen as on any other state, and all sorts of men may not go to school. 'I grant (quod the Archbishop) much of your meaning herein, as needful in a commonwealth; but yet utterly to exclude the ploughman's son and the poor man's son from the benefit of learning, as though they were unworthy to have the gifts of the Holy Ghost bestowed upon them as well as upon others, is as much to say as that almighty God should not be at liberty to bestow his great gifts of grace upon any person, nor nowhere else but as we and other men shall appoint them to be employed according to our fancy, and not according to his most godly will and pleasure.

In the end Cranmer carried the day, and provision was made at the school for 50 poor scholars.[40]

Another evangelical bishop eager to promote education in his diocese was Hugh Latimer, who asked Cromwell's mediation with the King in October 1538 for the guild school at Worcester. The Bishop himself, despite his poverty, had continued to support the schoolmaster after the dissolution of the guild 'because he is honest and bringeth up their youth after the best sort', but he hoped that Henry would grant the city the possessions of the Franciscans and Dominicans there for the maintenance of the school and for other municipal charges. The King in fact granted the two friaries to the city in 1543, having founded a school of his own there in the previous year which provided for 40 poor scholars and which was closely modelled on Cranmer's school at Canterbury. This establishment was attached to the cathedral and in December 1541 Henry commanded Sir Richard Riche to see that John Pether was admitted master there, as the King had heard 'by the credible report of divers of our chaplains' that Pether was fit for the office because of his sobriety and learning. The guild school, however, continued to exist independently with Latimer's support.[41]

Latimer also asked Cromwell to intercede with Henry for Warwick college so that it would be granted 'some piece of a broken abbey', and revealed that he himself had to pay the readers of the scripture lecture there because the college itself lacked funds to do so. The Bishop also mediated successfully with Cromwell for Lady Joan Cooke, widow of an alderman and mercer of Gloucester. She wished to buy monastic lands in order to found a free grammar school in the city in fulfilment of her husband's will, of which she was sole executrix. The school seems to have been functioning in the 1530s and its new building was completed by 1540. A cathedral school was also founded at Gloucester, but it failed to compete effectively with Lady Cooke's establishment.[42]

In Wales the dissolution was seen as an unprecedented opportunity to remedy the lack of learning and unreformed state of religion in the country. William Barlow, transferred to the neglected see of St David's in 1536, warned Cromwell that the reformation so successfully accomplished in England would not be extended to Wales unless more schools were established, since there was scarcely a learned man in his diocese apart from those Barlow himself had financed. In January 1541 he was granted monastic property in Brecknock in order to found a *'ludus Literarius'* there, and was licensed to convert the salaries of the collegiate church at Abergwilley (£53 a year) into wages for schoolmasters and divinity readers. In July 1542 a royal free school was established at Abergavenny. Tithes were granted to the town specifically for the payment of the master and undermaster, who received £13 6s 8d and £6 13s 4d respectively.[43]

One of Barlow's diocesan clergy, Thomas Lloyd, canon of St David's cathedral, decided to found a school at Carmarthen at his own expense. A licence of foundation was granted in January 1536, and some three years later the mayor and aldermen of Carmarthen petitioned Cromwell for the buildings of the Greyfriars there. They offered the King £40 for the land and Cromwell £20 for his trouble, and ingeniously pointed out that the property was of no practical or monetary value to the crown: 'there is no foot of lead upon any part thereof, and it were pity that such building in such a barren country should not be conveyed to some lawful and convenient use for the maintenance of the commonwealth.' In February 1543 the school was refounded as 'The King's School of Carmarthen of Thomas Lloyd's foundation', when it was granted additional lands.[44]

In England, too, monastic and collegiate property was converted into schools, usually (as in Wales) on the initiative of local clergy or lay inhabitants. Robert Holgate, Bishop of Llandaff and President of the Council of the North, was licensed to found two free grammar schools at Hemsworth and Old Malton in Yorkshire in April 1542. In October 1546 he received letters patent for the foundation of grammar schools there and at York. Interestingly enough, though Hebrew, Greek and Latin were to be taught free, the pupils' parents were expected to pay a quarterly sum for instruction in English writing and arithmetic. Presumably it was hoped that the boys would be encouraged to study the more difficult subjects because teaching was free.[45] In July 1545 John Hales of Coventry was licensed to found a free school there under the name of 'Henry VIII's School', and to grant the city lands to the value of 200 marks for its endowment, while in December the collegiate church at Ottery St Mary, Devon was dissolved and a royal free grammar school established in its place, with a stipend of £10 provided for its master. The Duke of Norfolk resolved to re-establish Thetford priory as a collegiate church on the model of Parker's college at Stoke-by-Clare, and consequently he wrote to the latter requesting his statutes.[46]

There were also advances in school education in the home counties. Ralph Radcliffe, a scholar of Cambridge and former tutor to the Marquess of Dorset's children, was granted the site of the Carmel at Hitchen. Here he opened a successful and lucrative school which achieved a modest fame for the drama productions which (as at Colet's school) were staged as a means of teaching rhetoric.

Leonard Coxe, who had taught in Poland and Hungary and had been master of the abbey school at Reading until the dissolution in 1539, was appointed master of Reading grammar school in February 1541 and granted the schoolhouse and a salary of £10. Coxe was a noted humanist, a correspondent of Erasmus and translator of his works; doubtless his pupils at Reading were thoroughly imbued with the new learning.[47]

Some of the former religious themselves attempted to use property released by the dissolution to found schools. Robert Ferrar, appointed prior of Nostell, Yorkshire, by Cromwell, asked his patron to persuade the King to re-establish the house as a school for the youth of the locality, while Robert Whitgift, prior of Wellow, continued to teach the sons of local gentlemen in the convent building.[48] Another learned religious, Richard Whitford the 'poor wretch of Syon', found refuge after the dissolution with Charles, Lord Mountjoy, son of his earlier patron; though Whitford turned his energies to devotional writing rather than to school teaching.

Mountjoy fully shared his father's predilection for learning, and there is one instance of his interest in school education. In a will of April 1544, made before he accompanied the King to France for the war, he provided for the establishment of lectures for the children of the Westbury-under-the-Plain, Wiltshire for two years. The reader was to be a 'godly and discreet man' and was to receive 20 marks a year. Mountjoy's instructions concerning the content of the lectures strongly recall Colet's precepts for the school of Jesus. The morning lecture was to be 'ordained for the catechism of the children, that they may thereby perfectly be instructed to know what they profess in their baptism, in their Pater Noster, how to pray in their Ave Maria, to know how Our Lord ought to be honoured, and in the ten commandments'. In addition there was to be a lecture on three afternoons a week in which the children would learn obedience to the King with the aid of scriptural and other texts. The reader was also to give 'interpretation of vice with their texts of scripture and promises to the well-doers with their texts of scripture'. Thus learning was to inculcate political obedience as well as morality.[49]

Cromwell, though not himself a founder of schools or of lectures for children, played an active part in promoting school education in various localities. Friar George Brown, for example, asked him to intercede with the bishop of Ely so that his 'own scholar' Robert Radcliffe could teach at the grammar school in Jesus college, Cambridge. Radcliffe, according to Brown, was an excellent scholar in Latin and Greek who had written against the schoolmen of Cambridge. In March 1537 William Sabyn and Willian Notyngham wrote to thank Cromwell for maintaining the borough school at Ipswich. They recommended as grammar master Richard Argentyn, who had been reading 'a lecture of Paul's epistles *ad Romanos*' twice a week since Christmas and as usher Richard Pykeryng. Argentyn was in fact successively usher and master of the school, besides being a practising physician and theologian. In the reign of Edward VI he published translations of Luther, Zwingli and Ochino, and was the author of a tract addressed to Oxford and Cambridge on the benefits of instruction in Arabic.[50]

Cranmer wrote to Cromwell in August 1538 on behalf of the schoolmaster of Ludlow, an acquaintance of the Archbishop from his Cambridge days. The master, whom Cranmer described as especially learned in Latin and well-read in 'eloquent authors', wished to renounce his priesthood but feared that he might lose his position if he did so. Accordingly Cranmer asked Cromwell's mediation with the guild at Ludlow, which had the appointment of the master. Cromwell himself, in a draft letter of January of that year, asked the new patron of the school of Week St Mary, Cornwall to give the mastership to John Poynt, who was 'lawful as I am credibly informed and sufficient for the room also, accustomed to bring up youth'.[51]

The school at Week St Mary was a remarkable establishment which deserves some description, though, largely because of its geographical position and consequent lack of pupils it was destined to last for only 40 years. The school was founded in 1506 by Thomasine Bonaventure, wife of Sir John Percival, who himself founded Macclesfield school in 1503. The latter was a chantry school, its master was to be a graduate, and grammar was to be taught free. Thomasine undoubtedly had Macclesfield in mind as a model when she established her own school. The master was to be a priest of virtuous character and a graduate in either arts or grammar, and teaching was to be free to all comers. Of the four masters whose names are known, two were not graduates, but one was a BA of New college and former usher of Winchester college, while the other was an MA. There is, however, no evidence that Cromwell's nominee Poynt actually came to the school, which had ceased to exist before the end of the reign.[52]

The monastic dissolution thus provided the opportunity for a number of educational endowments; Furnivall lists 14 schools founded in the years 1541–7, several of which were either new cathedral schools or re-foundations of existing ones.[53] However, because there was no official and universal scheme for the establishment and regulation of these potential centres of local education, progress and activity were haphazard and very much dependent on local enthusiasm. Westminster abbey and Worcester cathedral each maintained 40 scholars, Ely and Chester 24, Rochester and Peterborough 20 and Durham 18, but at the other end of the scale there was no cathedral school at Ipswich and those at Bristol and Gloucester failed to compete with the developing borough schools maintained independently of royal and ecclesiastical patronage.[54]

A recent study of the south west examines in detail the effect of the reformation on education in the region. The gains from the dissolution were four new endowed grammar schools at Bristol, Bath, Gloucester and Sherbourne, while the schools at Ottery St Mary and Crediton were given increased endowments by the crown. On the debit side, three public grammar schools and five elementary schools disappeared, while Winchcome lost its schoolhouse and was no longer free and Cirencester lost endowments worth £3. Most serious of all was the loss of the schools maintained by or connected with the religious houses. The school at Cirencester was closed in about 1540 and was not revived for another five years, when a chantry was converted by the local people to replace it. Bruton School, whose patron and trustee was the Abbot of Bruton, also suffered. In 1539 the schoolmaster, Hugh Sherwood, was allowed to continue to keep a school, though teaching would no longer be free, but in fact the school seems to have been suspended until its re-foundation in 1550. In September 1537 the abbot of Forde had appointed William Tyler, MA, to teach grammar and lecture on scripture in the refectory, but at the dissolution two years later Tyler was awarded a pension of £3 from the court of augmentations in place of his stipend of £3 6s 8d, and teaching came to an end. Sherborne abbey had supported three scholars at the grammar school in the town, but this, too, came to an end. In this last case, however, there was a new grammar school to make up for the loss of the monastery.[55]

Thus, though Traheron's report to Bullinger that 'some of the principal monasteries are turned into schools of studious men' is patently correct, the King and his advisers neither produced nor even envisaged a comprehensive scheme of grammar schools comparable to that propounded by Wolsey in the 1520s and it is hard to agree with Leach's praise of Henry VIII as 'in a sense, the greatest of school founders'.[56] The King failed to sustain the enthusiasm he had expressed in the Act concerning the new bishoprics which promised substantial increases in both school and higher education. At the same time, courtly and clerical interest in the matter was largely confined to a small group of evangelicals, of whom Cranmer, Latimer and Barlow were the most notable patrons of humanist education in the schools.

III

So much for the new schools founded during the reign. How far can studies at this level be considered humanistic? In the sphere of Latin instruction there was a gradual shift from the more old-fashioned grammatical works of Stanbridge, Horman and Whittinton to Lily's grammar, composed with Erasmus's help for Colet's school. Lily's rivals may themselves be regarded as humanists; indeed, the works of Horman and Whittinton were produced during the first wave of enthusiasm for the new learning. William Horman was a friend of More and his *Vulgaria*, published in 1519 by the royal printer Pynson and intended specifically for Eton (of which he was vice-provost) was prefaced by epigrams by Lily and Ritwyse. Robert Whittinton was schoolmaster to the King's henchmen, the author of elaborate Latin poems in praise of Anne Boleyn, and the translator of works by Cicero, Seneca and Erasmus. His *Vulgaria* was also published in 1519, and the rivalry between himself and Horman resulted in the so-called 'Grammarians' War'.[57]

It was increasingly felt, however, that Lily's grammar was the best and between 1528 and 1530 Eton abandoned Whittinton's work for Lily's. In 1540 Leonard Coxe presented Cromwell with a 'comment upon a book made some time by Master Lillie and corrected by Erasmus, which work of grammar is much set by in all schools both on this side the sea and beyond'.[58]

At about the same time the King decided that it would be desirable to have one authorised grammar for the whole realm and after consultations with Coxe and other scholars, Lily's work was selected for the honour and authorised by royal proclamation. From 1540 this grammar, with emendations drawn from the works of Linacre and Melanchthon, was printed with the royal proclamation as the 'King's Grammar'. The volume also contained a Latin–

English alphabet; the Pater Noster, Ave Maria, Apostles' Creed and ten commandments in English and Latin, with other prayers; the eight parts of speech; Lily's *Carmen de Moribus*; and Erasmus's *Christiani Hominis Institutum*.[59]

The royal grammar was welcomed by the King's humanist subjects. In the 1541 edition of his *Castle of Health* Elyot praised Henry, who 'hath not disdained to be the chief author and setter-forth of an introduction into grammar for the children of his loving subjects'.[60] John Palsgrave published *The Comedy of Acolastus* with a dedication to the King warmly acclaiming his desire to impose uniformity: 'For now is it intended that every school of your grace's realm should begin to wax one self school.' *Acolastus* itself was meant to be used in the teaching of Latin, and was to be read after the pupil had mastered the English part of the royal grammar and before he tackled the Latin section. Palsgrave claimed that it was the King's example which had spurred him on to produce the book:

> When I consider . . . how highly your grace doth tender the well bringing up of your youth in good letters, in so much, that where as it is clearly perceived, by your most prudent wisdom, how great a damage it hath heretofore been and yet is, unto the tender wits of this your noble realm, to be hindered and confounded with so many divers and sundry sorts of precepts grammatical: you have for the redress thereof, willed one self and uniform manner of teaching of all those grammatical enseignements, to be used throughout all your highness' dominions, and committed the disposing of that matter unto such singular personages, both of exact judgment, and thereto of excellent literature, that I for my part do not a little hereof rejoice, and earnestly do I wish, that I at these present days (which in that exercise, have spent no small time of my life) had observed but some one valuable document to bring to this Gazophilacium, some thing to help to furtherance of this your noble grace's so goodly, and thereto so godly and much fruitful a purpose.[61]

Though Palsgrave was obviously flattering his royal master, the publication of the King's grammar — with the weight of his authority behind it — was certainly a step forward for the new learning in the schools.

Advance in the teaching of Greek, on the other hand, was slow, and the main reason for this was scarcity of suitably qualified teachers. Colet was exceptionally lucky to have Lily as his first highmaster at St Paul's, but it seems that no Greek was taught in the school between 1532 and 1558.[62] It should be remembered in this context that the first Greek text printed in English, John Cheke's edition of two sermons by Chrysostom, was not published until 1543; presumably the very limited demand there was for Greek literature in the original could be satisfied by imported books. Obviously, too, those rare teachers equipped with Greek would gravitate to the universities rather than to schools.

School education in general was hampered by the fact that teaching children was not regarded as a desirable profession. Sir Anthony St Leger is credited with saying that three things would settle a state: good godfathers and godmothers performing their vows; good householders overseeing their families; and good schoolmasters educating youth. This last, he said, was 'the most useful, though the most contemptible profession'.[63] Scholars would undertake teaching out of financial necessity, but in general they felt aversion for the drudgery of instruction and resented the fact that it took up valuable time which could be spent on their own studies. In 1538 Richard Jones, highmaster of Colet's school, tried to persuade a friend named Welden to take on some teaching, but he was met by an unequivocal refusal:

> Now I will prevent to desire you, not to wish nor address unto me the cure and charge of no man his child or children. For I am now saved to my study and am able to live (I thank God and my master) without any such help and let of study. Wherewith I will not entangle nor cumber myself in no wise now, as I did in times past, nor with no other impediment, unless it be for a special friend. For I have lost too much time already, as you well know.[64]

Schoolteaching was usually regarded as a temporary expedient, resorted to by a scholar desperately short of funds or by an ambitious young cleric who saw it as a step to higher preferment. The task of instruction was often left to junior clerks and, considering that the master of an endowed school usually earned a stipend of £10 while beneficed clergy received between £10 and £20, it is not surprising that many schoolmasters accepted livings with alacrity. It should be remembered, too, that Wolsey began his career as a teacher at Magdalen school, and first attracted substantial patronage when he went home for the holidays with two of his pupils, the sons of the Marquess of Dorset.[65]

Despite the low status of teachers and other impediments many schools employed and educated humanists of note during the reign. Some of these masters and pupils have been described above. In addition, Reginald Pole began his famous humanist education at the school attached to the Charterhouse at Shene, and possibly passed from there to the Benedictine priory of Christchurch, Canterbury (where William Selling had probably taught Greek towards the end of the fifteenth century) before proceeding to Magdalen college, Oxford and thence to Italy.[66] Magdalen school numbered among its pupils John Parkhurst, William Tyndale and Edward Wotton; this last was a physician and medical writer and reader of the Greek lecture at Corpus Christi.[67]

The teachers at Magdalen school were also distinguished by their learning. Thomas Robertson, who was master in 1526, contributed a section to Lily's grammar in the edition of 1532 and worked on the Bishops' Book in 1537. Richard Sherry, master in 1534, translated Erasmus's educational treatise *Declamatio de Pueris Statim ac Liberaliter Instituendis* and composed a textbook on rhetoric. The master between 1542 and 1548 was the reformer John Harley, who was later tutor to the sons of the Duke of Northumberland.[68]

Eton, too, boasted a number of humanists as pupils and masters. Richard Morison was educated there, as were the Cambridge humanists Walter Haddon and Thomas Wilson.[69] Notable headmasters during the reign were Robert Aldrich (Erasmus's friend and later bishop of Carlisle), Richard Coxe and Nicholas Udall.

Though too colourful to be typical, Udall's career is useful as a reminder that there was no such thing as a standard or ideal humanist. His involvement in the Lutheran scandal at Cardinal college, Oxford, and his employment as one of the poets for Anne Boleyn's coronation have already been described. (See Chapter Three, above.) Possibly, as has been suggested, his Lutheran learnings partly explain his prosecution in 1541 for offences allegedly committed at Eton. Suspected of complicity in a robbery committed at the school by two of his pupils, Udall confessed to immoral relations with one of the accused and was confined in the Marshalsea. The following year he was deprived of his headship. Court influence eventually secured his release and the payment of his arrears of salary, though Wriothesley's attempt to have him reinstated at Eton was unsuccessful.

His moral failings apart, Udall produced an interesting literary output during Henry's reign. He published *Flowers for Latin Speaking Selected and Gathered out of Terence* in 1534 and a version of Erasmus's *Apothegmes* in 1542 and was general editor of the *Paraphrases of Erasmus*, translated under the auspices of Katherine Parr. His letter of thanks to Wriothesley is replete with classical examples of reformed characters, designed to emphasise 'mine honest change from vice to virtue, from prodigality to frugal living, from negligence of teaching to assiduity, from play to study, from lightness to gravity'. Eton probably benefited from his instruction, though his fellow humanists did not regard his educational practices with complete approval; Haddon called him 'the best schoolmaster of his time, as well as the greatest beater'.[70]

There is occasional evidence that other schoolmasters were well-educated men and quite possibly humanists. The foundress of the school of Week St Mary was unique in the west country in stipulating that the master should be a graduate, but university men were sometimes to be found in teaching posts. The master of Wilton School in the 1530s was Nicholas Hartwell, formerly of Winchester college and New college, with both a BA and an MA from the university. At Chipping Campden, Gloucestershire, two of the masters of the 1540s are known. James Dodwell was a former member of Magdalen college and MA of Oxford, while Robert Glassman, though not a graduate, had been a curate of William Latimer, the classical scholar and friend of Erasmus. As a modern commentator observes, it seems unlikely that Latimer would have employed an unlearned man. Similarly John Littleskill, master of the grammar school at Wells cathedral, was not a graduate, but in his will of 1539 he bequeathed Greek and Latin books to two Oxford scholars and mentioned five volumes he owned, including works by Ambrose, Cyprian, Chrysostom, Origen and Erasmus.[71]

As far as can be gathered from the paucity of information about schools in the reign of Henry VIII, elementary education was influenced to a significant degree by the new learning. Certain key institutions — most notably, the school of the Boy Jesus at St Paul's — were explicitly founded to provide humanist instruction at the most basic level, while there are also hints and glimpses of humanist educators at work in other schools. If no scheme of school endowment for the whole kingdom was implemented, this was due to political factors; the fall of Wolsey, and the negligence and self-interest of the King and his advisers in the wake of the monastic dissolution. Interest in the promotion of learning in the localities varied greatly and there was considerable apathy, but much ground was gained in certain areas through the initiative of individuals. If the Henrician achievement in school education seems limited compared with the large number of foundations under Edward and Elizabeth, it must be remembered that these later schools were established by or with the advice of men who had benefited from the humanist experiments of the earlier reign, and that the basis of education in the tongues and the classics laid down in the time of Henry VIII endured for almost four centuries.

Notes

1. For medieval education, Joan Simon, *Education and Society in Tudor England* (Cambridge University Press, Cambridge, 1966), Chapter 1, passim.

2. For Stanbridge and Banbury school, *The Vulgaria of John Stanbridge and the Vulgaria of Robert Whittinton*, Beatrice White (ed.) (Early English Text Society, Oxford University Press, London, 1932), pp. xvii–xviii. For Magdalen school, see Chapter 1, above.

3. Nicholas Orme, *Education in the West of England, 1066–1548* (University of Exeter Press, Exeter, 1976), p. 26.

4. Cf. Erasmus, *Lives of Jehan Vitrier and John Colet*, J. H. Lupton (ed.) (George Bell & Sons, London, 1883), pp. 36–7: 'The colleges established in England at a great and imposing cost he used to say were a hindrance to profitable studies, and mostly centres of attraction for the lazy.' On the school, R. B. Gardiner, *Admission Registers of St Paul's School* (2 vols., George Bell & Sons, London, 1884, 1906); M. F. J. McDonnell, *A History of St Paul's School* (Chapman & Hall, London 1909); and the *Lives* of Colet by Samuel Knight (J. Downing, London, 1724) and J. H. Lupton (George Bell & Sons, London, 1909).

5. Statutes printed in Lupton, *Colet*, Appendix A.

6. P. S. and H. M. Allen, H. W. Garrod (eds), *Opus Epistolarum Des. Erasmi Roterodami* (11 vols., Clarendon Press, Oxford, 1906–47), no. 593; trans. R. A. B. Mynors and D. F. S. Thompson, in Wallace K. Ferguson (ed.), *The Epistles of Erasmus* (6 vols., University of Toronto Press, Toronto, Buffalo, London, 1974–82). Hereafter cited when used in quotation as 'Toronto translation'.

7. Allen, *Erasmi Epistolae*, no. 341; cf. no. 227.

8. J. H. Rieger, 'Erasmus, Colet and the Schoolboy Jesus', *Studies in the Renaissance* vol. 9 (1962), pp. 187–94; Allen, *Erasmi Epistolae*, no. 260.

9. Richard Pace, *De Fructu Qui Ex Doctrina Percipitur*, F. Manley and R. S. Sylvester (eds and trans.) (Renaissance Society of America, Ungar, New York, 1967), pp. 20, 21.

10. Gardiner, *Admission Registers*, vol. 1, pp. 17–21.

11. N. H. Nicolas (ed.), *Privy Purse Expences of Henry VIII* (William Pickering, London, 1827), pp. 171, 186, 205, 231, 259, 280; PRO SP1/130, fo. 78, confession of John Ainsworth, March 1538. Calendared in *Letters and Papers, Foreign and Domestic, of the Reign of Henry VIII*, J. S. Brewer, J. Gardner, R. H. Brodie (eds) (21 vols., HMSO, London, 1962–1932), vol. 13, i, no. 533 (hereafter cited as *L&P*).

12. Simon, *Education and Society*, p. 95, PRO SP1/236, fo. 291 (*L&P*, Addenda, vol. 1, i, no. 717), Ritwyse to Henry VIII, 1530(?).

13. John Vowel alias Hooker, *Life and Times of Sir Peter Carew*, John MacLean (ed.) (Bell & Daldy, London 1857), pp. 5–6.

14. Allen, *Erasmi Epistolae*, nos. 237, 258.

15. Thomas Stapleton, *Histoire de Thomas More, grand chancelier d'Angleterre*, A. Martin and M. Audin (eds and trans.) (L. Maison, Paris, 1849), p. 32.

16. For lists of schools, Knight, *Colet*, pp. 90–2; F. J. Furnivall, *Manners and Meals in the Olden Time* (Early English Text Society, Oxford University Press, London, 1868), pp. liii–liv.

17. Edmund Chisholm Batten, *The Register of Richard Fox while Bishop of Bath and Wells* (Harrison & Sons, London, 1889), pp. 118–19; Orme, *Education in the West*, pp. 184–5.

18. Orme, *Education in the West*, pp. 105–6. Batten, *Register of Fox*, p. 129.

19. Godwin, *Catalogue of the Bishops of England*, quoted in Leslie Stephen and Sidney Lee (eds) *Dictionary of National Biography* (21 vols., Smith, Elder & Co., London, 1908–9), art. 'Oldham' (hereafter cited as *DNB*); A. A. Mumford, *Hugh Oldham* (Faber & Faber, London, 1936), p. 12.

20. W. R. Whatton, *History of Manchester School* (William Pickering, London, 1834), p. 24.

21. Simon, *Education and Society*, p. 91; Orme, *Education in the West*, pp. 117–23.

22. Orme, *Education in the West*, pp. 94, 100, 102, 112–13.

23. Ibid., p. 110, 186–90.

24. Ibid., pp. 129–30, 209, 213.

25. The Cardinal statutes are printed in *Statutes of the Colleges of Oxford*, E. A. Bond (ed.) (3 vols., J. H. Parker and Longman, Brown, Green & Longman, Oxford and London, 1853), vol. 2.

26. PRO SPL/32, fos. 43, 53–4, 55 (*L&P*, vol. 4, nos. 1459, 1470), letters from Warham to Wolsey, June and July 1525.

27. M. A. E. Wood, *Letters of Royal and Illustrious Ladies* (3 vols., Henry Colburn, London, 1846), vol. 2, pp. 21, 25, Elizabeth Dowager Countess of Oxford to Wolsey, 8 and 22 July 1528.

28. *L&P*, vol. 4, no. 4435, licence of foundation for Cardinal college, Ipswich.

29. *L&P*, vol. 4, no. 4691, printed in John Strype, *Ecclesiastical Memorials* (3 vols., Clarendon Press, Oxford, 1820–40), vol. 2, ii, pp. 139–41.

30. J. G. Nichols (ed.), *Narratives of the Days of the Reformation* (Camden Society, J. B. Nichols & Son, London, 1859), pp. 238–9.

31. Joan Simon compares this programme with that laid down for Colet's school in 1549. There the fifth form was to study Mantuanus and Terence; the sixth, Virgil and Cicero's epistles; the seventh, Sallust and the *Aeneid*; the eighth, Caesar, Ovid, Horace and Cicero's *De Officiis*. *Education and Society*, pp. 143–4.

32. PRO, SP1/52, fo. 127 (*L&P*, vol. 4, no. 5159), Goldwin to Wolsey.

33. Allen, *Erasmi Epistolae*, no. 2253 to Juan Vergara, c. 13 January 1530.

34. Furnivall, *Manners and Meals*, pp. liii–liv.

35. For what follows on Stoke, John Strype, *Life and Acts of Matthew Parker* (3 vols., Clarendon Press, Oxford, 1821), vol. 1, pp. 15–18.

36. *Correspondence of Matthew Parker*, John Bruce and Thomas Perowne (eds) (Parker Society, Cambridge University Press, Cambridge, 1853), no. 23, Parker to the Council of Katherine Parr, 1545; ibid., p. 33, note 2, Denny to the King's commissioners in Suffolk, 29 February 1548; Strype, *Parker*, vol. 1, pp. 41–2.

37. W. G. Searle, *History of the Queens' College* (2 vols., Cambridge University Press, Cambridge, 1867 and 1871), vol. 1, pp. 201–7; Orme, *Education in the West*, p. 54.

38. British Library, Cotton MS Cleop. E IV 302 (*L&P*, vol. 14, ii, no. 601).

39. Simon, *Education and Society*, pp. 184–6.

40. Morice's account is printed in Nichols, *Narratives*, pp. 263ff.

41. *Sermons and Remains of Hugh Latimer*, G. E. Corrie (ed.) (Parker Society, Cambridge University Press, Cambridge, 1845), p. 403; Simon, *Education and Society*, p. 186.

42. Latimer, *Remains*, pp. 396 and 418; Orme, *Education in the West*, pp. 64–5, 137–41.

43. PRO SP1/140, fos. 114–7 (*L&P*, vol. 13, ii, nos. 1072–3), Barlow to Cromwell (1538); *L&P*, vol. 16, ii, no. 503 (30), grants in January 1541, vol. 17, no. 556 (25), grants in July 1542.

44. PRO SPL/156, fo. 61 (*L&P*, vol. 16, ii, no. 787), mayor and aldermen to Cromwell (1539); *L&P*, vol. 18, i, no. 226 (22), grants in February 1543.

45. *L&P*, vol. 17, no. 283 (44), grants in April 33 Henry VIII; *DNB* art. 'Holgate'. Cf. PRO SP11/6, fos. 131b ff., Holgate's petition to Southwell, 1555. I am grateful to Joy Shakespeare for this last reference.

46. *L&P*, vol. 20, i, no. 1335 (38 and 39), grants in July 1545; ibid., vol. 20, ii, no. 1068 (45), grants in December 1545; Orme, *Education in the West*, pp. 167, 211; Strype, *Parker*, vol. 1, p. 25.

47. Charles Henry and Thompson Cooper, *Athenae Cantabrigienses* (2 vols., Deighton, Bell & Co. and Macmillan & Co., Cambridge, 1858, 1861), vol. 1, pp. 203–4; A. B. Emden, *A Biographical Register of the University of Oxford* (Clarendon Press, Oxford, 1974), pp. 154–5.

48. PRO SP1/136, fos. 93–4 (*L&P*, vol. 13, ii, no. 285), Ferrar to Cromwell; Furnivall, *Manners and Meals*, p. xix; Simon, *Education and Society*, p. 181.

49. British Library, Harleian MS 78 (78 vols. 18–23 (*L&P*, vol. 19, i, no. 431).

50. PRO SP1/246, fo. 96 (*L&P*, Addenda, vol. 1, Appendix 5); SP1/117, fos. 70–1 (*L&P*, vol. 12, i, no. 688); *DNB* art. 'Argentine'.

51. *Miscellaneous Writings and Letters of Thomas Cranmer*, J. E. Cox (ed.) (Parker Society, Cambridge University Press, Cambridge, 1846), p. 380; PRO SP1/128, fo. 120 (*L&P*, vol. 13, i, no. 105).

52. Orme, *Education in the West*, pp. 173–82.

53. Furnivall, *Manners and Meals*, pp. liii–liv.

54. Simon, *Education and Society*, p. 186.

55. Orme, *Education in the West*, pp. 28–32, 205, 211.

56. Quoted and seconded by A. G. Dickens, *English Reformation* (Fontana, London, 1973), p. 211.

57. White, *Vulgaria of Stanbridge*, pp. xxiv–xxv, xxx, xxxii, 146; William Nelson, *John Skelton, Laureate* (Columbia University Press, New York, 1939), pp. 148–53.

58. R. S. Stanier, *Magdalen School* (Basil Blackwell, Oxford, 1940), pp. 45–6.

59. Ibid., pp. 42–3; Simon, *Education and Society*, pp. 190–1.

60. Cf. Pearl Hogrefe, *Life and Times of Sir Thomas Elyot, Englishman* (Iowa State University Press, Iowa, 1967), pp. 249–51.

61. *John Palsgrave's Comedy of Acolastus*, P. L. Carver (ed.) (Early English Text Society, Oxford University Press, London, 1937), pp. 3–4.

62. Simon, *Education and Society*, p. 95.

63. David Lloyd, *State Worthies*, Charles Whitworth (ed.) (J. Robson, London, 1766), p. 103.

64. PRO SP1/133, fo. 47 (*L&P*, vol. 13, i, no. 1193).

65. Orme, *Education in the West*, p. 20 George Cavendish, *Life and Death of Cardinal Wolsey*, J. Singer (ed.) (Early English Text Society, Oxford University Press, London, 1959), p. 5.

66. Lodovico Beccatelli, *Life of Cardinal Reginald Pole*, Benjamin Pye (ed.) (C. Bathurst, London 1766), p. 13; Martin Haile, *Life of Reginald Pole* (Sir Isaac Pitman & Sons, London, 1910), pp. 6–7; F. A. Gasquet, *Cardinal Pole and His Early Friends* (G. Bell & Sons, London, 1927), p. 17.

67. Stanier, *Magdalen School*, pp. 63–5, 70–2.

68. Ibid., pp. 71, 73, 74–81.

69. Athenae Cantabrigienses, vol. I, pp. 434–7, 299–302; Lloyd, *State Worthies*, p. 113.

70. John S. Farmer (ed.), *Dramatic Writings of Nicholas Udall* (privately printed, London, 1906), p. 131n.; Cecilie Goff, *A Woman of the Tudor Age* (John Murray, London, 1930), p. 124; British Library, Cotton MS Titus B VIII fos. 386–8 (*L&P*, vol. 18, ii, no. 545); Emden, *Biographical Register*, pp. 586–8.

71. Orme, *Education in the West*, pp. 108, 127–8, 87.

5 The Wandering Scholar

I

The flowering of humanism in Henrician England must be seen as part of the wider field of European renaissance culture. Christendom — even after the Lutheran revolt — was conceived of as an entity, and the issues raised by scholarship were of universal concern. For scholars of all nations Latin was truly an international language which enabled them to benefit from instruction and from the conversation of the learned in centres of study as far apart as Oxford and Krakow, and there was great fluidity of movement between the scholarly communities of all the countries of Europe. Moreover — and despite its geographical position — England attracted foreign humanists not simply by the rumoured munificence of its patrons but also by its high reputation for scholarship. European humanists sought literary friendships with English scholars and favour from English patrons. They dedicated books to Englishmen and praised the kingdom in letters and literary works. They journeyed to England to study at the universities, transcribe manuscripts, make the acquaintance of the great and the learned and obtain employment and gifts from the court.

Nor was this traffic one-sided. Englishmen of the earlier sixteenth century were far from insular, even after Henry's breach with Rome. The University of Louvain alone records the names of 107 English scholars who matriculated there during the reign, and this is only a minimum number, since many students who 'went to university' did not register for degrees.[1] English scholars were also to be found at universities in France, Italy and Germany. Many of them were obscure, and of course not all were humanists, but a number of the most illustrious English exponents on the new learning received part of their education abroad, some of them holding public lectureships and professorial chairs in European universities.

The wandering scholar stood to gain much in terms of knowledge, intellectual stimulation and fame, but his lot was far from glamorous. Besides having to cope with the physical dangers and discomforts of travel — the state of the roads, the incidence of war and brigandage, the high price and poor quality of accommodation

— he was also at the mercy of financial necessity. Patrons tended to treat their scholarly protégés with the same nonchalence with which they considered other appeals for charity. Thus a timely epistle or dedication might call forth a gift, but few patrons were inclined to make more regular provision for their clients. They also had short memories, and even if a pension or exhibition were granted the absent scholar had to busy himself with constant reminders to his Maecenas to ensure that it was paid over. Scholars were therefore engaged in a constant battle with penury. Erasmus's complaints of his poverty are notorious and probably exaggerated, but even this highly eminent humanist fretted over the payment of his pensions from England and was once obliged to send his English patrons a sort of circular letter outlining his plans and hinting strongly at his need for 'a horse free from mortal sin'.[2]

Scholars less celebrated than Erasmus, with less hope of patronage, often found themselves in dire financial straits. In February 1539 Robert Farington, newly returned from his studies at Louvain, wrote to Cromwell of his disappointment at not obtaining a fellowship at King's Hall, Cambridge. He had counted on this and had sold part of his books, bedding and clothes, and his journey abroad with other expenses had cost him more than £60. Richard Morison, sick and penniless in Italy, was only saved by being taken into Pole's household and borrowing heavily from scholars whose resources were almost as scanty as his own.[3] Thus itinerant scholars, with a few individual exceptions, were not a privileged nor a comfortable class.

The most celebrated European humanist connected with England was Erasmus. Despite his complaints of the stinginess of his English patrons, England was the quarter from which he drew his most steady income. He had pensions from Warham and Mountjoy, and received besides occasional gifts from patrons ranging from the King, Queen Katherine and Wolsey through bishops Fisher, Fox and Tunstal to Christopher Ursewick, rector of Hackney and John Yonge, Master of the Rolls. Erasmus did not jealously guard his access to English patronage but was eager to assist other European scholars to employment or monetary reward. A letter to William Hermans of December 1498, though strictly speaking outside our period, is instructive in showing how scholars went about earning the favour of patrons, in this case Mountjoy:

This nobleman has the utmost confidence in anything you write;

so, if you make sure that the courier continually brings something new, you will not only please and help me a great deal but do yourself a service also. Above all, write to him as a friend: praise him for concentrating his admiration on letters despising all else; say that while few do so, they are a happy few indeed. Give him an account of the pleasures that literature affords. Extol the combination of scholarship and morality, putting in a word for me, while kindly offering your own services. Believe me, it will do your reputation good as well; for he is a most powerful figure in his own country, and in him you will find a disseminator of your books throughout England.[4]

Equally interesting is his letter of May 1527 to Nicholas Cannisius, an agent of his sent to England with a note to Warham:

You will enjoy your visit. You will meet many of the English nobles and men of learning. They will be infinitely kind to you, but be careful not to presume upon it: when they condescend, be you modest. Great men do not always mean what their faces promise, so treat them reverently, as if they were gods. They are generous and will offer you presents, but recollect the proverb, Not everything everywhere and from everyone. Accept gratefully what real friends give you. To mere acquaintances excuse yourself lightly; more art is needed in refusing graciously than in receiving . . . smile on as many as you please, but trust only those you know, and be specially careful to find no fault with English things or customs. They are proud of their country, as they may well be.[5]

Whatever his reservations about the sincerity of patrons, Erasmus was assiduous in recommending European scholars who went to England. Some of these were transient visitors. The Seigneur de Berghes sent his son to the English court with his tutor, Adrian Barland, and Erasmus took care to recommend them in letters to Pace, Lupset, Mountjoy, Tunstal, Wolsey and Sir Henry Guildford.[6] A wandering scholar of a rather different sort was Simon Grynaeus, who went to England in the summer of 1531 to search the libraries for old manuscripts to publish. Erasmus gave him letters of introduction to Mountjoy and Vulcanius, and possibly to others. Grynaeus evidently met and became friendly with Reginald Pole, then in England, and Vives in the Netherlands heard good reports of him from his English friends. He probably also met Claymond — a friend of Vives — with whom he later corresponded. Grynaeus also won the goodwill of More, who offered him hospitality, university contacts and an introduction at court. Grynaeus himself acknowledged to More's son John:

> Not only did your very illustrious father . . . not disdain to admit me, an obscure stranger, to his house; but, since his duties called him to court, I often accompanied him there . . . Although he knew for certain that my way of thinking on matters of religion was opposed to his on a number of points, his indulgent kindness was not diminished for a single instant. He helped me with his advice and his purse, and when the business which brought me to England was concluded to my satisfaction, he recommended me with such benevolence to his friends at Oxford that they opened to me their valuable library and allowed me to carry away a number of books of the greatest rarity, indispensable to the success of my literary labours. Thus heaped by More with favours, I left England bearing trophies of learning, more happy and more proud than if I could have had in my hands the most precious treasures of this rich kingdom.[7]

More must have been less than pleased at the consequences of his kindness, as Grynaeus pleased the King by his opinion on the royal marriage and agreed to canvass other judgements at Basle. (For Grynaeus and the royal divorce, see Chapter 2, above.)

Other scholars paid brief visits to England. The French humanist Christopher Longolius, who later became friendly with Pole at Padua, went to England in 1519 with a recommendation from Budé to More. He became friends with Linacre, who was generous to him during his stay and sent him a gift in 1521 in the care of Pole. Pace, too, was hospitable and Longolius on his deathbed, begged Pole to remember him to this English friend.[8]

A scholar who came to England in rather unusual circumstances was Thomas Murner, a Franciscan of Strasbourg, satirist, sometime poet laureate to the Emperor Maximilian and supporter of Reuchlin. He translated Henry VIII's *Assertio Septem Sacramentorum* into German and composed a defence of that work in 1522. In August 1523 More informed Wolsey that Murner

was out of Almaine sent to England by the mean of a simple

person, an Almain naming himself servant unto the King's grace, and affirming unto Murner that the King had given him in charge to desire Murner to come over to him in England, and by occasion thereof he is comen over, and hath now been here a good while.

Henry VIII pitied him and was grateful for the defence of himself, but he had little use for a foreign pamphleteer in England. However, he felt that Murner was an important orthodox influence in evangelical Strasbourg, so he graciously gave the friar a gift of £100 and a letter to the city magistrates. Murner, unfortunately, fared badly on his return. He began yet another defence of the King, but all but a printed fragment of this was destroyed when a mob ransacked his lodgings in 1524.[9]

Another unusual visitor to England was Ignatius Loyola, who came in 1530 to beg alms. Loyola knew Vives, and a modern Jesuit postulates that he received money from Katherine of Aragon; it is indeed quite likely that the Queen would favour a fellow countryman. The same commentator, perceiving traces of Richard Whitford's devotional thought in Loyola's writings, thinks that he visited the English scholar at Syon. However, little can be known of Loyola's stay in England, to which he himself made only a fleeting reference.[10]

Some scholars stayed for rather longer periods, seeking service at court or in noble households. The King continued his father's practice of employing Italians like Ammonio and Vergil on royal and papal business, but one Italian was markedly unsuccessful in gaining royal patronage. Alessandro Geraldini had been tutor to the daughters of Ferdinand and Isabella and accompanied Katherine to England, but he was dismissed for indiscreet gossip when she was widowed; she never forgave him for hinting quite wrongly that she was pregnant by Arthur and thus jeopardising her marriage with Henry.

Geraldini, made bishop of San Domingo in the new world at the request of Margaret of Austria, was naturally eager to return to Europe and obtain a more lucrative living, so he wrote Katherine a rather fulsome letter in January 1518. He had already sent one missive which he charitably supposed had not reached her, and now he sent an Indian ceremonial chair and robe, regretting that he could not send her parrots because they might not survive the change of climate. He hoped fervently that she would have a son, and said he intended to pay his respects once he got leave of absence. In May

Margaret, Katherine's former sister-in-law and companion in study, wrote to her in Geraldini's favour, and in November Leo X recommended him to both the Queen and King. Katherine, however, was unmoved, and Geraldini complained to Wolsey that Margaret, whom he had taught for only five months, had given him a bishopric but the Queen had given him nothing. It was characteristic of Katherine that once she felt her trust betrayed she would have nothing to do with the offender, and Geraldini never gained preferment in England.[11]

Most foreign scholars began by attempting to enter noble rather than royal service. In 1517 John Phrysius, a former *famulus* of Erasmus, departed for England with letters of recommendation from Erasmus to More (then at Calais), Fisher and Sixtinus. These letters reveal the mendacity of scholars when assisting each other. Erasmus told Fisher that Phrysius wrote very well in Greek and Latin and could help the Bishop with a book he wanted published, but he was more candid with More: 'I do not wish to impose this man on you; however, if you have need of a secretary he writes Latin and Greek well enough in a sufficiently correct and readable manner'. More evidently had no use for Phrysius, since he sent him on to England with ten groats for his travelling expenses.[12]

Others were more successful in finding employment. Gerard Phrysius, a countryman of John and a former pupil of Listrius, was in the service of Thomas Boleyn between 1529 and 1533 and possibly for a longer period; nothing is known of him beyond his two letters to Erasmus.[13] In 1529 he wrote on behalf of his master to commission a commentary on Psalm 22, and in 1533 he assured Erasmus that his pension from the see of Canterbury would continue despite Archbishop Warham's death.

As might be expected, Mountjoy was ready to offer employment to European scholars of good repute. In 1522 John Crucius of Louvain went to England and became tutor to Mountjoy's children. He stayed for five years, visiting many of his patron's properties around London, and in August 1527 he saw Pace at Syon. He returned to Louvain a few months later to lecture on Greek. Another graduate of Louvain who taught Mountjoy's son Charles was Peter Vulcanius of Bruges, a former pupil of Erasmus who may have owed his appointment to him.[14]

Gentian Hervet of Orleans, who studied with Erasmus and Lupset, received the patronage of the Pole family. Hervet was Lupset's pupil at Corpus, Oxford for two years and worked with him in Paris supervising the publication of one of Linacre's translations of Galen. He spent nine years serving the Poles in both a literary and a teaching capacity. In 1526, when he was described as 'a layman of the Countess of Salisbury's household', he translated Erasmus's *De Immensa Misericordia Dei* into English at her command. He was tutor to Geoffrey Pole's son, and at Geoffrey's request translated Xenophon's *Treatise of Household* from Greek to English. Arthur Pole he described as generous to learned men. Hervet shared the family's conservative religious views and followed Reginald to Padua and Venice. He also went to Avignon, and his *Opuscula*, including reminiscences of and epigrams on the Poles, Fisher and More, were printed at Lyons by Etienne Dolet in 1541.[15]

Another Frenchman of rather different religious views — and therefore of different English patronage — was the poet Nicholas Bourbon de Vandoeuvre. Bourbon was an evangelical who owed much to Anne Boleyn and William Butts. Anne's chaplain William Latymer records their intervention on his behalf:

Master Doctor Butts receiving letters out of France from one Nicholas Borbonius, a learned young man and very zealous in the scriptures, declaring his imprisonment in his own country for that he had uttered certain talk in the derogation of the Bishop of Rome and his usurped authority, made his suit to the Queen her majesty in his behalf: did not only obtain by her grace's means the King's letters for his delivery, but also after he was come into England his whole maintenance at the Queen's only charges in the house of the said Master Butts.

Bourbon alluded to Butts's and Anne's intervention in his *Nugae*, published by Dolet at Lyons in 1536 and 1538. There are verses of gratitude for his deliverance to the King and to Anne, who appointed him tutor to three young gentlemen at court. Butts received thanks as 'Maecenas' and 'father', and there are verses to other evangelical courtiers and clerics who Bourbon knew during his stay in England, including Cranmer, Cromwell, Hugh Latimer, Bainton, Dudley and William Boston. Bourbon probably left England on Anne's fall and subsequently gained the patronage of Margaret de Valois, who made him tutor to her daughter Jeanne d'Albret.[16]

Not all foreigners who took service with the English nobility were fortunate; indeed, the experiences of the Dutch humanist

Hadrianus Junius show clearly that scholars were mere servants to the great and very much at their caprice. Junius studied at Harlem and Louvain and graduated MD from Bologna. He was invited to England by Bonner, whom he encountered at the siege of Landrécy, but the Bishop apparently did nothing for him. Instead, in late 1543 or 1544, Junius entered Norfolk's service as a physician. Norfolk consulted him about the education of his grandchildren and Junius may have been their tutor; possibly he was the real author of the letter sent to Surrey from his children congratulating him on defeating the French at Boulogne. Certainly he resided at Kenninghall, whence he wrote bitterly of the insincere fawning and spurious friendship prevalent in the household and of the lack of good manners and interest in literature. His life was obviously made miserable by the uncouth retainers of the Howards. Surrey gave him a yearly pension of 20 nobles, but it is uncertain how long he remained in Norfolk's service. He did manage, however, to produce a Latin edition of Plutarch's *Symposia*, dedicated to the imperial ambassador Van der Delft, and a Greek and Latin lexicon, dedicated to Prince Edward.[17]

Some European scholars in England tried to avoid household service and private teaching and made instead for the universities. The presence of foreign students at Oxford and Cambridge was, of course, no new thing. John Sixtinus, for example, was in Oxford before October 1499, when he first wrote to Erasmus. A great friend of Tunstal, Sixtinus prospered in Henry VIII's reign. In 1513 he was one of the foreigners excused the subsidy, and in 1516 he acknowledged to Erasmus, 'I owe so much to our excellent, great, popular and kindly King for all he has done for me'. Sixtinus died in 1519, wealthy enough to leave £40 for exhibitions for poor scholars at Oxford and Cambridge, besides 20 marks to his executor Tunstal.[18]

Wolsey's and Fox's humanistic innovations at Oxford attracted a number of foreign scholars. Besides Hervet, at Corpus with Lupset, and Vives, reader of the public rhetoric lecture, there were several Europeans at Corpus and Cardinal. At the latter were to be found Peter Garsias de Lalo, formerly of the Sorbonne, and John de Coloribus, a Dominican who wrote a book against Luther at Wolsey's command. Matthew Culphurnius, himself a Greek, read Wolsey's Greek lecture.[19] Two notable beneficiaries of Fox's and Wolsey's patronage were Nicholas de Burgo and Nicholas Kratzer, whose respective careers illustrate the different ways in which scholars could gain employment and favour in England.

Nicholas de Burgo was a Franciscan of Florence who graduated BD from Paris. He probably came to Oxford about 1517 and was incorporated BD there in 1523 and DD in 1524. He succeeded Thomas Brynknell in Wolsey's theology lecture, a post he held from 1525 to 1535, and he was also lecturer in theology at Magdalen between 1526 and 1530.

Besides his academic duties, he was eminently useful in the King's 'Great Matter'. In 1530 he was one of the royal commissioners at Oxford charged with persuading the university to vote against the Aragon marriage. So zealous was he that the townswomen stoned him, but he was amply rewarded for his discomfort. The treasurer of the chamber's accounts record a reward of £5 in November 1528 and another of £6 13 4d in July 1529, when he is described as 'of the King's spiritual learned counsel'. He also received a grant of denization and a canonry in Romsey abbey, both in January 1530.

De Burgo was so deeply involved in the direction of Henry's case that Longland advised Cromwell against permitting him to visit Italy. In 1532 he was appointed to the theology lecture at Henry VIII's college in Oxford, though this particular piece of promotion was not entirely satisfactory; in January 1533 he complained that though he had performed his duties and even added public lectures, he had received no money from those who distributed the King's gifts. Even so, he was anxious to retain his preferments. In July 1537 he was abroad, and wrote begging Henry to be allowed to keep his benefice and college office and promising to return to England soon.[20]

Nicholas Kratzer of Bavaria was an acquaintance of Erasmus and Peter Gillis who studied at Cologne, Wittenberg and Oxford. A mathematician and astronomer, Kratzer was a tutor in More's household for a time, and in July 1517 Fox made him a fellow of Corpus. He was Wolsey's first mathematics reader and also lectured on astronomy at the King's command. In 1520 Tunstal, who met him at Lucca while Kratzer was on leave and he was on diplomatic business, described him as 'deviser of the King's horologies' and wanted to take him to the assembly of German electors, where he might prove useful. The treasurer of the chamber's accounts record payment to him as 'astronomer' of a quarter's wages of £5 at Christmas 1528. Evidently in favour at court, he received a payment of six shillings in April 1531 for mending a clock, and he composed his *Canones Horopti* at the request of William Tyler, groom of the chamber. In August 1538 Spalatin sent him a treatise on the consolation of princes to present to Cromwell, who forwarded it to the King in February 1539.[21]

After Erasmus the greatest European scholar to visit England and draw patronage from it was Juan Luis Vives. His experiences illustrate both the opportunities open to humanists and the discomforts and dangers the wandering scholar might face. A native of Valencia and former student at Paris, Vives settled in the Netherlands and was tutor to William de Croy, Chièvres's nephew and Cardinal-archbishop of Toledo. In 1519 Erasmus recommended him as tutor to Prince Ferdinand in a lavish encomium, though in the event Vives remained with Croy. After his pupil's premature death he hoped for employment in England (to be gained through More's mediation) which would leave him leisure to study. By July 1521 he was receiving financial support from Katherine of Aragon, and in 1522 he dedicated his commentaries on *The City of God*, prepared for Froben's edition of Augustine, to her husband. Henry replied with a gracious epistle promising that 'our favour and goodwill shall never fail in your affairs, whatsoever occasion shall be offered that may tend to your avail.'[22]

Thus encouraged, Vives came to England in spring 1523, armed with a letter of recommendation from Erasmus to Fisher. He spent part of each of the next five years in England. Despite his reluctance to teach he was appointed almost immediately to Wolsey's rhetoric lecture at Oxford, where the King and Queen went to hear him. His health suffered because of the dampness of Oxford, but the university had its compensations. He became friends with Claymond, and his teaching was well enough appreciated to be remembered a decade later.[23]

Apart from his duties at Oxford Vives was often required at court. Katherine consulted him about her daughter's education, and he often accompanied the Queen on journeys by river to the learned monastery at Syon. He knew Sir John Wallop, and at his request wrote a letter of advice for his brother Giles. He became friends with Linacre and Longland and caught the attention of Mountjoy, for whose son Charles he composed a short outline of studies. In material terms he was well off, since he received pensions from both the Queen and King as well as licences to export corn and import woad and wine. Katherine wanted him to settle in England, and sent his wife a gift and the promise of her protection if she would agree to reside here.[24]

Vives, then, was a highly-favoured scholar, but Erasmus warned him that the goodwill of Katherine and Henry would not keep body and soul together. Indeed, a vivid letter of Vives himself shows that even eminent humanists could complain of shabby treatment, and highlights the lowly position scholars occupied at a renaissance court:

> when I wish to return to my usual occupations, whether reading, writing or meditating, when I wish to seek refreshment by steeping myself again in that sort of life which was once familiar to me, there is no place left to me. My room is a tiny box, very narrow, where there is no table and scarcely a seat, and which is surrounded by other rooms full of noise and clamour, so that I cannot collect my thoughts without all my will and effort. Also I life quite far from the court, and so as not to lose the whole day in going and coming, once I have left the house in the morning I do not return until night. If I dine here, I cannot walk about in this narrow space (indeed, how could I?), so I curl up as though in a hole, and cannot devote myself entirely to my work. For I have to take care of my health, especially here where, if I fell ill, I would be thrown into some sewer and thought of only as a vile, sick dog.[25]

Cramped rooms and noisy neighbours were small troubles for Vives once the royal divorce was under way. The King subjected him to house arrest for assisting the Queen, and she took offence at unpalatable advice he offered. Hated by both parties and deprived of his royal pensions, Vives left England for ever in 1528. (For Vives and the royal divorce, see Chapter 2, above.) Thus his career shows both the shining prospects offered to foreign scholars in England and the difficulties — including political ones — they might encounter.

II

For their part, English scholars showed themselves eager for travel and study abroad, and some of them achieved international reputations. Foremost amongst these was Richard Croke, a protégé of Grocyn and product of Eton and King's, Cambridge. Croke was particularly famed as a Greek scholar. He studied at Paris under Aleandro, and it is thought that he was involved in the printing of

Erasmus's *Praise of Folly* by Gourmont; certainly he and Aleandro were godfathers to the printer's nephew. Croke was a gifted and promising pupil, but even so he was short of money at Paris, and Erasmus solicited Colet on his behalf.

After Paris Croke taught successively at the universities of Louvain and Cologne, and was invited by the Duke of Saxony to be Greek professor at Leipzig. Here he lectured on Theocritus, Herodotus and Plutarch, and won much admiration. Mucianus praised him to Reuchlin, and Erasmus told Linacre, 'Croke is the great man at Leipzig University, giving public lectures on Greek'. He became quite a celebrity in northern Europe, and the German humanist satire *Epistolae Obscurorum Virorum* contains 'criticism' of him by an ignorant monk as well as praise from Camerarius, Cruciger and Erasmus. Nor did his own country neglect him. He was recalled to England by Henry VIII, came under the patronage of Fisher, and in 1518 became Greek lecturer at Cambridge.[26]

Equally outstanding was Robert Wakefield, a brilliant protégé of Fisher. He taught his patron Greek, but was much more famed as a Hebraist and expert in Chaldee and Aramaic. Wakefield took his BA at Cambridge in 1514 and his MA in 1519 at Louvain, where he taught Hebrew in Busleyden's college dedicated to the three tongues. Also in 1519 he was elected fellow of St John's, and was thus equipped by Fisher with a stipend to assist his studies abroad. In 1522 he succeeded Reuchlin as Hebrew professor at Tübingen, where he also taught Greek. He returned to Cambridge by March 1524 and taught Hebrew there, becoming BD in the following year. Reginald Pole learned Hebrew from him, and he taught Hebrew, Chaldaic and Aramaic to his friend Pace. He composed an *Oratio de laudibus et utilitate trium linguarum Arabicae, Chaldaicae et Hebraicae*, published in 1524 and dedicated to Henry VIII.[27]

Another eminent wandering scholar was John Palsgrave, who spent a large part of his life in study and employment abroad. A graduate of Paris, he became schoolmaster to the King's sister Mary in 1513 and accompanied her to France for her marriage in 1514; doubtless he was chosen to assist her with her spoken and written French. He was among those of Mary's suite dismissed by the French King on the morrow of the wedding, but he had no desire to return to England; Mary wrote asking Wolsey to favour him, so that he could 'continue at school' and 'shall not need to come home'.

In December 1516 More informed Erasmus that Palsgrave, 'our friend, who has been completely devoted to you for a long time, as you know, is going to Louvain to devote himself to law while at the same time, as is his custom, addressing himself to Greek and Latin literature'. On his journeys between England and the Netherlands Palsgrave carried letters between Erasmus and More, and the latter presented him to a number of benefices between 1520 and 1524. Palsgrave later worked in England as tutor to a number of young gentlemen, but by July 1538 he was once more abroad, teaching in France.[28]

Palsgrave, Croke and Wakefield all proved useful to the King in the political sphere. Palsgrave and Croke were tutors to Henry's bastard son; their position was potentially influential because the boy was considered seriously as an alternative heir to the throne. When Henry resorted to divorce to settle his dynastic problem all three scholars employed their linguistic abilities in his service. Wakefield and Palsgrave produced literary propaganda, while Croke was sent to research the King's case in Italy and to justify the supremacy by sermons in England. (For Croke, Wakefield and Palsgrave during the divorce see Chapter 2 above.)

In contrast to the political work of these three scholars Leonard Coxe travelled widely but restricted himself to the academic field. Coxe's early life is obscure, but he matriculated in 1514 at Tübingen (where he met Melanchthon and was taught by Stoffler) and in 1518 at Krakow. Here he lectured on Livius, Quintilian and Jerome, and published two of the latter's epistles as well as Pontanus's *De laudibus divinis*. During the 1520s he taught at schools in Poland and Hungary, besides lecturing at Krakow on Cicero and Virgil. He was a correspondent of Erasmus, and his literary output was considerable. In 1524 he produced an edition of Adrian di Castello's *Venatio*, dedicated to Decius, and in 1526 he published two educational tracts, *De erudienda iuuentute* and *Methodus humaniorum studiorum*. He also produced an edition of Henry VIII's controversy with Luther and versions of Horace's *Epodes* and Cicero's *Orator*, besides other works. He became poet laureate and contributed verses to a number of books published at Krakow, including Erasmus's *Hyperaspistes* and *Epistola ad Sigismundum*. He returned to England by February 1530 and was schoolmaster at Reading before and after the monastic dissolution. He published an educational work, *The Art or Craft of Rhetoric*, in 1532, assisted in the production of Henry VIII's grammar, and contributed verses to Palsgrave's French grammar.[29]

Most Englishmen who were drawn to foreign universities went as students rather than teachers. Their length of stay depended on financial support, their patrons' plans for them and the availability of other opportunities, and often mere fragments of information survive about them. For example, in May 1540 John Shire, a student of Cambridge, received licence to go abroad for his 'further increase in virtue and cunning', and Christopher Hales, rector of Flaxbury, Worcestershire, was granted a licence to study abroad for seven years in May 1543. John Felymore, a student at Paris who knew John Bekynsaw, was evidently assisted there by Lady Lisle.[30]

A more distinguished traveller abroad was Edward Wotton of Magdalen, Oxford. Claymond recommended him to Fox in 1520 or 1521, and though the Bishop regretted that he could not make Wotton a fellow of Corpus for technical reasons, he did make him *socio comparem* and give him licence to study in Italy for up to five years. Wotton's chief reason for travelling was to learn Greek, but he really distinguished himself as a medical scholar. He gained his MD at Padua, and was possibly the Englishman 'Odoadus' who corrected the proofs of the Aldine edition of Galen with Clement and Lupset in 1525.[31]

Andrew Borde was another student of medicine who travelled widely. Originally a Carthusian, Borde was given licence to study medicine overseas by Prior Batmanson of the London Charterhouse and was away between 1528 and 1530. In the latter year he was ordered to wait on Sir Robert Drury and was consulted by Norfolk about an illness. Norfolk arranged for him to see the King, and probably as a result he went abroad again to study at Orleans, Poitiers, Montpellier, Toulouse and Wittenberg. He also visited Compostella and Rome. He returned to London by May 1524, when he swore to the succession and the supremacy. As a result the Carthusians imprisoned him, but he was freed by Cromwell. He gave the minister his *Itinerary of Europe*, which is no longer extant: 'one Thomas Cromwell had it of me. And because he had many matters [of state] to despatch for all England, my book was lost.'[32]

Borde's familiarity with the French universities was undoubtedly the reason Cromwell sent him to report on their feelings about the King's proceedings. Borde also wrote to Cromwell in 1536 from 'a little university called Glasgow' where he had gone to study and practise medicine; he reported that apart from 'some scholastic men' there was great support for Henry. Borde was in Cambridge in August 1537 but soon went on his travels again, visiting or passing through Calais, Gravelines, Antwerp, Cologne, Coblenz, Worms,

Venice, Rhodes, Joppa and Jerusalem. He settled for some time at Montpellier, which he described as 'the most noblest university of the world for physicians and surgeons'. Here he composed three books; his *Breviary of Health*, *A Compendious Regiment or Dietary of Health* (dedicated to Norfolk and published in 1542), and his *Introduction of Knowledge*.[33]

This last work, published in 1547 or later and dedicated to Princess Mary, is interesting for showing a wandering scholar's impressions of his surroundings. Louvain was 'a good university', as were Toulouse and Montpellier, but the Saxons and Bohemians were rank heretics. Borde described the university of Salerno but thought it better to pass over in silence the differences between the Greek and Latin churches. He commented on the abominable vice of Rome and decayed state of the city, especially St Peter's, and lamented the decline of the Hebrew language: 'the Hebrew which the Jews doth speak now, these days, doth alter from that true Hebrew tongue (except the Jews be clerks) as barbarous Latin doth from true Latin, as I have known the truth when that I did dwell amongst them.'[34] With its wealth of comment the *Introduction of Knowledge* must have been useful as a sort of handbook for wandering scholars.

As noted above, a comparatively large number of English students spent some time at Louvain. Nicholas Daryngton was there in April 1522, having been promised an allowance from his Cambridge college, Christ's. He did not matriculate, however, and his length of stay is unknown. William Warham, nephew of the Archbishop, was abroad with the King's licence by July 1537, when he received another licence to remain abroad for the attainment of learning. Nothing more is known of his time in Europe, except that he matriculated at Louvain in 1541.[35]

As might be expected, university life abroad was not free from troubles and quarrels. Christopher Joy matriculated at Louvain in 1531 as did his friend Henry Phillips in 1534. Joy returned to England by January 1538 but Phillips stayed on, apparently in some sort of trouble. He wrote to Joy of his misery and the calumny spoken against him, and asked him to forward a letter to his patron Thomas Bryerwood, chancellor to the bishop of Exeter. In this letter he complained that Bryerwood, his 'sole Maecenas', had not answered his letters, though he knew from Richard Leighton — whose brother William was also a student at Louvain — that he wished to advise him. Phillips wanted to continue his studies and claimed to have travelled over Europe learning the languages, customs and laws of the different nations. He had even served as a soldier in Charles V's army 'for the sake of bread', but asked to be saved from the need to do this. He also hoped that Bryerwood would be the means of reconciling him with his father.[36]

Phillips surfaces about a year later in a letter from Richard Leighton to Cromwell; this is mutilated, so Phillips's alleged doings, though sinister, are obscure. Phillips, Leighton said, 'robbed his own father, and so at that time had more money than all the Englishmen that were there [in Louvain], and anon after Tyndale's taking he began to betray his country, as keeping certain Englishmen there at Louvain prisoners'. These were alleged to have said that they would not return to England until they saw a better world and a change, but Leighton strenuously denied this to be true and protested the innocence of his brother William, whose only friends were Tunstal and himself.[37]

A number of scholars were sent abroad by the King. Henry's motives here were undoubtedly mixed; these protégés would exhibit the royal munificence as well as the famous learning of the English. The King could be generous on occasion, as he was to John Cheke and Thomas Smith. Both these Cambridge scholars owed their advancement to the ubiquitous Dr Butts. About 1534 he recommended them to Henry, in particular for their skill in Greek, and they were given exhibitions for study abroad. Nothing is known of their travels but in 1540, as has been seen, they were appointed respectively to the Regius chairs of Greek and civil law at Cambridge. Smith's promotion caused something of a furore, as many felt that he was not sufficiently versed in law, so he spent the next two years studying at Orleans, Paris and Padua. He took up his professorial duties on his return and in 1543 became vice-chancellor of the university. Cheke, too, was prominent in Cambridge affairs, and also held the important post of tutor to Prince Edward.[38]

The scholar whose studies abroad were most highly favoured by Henry was Reginald Pole. Pole was one of his closest male relatives, and the King's generosity to him can be seen as part of his general programme of reparation to the Pole family, descendants of his attainted great uncle the Duke of Clarence. As a younger son Pole was probably intended for the church from an early age, and so it is not surprising that Henry's munificence should take the form of educational sponsorship. The King undoubtedly intended his cousin for high office in the English church, and Pole's sojourn abroad was perhaps meant to make him familiar to the Italian prelates, as well as to enable him to study theology and other disciplines necessary to his future greatness. In 1521 Pole went to Italy with a recommendation from Henry to the Venetian *Signoria* and a pension of £100. The King gave him other sources of revenue, too. He received a pension from the prior of St Frideswide's at Henry's request; had two prebends in Salisbury cathedral; and was appointed dean of Wimborne and dean of Exeter.[39]

Once abroad, Pole was as much a royal representative as an admired scholar. He owed his popularity and celebrity partly to his relationship to Henry, and acknowledged this himself in a letter to Wolsey of July 1525. In January 1524 Clement VII was careful to send him a letter of compliments which not only urged him to study but also expressed the new Pope's obligations to Henry and the English in general. However, Pole also earned respect for his own scholarly merits. More described him to Margaret Roper as 'as noble as he is learned in all branches of letters, nor less conspicuous for his virtue than for his learning'. He was warmly praised by Erasmus, who recommended John a Lasco to him, by Lupset, who helped him with his studies at Padua, by John Botzheim, Leonard Casembroot and Germain de Brie.[40]

Pole was taught at Padua by the noted Grecian scholar Niccolò Leonico and by the classicist Romolo Amasei. Leonico was appointed his tutor by the Venetian *Signoria* out of respect for the English King, though Pole also carried a letter of introduction to him from William Latimer. Pole tried unsuccessfully to persuade Amasei to be Wolsey's rhetoric reader at Oxford. Like many wandering scholars, he collected manuscripts which he brought to England when he returned with Lupset in October 1526.[41]

During the royal divorce it became clear that Henry expected some return for his generosity to Pole, who was sent to Paris in 1529 to persuade the university to favour the King. After this mission, which he accomplished more or less successfully, he returned to his studies, first in Avignon and then in Italy. He retained Henry's goodwill until the publication of his *De Unitate Ecclesiae* in 1536 showed the King that he would not countenance the breach with Rome. (For Pole's somewhat problematical role in the divorce and his subsequent breach with Henry, see Chapter 2 above.)

Wolsey imitated Henry's patronage of Pole by having his bastard son educated extensively and expensively abroad. Thomas Wynter, like Pole, was endowed with numerous church revenues and livings from a very tender age, and numbered among his titles dean of Wells, archdeacon of Richmond and provost of Beverley. Thus Wolsey showed himself the King's equal in munificence and encouragement of learning, but Wynter was not the intellectual equal of Pole. Indeed his career abroad reads at times like an unkind parody of the latter's.

In 1518, while still a minor, Wynter matriculated at Louvain with his tutor Maurice Birchenshaw, a friend of Lupset and former teacher at Magdalen school and St Paul's. Birchenshaw returned to England in 1522 but Wynter proceeded to Italy. Wolsey may have sent him to Padua with Lupset, and he may have lived in Pole's household there. Nothing is known of his studies, and his movements are obscure. He may have wintered in Louvain in 1523 to 1524 because of ill health, and at some point he returned to England. In October 1526 he was escorted to Paris by the English ambassador John Clerk. He stayed there for several years, studying and frequenting the court, and he met up with Pole again during his mission to the university.

Wynter was not an able scholar, and seems to have enjoyed travel for its own sake rather than for the opportunities of study it afforded. In January 1527 Sir John Russell reported that Wynter was praised for his own merits as well as for Wolsey's sake and that learned and worshipful men resorted to him; but he said frankly that a more splendid household might encourage him to apply himself to study. Lupset joined Wynter early in 1528 to regulate household expenses and supervise Wynter's studies. The latter himself wrote to the Cardinal at intervals in adequate Latin and a fine Italian hand, but perhaps Wolsey sent Lupset to him because he was uneasy about his progress.[42] This was certainly slow. In March 1528 George Hampton wrote to Wolsey with evident relief in favour of one Cyprianus, from whom Wynter had profited more than any other teacher in Paris. Wynter himself wrote to his father about Cyprianus, who was not only a diligent teacher but a dear friend, instructing him by reading and delighting him by his conversation. Over the past year they had read Mela or Pliny together almost every day. Cyprianus had spent his youth in England and wished to return there, so Wynter asked Wolsey to give him a benefice.[43]

Wynter's letters to his father tend to be pious, stilted and embellished with schoolroom commonplaces. Perhaps he was overwhelmed by the rigorous programme of study designed for him. In December 1528 he told Wolsey that he was studying Latin,

Greek, the rudiments of astronomy and mathematics, and scholastic questions. Rather surprisingly, considering that these last were anathema to many humanists and of only secondary importance to others, he declared that he preferred them above any other study because of their ingenious subtlety, since the schoolmen got to the heart of the matter while other authors merely skimmed the surface. Perhaps in this he was simply parroting the Venetian ambassador, who had talked to him about scholasticism and made flattering allusions to Wolsey's knowledge. By the following June Wynter still had not learned French, and Wolsey suggested he lodge in a French household in order to remedy this. Wynter gravely recorded his approval of this course, and aired his knowledge of Erasmus's *Adagia* by alluding to the well-worn proverb about the sow teaching Minerva. Clearly his scholarship was not outstanding.[44]

After Wolsey's fall Wynter was deprived of his revenues and benefices, but he was able to turn to his father's former clients Gardiner and Cromwell for help in gaining the King's favour. He was in Venice by July 1531 but returned to England soon after. In January 1532 he was granted licence to leave the country, and in February he sent Cromwell a letter of thanks from Calais.[45]

Wynter proceeded to Paris — where he met Pole and learned of the high cost of living in Italy — and thence to Padua. In August he complained to Cromwell that he was unable to buy books and could not make friends with the learned because of his shabbiness. In March 1534 he declared petulantly that he loved letters but also wanted to keep his preferments. More sententiously, he observed that riches were a great assistance to study and an ornament to life not to be rejected. In July he returned to England and on Cromwell's advice went to court to salute Anne Boleyn. She promised him favour, and he planned to return to Italy, but by January 1536 he was still in London complaining of his 'small fortune'. In February 1537 his finances seem to have reached their lowest ebb. He sent Cromwell a pathetic letter written in English rather than Latin, a sure sign that he had been without teachers for some time; indeed, he declared that he had been absent from his learning for 44 months. Thus Wynter's career as a wandering scholar petered out somewhat ingloriously.[46]

Both Wynter and Pole were important quite apart from their own studies; their households in Paris and Padua were homes or meeting places for a number of English scholars. These came from a variety of backgrounds. Some were equipped with exhibitions from Henry

VIII or other patrons, some were quite penniless; some were in the service of Pole or Wynter, others appeared in their households only intermittently. They were drawn by a number of considerations; the hope of favour or promotion through association with the King's or Cardinal's kinsmen, the opportunities for study, the availability of new books, and the chance of meeting foreign humanists and patrons.

John Bekynsaw received patronage from a number of sources. Originally sent to Paris by his Oxford college, which considered him 'an admirable Grecian', Bekynsaw also received two payments from the King's privy purse, £4 13 4d in February 1530 and £5 in April. He seems to have lodged in Wynter's household; the previous spring Wynter and Volunzenus had recommended him to Cromwell, who may have brought him to Henry's notice. He was also in receipt of funds from Anne Boleyn, who allegedly gave him £40 a year for study in Paris. Her gifts were thus considerably larger than the King's, and on her fall Bekynsaw was in financial difficulties. By June 1537 he had attached himself to William Knight, who advised him to seek service in France. Bekynsaw, however, declared that he would be forced to return to England by midsummer, 'because of uncertainty of my living and despair of any more friends'. Poverty was interfering with his studies and he longed for a quiet life in England:

> I live in langour and go not to my book as my heart would. If I might lie in a corner where I might without any trouble serve God and daily pray for your mastership and other my friends and so quietly study . . . I would think myself to have gotten the greatest felicity I sought ever for. God knoweth my mind, and so, I think, do you.

In the event Bekynsaw remained in Paris until at least 1539 and taught Greek at the university. He also had dealings with Lady Lisle, and advised her about her son's education. When he returned to England he prospered. In May 1544 he was pardoned of any treason possibly committed through his dealings with Pole and Richard Pate, for whom he had carried letters, and in July Henry VIII appointed him gentleman usher. In 1546 he published a treatise on the royal supremacy, *De Supremo et absolutio regis imperio*.[47]

John Mason was one of the most successful of the scholars taken

into the King's favour and associated with Pole and his friends. His
studies at Paris were supported by funds from the privy purse. In
December 1529 he received £3 6 8d by way of exhibition and the
same sum in September 1530. In 1531 he was given a reward of 40
shillings and in January and October 1532 he was paid £6 13 4d for a
year's exhibition. He visited Padua, and was in Valladolid in July
1534, whence he sent impressions of Spain and news of England to
Starkey at Padua. In 1535 he visited Sardinia, Corsica, Sicily and
Naples (again sending descriptions to Starkey) and in 1536 he was in
Venice. Later he would be suspected of 'injudicious conferences'
with Pole.

The antiquary David Lloyd suggested that Mason's travels were
intended to equip him for state service, and this may be true. In 1537
he became secretary to Sir Thomas Wyatt, ambassador in Spain.
Recalled to England in 1541, he became the King's French secretary
in 1542 with a salary of £40 a year. In May 1543 he became one of the
clerks of the privy council for life, with a stipend of £20 a year, and
later received other grants and offices from the King.[48] Similarly
Starkey and Morison, both members of Pole's household, were able
to use the fruits of their study abroad in the royal service. (See
Chapter 2, above.)

Other scholars were briefly associated with Wynter or Pole.
William Swerder was a friend of George Lily and client of Cromwell
who studied at Paris. He gave Cromwell useful information
occasionally, and in 1539 sent him a little book on commonwealths
as a gift. John Frier lived with Pole in Padua but his patron (who
presumably supported him) was Edward Foxe. On Starkey's
instructions Frier followed Foxe to Germany later in 1535 and
attended him at the Diet of Smchalkalde. A notable itinerant was
the Scots humanist Voluzenus. He was Wynter's tutor in Paris and
used by him as a messenger to his father. On Wolsey's fall and
Wynter's return to England he entered the service of the bishop of
Paris, though he relied on Cromwell for advancement and protection. In April 1531 he sent him a 'treaty of histoire' as a gift and later
dedicated his version of Cicero's *Scholia seu commentariorum in
Scipionis somnium* to Cromwell's son Gregory. By November 1535
he was in Lyons, where he informed Starkey that Sadoleto, the
humanist Bishop of Carpentras, had offered him a teaching post
with a salary of 70 crowns. He reminded Starkey that the previous
summer in Bonvisi's garden in London he had advised him to choose
Carpentras as his place of study. Volunzenus was back in Paris in

June 1536, whence he wrote asking Cromwell's protection and interest in his affairs.[49]

Not all Wynter's and Pole's associates found favour in England; two at least followed Pole in adherence to Rome. Richard Pate, nephew of Bishop Longland and former pupil of Vives at Bruges, took his MA at Paris and was a frequent visitor at Wynter's house. He was ambassador to Charles V in 1533 and 1540, but in the latter year he fled to Italy because he could no longer condone Henry VIII's religious policies. He was attainted of high treason with Pole in 1542, and like him remained in exile until Mary's reign.

A scholar of similar views was Pole's chaplain Thomas Goldwell. He may have been the Goldwell of Canterbury college, Oxford who was questioned in 1531 or 1532 about books written in Katherine of Aragon's defence. By July 1532 he was in Padua, receiving ample funds from his father William, who urged him to write in Greek to Archbishop Warham to thank him for a gift of £10 and to do the King any service he could. In July 1536 he matriculated at Louvain, and he travelled to Italy by way of the universities of Heidelberg and Ingoldstadt. He reached Padua by April 1538 and met Pole, but he told his father he would not stay there for the whole summer and asked him to forward his letters to Rome in the care of William Elston, the Observant forced into exile by his support of Queen Katherine. Goldwell was in Rome by May 1538. He only returned to England in 1553, in Pole's retinue.[50]

Scholars in Pole's household had opportunities of study and of meeting foreign humanists. While in Provence Pole became intimate with Sadoleto, who gave him one of his books to present to Bembo and letters to the bishop of Verona and to his friend Lazaro, whom Pole later made his tutor. He became friends with the bishop and Contarini as well as with scholars more or less resident at Padua and Venice. Books were in more plentiful supply than in England. Pole wrote to Alvise Priuli in May 1535 requesting books, as he intended to read rather than write during the hot summer. He wished for Sadoleto's book on philosophy, and also wanted Lazaro to send some commentaries on Euclid. After his return to England Starkey relied on Bernardino Sandro of Pole's household to tell him what printed books were available in Italy. In April 1535 Sandro sent him the sayings of Pasquino, and in December informed him that Pole had received a manuscript copy of Sadoleto's *Hortensio* from Bembo and that this would soon be published. In May 1536 he regretted that there was currently no means of sending books to

England, but sent Starkey a list of the latest printed books in Greek and Latin including works by Proclus, Eusebius and Marc'Antonio Flaminio.[51]

The household was very studious. In December 1535 Frier told Starkey that Pole was devoting himself to theology. Morison battled with his poverty to continue his Greek studies. In August 1535 he was hoping to read the whole of Aristotle, and in March 1536 he appealed to Starkey for money for his journey to England and for the purchase of certain Greek books which were either expensive or unobtainable in England. George Lily told Starkey in April 1535 that he was studying Latin and reading the most approved authors, besides hearing Egnatius lecture on Latin. Lily had no tuition in Greek but hoped to have private instruction soon. This was evidently forthcoming, for in December he reported that he had been able to read unaided Sophocles, Euripides, Aristophanes, Xenophon and Plutarch. He was taught Greek by Egnatius and Faustus and also profited from Morison's presence. In 1535 members of the household were hard at work preparing an edition of Basil for publication and collating the text with manuscripts in St Mark's library.[52]

Life in the household could also have its drawbacks. Pole lived in seigneurial fashion, and the scholars who lodged with him could not retreat completely into private study; rather, they were expected to entertain visitors and accompany Pole on outings as members of the retinue of a great lord. Sandro complained in October 1535 of the entertainment of distinguished guests. They were keeping open house, he said, and Pole had given three or four banquets to the French ambassadors. A number of Italian scholars — Lazaro, Lampridio, Boemo and Priuli — had come to lodge as though the house were their own. Priuli had stayed for months and then made Pole go to his own house in Padua. Since then they had lived in Pole's house at Murano and Harvel's house at Venice, and now Pole was planning to visit Verona. They were all sick, said Sandro, of this way of living. Later in the same month George Lily grumbled at having to wait on Pole and attend to his wishes because of the lack of servants, so that he had no leisure for study.[53]

The disadvantages of a scholar's life abroad did not deter people from travelling. The King granted exhibitions to the antiquary Leland, who received a quarter's wages of £25 at Christmas 1528, and to one William Brograve, who had a yearly 'exhibition beyond the sea' of £13 6 8d. Some nobles and courtiers followed Henry's

example in educating their relatives overseas. Lord Cobham
sent his two sons to Louvain and Venice respectively. (See Chapter
7 below.) Sir Anthony Denny (who as yet had no son of his own)
sent his nephew John to study at Venice under Edmund Harvel's
practical eye. He was there by May 1543 but evidently not making
satisfactory progress, since Harvel excused him to his uncle on
the grounds of poor health. By June John learned that Sir Anthony
wished him to return to England by Michaelmas, and wrote
asking permission to study in Italy for a year or two longer as
he had made such a good beginning; certainly, his letter shows
that he had learned Italian. Harvel, too, wrote in support of his
charge:

> who certainly ceaseth not of diligence to exercise himself daily in
> luting, vaulting, and also the Italian tongue as far as his tender
> nature can extend. And hereto hath profited not meanly, and
> trust daily shall do more and more; trusting that he shall answer in
> some part to your expectation.

It is not, unfortunately, known whether Sir Anthony relented.[54]

III

Besides pursuing their studies abroad, humanists were eager for
friendships with scholars of other nations. These might be initiated
by a mutual friend, such as Erasmus, and would be conducted
largely or wholly by letter, since the parties concerned met rarely, if
at all. The most notable epistolary friendship was that of Reuchlin
and Fisher.

The celebrated and persecuted German hebraist quickly won the
approval of English humanists, most notably Colet and Fisher.
Colet's interest in Reuchlin's works diminished as he himself
became exclusively Christocentric, but Fisher proved more steadfast. Indeed, his enthusiasm for Reuchlin's cause passed well
beyond the bounds of polite interest, and through Reuchlin and his
works the bishop became a fervent advocate of Hebrew studies. In
spring 1515 Fisher told Erasmus of his admiration for Reuchlin, and
asked him to send his works and to question him about the genealogy
of the Virgin. Fisher declared, 'I find his type of scholarship very
congenial; in fact, I know no one else who comes closer to Giovanni

Pico.' The following summer Fisher praised Reuchlin warmly: 'He seems to me, in comparison with everyone else whose works I have read, to be the best man alive today, especially in knowledge of the recondite field that lies between theology and philosophy and touches on both.' So enthusiastic was he that, despite his age, he planned to visit Reuchlin in Germany. Reuchlin begged Erasmus to dissuade him for fear he would be disappointed, but as late as November 1520 Fisher was still planning the journey.[55]

In March 1517 Erasmus sent More a volume of writings on Reuchlin's trial at Cologne which he was to lend Fisher, while Reuchlin himself sent two copies of *De Arte Cabalistica* for Fisher and Erasmus. Neither this work nor the *Speculum Oculi* reached the bishop quickly, however, as More kept them to read himself. In addition, and ironically in view of later reformation history, Erasmus advised Reuchlin to sent his great-nephew Philip Melanchthon to Fisher with a letter of recommendation; it is interesting to imagine the future leader of Lutheranism under the tutelage of one of its most determined opponents. It may be noted that Fisher's support of Reuchlin was more firm than even Erasmus's; the latter excused himself to Wolsey in May 1519 by saying that he had got little from the Talmud or Cabala and was not very close to Reuchlin, with whom he had only a sort of official friendship between learned men.[56]

This particular literary friendship was not merely for the exchange of compliments, but for the increase of learning. The fruit of Fisher's association with Reuchlin appears in the statutes he issued to St John's, Cambridge, which provided for the study of Hebrew.

Englishmen abroad for study or diplomacy might have opportunities of meeting foreign scholars, and sometimes a European humanist might act as intermediary between his English and continental friends; this was a role Erasmus often played. Two notable examples of European scholars with a number of English friends were Leonico and Budé.

Leonico had known William Latimer and Tunstal when they were students at Padua; the former gave Pole an introduction to him, and the latter commended Lupset to him. He met Lupset and Pace while they were in Italy on scholarly and diplomatic business, and dedicated his *De Varia Historia* to Tunstal. On 19 January 1524 he sent copies of his version of Aristotle's *De Parva Naturalia* to Linacre and More. In return, he asked Linacre for one of his medical commentaries and More for a copy of *Utopia*; this was sent to Padua in the care of John Clement a few months later. Leonico was also acquainted with Claymond, whom he described to Lupset as 'that most holy old man'.[57]

The French scholar Budé came to know English scholars through both personal contact and the recommendations of Erasmus. In June 1516 Erasmus told Budé of Linacre's admiration for his scholarship, and the following month the two met in Paris; Linacre had gone to France in Mary Tudor's suite in 1514, and had stayed to see his translation of Galen's *De Sanitate Tuenda* through the press. Budé told Erasmus that he was favourable impressed by Linacre: 'He seemed to me a man of high character, kindly, and devoid of all self-importance.' Budé had sent Linacre a copy of his own *De Asse* and had sought his friendship. He also helped correct *De Sanitate* for the press, and in June 1518 Linacre sent him his thanks and some cramp rings blessed by Henry VIII. Budé replied that he did not regret the time spent on Galen, and joked that *De Asse* was no gift but a fee to buy Linacre's voice for him in England. The following September Budé expressed approval of the specimen of Galen which Lupset had shown him, and told Linacre to introduce himself as his friend to members of the French embassy in England.[58]

Budé's relations with Tunstal were not quite as warm, possibly because Tunstal, a diplomatist as well as a scholar, was inclined to be mistrustful of the French. In October 1516 Erasmus wrote to Budé in praise of Tunstal, then ambassador to Charles of Castile in the Netherlands. He exhorted Tunstal twice to write to Budé, and he complied in April 1517 with a letter praising the scholarship of Budé and Erasmus, commenting in particular on Budé's skill in Greek. At the same time, however, Tunstal told Erasmus that he was very busy and had only written to honour Erasmus's promise to Budé and to gain the favour of a learned man. Francis I had been trying through Budé to persuade Erasmus to settle in France, and Tunstal warned against this: 'I am a little afraid that your friends, desirous of seeing you, have in writing to you inflated the royal command the better to attract you, and have made a mountain out of a molehill.' In October 1517 Erasmus informed Budé that Tunstal, who was very ill, had returned to England, and advised him to write to him now and then, as no one was more loyal and devoted to him. However, Budé replied in December that he had nothing to write to Tunstal, as the latter had not replied to his letter of the previous May.[59]

Budé was more happily familiar with two other humanist diplomats, More and Pace. It is too often assumed that More's reputation for amiability depends exclusively on posthumous hagiographical accounts; the testimony of Erasmus and others shows that this is not so. Erasmus was always eager to commend him, and besides the famous verbal portrait he composed for Hutten in 1519 he sent an extended panegyric to John Froben.[60] As for Pace, Erasmus tell us that he resembled More like a brother. The two inspired affection as well as respect in European scholars.

More came to know a number of continental humanists through his friendship with Erasmus, his diplomatic missions and his literary works. In spring 1515 he and Tunstal went to the Netherlands to negotiate a commercial treaty. Their mission had two important consequences: More began work on *Utopia*, and both ambassadors made contact with foreign scholars. Erasmus recommended them to Peter Gillis as 'two of the best scholars in the whole of England' and advised him that any service he could do them would be worthwhile. Gillis became a firm friend of both. He and Erasmus arranged for Metsys to paint their portraits as a gift for More, and Tunstal was godfather to Gillis's child. More also met Jerome Busleyden and composed three epigrams on his house at Mechlin, his Muse and his coin collection. In October 1517 he told Erasmus that he had been greatly affected by the death of Busleyden, 'a man of uncommon erudition who showed friendship for us and for everyone'. When More returned home Tunstal stayed with Erasmus in Brussels, and spent his time collecting ancient coins and reading Erasmus's *De Copia* and Budé's *De Asse*.[61]

In autumn 1517 More accompanied Wolsey to the diplomatic conferences at Calais and Bruges. Though dissatisfied at being on embassy, More had a few consolations. He was entertained by Anthony of Bergen, the scholarly abbot of St Bertin, and he had Pace for a colleague; Erasmus envied them being together in Bruges, like Hercules and Theseus. In 1520 More was present at the Field of Cloth of Gold and the meeting of Henry VIII and Charles V at Bruges. Erasmus went to Calais to greet his English friends and patrons and More stayed with him at Bruges for a few days. Here Erasmus introduced him to Craneveld, and the two became firm friends. On his departure More gave Craneveld some Roman coins and a ring for his wife, and Craneveld thanked Erasmus for the introduction, more valuable to him than the riches of Croesus. The two met again in July 1527, when More was at Calais with Wolsey.[62]

Through Erasmus, More also became friendly with Budé and Conrad Goclenius. To Budé he sent gifts of cramp rings and dogs, as well as praise of *De Asse*. Budé, like Busleyden, contributed a letter to *Utopia*, and in August 1519 recommended Longolius to More; the French scholar was on his way to England, and planned to visit him.[63]

Besides these international friendships, there was a less pleasant aspect of the scholarly community; their readiness to enter into acrimonious controversy with each other. In 1519 Fisher argued with Jacques LeFèvre d'Etaples over the identity of Mary Magdalen. He was encouraged to write his *De Unica Magdalena* by Stephen Poncher, bishop of Paris, who was French ambassador in England in 1517. Erasmus feared that such a controversy would harm the new learning, especially as LeFèvre was already under attack from the Dominicans of Paris because they suspected him of favouring Reuchlin. Though praising Fisher's learning to Poncher, Erasmus deplored his enthusiasm for the fight. Fisher was

> a learned and pious man in all, but of such a spirit that he does not give in easily when heated in discussion. Would it had pleased heaven that he had first of all tempered his sarcasms! . . . What ill spirit is it that troubles the tranquillity of studies by polemics of this kind? How much better it is to wander in the gardens of the Muses and to live in good understanding.[64]

Erasmus himself, however, was rather throwing stones in a glasshouse, as he had been in bitter controversy with Edward Lee since 1518. Lee had taken exception to some points of interpretation in the Greek new testament, and Erasmus complained to many of his correspondents that Lee had ceased to be his friend. Lee's language to him was caustic in the extreme, and Erasmus replied vigorously in kind. It must be admitted that Erasmus feared for the future of biblical studies as well as his own safety from charges of heresy, and on the other side Lee was acutely aware of the potential dangers of the 'open bible'. The quarrel, emotional and acerbic, ended unexpectedly in June 1520 when they met by chance at Calais and shook hands by way of reconciliation.[65]

More, meanwhile, enjoyed a controversy with the French humanist Germain de Brie (Brixius) which was based on nothing more than chauvinism. Brie's *Chordigera* of 1513 was a patriotic account of the fight between the French ship *Cordelière* and the English *Regent* in August 1512 which exalted the French and derided the English. Among More's epigrams published in 1517 were a few

168 The Wandering Scholar

which attacked Brie's poem. The Frenchman replied with his *Antimorus*, and More published his *Epistola contra Brixium* and a new edition of the *Epigrammata* in 1520. The battle took a personal turn when Brie hinted — quite dangerously — that More had praised Henry VIII in order to criticise his father, and sneered that More's family concerns had hindered his studies. The battle was fought vigorously and apparently petered out inconclusively. The height of irony came in April 1520 when Erasmus and More almost simultaneously urged each other to moderation in their respective quarrels.[66]

Richard Pace's career as humanist and diplomat ended in tragedy. Pace, Erasmus said, was born for the Muses, and his friends included Pole, Lupset, Leonico and Budé, besides Erasmus himself. However, much of his time was spent on diplomatic missions, a circumstance which Polydore Vergil attributed to the jealousy of Wolsey:

> Pace was a most virtuous individual and gave upright advice in the royal council; moreover his manners were most polished, he was well-educated, musical and witty and greatly delighted the King, who willingly listened to his advice even in matters of the gravest importance. Yet the more dear he became to the King, the more hateful he was to Wolsey, who wished above all to play the chief part with the King: and so the Cardinal took the utmost care that the man should be as far distant as possible from Henry, from his home, from his native land, under the guise of fulfilling . . . diplomatic tasks.

Worse still, these strenuous and unnecessary missions caused the breakdown of Pace's mental health: 'he was worn down by being frequently sent on embassies . . . suffering from virtual exile from his native land, his mind as a result was so impaired that he shortly after began to have periods of madness.'[67]

Vergil's account is undeniably coloured by hatred of Wolsey; indiscreet criticism of the Cardinal had landed him in the Tower in 1515, and the injury rankled. However, his allegations bear some resemblance to the facts. Pace was indeed kept abroad for long periods and he found so little to occupy him that he took up literary projects. In 1522 he worked on translations of Plutarch in Rome and translated Chrysostom and Paul in Venice, besides publishing his own works and Leonico's. In 1525 in Venice he translated the psalms, and he suffered a nervous breakdown in Padua where Lupset nursed him; Erasmus blamed 'these embassies and counter-embassies'. Though judged fit enough in 1527 to be employed on divorce business he relapsed into hopeless insanity within a few years.[68]

Not all humanist diplomats were as unfortunate as Pace, and many took the chance to meet foreign scholars. On his embassy to Italy in 1527 Sir Thomas Wyatt met Castiglione and Navagero in Venice and Ghiberti and his secretary Berni in Rome. Sir Thomas Elyot, Henry's ambassador in the Netherlands in the early 1530s, met a number of friends and acquaintances of Erasmus; Anthony of Bergen, John Carandolet, Philip de Lannoy and Philip de Croy. Cranmer, the King's envoy to the Diet of Ratisbon in 1533, won praise from Zuichemus, and was entrusted by John Dantiscus with the education of a boy who remained with him until 1540. Edmund Harvel at Venice, though not an accredited ambassador, looked after English interests in the Republic and represented Henry VIII with the *Signoria*. He assisted the English students at Venice and Padua, and also tried to help Italian scholars gain patronage in England. In 1542 he sent Henry a book which Pietro Aretino had dedicated to the King, presumably in gratitude for a gift of 300 crowns and in the hope of more. Similarly in 1546 he sent a book of geometry by Niccolò Tartaglia also dedicated to Henry.[69]

Some foreign ambassadors in England were also interested in the new learning. The Venetians Giustinian and Sagudino were correspondents of Erasmus and acquaintances of More. Sagudino was present at More's house when a letter from Erasmus was read out there in June 1517, and More sent Giustinian's letters on to Erasmus. More found Giustinian an eager student of sacred literature, though very fond of scholastic 'questions', and he believed him honest, knowledgeable and very sympathetic to Erasmus. In June 1517 Sagudino was spending two hours a day reading Erasmus's *Chiliades*, while Giustinian expressed admiration for both the *Adagia* and the edition of Jerome. Some ten years later the Venetian envoy Gasparo Spinelli visited Pace at Syon and reported that he was leading 'a blessed life in that beautiful place', had made himself an excellent Chaldee and Hebrew scholar, and was busy correcting the old testament.[70]

Some of the imperial ambassadors to England were learned men. Louis de Flandres, Seigneur de Praet, was a corespondent of Erasmus, who praised him in the preface to a Chrysostom miscellany published in 1529. De Praet had been educated by the Brethren of the Common Life at Ghent and at Louvain, and he received a stream of dedications from Badius, Vives and other humanists. The German scholar Henry Cornelius Agrippa von Nettesheim was a member of the Emperor's embassy to England in 1510. He stayed with Colet at St Paul's and Stepney and studied the Pauline epistles. He was involved again in English affairs when his friend Chapuys tried to persuade him to write in support of Queen Katherine.[71]

Chapuys himself, a native of Savoy, was Charles V's ambassador to England from 1529 to 1545. He had obtained a doctorate in law from Turin, where he also pursued humanist studies and became friends with Agrippa. As ambassador of the Queen's nephew Chapuys's position was too delicate for him to associate much with English scholars, but he took note of new books, helped Erasmus secure his pension from Canterbury after Warham's death, and himself composed a humorous Latin poem on the radical English reformers. Late in life he founded a grammar school in Annecy, his birthplace, and the Collège de Savoie in Louvain.[72]

This survey of contacts between English and European scholars shows the high esteem in which English scholarship was held. Moreover, it emerges that in terms of learning England was never insular and introspective, even after the breach with Rome. The number of English scholars studying abroad did not decrease or increase significantly as the reign wore on, though a number of eminent conservatives were forced to join their evangelical brethren in exile. Despite the immense shock felt by Catholics and Protestants alike at the executions of Fisher and More, foreign scholars did not cease to laud England as a temple of the Muses, to dedicate works to Englishmen, and to seek favour and employment here.

Notes

1. A. Schillings (ed.), *Matricule de L'Université de Louvain* (10 vols., Palais des Academies, Brussels, 1952–67), vols. 3 and 4, passim.

2. P. S. and H. M. Allen, H. W. Garrod (eds), *Opus Epistolarum Des. Erasmi Roterodami* (11 vols., Clarendon Press, Oxford, 1906–47), nos. 781–7.

3. Schillings, *Matricule de Louvain*, vol. 4, p. 124; J. S. Brewer, J. Gairdner, R. H. Brodie (eds), *Letters and Papers, Foreign and Domestic of the Reign of Henry VIII* (21 vols., HMSO, London, 1862–1932), vol. 14, i, no. 389, Robert Farington to Cromwell, (28) February 1539 (hereafter cited as *L&P*). For Morison's poverty, *L&P*, vol. 10, nos. 320–2, 417–9, 661; vol. 11, nos. 101–2.

4. Allen, *Erasmi Epistolae*, no. 81, trans R. A. B. Mynors and D. F. S.

Thomson, in Wallace K. Ferguson (ed.), *The Epistles of Erasmus* (6 vols., University of Toronto Press, Toronto, Buffalo, London, 1974–82). Hereafter cited when used in quotation as 'Toronto translation'.

    5. Allen, *Erasmi Epistolae*, no. 1832. Trans. J. A. Froude, *Life and Letters of Erasmus* (Longmans & Co, London, 1894–95), p. 351.

    6. Allen, *Erasmi Epistolae*, nos. 1025, 1026, 1028, 1029, 1031, 1032.

    7. Simon Grynaeus (ed.), *Platonis Omnia Opera* (apud Ioan. Valderum, Basle, 1534), preface. See also Allen, *Erasmi Epistolae*, nos. 2459 and 2460 to Mountjoy and Vulcanius; 2526 to Pole; 2502 from Vives; and Allen's note, vol. 6, p. 245.

    8. *L&P*, vol. 3, no. 1267, Longolius to Linacre, 7 May 1521; nos. 2460 and 2465, Longolius to Pole, 22 and 25 August 1522.

    9. *State Papers Published Under the Authority of His Majesty's Commission.* Volume I, King Henry the Eighth (HMSO, London, 1830), pp. 125–7, More to Wolsey, 26 August 1523; Allen, *Erasmi Epistolae*, note on no. 1397; Erwin Doernberg, Henry VIII and Luther, *An Account of their Personal Relations* (Barrie & Rockliff, London, 1961), pp. 26, 37–40, 10.

    10. A. M. Peters, S. J., 'Richard Whitford and St Ignatius' Visit to England', *Archivum Historicum Societatis Jesu*, vol. 25 (1956), pp. 328–50.

    11. *L&P*, vol. 2, no. 3871, Geraldini to Katherine; PRO SP1/16, fo. 293 (*L&P*, vol. 2, no. 4195), Margaret of Austria to Katherine; ibid., fos. 464–9 (*L&P*, vol. 2, nos. 3774–5), Leo X to Henry and Katherine: *L&P*, vol. 2, no. 4196, Geraldini to Wolsey. For Katherine's attitude to another servant by whom she felt betrayed, Francisca de Carceres, Garrett Mattingly, *Catherine of Aragon* (Jonathan Cape, London, 1944), pp. 97–8, 121–2.

    12. Allen, *Erasmi Epistolae*, nos. 667 to Fisher, 668 to Sixtinus, 683 from More.

    13. Ibid., nos. 2232, 2825 from Phrysius.

    14. Ibid., nos. 1932 from Crucius, 2459 to Mountjoy, 2460 to Vulcanius. For Charles Blount's education, see Chapter 6 below.

    15. Gentian Hervet, *Opuscula* (Dolet, Lyons, 1541); cf. the prefaces to his *De Immensa* and *Treatise of Household*; A. W. Reed, *Early Tudor Drama* (Methuen & Co, London, 1926), p. 170; Pearl Hogrefe, Life and Times of Sir Thomas Elyot, Englishman (Iowa University Press, Iowa, 1967), pp. 232 and 387; J. A. Gee, *Life and Works of Thomas Lupset* (Yale University Press, New Haven, 1928), p. 97.

    16. William Latymer, 'A Brief Treatise or Chronicle of the Most Virtuous Lady Anne Boleyn', Bodleian Library, Oxford, MS C Don 42 fo. 27b; Bourbon, *Nugae* (Dolet, Lyons, 1538), passim; see also J.-A. Jaquot, *Notice sur Nicolas Bourbon de Vandoeuvre* (Bouquot, Troyes, 1857).

    17. *Hadrianus Junius Epistolae* (Vincent Caimax, Dordrecht, 1602), 'Vita', pp. 89 and 459. Most of these letters are without date, and so it is impossible to be precise about Junius's movements. See also G. F. Nott (ed.) *The Works of Henry Howard Earl of Surrey and of Sir Thomas Wyatt the Elder* (2 vols., Hurst Rees Orme & Brown, London, 1815–16), vol. 1, pp. xvi–xvii, lxii, 290–3.

    18. Allen, *Erasmi Epistolae*, nos. 112–13, 430, 545. See also Samuel Knight, *Life of Dean Colet* (J. Downing, London, 1724), pp. 191–3.

    19. Richard Fiddes, *Life of Cardinal Wolsey* (J. Knapton, London, 1726), pp. 198–205, 353. For the Oxford lectureships, see Chapter 1 above.

    20. A. B. Emden, *A Biographical Register of the University of Oxford, 1501–1540* (Clarendon Press, Oxford, 1974), pp. 85–6; Sir Henry Ellis (ed.), *Original Letters Illustrative of English History* (11 vols., 3 series, Harding Triphook & Lepard, London, 1824, 1827, 1846), series 3, vol. 2, p. 111, Longland to Cromwell; PRO SP1/74 fos. 80–1 (*L&P*, vol. 6, no. 75), De Burgo to Cromwell, 26 January 1533; British Library, Cotton MS Vit. B XIV 247 (*L&P*, vol. 12, ii, no. 282), Frater Nicolaus to Henry VIII, 18 July 1537.

    21. Allen, *Erasmi epistolae*, no. 515 from Gillis, 18 January 1517; Ellis, *Original*

172   *The Wandering Scholar*

Letters, series 3, vol. 1, p. 230, biographical note on Kratzer, p. 231, Tunstal to Wolsey, 15 October 1529; Fiddes, *Wolsey*, pp. 198–205; *L&P*, vol. 5, p. 305, treasurer of the chamber's accounts; Sir N. H. Nicholas (ed.), *Privy Purse Expences of Henry VIII* (William Pickering, London, 1827), p. 130; British Library, Cotton MS Vit. B XIV 276 (*L&P*, vol. 13, ii, no. 179), Kratzer to Cromwell, 24 August 1538; G. R. Elton, *Reform and Renewal* (Cambridge University Press, Cambridge, 1973), p. 17.

22. Allen, *Erasmi Epistolae*, nos. 917 to Juan de la Parra, 13 February 1519, 1222 from Vives, 10 July 1521. Henry VIII's letter is prefixed to *St Augustine of the City of God: With the Comments of J. Lud. Vives* (George Eld, London, 1610).

23. Henry de Vocht, 'Vives and his Visits to England', *Monumenta Historica Lovaniensa* (Louvain University Press, Louvain, 1934); Vives, *Opera Omnia*, G. Majansius (ed.) (8 vols., In Officina Benedicti Monfort, Valencia, 1782–90), vol. 1, p. 76, 'Vita'; ibid., vol. 7, p. 207, letter to Hector Decamious from Oxford, p. 214, letter to Claymond. For Vives's lasting reputation at Oxford, PRO SP1/82, fos. 173–4 (*L&P*, vol. 7, no. 308), Michael Drome to William Marshall, 9 March 1534.

24. Vives, *Opera*, vol. 7, pp. 208–11, letter to Giles Wallop, pp. 207–8, to Linacre, pp. 212–13 to Longland; *L&P*, vol. 4, nos. 1293, 1298, import and export licences. For Vives's *De Ratione Studii Puerilis* composed for Charles Blount, see Chapter 6 below; for Vives and Princess Mary's education, Chapter 7 below.

25. Vives, *Opera*, vol. 7, pp. 201–3, letter to Miranda.

26. Allen, *Erasmi Epistolae*, nos. 227 to Colet, 256 from Aleandro, 415 to Linacre; J. T. Sheppard, *Richard Croke, A Sixteenth Century Don* (W. Heffer & Sons, Cambridge, 1919), pp. 3, 12, 14, 15, 17; E. P. Goldschmidt, *The First Cambridge Press in its European Setting* (Cambridge University Press, Cambridge, 1955), p. 2. See also Chapter 1 above.

27. Allen, *Erasmi Epistolae*, no. 1311 to Fisher; Schillings, *Matricule de Louvain*, vol. 3, p. 597; Goldschmidt, *First Cambridge Press*, p. 58; E. L. Surtz, *Works and Days of John Fisher* (Harvard University Press, Cambridge, Mass., 1967), pp. 143–5.

28. *L&P*, vol. 1, no. 3434, Mary of France to Wolsey; Allen, *Erasmi Epistolae*, nos. 499, 607, 623; *John Palsgrave's Comedy of Acolastus*, P. L. Carver (ed.) (Early English Text Society, Oxford University Press, London, 1937), pp. xvii–xviii.

29. Allen, *Erasmi Epistolae*, nos. 1803, 1824. Coxe's life is obscure at many points; the best summary is Allen's note to no. 1803.

30. *L&P*, vol. 15, no. 733 (22) and vol. 18, i, no. 623 (69), licences to Shire and Hales; for Felymore, see Muriel St Clare Byrne (ed.), *The Lisle Letters* (6 vols., University of Chicago Press, Chicago and London, 1981), vol. 5, pp. 683–4.

31. P. S. and H. M. Allen (eds), *Letters of Richard Fox* (Clarendon Press, Oxford, 1929), no. 74 to Wotton, 2 January 1520–1. J. A. Gee thinks that 'Odoardus' is David Edwards; *Lupset*, pp. 117–18.

32. *Andrew Boorde's Introduction and Dyetary*, F. J. Furnivall (ed.) (Early English Text Society, Kegan Paul, Trench, Trubner & Co., London, 1870), p. 145. This perhaps explains why so many scholars who approached Cromwell with literary offerings were unsuccessful in their suits; for a list of these, Elton, *Reform and Renewal*, pp. 20–3.

33. Borde, *Introduction*, pp. 36–40, 59, 194, Leslie Stephen & Sidney Lee (eds), *Dictionary of National Biography* (21 vols., Smith Elder & Co, London, 1908–9), article on 'Boorde'.

34. Borde, *Introduction*, pp. 151, 194, 164–7, 173–6, 178, 221.

35. PRO SP1/24, fo. 98 (*L&P*, vol. 3, no. 2204), Daryngton to Henry Golde, 28 April 1522; *L&P*, vol. 12, ii, no. 411, grants in July 1537; Schillings, *Matricule de Louvain*, vol. 4, p. 236.

36. PRO SP1/128, fos. 113, 114 (*L&P*, vol. 13, i, nos. 98, 99), Phillips to Joy and to Bryerwood, 17 January 1538; Schillings, *Matricule de Louvain*, vol. 4, pp. 49, 116.

37. *L&P*, vol. 14, i, no. 393. Only the lower half of each page remains, so the letter is somewhat obscure.

38. John Cheke, *D. Ioannis Chrysostomi homiliae duae* (Reyner Wolfe, London, 1543), preface to Henry VIII; John Strype, *Life of the Learned Sir John Cheke* (Clarendon Press, Oxford, 1821), p. 6 and *Life of the Learned Sir Thomas Smith* (Clarendon Press, Oxford, 1820), p. 8; Mary Dewar, *Sir Thomas Smith, a Tudor Intellectual in Office* (Athlone Press, London, 1964), Chapter 2, passim.

39. For Pole's early life, education and preferments, Lodovico Beccatelli, *Life of Cardinal Reginald Pole*, Benjamin Pye (ed.), (C. Bathurst, London, 1766), pp. 13–17; Martin Haile, *Life of Reginald Pole* (Sir Isaac Pitman & Sons, London, 1910), pp. 6–7; Charles Edward Mallet, *A History of the University of Oxford* (3 vols., Methuen & Co, London, 1924, 1927), vol. 2, p. 30.

40. British Library, Cotton MS Vesp. F XIII 206b (*L&P*, vol. 4, no. 1529), Pole to Wolsey; *L&P*, vol. 4, no. 79, Clement VII to Pole; Allen, *Erasmi Epistolae*, nos. 1595 from Lupset, 1627 to Pole, 1650 from Casembroot, 1817 from Brie. See also *L&P*, vol. 4, no. 938, Bembo to Pole.

41. Allen, *Erasmi Epistolae*, nos. 1627 (introductory Note), 1817; Beccatelli, *Life of Pole*, p. 17. Some of the manuscripts owned by Pole can be identified, though none can be said with certainty to date from this first sojourn in Italy. Cf. E. Lobel, 'Cardinal Pole's Manuscripts', *Proceedings of the British Academy*, vol. 17 (1931), pp. 1–7.

42. Schillings, *Matricule de Louvain*, vol. 3, p. 592; Allen, *Erasmi Epistolae*, no. 1360 from Lupset, 21 April 1523; British Library, Cotton MS Vit. B V 234, (*L&P*, vol. 3, no. 3594), Clerke to Wolsey, 2 December 1523; ibid., Calig. D X 130 (*L&P*, vol. 4, no. 2805), Russell to Wolsey, 16 January 1527; PRO SP1/47, fos. 69–70, (*L&P*, vol. 4, nos 4022, 4216), Lupset to Wolsey, 6 March and 28 April 1528. For Wynter's letters to Wolsey, PRO SP1/47, fos. 71–2, 258–9, (*L&P*, vol. 4, nos. 4023, 4214). For his education in general, Gee, *Lupset*, pp. 103, 105–7, 110, 124, 126–31; W. Gordon Zeeveld, *Foundations of Tudor Policy* (Harvard University Press, Cambridge, Mass, 1948), pp. 60–71.

43. PRO SP1/53, fos. 127–8 (*L&P*, vol. 4, no. 5382), Wynter to Wolsey, 15 March 1529; Cf. *L&P*, vol. iv, no. 4064, Hampton to Wolsey, 13 March 1528.

44. PRO SP1/51, fos. 102–3; SP1/53 fos. 127–8 (*L&P*, vol. 4, nos. 5019, 5624), Wynter to Wolsey, 9 December 1528 and 5 June 1529.

45. John Strype, *Ecclesiastical Memorials* (3 vols., Clarendon Press, Oxford, 1820–40), vol. 1, ii, pp. 137–8, Wolsey to Gardiner, 23 July 1530; British Library Cotton MS Nero B VI 163 (*L&P*, vol. 5, no. 338), Wynter to Cromwell, 14 July 1531; *L&P*, vol. 5, no. 766 (12), licence to Thomas Wynter, the King's chaplain; *L&P*, vol. 5, Appendix 24, Wynter to Cromwell, 7 February 1532.

46. PRO SP1/73, fo. 174 (*L&P*, vol. 5, Appendix 27), Wynter to Cromwell, 18 February 1532, Paris; SP1/70, fos. 203–4 (*L&P*, vol. 5, no. 1210), Wynter to Cromwell, 2 August 1532, Padua; SP1/74, fos. 192–3 (*L&P*, vol. 6, no. 172), 20 February 1533, Padua; British Library, Cotton MS Nero B VI 122 (*L&P*, vol. 6, no. 314), Wynter to Cromwell, 7 April 1533, Padua; PRO SP1/82, fo. 247 (*L&P*, vol. 7, no. 2801), Wynter to Cromwell, 2 March 1534, Ferrara; SP1/85, fos. 54–5 (*L&P*, vol. 7, no. 964), Wynter to Cromwell, 9 July 1534; British Library, Cotton MS Nero B VII 92 (*L&P*, vol. 8, no. 132), Harvel to Starkey, 30 January 1535; PRO SP1/101, fo. 2 (*L&P*, vol. 10, no. 2), Wynter to Cromwell, 1 January 1536, London; British Library, Cotton MS Titus B I (*L&P*, vol. 12, i, no. 447), Wynter to Cromwell, 17 February 1537.

47. Nicholas Harris Nicholas, *Privy Purse Expences of Henry VIII* (William Pickering, London, 1827), p. 23; Latymer, *Brief Treatise*, fo. 28b; Zeeveld, *Tudor Policy*, pp. 62ff; PRO SP1/121, fos. 58–9 (*L&P*, vol. 12, ii, no. 39), Bekynsaw to Knight; Emden, *Biographical Register*, p. 37.

48. David Lloyd, *State Worthies*, Charles Whitworth (ed.) (J. Robson, London, 1766), pp. 225–8; Patricia Thomson, *Sir Thomas Wyatt and his Background* (Routledge and Kegan Paul, London, 1964), p. 48; Zeeveld, *Tudor Policy*, p. 99. For Mason's correspondence with Starkey, *L&P*, vol. 7, no. 945, vol. 9, no. 981; for his promotions, ibid., vol. 17, no. 1012, vol. 18, i, no. 623, vol. 20, ii, no. 910.

49. For Swerder, Elton, *Reform and Renewal*, p. 23; PRO SP1/155, fos. 53–4 (*L&P*, vol. 14, ii, no. 605), Swerder to Cromwell, 29 November 1539; *L&P*, vol. 9, no. 673, George Lily to Starkey, 23 October 1535. For Frier, Emden, *Biographical Register*, pp. 220–1; *L&P*, vol. 9, nos. 917, 1011, vol. 10, no. 321. For Voluzenus, PRO SP1/51, fos. 102–3, SP1/53 fos. 127–8 (*L&P*, vol. 4, nos. 5019, 5382), Wynter to Wolsey, 9 December 1528 and 15 March 1529; SP1/237, fo. 17 (*L&P*, Addenda, vol. 1, i, no. 731), Voluzenus to Cromwell, 12 April 1531; British Library, Cotton MS Nero B VI 20 (*L&P*, vol. 9, no. 867), Voluzenus to Starkey, 21 November 1535; PRO SP1/104, fos. 194–5 (*L&P*, vol. 10, no. 1169), Voluzenus to Cromwell, 20 June 1536. See also M. P. D. Baker-Smith, *The Writings of Florens Wilson in Relation to Evangelical Humanism* (unpublished PhD Dissertation, Cambridge, 1970), passim.

50. For Pate, Emden, *Biographical Register*, pp. 435–6; Vives, *Opera*, vol. 7, pp. 141–2. For Goldwell, PRO SP1/69, fo. 86, (*L&P*, vol. 5, no. 757), warden of Canterbury college to Cromwell; SP1/70, fo. 168 (*L&P*, vol. 5, no. 1155), Thomas Goldwell to William, 26 April 1538; SP1/132, fos. 41–2 (*L&P*, vol. 13, i, no. 935), Thomas Goldwell to William, 5 May 1538. See also Schillings, *Matricule de Louvain*, vol. 4, p. 139; Emden, *Biographical Register*, pp. 239–40; Zeeveld, *Tudor Policy*, pp. 83–4, 117.

51. *L&P*, vol. 8, no. 761, Pole to Priuli, May 1535; vol. 9, no. 1028, vol. 10, no. 945, Sandro to Starkey, 28 December 1535 and 23 May 1536.

52. *L&P*, vol. 9, no. 917, Frier to Starkey, 1 December 1535; vol. 9, no. 103, vol. 10, no. 565, Morison to Starkey, 16 August 1535 and 27 March 1536; vol. 8, no. 581, vol. 9, no. 1034, George Lily to Starkey, 22 April and 29 December 1535; vol. 9, nos. 512, 659, 1028, Sandro to Starkey, 1 October, 21 October and 28 December 1535.

53. *L&P*, vol. 9, no. 512, Sandro to Starkey, 1 October 1535, no. 673, Lily to Starkey, 23 October 1535.

54. *L&P*, vol. 5, pp. 303ff., treasurer of the chamber's accounts; PRO SP1/178, fo. 63 (*L&P*, vol. 18, i, 576), Harvel to Sir Anthony Denny, 20 May 1543; SP1/179, fo. 43 (*L&P*, vol. 18, i, no. 714) John Denny to Sir Anthony, 15 June, 1543; ibid., fo. 53 (*L&P*, vol. 18, i, no. 725), Harvel to Sir Anthony.

55. Allen, *Erasmi Epistolae*, no. 324 to Reuchlin, 1 March 1515; no. 432 from Fisher, c. 30 June 1515; no. 457 to Reuchlin, 27 August 1516.

56. Ibid., nos. 543 to More, 562 from Reuchlin, 592 from Fisher, 784 to Fisher, 457 to Reuchlin; no. 967 to Wolsey, 18 May 1519.

57. For the letters of Leonico, F. A. Gasquet, *Cardinal Pole and his Early Friends* (G. Bell & Sons Ltd, London, 1927), passim.

58. Allen, *Erasmi Epistolae*, no. 421 to Budé, c. 9 June 1516; no. 502 from More, 15 December 1516; no. 435 from Budé, 7 July 1516; *Budaei Epistolae* (apud Io. Badium Ascensium, Paris, 1531), Book 1, pp. 17b, 14b, 18b.

59. Allen, *Erasmi Epistolae*, no. 480 to Budé, 20 October 1516; no. 571 Tunstal to Budé, April 1519; no. 572 from Tunstal, 22 April 1517; no. 689 to Budé, 26 October 1517; no. 744 from Budé, 21 December 1517; no. 583 Budé to Tunstal, 19 May 1517.

60. Ibid., nos. 999 to Hutten, 635 to Froben.

61. Ibid., no. 332 to Gillis, 7 May 1515. For the Metsys portraits, nos. 515, 584, 683.

62. Ibid., nos. 683, 741, 761. For More and Craneveld, nos. 1145, 1173, 1850; Henry de Vocht, *Monumenta Humanistica Lovaniensa* (Louvain University Press, Louvain, 1928), pp. xlviii–xlix, 312 and epistles 115, 151, 156, 177, 242, 262.

63. Allen, *Erasmi Epistolae*, nos. 1220, 1223, 1765.

64. Ibid., no. 1016 to Poncher. Cf. nos. 936, 1068 to Fisher.

65. For the Erasmus–Lee controversy, ibid., nos. 886, 993–8, 1037, 1061, 1074, 1083–6, 1089–90, 1095, 1098–9. For its end, no. 1118.

66. For the More–Brie controversy, ibid., nos. 620, 1045, 1087, 1093, 1096; Hoyt Hopewell Hudson, *The Epigram in the English Renaissance* (Princeton University Press, Princeton, 1947), pp. 49–58. For More's and Erasmus's mutual exhortations to moderation, Allen, *Erasmi Epistolae*, nos. 1090, 1093.

67. Polydore Vergil, *Anglica Historia*, Denys Hay (ed.) (Camden Society, Offices of the Royal Historical Society, London, 1950), pp. 293, 329. For a parallel account of Wolsey's jealousy of More and hopes of sending him on embassy to Spain, William Roper and Nicholas Harpsfield, *Lives of St Thomas More*, E. E. Reynolds (ed.) (Everyman, London, 1963), pp. 10–12, 70–2.

68. Allen, *Erasmi Epistolae*, no. 1624 to Lupset; Jervis Wegg, *Richard Pace, a Tudor Diplomatist* (Methuen & Co, London, 1932), passim.

69. A. K. Foxwell (ed.), *The Poems of Sir Thomas Wiat* (2 vols., University of London Press Ltd, London, 1913), vol. 2, pp. vi–vii; Hogrefe, *Elyot*, p. 186; J. E. Cox (ed.), *Miscellaneous Writings and Letters of Thomas Cranmer* (Parker Society, Cambridge University Press, Cambridge, 1846), pp. 402–4; PRO SP1/173, fos. 62–3 and SP1/223, fo. 34 (*L&P*, vol. 17, no. 841 and vol. 21, i, no. 1482), Harvel to Henry VIII, 24 September 1542 and 20 August 1546.

70. On the Venetians, Allen, *Erasmi Epistolae*, nos. 461, 559, 601.

71. For de Praet, Allen, ibid., nos. 1191, 2093. For Agrippa's stay in England, Henry Morley, *Life of Henry Cornelius Agrippa von Nettesheim* (2 vols., Chapman & Hall, London, 1856), vol. 1, pp. 226–50.

72. Garrett Mattingly, 'A Humanist Ambassador', *Journal of Modern History*, vol. 4, no. 2 (June 1932), pp. 175–85; J. G. Ritz, 'Un ambasadeur de Charles-Quint à la cour d'Henry VIII', *Cahiers d'Histoire*, vol. 11, part 2 (1966), pp. 163–79.

6 The Renaissance English Gentleman

I

Although humanism is usually considered in relation to reform of the church and education of the clergy, the precepts of the new learning were also meant to apply to the education of laymen, particularly to the nobility and gentry who held positions of responsibility in society and the state. For them, learning was not to be merely ornamental, though they were expected to have all the graces of the courtier. Humanism was to inculcate piety and morality through the reading of good literature, which also furnished useful advice and good and bad examples of rulers and administrators. Consequently gentlemen should learn the tongues, and the study of rhetoric would equip them with that eloquence essential to ambassadors and ministers and admirable in courtiers. Thus for Henrician laymen humanist education could not be the exclusive preserve of scholars and churchmen.

A comparatively small number of educational treatises was available for the guidance of parents and teachers. Some were the work of foreign scholars, and could be consulted in Latin or in English translation. Two major works of Erasmus, his *Institutio Christiani Principis* and *Declamatio de Pueris Statim ac Liberaliter Instituendis*, were influential in England. Erasmus himself sent a copy of the *Christian Prince* to Henry VIII in 1517, while Elyot recommended it in *The Governor*: 'there was never book written in Latin that, in so little a portion, contained of sentence, eloquence and virtuous exhortation, a more compendious abundance.' The other treatise was partially translated into English by Richard Sherry, Master of Magdalen school. Similarly, two educational tracts by Vives were read and used in England. His *De Ratione Studii Puerilis* was published in Latin at Antwerp with a dedication to Charles Blount, son of Lord Mountjoy, and his *Introductio ad Sapientiam* was translated into English by Richard Morison, dedicated by him to Cromwell's son, and published in 1540.[1]

Works of educational theory were also produced by English scholars. Like Vives, Thomas Lupset composed an educational treatise for an individual student. This was his *Exhortation to Young*

Men, persuading them to walk in the pathway that leadeth to honesty and goodness, published in 1535 and addressed to his pupil Edmund Withypoll, son of a London merchant. Richard Pace's *De Fructu Qui Ex Doctrina Percipitur* was published at Basle in 1517, when the new learning was still fighting hostility and criticism in England. Its dedication to Colet and frequent allusions to his school indicate that it was intended as much for lay as for clerical education. Thomas Starkey's *Dialogue of Lupset and Pole*, composed in the early 1530s, contains important material about the utility of learning and the education of the nobility. Though not published until the last century, the ideas expressed in it undoubtedly received discussion in the 'Paduan' circle of humanists around Reginald Pole.[2]

The greatest English educational writer of the reign was Sir Thomas Elyot, and his *Book Named the Governor* of 1531 presents one of the most highly-developed systems of instruction produced in Europe in the period. Its numerous editions attest its influence and popularity.[3] Elyot also translated classical educational works for the benefit of his English audience. Isocrates's oration to Nicocles appeared as *The Doctrinal of Princes*, Eucolpius's account of Alexander Severus was published as *The Image of Governance*, and Elyot translated Plutarch's treatise *On the Education or Bringing Up of Children*.

These works will be discussed in the light of what they say about the application of humanist scholarship to laymen. It may be taken as read that the theorists felt that gentlemen should be concerned with the health of the body as well as of the mind and soul, and that they should master such non-academic skills as the arts of war and of the hunt, sports like fencing, wrestling and running, and music and dancing. (Indeed, Elyot went some way towards the modern image of the renaissance man by insisting that painting and carving were fit subjects for a gentleman's study.) This chapter, then, will be concerned with the academic studies of laymen, not their social and martial accomplishments.

These treatises were aimed at a noble and gentle audience, but the authors did not exclude other orders of society from education on any ground of principle. Elyot made Plutarch deny that his precepts were only for the sons of the rich; if a poor man lacked the means to follow his advice he must blame fortune, not the philosopher. Erasmus made it clear in *De Pueris* that he did not intend to keep the poor from instruction and declared that the rich should assist those who were gifted but penurious:

But, you ask me, what shall the poor do who have difficulty in feeding their children . . . ? To that I have nothing to reply except the verse of the comic poet, 'We do what we can, we cannot do what we wish'. We deliver here an excellent method of instruction, but we cannot bestow fortune.[4]

Scarcity of evidence makes it impossible to assess the impact of humanism on the non-gentle classes; though Cranmer and other school founders were concerned that provision was made for poor scholars on their establishments. (See Chapter 4 above.)

One of the first aims of the theorist was to show that education was valuable to gentlemen, and to refute those who thought otherwise. Pace in *De Fructu* told an anecdote about a nobleman with a hunting horn round his neck who angrily denounced the new learning and said that he would rather see his son hanged than a scholar. Pace's reply was straightforward:'

if some foreigner came to the King, a royal ambassador, for example, and he had to be given an answer, your son, brought up as you suggest, would only blow on his horn, and the learned country boys would be called on to answer him. They would obviously be preferred to your son, the hunter or hawker, and using the freedom that learning gives they would say to your face, 'We would rather be learned, and thanks to learning no fools, than to be proud of our stupid nobility'.

Starkey in *Lupset and Pole* was equally scathing about the values of the nobles:

First and most principal of all ill customs used in our country . . . is that which toucheth the education of the nobility, whom we see customably brought up in hunting and hawking, dicing and carding, eating and drinking, and, in conclusion, in all vain pleasure, pastime and vanity. And that only is thought to pertain to a gentleman, even as his proper fait [activity], office and duty, as though they were born thereto, and to nothing else in this world of nature brought forth.

In *The Governor* Elyot recorded the widespread opposition to the education of the gentry:

For of those persons be some which, without shame, dare affirm that to a great gentleman it is a notable reproach to be well learned and to be called a great clerk: which name they account to be of so base estimation, that they never have it in their mouths but when they speak anything in derision.[5]

Similarly, in *The Image of Governance* Elyot observed that 'many, being ignorant of good letters, do universally reprove them that be studious in learning'; he replied that 'by knowledge most chiefly, a man excelleth all other mortal creature, and thereby is most like unto God'. Vives likewise declared, 'This is the cause of most absolute wisdom, whereof the first step is to know thyself, and the last of all, to know God.' Elyot vigorously asserted the right of laymen to learning in his *Preservative Against Death*, dedicated to his friend Sir Edward North. North was a busy man, constantly serving the King as chancellor of the court of augmentations, but 'at the least way, either by day or by night, Martha shall find opportunity to sit down by her sister; if not she shall find but little thank for all her good housewifery'.[6]

Erasmus declared in *De Pueris* that without education a man was not truly a man, but a monster or beast in a man's body. For Vives studies had a good effect on man's behaviour and helped him bear the vicissitudes of fortune:

Nothing can be imagined more pleasant than the knowledge of many things, few or none more fruitful than the intelligence of virtue. Studies be of such efficacy and strength that they temper prosperity, they mitigate adversity, they keep under the hasty and rash motions of youth, they delight and comfort crooked and painful age, being with us at home. Abroad, in public and private business, when we are alone, when we be accompanied in idleness, in labours, never absent, but always ready to help and aid us.[7]

An increase in lay learning would also be good for the kingdom at large. Thus Elyot in the preface to the second edition of his *Dictionary* in 1542 praised Henry VIII for exhorting the young nobility and gentry to study, as this would benefit the whole community.

A theme which recurs in all these works is that true nobility does not depend on land, riches, titles or genealogy but on virtue, which was implanted and nourished by education: *generositas virtus non sanguis*. This does not imply egalitarianism, however; the aim was to improve the existing nobility, not to replace it with a learned meritocracy.[8]

The theorists agreed on several practical points. The child was to be taken from the company of women as soon as possible, lest he be over-indulged or his character tainted by frivolity and wantonness.[9] His education was to begin at an early age. Erasmus advised that he commence at three or four years by learning proper speech and pronunciation. Elyot in *The Governor* argued against Quintilian that children should begin their education before the age of seven. They should not be forced to it by violence, but their letters should be drawn attractively for them. As for grammar, there were many good works for both Latin and Greek which were suitable for a young child. A father should not shrink from instructing his own son, as the Emperor Augustus had not disdained to do so.

Whether or not the child benefited from parental teaching, the choice of a tutor was a crucial matter. Elyot was scathing about those who were influenced in this respect by avarice, and who took more care choosing a falconer than a teacher: 'if they hire a schoolmaster to teach in their houses, they chiefly enquire with how small a salary he will be contented, and never do ensearch how much good learning he hath, and how among well learned men he is therein esteemed.' Erasmus used violent language about such negligent parents, calling them worse than infanticides: 'May heaven make less numerous those who spend more on a diseased prostitute than on the education of a son.' In *The Christian Prince* he stressed that the tutor should be morally upright as well as of impeccable scholarship, a man

> of good character, unquestioned principles, serious, of long experience and not merely learned in theories — to whom advancing years provide deep respect; purity of life; prestige; sociability and an affable manner, love and friendship . . . Such a man should the future prince's tutor be (as Seneca elaborately sets forth), that he can scold without railing, praise without flattering, be revered for his stainless life, and loved for his pleasing manner.

Elyot painted a similar picture of learning and rectitude:

such a master as is excellently learned both in Greek and Latin, and therewithal is of sober and virtuous disposition, specially chaste of living, and of much affability and patience: lest by any unclean example the tender mind of the child may be infected, hard afterward to be recovered . . . Also by a cruel and irous master the wits of children be dulled; and that thing for the which children be oftentimes beaten is to them ever after fastidious.

Vives was insistent on the respect due a teacher. In the *Introduction to Wisdom* he expatiated on the debt the pupil owed his master, and in *De Ratione Studii* he urged the child to love, honour and emulate his tutor:

By obeying his precepts closely and modestly, and by observing, honouring him in all he says or does, or esteems in life or speech, so act that he will feel that you also approve it. If he disapproves anything, then do you also shun it. Listen to him intently — to his words, his forms of speech, note down his opinions, and make yourself as far as possible like him; take him for example, because when the teacher shall see this he will take pains that you shall not possibly receive from him anything which would be unworthy of imitation.[10]

Having settled the question of the tutor the theorists addressed themselves to methods of teaching and works to be read. Here, it is best to consider each author individually, as each had a different objective in writing and their treatises took different forms, varying from detailed schemes of instruction to simple lists of precepts.

Vives's *De Ratione Studii Puerilis* (Plan of Boys' Studies) was addressed to Charles Blount, but its immediate publication shows that it was a general treatise rather than a private letter of advice. Vives began with some salutary religious precepts:

Since wisdom, virtue and knowledge come from God alone, it is fitting that the first entrance to all these should be through God, towards whom it behoves thee always to comport thyself with the greatest piety, and in his affairs to bear a most religious mind, nor to carry out any work of his in a light, sluggish or perfunctory manner. Since God does not give his gifts to idle people, there is need of labour and diligence in the pursuit of letters and virtue.

The boy should cultivate the art of memory and make notes on Latin vocabulary in a paper book. Only the best modern Latin grammars should be used, such as those by Aldo and Nebrissensis. He should take notes from his reading and from what his tutor said, and in more formal writing was to practise his literary style. He must not be afraid to ask questions, and should engage in friendly rivalry with his schoolfellows.

The student's Latin vocabulary was to be increased by reading. Terence was good for words useful in daily conversation, as were Erasmus's colloquies and the letters of Cicero, the younger Pliny, Poliziano and other ancient and modern writers. Histories — by Livius, Suetonius, Tacitus, Caesar and Sallust — were primarily valuable for building up knowledge of language and fluency, while agricultural writers like Cato and Columella were useful for specialised vocabulary, as was the architect Vitruvius.

Poetry was to be considered:

Poets are also to be studied for the sake of the mind; for they often relieve the tedium of business, and of the reading of unfettered speech. This alternation of verse and prose keeps the mind intent on studies for a longer time . . . The poets are in invention sublime, pleasant, keen, weighty, facile; in words sweet, charming, gay. They raise up every emotion as the occasion demands.

Virgil was the finest, and Horace, Seneca, Silius Italicus and Lucan were also recommended. Besides the Roman classics, Christian poets like Prosper, Prudentius and Juvencus should be read for the sake of piety as well as style.

The boy should learn Greek as well as Latin:

To the one who has acquired the knowledge of the Greek tongue, the fountains of all branches of learning stand open, for these have issued from the Greeks. He is admitted to the knowledge of the greatest minds in which Greece was always so prolific. Moreover, his copiousness of Latin speech is deeper founded.

Following Quintilian, Vives thought that Greek and Latin letters should be learned simultaneously, and that the pupil should gain his first knowledge of Greek vocabulary by hearing his teacher read short works such as those of Aesop and Isocrates. His own reading should begin with the orators — Aristotle, Isocrates, Demosthenes and part of Lucian. Philosophical works by Plato, Aristotle, Xenophon and Theophrastus should be next studied, and then the historians Thucydides and Plutarch. Finally, the poets should be tackled, beginning with the Attic writers because they were the easiest. In order, the boy should read Aristophanes, Homer ('the fountain of the rest'), Euripides and Sophocles. He should use a lexicon and a Latin–Greek dictionary, and should compare the Greek originals with Latin translations.

Some of the precepts and instructions of *De Ratione Studii* are echoed in Vives's *Introduction to Wisdom*, though this second work is more concerned with moral and religious guidance than with directions for study. There are, for example, chapters on religion and on Christ which warn of the limitations of human achievement: 'All human wisdom, compared with Christ's religion, is but dirt and very foolishness'; 'Perfect wisdom is to know this religion and to live according to it is perfect virtue.' Everything good in pagan literature is found more purely, rightly, openly and easily in Christian writings. Scripture should not be used for jokes or bawdy tales, and the reader should be present when the word of God was read and preached. The chapter on speech and communication is not concerned with wit or elegance of diction, but with the avoidance of flattery, anger and spite, and the need to bridle the tongue.

Indeed, even the practical advice to the student in this work has a strongly didactic flavour. He should carry his paper book with him at all times, so as to note down any wise sayings he might hear. He should avoid 'lewd authors' and beware of the religious opinions of pagan and heretical authors. He should exercise his memory and avoid arrogance, which hinders study, and he should write letters as an academic exercise every second or third day.[11]

Lupset's *Exhortation to Young Men*, dedicated to his pupil Edmund Withypoll, was composed in 1529 but not published until 1535, some six years after his death; thus it is a rather more personal document than Vives's *De Ratione Studii*. According to the *Exhortation*, care of the soul was man's first concern, and Lupset recommended that his pupil read scripture and the fathers. He also foreshadowed Elyot in urging Withypoll not to inquire into doctrine, but to be meekly devout:

take in your hands the new testament and read it with a due reverence. For I would not have you in that book forget with whom you talk. It is God that there speaketh, it is you, a poor creature of God, that readeth. Consider the match, and meek down your wits. Presume not in no case to presume that you understand aught; leave devising thereupon; submit yourself to the expositions of holy doctors; and ever conform your consent to agree with Christ's church. This is the surest way that you can take before God and man. Your obedience to the universal faith shall excuse you before God, although it might be in a false belief; and the same obedience shall also keep you out of trouble in this world.[12]

Such a vigorous assertion of orthodoxy is an apt reminder that English humanism was not invariably evangelical. Withypoll should choose the fathers Chrysostom and Jerome as commentators on the gospel, not the schoolmen. Aristotle's *Ethics* was the work next in importance to scripture and the fathers.

For moral philosophy he should also read Cicero's *De Officiis*, *De Fato*, *De Senectute* and other works, besides Seneca, 'of whom ye shall learn as much of virtue as man's wit can teach you'. Withypoll should also 'let Plato be familiar with you, specially in the books he writeth *De re publica*', and he should read Erasmus's *Enchiridion*, 'a work doubtless, that in few leaves containeth an infinite knowledge of goodness'. He was to read no religions or philosophical books but these.

Lupset offered practical advice on care of the body, recommending that Withypoll read Galen's *De bona valetudine tuenda*. Friends were a great worldly treasure, as Withypoll would learn from Cicero's *De Amicitia*. Xenophon's *Oeconomia* was recommended for housekeeping, and Aristotle's *Politics* for the upbringing of children. Anger — an enemy to prosperity — should be kept in check, and Plato and Seneca would help Withypoll achieve this.

Piety, however, was the paramount concern, and once more Lupset exhorted his pupil to an unquestioning and devout orthodoxy:

Go you forth your way after the meek steps of a true Christian man . . . For under the cloak of obedience, chance what chance shall, your soul is ever sure for taking any hurt . . . Leave, therefore, my good Edmund, all manner of meddling, and pray to God to accept your obedience. Pray also bitterly, that his will may be fulfilled in this world among us, as the angels fulfill it in heaven. Thus pray, and meddle no further. For I assure you, it is so to be done.[13]

Elyot's *Governor* laid down an extremely detailed plan of instruction which was to last from infancy to maturity. Like Vives, Elyot believed that Greek and Latin should be learned simultaneously:

> And if a child do begin therein at seven years of age, he may continually learn Greek authors three years, and in the meantime use the Latin tongue as a familiar language: which in a nobleman's son may well come to pass, having none other persons to serve him or keeping him company, but such as can speak Latin elegantly.[14]

Elyot warned that grammar lessons should not be too prolonged or tedious, lest they discourage the child from learning, 'For a gentle wit is therewith soon fatigate.' The young child should read Aesop's fables for their moral as well as their linguistic value. He might read some of Lucian's dialogues, but care must be taken in selecting them; 'it were better that a child should never read any part of Lucian than all Lucian.' Aristophanes's comedies might be substituted, and as they were metrical they could easily be learned by heart.

Homer was an extremely important author, but very long for a child, so one of Virgil's works should be read at the same time for variety: 'this noble Virgil, like to a good nurse, giveth to a child, if he will take it, everything apt for his wit and capacity; wherefore he is in the order of learning to be preferred before any other author Latin.' Elyot also recommended Ovid's *Metamorphosis* and *Fasti*, but since they were both long and complex the tutor might substitute Horace, 'in whom is contained much variety of learning and quickness of sentence'. Lucan and Silius Italicus were also suitable, and the pupil might be encouraged to write poetry himself:

> And if the child were induced to make verses by the imitation of Virgil and Homer, it should minister to him much delectation and courage to study. Nor the making of verses is not discommended in a nobleman, since the noble Augustus and almost all the old emperors made books in verses.

This rather formidable programme was to last until the child reached 14, after which studies became more complex.[15] Firstly, the child should study logic and rhetoric from Cicero, Rudolph Agricola, Quintilian, Isocrates and Erasmus. Elyot stressed the value of rhetoric for nobles and gentlemen:

> The utility that a nobleman shall have by reading these orators is that, when he shall hap to reason in council, or shall speak in a great audience, or to strange ambassadors of great princes, he shall not be constrained to speak words sudden and disordered, but shall bestow them aptly and in their places.

However, eloquence in Latin without true learning was worthless:

> There be many nowadays in famous schools and universities which be so much given to the study of tongues only, that when they write epistles they seem to the reader that, like to a trumpet, they make a sound without any purpose, whereunto men do harken more for the noise than for any delectation that thereby is moved.

The boy must study cosmography and then history, which was a most valuable discipline. The tutor should show his pupil 'what incomparable delectation, utility and commodity shall happen to emperors, kings, princes and all other gentlemen by reading of histories'. The recommended authors were Titus Livius, Xenophon, Quintus Curtius, Sallust and Caesar. All these gave good and bad examples of character and conduct, and practical instruction in the arts of peace and war. Thus they were useful to those who held office in the state.

Finally, at the age of 17 the pupil should study moral philosophy. Aristotle's *Ethics* should be read to him in Greek (as there was no good translation available), and he should read Cicero's *De Officiis*. Above all, 'the works of Plato would be most studiously read when the judgment of a man is come to perfection.' The mature man should also read Solomon's Proverbs, Ecclesiastes and Ecclesiasticus with the historical parts of the bible; but the rest, especially the new testament, was 'to be reverently touched, as a celestial jewel or relic, having the chief interpreter of those books true and constant faith, and dreadfully to set hands thereon'.[16]

Elyot's translation of Plutarch's treatise on education contains useful precepts and guidelines for parents. Children were taught by exhortation, reasoning and judicious praise, not by beating. The faculty of memory should be developed, and history was an important study: 'verily, remembrance of affairs done in time past is an example and mirror, the better to consider things to come.' Eloquence, which saved Ulysses from the Cyclops, was invaluable. Education should not stop when a boy came of age, because while the faults of children were easily corrected young adults were prone to more grievous sins. Learning, however, would implant and develop virtue: 'Therefore truly the thing that in us is divine and immortal is learning.'

Remarks on education appear in Elyot's other works. *The Image of Governance* contrasted the career of Heliogabalus, eventually deposed and murdered because of his 'lascivious and remiss education', with that of the successful Alexander Severus, who learned Greek and Latin grammar and literature; wrote Greek verses and enjoyed music; excelled in geometry, arithmetic and astronomy; and wrote the lives of good princes in verse. *The Doctrinal of Princes* furnished advice about study. Once more, history was particularly valuable. The importance of the prince's education for the good of the whole realm and the consequent responsibility of his tutor were emphasised, though the prince was also responsible for his own instruction. Philosophy was perhaps the best study for a prince:

> If thou wouldst perfectly know that which belongeth to kings to perceive, give thee to experience and study of philosophy. For philosophy shall declare unto thee the means or ways how to bring to pass thine affairs; experience in semblable business shall make thee able to do or sustain them.

Elyot, like Erasmus, hoped for the Platonic ideal of the philosopher–king, brought into being by humanist study. Indeed, Erasmus's *Institutio Christiani Principis* was designed to teach princes about their duties. It also contained practical advice about the instruction of a ruler which could apply to men of lesser rank.

Since most princes were born for rule rather than elected, it was their tutors' responsibility to see that they were thoroughly trained in virtue and in the arts of government. The child prince must be kept away from corrupt and frivolous company and from flatterers, and should get used to his duties at an early age. He should learn virtue through fables, especially those of Aesop, and through myths:

When he has learned with pleasure the story of Phaeton, the teacher should show that he represents a prince, who while still headstrong with the ardour of youth, but with no supporting wisdom, seized the reins of government and turned everything into ruin for himself and the whole world. When he has finished the story of the Cyclops, who was blinded by Ulysses, the teacher should say in conclusion that the prince who has great strength of body, but not of mind, is like Polyphemus.[17]

Christian religion, however, was the most important aspect of the prince's education:

Before all else the story of Christ must be firmly rooted in the mind of the prince. He should drink deeply of his teachings, gathered in handy texts, and then later from those very fountains themselves [the gospels], whence he may drink more purely and more effectively. He should be taught that the teachings of Christ apply to no one more than to the prince.

Erasmus, like Vives, stressed that undesirable books should be excluded. Romances about Arthur or Lancelot should be avoided, for example, not only because they concerned tyrants but because they were poorly written, stupid and superstitious. Non-Christian works must be treated with caution:

the prince must be forearmed with an antidote, after this fashion: he whom you are reading is a pagan; you who are reading, are a Christian. Although he speaks with authority on many subjects, yet he by no means gives an accurate picture of the good prince. Look out that you do not chance upon something in his works which you think you must therefore imitate directly. Measure everything by the Christian standard.[18]

The prince should begin his reading with Solomon's Proverbs, Ecclesiasticus and Wisdom; biblical books which Elyot reserved for maturity. After these he should read Plutarch's *Apothegmata*, *Morals* and *Lives*, the works of Seneca, Aristotle's *Politics* and Cicero's *De Officiis*. Plato was the most important source for statecraft. The classical historians should be read, but with great reservation: Xenophon, Herodotus, Sallust and Livius were pagans, and the heroes they celebrated were often bad examples for a Christian prince. He should exercise equal discretion with the old testament:

> The prince should have thorough warning that not all of the things he reads in the holy scriptures are to be straightway imitated. Let him learn that the battles and the butcheries of the Hebrews, and their barbarity towards their enemies, are to be interpreted allegorically; otherwise it would be most disastrous to read them. One course was allowed that people because of the standards of the time; quite a different one is laid down for the heaven-blessed Christian peoples.[19]

Thus the prince was to read widely but with discrimination, to model himself on the good examples in literature and take warning from the bad ones.

Erasmus's *Declamatio de Pueris* concerned the education of very young children. Erasmus exhorted parents not to be parsimonious about spending money on education, warned that true honour lay in culture, not riches, and adjured them to avoid cruelty, which discouraged children from learning. Again, the child should learn philosophy and morality from Aesop's fables and from myths; the story of Circe, for example, taught that man without reason was a beast. He should also, like Elyot's young pupil, study bucolic poems and comedies.[20]

Pace's *De Fructu*, like these works of Erasmus, was more a defence of education than a plan of studies. Pace sang the praises of all the arts, including music. The value of philosophy was summed up succinctly: 'the benefit therefore of this branch of learning is extremely rich, though it can be expressed in a few words: it teaches us on every occasion to seek out honour, avoid disgrace, flee from evil, and pursue virtue.' Similarly, Pace observed simply that without Greek no one was truly learned. Rhetoric was important because eloquence ensured immortality through the praise accorded it, and also persuaded the hearer to virtue and dissuaded him from evil. Christ used eloquence to build his church on earth, and Paul, Augustine and Jerome were eloquent.[21]

Pace gave useful advice about the method of learning. The student should read only the best authors and should heed the old adage, 'Read not many, but much.' Plutarch was especially useful because he wrote about so many kinds of knowledge. Following the younger Pliny, Pace advised that the student practise composition by imitating the ancients and arguing against the best authors; if he won the argument he would earn praise, if he lost he would at least have learned something. Following Quintilian, Pace recommended translation from Greek to Latin and vice versa, and like Vives, he advised the student to write epistles as a literary exercise. If he wanted a rest he might write a song, but he should keep it short as this was only really suitable for those who wished to become poets.[22]

These, then, were the educational handbooks available to Henrician gentlemen. The educated layman should, in theory, have a thorough knowledge of Greek and Latin and have read scripture, the classics and modern humanist writings. He should study eloquence and cultivate a good literary style, and he might also compose poetry. There are some interesting omissions from these treatises. None of them mentions the study of Hebrew. This may be due simply to the lack of qualified teachers, who were scarce even in the universities, but it might also reflect the belief that laymen need have nothing to do with theology and so Hebrew was unnecessary to them. A rather surprising omission is the mention of modern languages. True, Erasmus expressed a certain contempt for the vernacular, yet Elyot was deeply concerned to enrich English and use it as the medium for scholarly works. In reality, many gentlemen knew French and some learned Italian and Spanish. Indeed, the real renaissance gentleman was a somewhat different creature from the one depicted by the theorists.

II

To what extent did Henrician laymen follow the precepts of the humanist educators? Numerous contemporary satires complained that court life left little time for study. Thus, for example, Alexander Barclay's *Miseries of Courtiers*:

> But as for courtiers, as well early as late
> Be of this pleasure utterly private [deprived].
> Though they live idle, their pains infinite
> To godly works them granteth no respite.
> Alway in clamour remain they, and in press,
> And lewd acquaintance will them no time release.
> But if that they choose some season secretly
> To some good study their minds to apply,

To write or read, anon some wretch is fain
And glad them to vex and to disturb again.
But if all other be absent and at rest
The near their chamber the kitchen clerk is prest,
Jangling his counters, chatting himself alone;
Thus seek all corners quiet, thou findest none.
So must one despise those noble orators,
The famous poets and excellent doctors,
And live among men a-void of virtues all,
That rather a man rude beasts may them call.[23]

Even so, some humanists at court tried to continue their reading. Erasmus worried about the health of John Clement, who spent long hours in study after working hard in Wolsey's service, and he fretted about Mountjoy. He told Charles Blount in 1530:

in one respect I should not wish you to be too like your parent. He is wont day after day to pore over books from dinner to midnight, with some inconvenience to his wife and lackeys, and no little grumbling among the servants; and, although he has been able to do so up to this time without loss of health, I do not deem it prudent for you to play the same game, which may not turn out so lucky in your case.

As chamberlain to Katherine of Aragon and holder of other royal offices Mountjoy was certainly kept busy, but he pursued his studies with zeal. Ammonio dedicated a printed collection of poems to him in 1511, contrasting his austerity of life and passion for study with the idle amusements of the majority of nobles and praising Mountjoy's enthusiasm for philosophy and history.[24]

Mountjoy was assiduous in choosing tutors for Charles. Between 1522 and 1527 John Crucius of Louvain filled this position. He was apparently succeeded by Peter Vulcanius of Bruges, a graduate of Louvain and former pupil of Erasmus. Vulcanius was himself an excellent teacher and Charles advanced rapidly under his guidance. Erasmus praised Charles's skill in Latin and congratulated Mountjoy on having such a son. Charles himself later tried to engage Ascham as secretary to himself and tutor to his son James, though the attempt was unsuccessful.[25]

At some point Charles Blount was taught with other sons of courtiers by John Palsgrave, whose grammar *L'Eclaircissement de la*

Langue Française of 1530 contained a letter from Andrew Bainton, son of Sir Edward, to 'the right noble and excellent young gentlemen, my lord Thomas Howard, my lord Gerald and Master Charles Blount, son and heir to the Lord Mountjoy, his late school-fellows'. 'My lord Gerald' was probably 'Silken Thomas', a later tenth Earl of Kildare, who was born in 1513 and spent much of his life in England. An inventory of his father's books reveals a surprising catholicity of taste, from schoolmen like Hugh of Vienne and medieval chronicles and romances to the fathers, classics, More's *Utopia*, Henry VIII's answer to Luther, and Latin and French scriptures. The Thomas Howard addressed here must be the son of the second Duke of Norfolk, who was also tutored by John Leland at Lambeth before his father's death in 1524. Anne Boleyn's French protégé Bourbon was appointed by her to teach Henry Carey, Henry Norris and Thomas Howard. This could be the pupil of Palsgrave, though equally it could be his nephew Thomas, son of the third Duke and brother of Surrey.[26]

Thomas More is justly famous for the education he gave his children. They were taught by a number of humanists, including Erasmus's friend William Gonnell, John Clement and Nicholas Kratzer. There seems to be no foundation for the legend that More's only son was an imbecile. More himself spoke favourably of his son's abilities, and in 1523 John received from Erasmus the dedication of Ovid's *Nux*. In 1533 he assisted his father in the literary battle against heresy by translating Nausea's *Sermon of the Sacrament of the Altar*. John More's sole disadvantage was the fact that he was over-shadowed by his brilliant father and extraordinary sisters.[27]

A man similar to More in his care for the children in his charge was Sir Humphrey Wingfield. In *Toxophilus* Ascham expressed his gratitude to Wingfield, who had brought him up:

> to whom next god I ought to refer for his manifold benefits bestowed on me, the poor talent of learning which God hath lent me . . . Would God all England had used or would use to lay the foundation of youth after the example of this worshipful man, in bringing up children in the book and the bow.[28]

Thomas Cromwell took immense pains over the education of his son Gregory, though the boy's studies were not always conducted along humanist lines. As a small boy in the 1520s Gregory was brought up by Margaret Vernon, prioress of the Benedictine house of Little Marlow, Buckinghamshire; though Erasmus in *De Pueris* expressed disgust at the practice of putting nuns in charge of the education of boys. On one occasion she told Cromwell that the tutor, Copland, gave a Latin lesson each morning to Gregory and to Nicholas Sadler. Another time she reported that 'your son is in good health and is a very good scholar, and can construe his Pater Noster, Ave and Creed. I doubt not but at your coming next to me you shall like him very well'. Another letter concerned a priest Cromwell had promised to send as a teacher. Margaret recommended a friend of her own, William Inglefield, MA and fellow of Lincoln college, Oxford. She would prefer him to be appointed because of her own interest in Gregory's education:

> good Master Cromwell, if it like you to call unto your remembrance, you have promised me that I should have the governance of your child till he be twelve years of age . . . and if he should have such a master which would disdain if I meddled, then it would be to me great unquietness, for I assure you if you sent hither a doctor of divinity, yet will I play the smatterer.[29]

In 1531 Gregory was at Bromehill, a living which belonged to Christ's, Cambridge, in the charge of Roland Lee. He had schoolfellows there, for in January Lee wrote to Cromwell 'among a houseful of children, God help'. In December, he wrote from Ashden that 'your little man is merry, thanked be God, and not only well and cleanly kept but also profits in his learning'. During the next few years Gregory was apparently under the occasional tuition — or at least, supervision — of Henry Lockwood, promoted Master of Christ's in 1531 by Cromwell. Indeed, in 1532 Lockwood hinted at a benefice Cromwell might help him to, adding the inducement that 'Gregory might lie of it, that I might see to his tuition'.[30] Gregory sometimes resided at Christ's, but about 1535 he was taught elsewhere by Henry Dowes.

Dowes's two letters to Cromwell provide a detailed account of Gregory's education, which was sadly not far advanced. In a letter dated 6 September Dowes regretted that 'summer was spent in the service of the wild goddess' (Diana, patron of hunting), but reassured Cromwell by describing Gregory's studious routine. After hearing mass in the morning he would read Erasmus's colloquy *Pietas puerilis*, 'wherein is described a very picture of one that should be virtuously brought up'. Dowes had made an English translation of this for Gregory, 'so that he may confer them both together', whereof (as learned men affirm) cometh no small profit'; Vives, one might recall, expected Charles Blount to compare Greek texts with Latin translations. For the rest of the day Gregory would practice his handwriting, read Fabian's Chronicle in English, play upon the lute and virginals, and go hunting, shooting and hawking.

By the following April Gregory's programme had expanded greatly. Dowes spoke of the ripeness and maturity of his wit which, he tactfully told Cromwell, was not 'of that hasty sort that by and by do bring forth their fruit' but 'doth daily grow to a more docility and apt readiness to receive that that shall be showed him by his teachers'. His plan of studies, 'as the hours limited for the French tongue, writing, playing at weapons, casting of accounts, pastimes of instruments and such others', had been devised by Master Southwell who, with Vallence the French tutor (who may also have taught the young Earl of Lincoln) now assisted Dowes. Southwell spent a lot of time teaching Gregory the correct pronunciation of English, and a healthy spirit of competition — as recommended by the humanist educators — was maintained in the classroom. Altogether, things were going so well that Dowes hoped for a profitable summer: 'whereas the last Diana, this shall (I trust) be consecrated to Apollo and the Muses, to their no small profit and your good contentation and pleasure.'[31]

Gregory received dedications to three humanist works: Voluzenus's version of Cicero's *Dream of Scipio*; Morison's translation of Vives's *Introduction to Wisdom*; and David Clapham's translation of Agrippa's *Commendation of Matrimony*. The translators were doubtless looking to Thomas Cromwell rather than his son, but these books were probably intended to be used in the instruction of Gregory. Three letters from Gregory to his father survive which are brief, in English, devoid of literary allusion and conventional in the expression of filial piety. In 1539 Dowes sent his pupil an account of William Jerome's recantation sermon; this, too, is in English, but presumably Dowes expected Gregory to appreciate Jerome's reference to scripture, Augustine, Homer, Cicero and Demosthenes.[32]

George Brooke, Lord Cobham sent his sons abroad for their education. In February 1540 Lord Lisle heard that Cobham had intended to send two sons to Germany with the chancellor of the Duke of Cleves, but that Cromwell — possibly worried about the diplomatic situation — had refused to allow them to go. However in

July 1541 William, the eldest son, was granted a safe-conduct to go overseas 'for his further increase of virtue and learning'. Before he left for Louvain university his father gave him a set of instructions which were both sententious and practical, and which would have delighted the humanist theorists.

Each morning William was to say his prayers and — despite the breach with Rome — 'to hear mass devoutly upon your knees and pray fervently at that time'. He was 'to apply your learning diligently, and that of your own mind without any compulsion; your learning shall be the civil law, rhetoric and Greek'. Moreover he was 'to be obedient in all points to your tutor, and to do nothing without his advice and counsel'. He was to play on the lute and other instruments, send frequent letters to his father, and note and use the best customs of the country. Cobham's final precept, though worthy of Polonius, was apt for a Henrician gentleman: 'Item, to take heed that you do not speak to think.'

Cobham's younger son George was in Venice by January 1546. Edmund Harvel told his father:

> Your son is with a man of singular honesty and learning, and that taketh great care to see him profit as well in the tongues both Latin, Greek and Italian as also in civil and virtuous customs; not doubting but your lordship shall have cause to rejoice greatly at his education in these parts.[33]

Sir Thomas Wyatt expressed his concern with his son's education and well-being in two letters of advice, written in 1537 when he was abroad on embassy. The letters do not lay down any plan of study for the younger Thomas, but they recall the moral emphasis of educational writers like Erasmus, Vives and Elyot.

Like the theorists Wyatt emphasised the importance of good and bad example. Thomas was to avoid temptation to do wrong by imagining himself in the presence of some honest man like his grandfather Sir Henry Wyatt, his father-in-law Sir William Hawte, or Sir John Russell. Conversely, he might learn from Wyatt's own tumultuous career: 'I may be a near example unto you of my folly and unthriftness that hath, as I well deserved, brought me into a thousand dangers and hazards, enmities, hatreds, prisonments, despites and indignations.' Thomas should study the moral philosophers, especially Seneca and Epictetus, and above all must remember God, respect his fellows and imitate honest men:

Begin therefore betimes, make God and goodness your foundations. Make your examples of wise and honest men; shoot at the
mark; be no mocker — mocks follow them that delight therein. He
shall be sure of shame that feeleth no grief in other men's shames.
Have your friends in a reverence and think unkindness to be the
greatest offence.

Whether or not Thomas followed his father's precepts, he preserved
both letters carefully.[34]

Thus a number of gentlemen were actively concerned with their
sons' education. Interest in learning was far from universal,
however, and despite the propaganda of the humanist theorists the
status of tutors remained low. 'Teaching representeth the authority
of a prince', said Elyot in *The Governor*, but the Dutch scholar
Junius experienced discourtesy and lack of respect for learning while
he was tutor in the Howard household. One Taylor, preceptor to the
Marquess of Exeter's son, actually fled to Louvain rather than
continue his duties. According to John Hutton, who tracked him
down:

> the cause of his so sudden departing was to avoid further displea-
> sure, for he, obeying your lordship's and my lady's
> command[ment] in ministering correction to my lord your son,
> was threatened by certain young gentlemen of your lordship's
> household, and put in such fear that he durst no longer to
> remain.[35]

Such instances of intimidation were probably quite common.

How widespread was knowledge of the tongues among English
laymen? Given the dearth of qualified teachers, it seems unlikely
that any gentleman mastered Hebrew. More, like his clerical friend
Fisher, was interested in the trial of Reuchlin, but it is doubtful that
he knew Hebrew.

Scarcity of teachers may also explain why few gentlemen learned
Greek. However More, like William Lily, certainly knew it, was the
translator of some of Lucian's dialogues, and ensured that his
children learned Greek. Elyot, a friend of More though not necessarily a formal student in his 'school', also knew Greek. He translated Isocrates directly from the Greek, and though his version of
Plutarch's work on education was taken from a Latin translation by
Guarino da Verona, Elyot's edition seems to show knowledge of the

original. Other gentlemen-scholars were more circuitous, and probably had little or no knowledge of Greek. Wyatt translated Plutarch's *Quiet of Mind* for Katherine of Aragon from Budé's Latin version, while Lord Morley took his translation of Plutarch's *Life of the Good King Agesilaus* from a Latin version.

Knowledge of humanist Latin was much more frequent among English laymen and became increasingly so as the reign progressed. Mountjoy, who had been Erasmus's pupil in Paris, was proficient in Latin, and his son learned it. More, of course, was fluent, and his children were noted Latinists. Elyot made translations from Latin, while Morley translated a wide variety of Latin works by Aquinas, Anselm, Turrecremata, Seneca, Plutarch, Athanasius and Boccaccio.[36] Cromwell's correspondence shows that he, too, was fluent in Latin, though it is impossible to corroborate John Foxe's story that he mastered the language — and was converted from wickedness — by reading Erasmus' *Novum Instrumentum* on his youthful travels. Sir Thomas Boleyn probably read Latin, since he owned a printed copy of Martial's *Epigrams* and commissioned three works from Erasmus. It seems unlikely that he could write it, however; his correspondence with Erasmus was conducted by a secretary, and a personal postscript to one letter is in English. Boleyn's son George understood Latin but his proficiency is questionable. He told a corespondent, 'I do not direct my other letters to the bishop of Worcester nor Sir Gregorio [Casale], because I can neither write Latin nor Italian well.' Similarly Sir Francis Bryan, sent on embassy to France, was ordered to leave serious negotiation to his clerical partner Dr Foxe, as his Latin was not adequate for the complexities of diplomatic bargaining.[36]

On the other hand Henry Howard, Earl of Surrey, was able to write as well as read Latin. In December 1529 the imperial ambassador was at dinner with Surrey's father:

> During the repast [Norfolk] showed me a letter from his son in very good Latin, which he desired me to read and give my opinion upon . . . he said to me: 'I told you that I was on many accounts delighted to see my son making so much progress in his studies, and following the path of virtue . . . the King has entrusted to me the education of his bastard son, the Duke of Richmond, of whom my own son may become in time preceptor and tutor, that he may attain both knowledge and virtue.[37]

Surrey was indeed Fitzroy's companion at Windsor and in France, though there is no evidence that he taught him. His poetry includes translations of Martial and of part of *The Aeneid*, and the influence of Horace is perceptible in his work. It is a sign of the progress of lay learning that in 1520 Barclay had dedicated his English version of Sallust's *Jugurthine War* to Surrey's grandfather, reserving the Latin text for a cleric, John Veysey, bishop of Exeter. Certainly by the end of the reign considerably more English gentlemen were conversant with Latin than had been the case at the beginning.

Knowledge of modern languages was much more widespread among laymen than was mastery of the ancient tongues. French was by far the most popular language, for two reasons. Firstly French, more than any other modern tongue, was the language of diplomacy, and proficiency would open the door to ambassadorial appointments. Secondly, it was to a large extent the language of the court, and fluency in French is supposed to have advanced the careers of Thomas Boleyn and his children. If the belief persisted in some quarters that lack of Latin was no hindrance to a gentleman, the same could not be said of French.

Grammatical works abounded. Alexander Barclay, encouraged by 'the motion of certain noble gentlemen' and commanded by the second Duke of Norfolk produced his *Introductory to Write and to Pronounce French*, and about 1525 Giles Duwes prepared a French grammar for his pupil Princess Mary, first published in the mid-1530s. Both works were mentioned in Palsgrave's *L'Eclaircissement de la Langue Française*, which also reveals that Charles Brandon, Duke of Suffolk, encouraged 'Master Petrus Vallensis, schoolmaster to his excellent young son the Earl of Lincoln' to compose a French grammar. *L'Eclaircissement* was first published in 1530 but was begun about 1513, when Palsgrave was tutor to Mary of France, Henry VIII's sister and later Suffolk's wife. In it Palsgrave announced his intention of writing another book on French: 'there is no tongue more abundant of adages or dark sentences comprehending great wisdom. But of them I defer at this time to speak any more, intending by God's grace to make of these adages a book apart.' Unfortunately, the press of other commitments seems to have prevented him.

Palsgrave's grammar enjoyed some popularity. The mercer Stephen Vaughan, Cromwell's agent in the Netherlands, told him that he was 'much desirous to attain the knowledge of the French tongue'. He had 'made not a little labour to master Palsgrave to have one of his books'; but the jealous author had refused and ordered the printer

> to sell none of them to any other person than to such as he shall command to have them, lest his profit by teaching the French tongue might be minished by the sale of the same to such persons as, besides him, were disposed to study the same tongue.

Vaughan implored Cromwell to get him a copy, even asking for the one Palsgrave had given him, for 'if I had one, I would no less esteem it than a jewel'.[38]

A number of gentlemen read French. John Bourchier, Lord Berners, translated Froissart's chronicles into English at the King's command, and at the 'insistent desire' of his nephew Sir Francis Bryan he translated Guevara's *Golden Book of Marcus Aurelius* from a French version. Bryan himself later translated Guevara's *Dispraise of the Life of a Courtier* from a French edition. George Boleyn was proficient in French. He owned a manuscript volume of Jean Le Fèvre's *Lamentations de Matheolus* which is interesting for the signatures, mottoes and verses scribbled on its pages by other courtiers, including Wyatt.[39]

Italian, too, was learned by laymen. It has been seen that George Boleyn could write it, though indifferently. Wyatt was well-read in Italian and familiar with the complexities of Italian verse-making. He followed the Florentine Alamanni in his penitential psalms and satires. Other poems are based on sonnets by Petrarch, and Wyatt also imitated the *stambotto*, and eight-line verse form used by Serafino. His jottings in Boleyn's copy of Le Fèvre are in Italian, French and Spanish. Surrey, too, used Petrarch as a model and a source, though a modern critic sees Virgil and the Latin poets as his main influence rather than the Italians. Petrarch's influence may be discerned in many of the love sonnets and other poems. Surrey may have met Alamanni at the French court, but the Florentine had no apparent impact on his poetry.[40]

Surrey's fluency in a number of languages is attested by dedications to him from John Clerke, his father's secretary. The *Opusculum Plane Divinum de Mortuorum Resurrectione et extremo iuditio* is a devotional work in English, Latin, Italian and French. Clerke's English version of a romance by Diego de San Pedro, *L'Amant Mal Traité de Sa Mie*, mentions Surrey's own linguistic skills, praising

> not only the great wisdom and singular judgment wherewith God
> the disposer of all things hath most abundantly endowed you, but
> also the exceeding great pains and travails sustained by yourself
> in traductions as well out of the Latin, Italian as the Spanish and
> French, whereby your lordship surmounteth many others, not
> only in knowledge but also in laud and commendation.

Clerke also published short works on the declension of French and
Italian verbs, and the latter is claimed as the first Italian grammar
printed in England. His gifts as an author, translator and
grammarian have been questioned, but even so his work must have
helped spread the knowledge of Italian.[41]

Cromwell, who was supposed by Chapuys and John Foxe to have
travelled in Italy, owned a number of Italian books. Edmund
Bonner asked to borrow some in 1530:

> where ye, willing to make a good Italian, promised unto me long
> ago the Triumphs of Petrarch in the Italian tongue, I heartily pray
> you at this time . . . to send me the said book with some other at
> your devotion, and especially, if it please you, the book called
> *Cortegiano* in Italian.

In February 1539 Morley sent Cromwell two works by Machiavelli
'to pass the time withall', and pointed out their political uses. The
first was *The Prince*, 'surely a very special good thing for your
lordship, which are so nigh about our sovereign lord in counsel, to
look upon for many causes'. Reginald Pole recalled in his *Apology*
that some years earlier Cromwell had been familiar with this work
and had advised him to follow its precepts. The other work Morley
sent was the *Florentine History*. Speaking of the Pazzi War between
Florence and the papacy, Morley tried to show how similar the cause
of the Florentines under Lorenzo the Magnificent was to that of
Henry VIII. In fact, the two cases bear no comparison, and
Cromwell never used the book for propaganda purposes.[42]

The only other modern language apparently studied by the
English nobility and gentry was Spanish, though evidence is meagre.
There are Wyatt's doodlings in the pages of Le Fèvre and Clerke's
allusion to Surrey's translations (which are apparently not extant);
and Berners translated *The Castle of Love*, another romance by
Diego de San Pedro, directly from Spanish.[43]

A study of the circulation and ownership of books during the reign affords some clues as to how far the reading public may be termed humanistic in its interests. About 1525 the printer Robert Copland complained about current reading tastes in the prologue to his *Seven Sorrows that Women Have When Their Husbands Be Dead*. Copland wished to offer his readers 'a very proper book of moral wisdom' or 'a book of common consolation', but they clamoured for ballads, sensational news-sheets or amusing pieces like *The Merry Jests of the Widow Edith*. His lament would have been echoed by the humanist educators, for despite their precepts the English nobility continued to delight in romances and other despised works. None the less humanist material was produced.

Of the classics Aesop, Ovid, Virgil, Terence and Cato had been available in the middle ages in the form of (largely-non-classical) collections of wise sayings, and these continued to be printed in the early years of Henry VIII. Fresh humanist editions and translations also appeared. Erasmus's compilation containing Cato's *Disticha* and other works was printed by Wynkyn de Worde in 1532. In 1540 Richard Taverner published Erasmus's Latin text with an English translation, and in 1545 Robert Burrant produced an English version, dedicated to Sir Thomas Cawarden. Terence was put into humanist form by Nicholas Udall, whose *Flowers for Latin Speaking Selected and Gathered out of Terence* was published in 1534, 1537 and 1544.[44]

Plutarch appeared always in Latin or English translation. Wyatt translated his *Quiet of Mind*, Elyot *How One May Take Profit of his Enemies* and the tract on education. And English translation of Erasmus's *De Tuenda Sanitate Praecepta* was printed by Wyer about 1530, and it was translated again in 1543 by John Hales and dedicated to Sir Thomas Audley.

Cicero appeared in the original or in English several times. The *Phillipics* were printed by Pynson in 1521 and the *Epistles* were published in Oxford about 1519. Robert Whittinton translated *De Senectute*, *De Officiis* and *Paradoxa*. Voluzenus's edition of *Scholia seu commentariorum in Scipionis somnium* was published by Redman, while the translation of *De Amicitia* by John Tiptoft, Earl of Worcester — one of the earliest English humanists — was reissued by Rastell about 1530.

Lucian was quite widely published in translation. The Latin versions of selected dialogues by Erasmus and More were printed in Basle in 1517 and in London in 1528 and 1531. Elyot translated *Cynicus* into English from More's version; *Menippus*, possibly translated by Rastell, was printed about 1513; and Henry Bullock's translation of the *Opusculum* was published in Cambridge by Siberch in 1521. Galen was available in the Latin translations of Linacre. *De Temperamentis* was printed by Siberch in 1521, and in the early 1520s Pynson published *De Naturalibus Facultatibus*, *De Symptom Differentiis* and *De Pulsum Usu*.

Robert Whittinton translated Seneca's *Ad Gallionem* into English in 1547, besides two works attributed to the same author: *The Form and Rule of Honest Living* and the *Mirror or Glass of Manners and Wisdom*, both published in 1547 with dedications to Bryan. An edition of Caesar's *Commentaries* in Latin and English appeared in 1530, as did an English translation of part of *De Bello Gallico*, taken from Gaguin's French version.

Other classical authors were more thinly represented. No work by Aristotle appeared except *De Cursione Lune*, a treatise attributed to him which was published by Faques in 1530 and Wyer in 1535. A sole edition of Apthonius's *Sophistae Praexcertatimenta*, edited by Gentian Hervet, was printed by Pynson about 1520. A single work of Xenophon, *Oeconomicus*, was translated by Hervet at the command of Geoffrey Pole and published in 1532. Frontinus's *Stratagems, Sleights and Policies of War* appeared in one English translation by Morison in 1539. Virgil was only available in his 'medieval' form; though Surrey translated parts of *The Aeneid*, they were not published during his lifetime.

Livius was only represented by the *History of Hannibal and Scipio*, translated into English from several sources by Anthony Cope in 1544, though Erasmus's edition of the *Histories*, printed in Basle in 1531 with a dedication to Charles Blount, would have been accessible to Englishmen. The only work of Euripides published in England was Erasmus's Latin metrical version of *Iphigenia in Aulide*; though again, Erasmus translated *Hecuba* into Latin and published it abroad with a dedication to Warham.

In fact, a number of Erasmus's translations and editions were dedicated to English clerics, both in compliment to individual patrons and to ensure them a friendly reception in England. Thomas Ruthal received Seneca's *Lucubrationes*; Plutarch's *De utilitate capienda ex inimicis* went to Wolsey; and the same author's *De tuenda bona valetudine praecepta* went to John Yonge, Master of the Rolls.

English laymen received dedications to modern humanist works printed at home and abroad. Erasmus dedicated all the editions of his *Adagia* from 1500 to 1528 to Mountjoy, the later editions including Charles Blount in the dedication. Mountjoy also received Paynell's *Precepts Teaching a Prince or a Noble Estate his Duty*. Erasmus addressed his *Praise of Folly* to More and his *Commentarius in Nucem Ovidii* to John More, who also received Grynaeus's *Platonis Omnia Opera* in compliment to his father as well as himself. Thomas Boleyn, as a move in the propaganda war during the royal divorce, commissioned three works from Erasmus in order to establish his family's humanistic and pietistic credibility: *Enarratio Triplex in Psalmum XXII* (Basle, 1530); *Dilucida et Pia Explanatio Symboli Quod Apostolorum Dicitur* (Basle, 1533); and *De Praeparatione ad Mortem* (Basle, 1534). The last two works were translated into English and published as the *Plain and Godly Exposition of the Common Creed* (translated by William Marshall and printed by Redman in 1533) and *Preparation to Death* (Berthelet, 1538).[45]

In 1544 Peter Betham addressed his version of Jacopo di Porcia's *Precepts of War* to Audley, and Sir Ralph Sadler received Peter Assheton's *Short Treatise upon the Turks' Chronicles* in 1546. Cromwell received Erasmus's *Laud and Praise of Matrimony* from Taverner and *The Castle of Health* from Elyot. Sir Anthony Denny was the recipient of Thomas Langley's *Abridgement of the Notable Work of Polydore Vergil*, and Sir Henry Knevet received Thomas Chaloner's version of Gilbertus Cognatus's *Of the Office of Servants*. The King's two sons received dedications. Fitzroy's was a medical work, David Edgar's *De Indiciis et Praecognitionibus*, while Edward received from David Talley *Progymnasmata Graecae grammatices* and from Philip Gerard Erasmus's *Very Pleasant and Fruitful Dialogue called the Epicure*.

Nobles and gentlemen often received dedications to humanist devotional works. John Pylbarough addressed his *Commendation of the Inestimable Graces and Benefits of God* to Cromwell. Denny received two patristic works, Paynell's *Sermon of St Cyprian made on the Lord's Prayer* and Thomas Chaloner's *Homily of St John Chrysostom*. Lord Hussey received from John Fewterer of Syon *The Mirror or Glass of Christ's Passion*, while Sir Edward North received Elyot's *Preservative Against Death*. Thomas Becon's early works were dedicated to (presumably) godly-minded Kentish nobility and gentry, among them Wyatt and Cobham.[46]

Several humanist religious works were addressed to English clerics or women. Erasmus's *De Immensa Misericordia Dei* was translated by Hervet, his *De Contemptu Mundi* and *Comparition of a Virgin and a Martyr* by Paynell. Erasmus dedicated many of his pietistic, scriptural and patristic works to English patrons, among them editions of Jerome and Chrysostom and the paraphrase of the epistles of Peter and Jude.[47] Other humanist devotional works appeared without benefit of patronage, such as Lupset's *Treatise of Charity* and *Compendious and Very Fruitful Treatise Teaching the Art of Dying Well*. Richard Whitford, the 'poor wretch of Syon', composed a number of devotional tracts, including *Work for House- holders*, *Preparation unto Houseling* and *Daily Exercise and Experience of Death*.

At the same time, however, the nobility and gentry were eager for non-humanist works, including the romances so vigorously proscribed by the educators. Charles Somerset, Lord Herbert commissioned an edition of Lydgate's *Governance of Kings and Princes*. Edward Stafford, Duke of Buckingham commissioned versions of two medieval romances, *Helyas Knight of the Swan* and a work which concerned Hetoum, Prince of Gorigos. Dedications to the three generations of the Howard family reveal a notable variety of taste. The second Duke of Norfolk, who died in 1524, commis- sioned Barclay's French grammar and received from him English translations of Sallust and of Spagnuoli's *Life of St George*. His son the third Duke received John Hardyng's *Chronicle* and Borde's *Dietary of Health*. His grandson Surrey was the recipient of a romance and a devotional work from Clerke, a medical treatise, *In Anatomicen Introductio* by David Edgar, and verses by Leland mourning the death of Wyatt.

A general view of the reading tastes of the age may be gained from a glance at the works dedicated to Henry VIII, who was naturally the patron most frequently addressed by authors. Leaving aside polemical theological works, editions of the bible, political propaganda and schemes for reforming the laws, there is an interesting variety of reading matter.

There is a small number of medieval works: Lydgate's *Fall of Princes* and *History, Siege and Destruction of Troy*; Froissart's *Chronicles* and Gower's *Confessione Amantis*; and the works of Chaucer, edited by William Thynne. Erasmus dedicated his version of Plutarch's *How to Tell a Friend from a Flatterer* to the King, who also received Whittinton's editions of Cicero and Morison's version of Frontinus. Henry was also the recipient of Linacre's translation of Galen's *Methodus Medendi*, Paynell's *Conspiracy of Lucius Catiline* and Cope's *Hannibal and Cicero*.

There are also editions of the fathers and devotional works based on scripture. Vives offered his commentaries on Augustine's *City of God*, Cheke two volumes of Chrysostom. Erasmus dedicated his paraphrase of Luke to Henry, while Morley and Sampson offered expositions of psalms. Finally there are humanist educational works: Whittinton's *De Nominum Generibus* and Wakefield's *Oratio de Laudibus et Utilitate Trium Linguarum Arabicae, Chaldaicae et Hebraicae*; the French grammars of Palsgrave and Duwes; Elyot's *Governor, Banquet of Sapience* and *Dictionary*; Palsgrave's *Comedy of Acolastus*, and Ascham's *Toxophilus*.

Besides the evidence of dedications, there are some scattered indications of reading, such as the list of books owned by Kildare mentioned above. Both Erasmus and Ammonio described Mountjoy's avid reading of histories which, as Barclay told the second Duke of Norfolk in the preface to the *Jugurthine War*, were profitable to all classes, 'but specially to gentlemen which covet to attain to clear fame and honour by glorious deeds of chivalry'. This would have horrified Erasmus and Vives, though Barclay did go on to cite Quintilian and Cicero on the utility of history to governors.

The third Duke of Norfolk exclaimed in public in 1541 that he thanked God he had never read scripture and never would However, in 1546 while confined in the Tower he requested books of a humanistic nature, perhaps hoping to reassure Henry about his loyalty:

> I would gladly have licence to sent to London to buy one book of St Austin's, *De Civitate Dei*; and of Josephus, *De Antiquitatibus*; and another of Sabellicus, who doth declare most of any book that I have read how the Bishop of Rome from time to time hath usurped his power against all princes, by their unwise sufferance.

The Duke's desire for books was not merely politic; he declared, 'unless I have books to read, ere long I fall asleep, and after I wake again I cannot sleep, nor did not this dozen years'.[48] By contrast to Norfolk's choices, books left at Bedington by Sir Nicholas Carew were exclusively medieval and mostly manuscript rather than printed: Gower's *Confessione Amantis*; tales of Enguerrain de Monstrelet and Lancelot; Froissart, and other chronicles of France and of the crusades. Clearly Carew looked to a chivalric past rather than a humanist present.[49]

Some English gentlemen produced literary works themselves. Elyot and Morley, as has been seen, were prolific as translators; Elyot in particular felt it his duty (as he put it) to use the one talent God had lent him for the benefit of his fellows. More's output, like Elyot's, was diverse. The translator of Lucian and author of *Utopia* and of lighthearted epigrams was also unique among English laymen in engaging in theological controversy. He was also the author of devotional treatises. External events — the rise of heresy, the King's 'Great Matter' — dictated that More's literary concerns should change. However, it seems difficult to accept the view that More ceased to be a humanist. Rather, his diversity was the result of humanist study and — as with Elyot — of the humanist sense of responsibility for exposing and remedying abuses in church and society.[50]

Poetry often exercised the pens of English gentlemen, though here it is important to distinguish between the gentlemen-poets and those lesser mortals employed to write verses for state occasions and court entertainments. The King himself set the pace by writing verses and lyrics. As might be expected, the productions of the noble and gentle amateurs were of variable quality. Morley, for example, tried his hand at English verse, but the results are not outstanding.[51]

Courtiers sometimes scribbled verses on the blank leaves of manuscript books, such as George Boleyn's copy of *Matheolus* and Elizabeth Carew's copy of Lydgate. The existence of 'court albums' shows that the gentlemen-poets took their work seriously. Some albums, such as the Devonshire and Blage manuscripts which contain some of Wyatt's work, are collections of poetry by different authors. It seems that these were passed around and added to, and it is often impossible to ascribe the verses positively to particular poets. For instance, George Boleyn achieved posthumous fame as a poet, but if his efforts survive they are not known.[52]

The collection *Songs and Sonnets*, known as 'Tottel's Miscellany' and first published in 1557, contains poems by Henrician gentlemen, including Wyatt and Surrey, though again, verses are not attributed to particular writers. A manuscript poem by Bryan in which he 'counsels man the right' has been found in the Huntington Library; comparison with number 286 of Tottel's Miscellany, 'That few words show wisdom, and work much quiet', shows that he was probably also the author of this poem. Bryan's translation of Guevara was republished in 1575 with some rather pedestrian verses

in his praise which help to convey his reputation as a gentleman and
a poet:

> A worthy knight of English court
>   Whom Henry King did love,
> First to translate from foreign phrase
>   Into our mother tongue,
> Investing it with English robe
>   As good for old and young.
> For pleasure and for profit both
>   To recreate the mind,
> And reaping thence commodity
>   Ease for themselves to find.
> One not unlike to Xenophon
>   Whose shape his countrymen
> Set up with sword in right hand clasped
>   In left, a writing pen.
> In like sort lived this worthy knight
>   In martial feats well-tried
> With lance, spear, targe; in time of peace
>   His pen good works descried.[53]

Similarly, Thomas Churchyard, Surrey's page, later praised his
master for the diversity of his gifts:

> An earl of birth, a god of spirit, a Tully for his tongue;
> Methink of right the world should shake when half his praise were
>   rung.
>
>   *   *   *
>
> His knowledge crept beyond the stars and wrought to Jove's high
>   throne,
> The bowels of the earth he saw, in his deep breast unknown.
> His wit looked through each man's device, his judgment
>   grounded was,
> Almost he had foresight to know, ere things should come to pass.
>
>   *   *   *
>
> In every art he feeling had, with pen past Petrarch sure,
> A fashion framed which could his foes to friendship oft allure.

Surrey was praised by Wharton in the eighteenth century as 'for his
justness of thought, correctness of style, and purity of expression

. . . the first English classical poet'. His sonnets are in the pastoral vein, and contain nothing of the medieval concept of courtly love. Among other achievements, he established iambic measure as the standard for English verse. In 1540 Surrey was praised by the French King's sons (who knew him) 'as well for his wisdom and soberness as also good learning'. His house near Norwich, Mount Surrey, is said to have been the earliest classical building in England.[54]

Some of Surrey's own verses on the death of Wyatt might serve as an introduction to that complex character. They also emphasise that a gentleman-poet must have many gifts and occupations:

A head where wisdom mysteries did frame;
Whose hammers beat still in that lively brain
As on a stithy, where that some work of fame
Was daily wrought to turn to Britain's gain.

A hand that taught what might be said in rhyme;
That reft Chaucer the glory of his wit;
A mark the which, unparfited for time,
Some may approach, but never none shall hit.

A tongue that served in foreign realms his King;
Whose courteous talk to virtue did inflame
Each noble heart; a worthy guide to bring
Our English youth by travail unto fame.[55]

Wyatt's poetry, like his letters to his son, is intensely didactic. His satires are cautions against the allurements of court life and of lucre, his version of the penitential psalms conveys strongly the agony of the sinner. In the love poetry — and despite the traditional pose of the unhappy courtly lover — the bitterness at treachery and perfidy is far more vehement than convention warranted. Despite his literary connection with Katherine of Aragon, Wyatt is traditionally linked with Anne Boleyn and her circle, and certainly the scriptural piety of many of his poems recalls Anne's preoccupations. For Wyatt, poetry was not merely a courtly accomplishment and amusement, but a vehicle for moral instruction and religious reflection.

III

Some idea of how far the new learning gained royal and courtly approval may be gained by a study of the education of the King's two sons. For both Fitzroy and Edward humanist instruction was a method of preparation for the throne. Their cases illustrate both the application of humanist theory and the practical problems faced by tutors.

Henry Fitzroy was born in 1519, and throughout his childhood he was a serious alternative candidate to Mary for the succession. Important foreign marriages were considered for him, and there were rumours that Henry would make him king of Ireland.[56] In 1525, amid much pomp and ceremony Fitzroy was created Duke of Richmond and Somerset, Earl of Nottingham and Knight of the Garter, and was appointed lord high admiral, lieutenant general north of Trent, keeper of the city and castle of Carlisle, warden general of all the marches towards Scotland, and receiver of Middleham and Sheriff Hutton. In all, lands worth £4,000 were bestowed on him.

In 1525 Fitzroy and Mary were both sent to different parts of the realm, to be the figureheads of regional councils and to be displayed as potential successors to Henry. While Mary went to the Welsh Marches Fitzroy, following a precedent of Richard III's reign, went to reside in the north, principally at Sheriff Hutton. He was placed officially in the care of both his godfathers, Wolsey and Norfolk, but it was the Cardinal who controlled his household and supervised his education.

Fitzroy's first tutor, from 1525 to February 1526, was John Palsgrave; the grateful tone of a letter he sent More suggests that the latter may have recommended him for the post. Certainly More played a prominent part in Fitzroy's creation ceremony and was consulted by the King as to whether the Duke should learn Greek and Latin simultaneously.

Palsgrave prepared himself diligently for his charge, consulting (among others) William Horman, John Ritwyse and William Gonnell. He also studied educational authorities, including Quintilian, Mapheus Vegius, Otho Brunfels, Guarino da Verona and 'especially Erasmus'. The King himself ordered Palsgrave to prepare two books for Fitzroy's use, and he set to work to improve the boy's barbaric Latin, instruct him in the rudiments of Greek, and read with him an eclogue of Virgil and two scenes of the *Adelphi*.[57]

Palsgrave was immediately involved in a confrontation between the humanist ideal of a prince versed in the tongues and good literature and the old-fashioned image of a sporting nobleman generous with his friends and contemptuous of learning. Henry VIII told Page, Parr and Palsgrave that he had committed to them his 'worldly jewel' so that the household officials should train him in body and the tutor bring him up in virtue and learning. The household as a whole, however, quickly concluded that the worldly jewel would be best employed in hunting and in obtaining preferment for themselves. Palsgrave complained to the Duke's mother, and told More that the servants tried to distract Fitzroy from learning with hunting and hawking:

> God hath given him a great aptness both to learning and all manner such qualities as should become such noble person to have, which in my mind were great pity but that it should be employed to the best effect; wherein I shall ever do my best according as for his age shall be requisite. And albeit that some here which be high shaven murmur against it, and . . . let not to say that learning is a great hindrance to a nobleman, I hear them with Ulysses' ears.

In February 1526 Palsgrave was succeeded by Richard Croke, but Croke's European reputation as a classical scholar failed to impress Fitzroy's household, who took every opportunity of undermining his authority. The tutor complained to Wolsey of the machinations of George Cotton (the Duke's gentleman-usher and later his governor) who not only encouraged Fitzroy and his schoolfellows to taunt their teacher and skip lessons but also made them despise the fine Roman handwriting Croke prized and himself taught them secretary hand.[58]

Croke detailed his troubles in a series of bitter letters, one of which culminated in a list of demands for Wolsey to transmit to Fitzroy's council. Croke alone was to decide the times of the lessons, and only those he thought fit for instruction were to remain in Fitzroy's chamber. The Duke was not to waste time writing to abbots and 'mean persons' after dinner, to the detriment of his digestion and powers of concentration, and he was to write nothing but Latin, particularly to the King and Wolsey, 'to the intent he might more firmly imprint in his mind both words and phrases of the Latin tongue, and the sooner frame him to some good style in writings whereunto he is now very ripe'. Lessons were not to be interrupted for every trifle, but only for important visitors to whom the Duke could show off his learning, as this would inspire him to excellence. 'Finally,' Croke said,

> that no ways, colour ne craft be taken to discourage, alienate or avert my said lord's mind from learning, or to extinct the love of learning in his estimation, but that he be induced most highly to esteem his book of all his other studies.[59]

No order from Wolsey about discipline in the ducal schoolroom is extant but Croke, aided by Leland's gift to Fitzroy of a copybook, managed to teach him an exceptionally fine Roman hand. He reported that at the age of eight his pupil could translate Caesar with a due appreciation of grammar and expression, and indeed, the only literary reference in Fitzroy's letters concerns a request to the King for a military harness 'to exercise myself in arms according to my erudition in the commentaries of Caesar'.

On the other hand, Croke did not ensure that Fitzroy wrote only in Latin, and as his letters were meant to be exercises in composition this was a signal failure. Furthermore, most of his surviving letters are written in favour of servants and household officials, and they are nowhere near the standard of the more strictly disciplined Prince Edward.

If Fitzroy's tutors failed to produce the perfect humanist prince, the reason lay in their geographical isolation from the busy overseers of the Duke's education — which served to undermine their own authority — and in the tractability of the material with which they had to work. Nevertheless it is evident from Henry VIII's expressed interest in his son's instruction and from Wolsey's careful selection of teachers that they intended to equip Fitzroy for possible rule by humanist education.

Prince Edward, born in 1537, was in a stronger position than Fitzroy. He was the undisputed heir; he lived either at or not far from court; and those who had charge of his studies could draw on the experience of Fitzroy's and Mary's education.

It is often asserted that Edward was taught with his sisters in a humanist 'royal nursery' directed by Katherine Parr, but this is not so. Katherine herself was not qualified to run a humanist 'school'; the three children did not live together at court; and even when Edward and Elizabeth shared a house they had separate tutors and lessons because of the different in age and sex. Moreover, following humanist theory Edward was taken from female company at an early age. He later recalled in his journal:

> was brought up, till he came to six years old, among the women. At the sixth year of his age he was brought up in learning by Master Doctor Coxe, who was after his almoner, and John Cheke, Master of Art; two well learned men who sought to bring him up in learning of tongues, of the scriptures, of philosophy, and all liberal sciences. Also John Belmaine, Frenchman, did teach him the French language.[60]

A glance at the careers of Edward's principal tutors reveals their links with the humanist community at Cambridge and the reform faction at court led by Denny and Butts. Richard Coxe had been involved in the Cardinal college heresy-hunt of 1527 but had since been chaplain successively to Goodrich and Cranmer.[61] The latter as the Prince's godfather played Wolsey to Edward's Fitzroy, and may have procured Coxe's appointment as tutor. Cheke was a client of Butts and a member of Denny's Cambridge college, St John's.

Two other St John's men were involved in the education of the King's younger children. In 1544 William Grindal, a pupil of Ascham, was made tutor to Elizabeth after Ascham sent him to court with a letter of recommendation to Cheke. Ascham himself was evidently Elizabeth's writing-master, and he later told Cecil that 'Many times by mine especial good master Master Cheke's means I have been called to teach the King [Edward] to write in his privy chamber.' He may also have taught Edward during his father's lifetime.[62]

Following humanist theory Edward was educated in the company of schoolfellows. The antiquarian Nichols drew up a list of potential study-companions for him, including the six youths sent as hostages to France in 1550 who, Ascham states, were educated with Edward after his accession; at least some of these may have shared his studies as Prince.[63]

Of the two young Dukes of Suffolk who died of the sweat at Cambridge in 1551 Henry, two years Edward's senior, was definitely educated with him by Coxe and Cheke, while Charles, born the same year as Edward, is a possibility. Their father, who died in 1545, asked Henry VIII in his will to advance 'the honest bringing up of my sons in learning and other virtuous education, and most especially of Henry my eldest son, whereby he might the rather attain to be able so to serve his most excellent majesty'. In his funeral sermon for the young Dukes Haddon observed that Henry delighted in literature and the conversation of learned men, to whom he was introduced by his mother Katherine. The brothers learned their handwriting from Ascham, who also taught Charles Greek.[64]

Another potential schoolfellow was James Blount, son of Charles, Lord Mountjoy, while Barnaby Fitzpatrick, who was urged by Ascham to model himself on Edward for study and virtue, was the latter's companion before as well as after his accession. Other possible classmates, cited by Nichols are Edward's maternal cousins, two sons of Edward Seymour: Henry, Lord Hastings, who shared Edward's studies as King; and Henry, Lord Stafford, though he was considerably older than the Prince. In addition Coxe suggested that Paget's eldest son Henry, his own godson, should be educated with Edward 'as others be', while Cecil later believed that Elizabeth had a good opinion of Thomas, Earl of Ormonde — born in 1532 and brought up at the English court — because of 'the memory of his education with that holy young Solomon, King Edward'. Edward's schoolroom seems to have been free of the disruption of Fitzroy's, perhaps because early in their association Coxe took a stick to 'Captain Will', as he termed Edward's disobedience.[65]

Edward's epistles to his relatives, godfather and tutor provide a fair amount of information about his studies. His textbook for letter-writing was probably Erasmus's *De Conscribendis Epistolis*, and his letters are formal notes expressing such commonplaces as thanks for a gift, enquiries after health and regrets for absence. At all times he embellished his sentiments with salutory quotations from scripture or the classics. For example, he excused the brevity of a letter to Coxe by quoting Cato, and exhorted him to be patient as Job in the face of illness.

Among this rather self-conscious exhibition of his reading, personal concerns occur only rarely. One such instance is the notorious letter to Katherine Parr asking her to dissuade Mary from 'Foreign dances and merriments which do not become a most Christian princess' — activities which evidently rankled with the eight-year-old Prince. The other is a somewhat anxious enquiry about the Latinity of the French admiral, to whom he had to make a welcoming oration.[66]

Edward was familiar with the old and new testaments, particularly the Pauline epistles. He read Solomon's Proverbs daily during mass, and his letters contain references to Esther, Aaron and Samuel. Patristic writers are not cited in his letters, though his library contained works by Ambrose, Basil the Great and Chrysostom.

Letters from Coxe reveal Edward's early progress. By December 1544 he felt that his pupil was ready to commence Cato and Aesop, and in January 1546 he told Cranmer that Edward had learned almost four books of Cato, besides biblical texts, Aesop's fables and Vives's *Satellitium*, composed for Mary some 20 years earlier. There are several quotations from Vives in Edward's letters, and he owned copies of *De Officio Mariti* and *De Institutione Fœminae Christianae*. In addition, George Day sent him some of Cicero's works as a new year's gift for 1547.[67]

It seems unlikely that Edward made much progress in Greek before his accession, as his first extant exercise is dated 6 March 1551. He began to learn French on 12 October 1546, and in that year he wrote to Elizabeth in French.[68]

In Edward, the long-awaited male heir to the kingdom, is seen the humanist education of a gentleman at its fullest extent. Like his eldest sister he studied scripture and the tongues, and thus if one speaks of his 'Protestant' education one must extend the doctrinal implication to Mary. In fact, Edward was not brought up in radical fashion as a godly young Josias, but after the renaissance model of a Christian prince delineated by Erasmus, Vives and other humanist educators.

Notes

1. Erasmus, *The Education of a Christian Prince*, Lester K. Born (ed. and trans.) (Columbia University Press, New York, 1936), and *Declamatio de Pueris statim ac Liberaliter Instituendis*, Jean-Claude Margolin (ed. and trans.) (Travaux d'Humanisme et Renaissance, no. 77, Geneva, 1966); Vives, *de Ratione Studii Puerilis*, printed in *Opera Omnia*, G. Majansius (ed.) (8 vols., in officina Benedicti Montfort, Valencia, 1782–90) and translated in Foster Watson, *Vives and the Renascence Education of Women* (Edward Arnold, London, 1912), pp. 241–50; Vives, *The Introduction to Wisdom*, Richard Morison (trans.) (Berthelet, London, 1540).

2. Lupset, *Exhortation to Young Men*, printed in J. A. Gee, *Life and Works of Thomas Lupset* (Yale University Press, New Haven, 1928); Pace, *De Fructu Qui Ex Doctrina Percipitur*, F. Manley and R. S. Sylvester (eds and trans.) (Ungar, New York, 1967); Starkey, *A Dialogue Between Reginald Pole and Thomas Lupset*, Kathleen M. Burton (ed.) (Chatto & Windus, London, 1948).

3. Elyot, *The Book Named the Governor*, H. H. S. Croft (ed.) (2 vols., Kegan Paul Trench & Co, London 1883).

4. Elyot, *Plutarch on the Education or Bringing Up of Children* (Berthelet, London, c. 1535), Chapter 8; Erasmus, *De Pueris*, pp. 439–40.

5. Pace, *De Fructu*, pp. 22–5; Starkey, *Lupset and Pole*, p. 123; Elyot, *Governor*, vol. 1, p. 99.

6. Elyot, *The Image of Governance* (Berthelet, London, 1544); Vives, *Wisdom*, pp. 120–1; Elyot, *A Preservative Against Death* (Berthelet, London, 1545), preface.

7. Vives, *Wisdom*, pp. 42, 90; Erasmus, *De Pueris*, pp. 388–90.

8. Cf. Pace, *De Fructu*, pp. 120–6; Erasmus, *De Pueris*, p. 418 and *Christian Prince*, pp. 151ff; Vives *Wisdom*, pp. 18–30; Elyot, *Governor*, vol. 2, pp. 29–30, 37–8; Starkey, *Lupset and Pole*, p. 109.

9. Erasmus, *De Pueris*, p. 408 and *Christian Prince*, pp. 193–4, 142–3; Elyot, *Governor*, vol. 1, pp. 29–31 and *Plutarch*, Chapter 3.

10. Erasmus, *De Pueris*, p. 416; Elyot, *Governor*, vol. 1, pp. 31–4; ibid., p. 113; Erasmus, *De Pueris*, pp. 395, 403–5; Erasmus, *Christian Prince*, p. 142; Elyot, *Governor*, vol. 1, pp. 50–1; Vives, *Wisdom*, p. 101, *De Ratione Studii*, pp. 242–3.

11. Vives, *Wisdom*, pp. 58, 54, 74ff, 29, 30, 36, 37, 38–9, 41.

12. Lupset, *Exhortation*, pp. 244.

13. Ibid., pp. 256–7.

14. For education between the ages of seven and 14, Elyot, *Governor*, vol. 1, pp. 53–71.

15. Ibid., vol. 1, pp. 72–98, 116–17, for education from adolescence to maturity.

16. Ibid., vol. 1, p. 97.

17. Erasmus, *Christian Prince*, pp. 143, 183, 147.

18. Ibid., pp. 148, 199.

19. Ibid., pp. 200–01.

20. Erasmus, *De Pueris*, pp. 403–6, 412, 413, 417, 418, 425–42, 443, 444.

21. Pace, *De Fructu*, pp. 36, 37, 126, 127, 188–93.

22. Ibid., pp. 134–8.

23. *The Eclogues of Alexander Barclay*, Beatrice White (ed.) (Early English Text Society, Oxford University Press, London, 1928), p. 127. Barclay's source was the *Miseriae Curialium* of the Italian humanist Aeneas Sylvius Piccolomini, later Pope Pius II.

24. P. S. and H. M. Allen, H. W. Garrod (eds), *Opus Epistolarum Des Erasmi Roterodami* (11 vols., Clarendon Press, Oxford, 1906–47), no. 2435; translated in F. M. Nichols, *The Hall of Lawford Hall* (privately printed, London, 1891), pp. 319–20; cf. no. 2735 to Quirinus Talesius. See also Andrea Ammonio, *Carmina Omnia*, Clemente Pizzi (ed.), (Leonis S. Olschki, Florence, 1958), pp. 3–5.

25. Allen, *Erasmi Epistolae*, nos. 1932, 2459, 2460; Roger Ascham, *Whole Works*, Rev. Dr Giles (ed.) (3 vols., J. R. Smith, London, 1865/64), vol. 1, epistle 19 to Charles Blount, 20 to Redman.

26. G. F. Nott, *Works of Henry Howard, Earl of Surrey and of Sir Thomas Wyatt the Elder* (2 vols., Hurst Rees Orme & Brown, London, 1815–16), vol. 1, appendix XLIX (misdated 1526); Edward Burton (attr.), *Life of John Leland* (Alfred Cooper, London, 1896), p. 10; Nicholas Bourbon, *Nugae* (Dolet, Lyons, 1538), Book 7, no. 15.

27. Allen, *Erasmi Epistolae*, no. 1402 for the dedication to Ovid. John More's translation of Nausea's sermon was published by Rastell in 1533. For education in the More household, see Chapter 7 below.

28. *Roger Ascham, English Works*, William Aldis Wright (ed.) Cambridge University Press, Cambridge, 1904), p. 97.

29. For Margaret Vernon's letters to Cromwell, M. A. E. Wood (ed.), *Letters of Royal and Illustrious Ladies* (3 vols, Henry Colburn, London, 1846), vol. 1, pp. 57–60; Henry Ellis (ed.), *Original Letters Illustrative of English History* (11 vols., 3 series, Harding, Triphook & Lephard, London, 1824, 1827, 1846), series 3, vol. 3, p. 11.

30. PRO SP1/237, fos. 5 and 65, calendared in *Letters and Papers, Foreign and*

Domestic, of the Reign of Henry VIII, J. S. Brewer, J. Gairdner, R. H. Brodie (eds) (21 vols., HMSO, London, 1862–1932), Addenda, vol. 1, i, nos. 724 and 744 (hereafter cited as *L&P*); PRO SP1/71, fos. 30–1 (*L&P*, vol. 5, no. 1309), Lockwood to Cromwell, 12 September 1532.

31. Dowes's two letters to Cromwell are in Ellis, *Original Letters*, series 3, vol. 1, pp. 341–3. Ellis reverses their order, but this has been corrected in view of the references to Diana and Gregory's expanded programme of studies.

32. Ibid., series 3, vol. 1, pp. 338–40, series 3, vol. 3, p. 258, letters of Gregory Cromwell and Dowes.

33. *The Lisle Letters*, Muriel St Clare Byrne (ed.) (6 vols., University of Chicago Press, London and Chicago, 1981), vol. 6, p. 28; British Library, Harleian MS 283, fo. 133 (*L&P* vol. 16, no. 893 (2)), 'remembrances for Master William'; *L&P*, vol. 16, no. 893, safe-conduct for William Brooke; A. Schillings (ed.), *Matricule de l'Université de Louvain* (10 vols., Palais des Academies, Brussels, 1952–67), vol. 4, p. 236; British Library, Harleian MS 283, fo. 343, Harvel to Cobham, 10 January 1546.

34. Wyatt's letters to his son are printed in Kenneth Muir, *Life and Letters of Sir Thomas Wyatt* (Liverpool University Press, Liverpool, 1963), pp. 38–43.

35. PRO SP1/135, fo. 252 (*L&P*, vol. 13, ii, no. 217), John Hutton to Exeter, 29 August 1538.

36. For Morley's translations, Turrecremeta's exposition of Psalm 26; Aquinas's work on the angelic salutation; Anselm on the life, stature and form of the Virgin; two epistles of Seneca; Plutarch's lives of Theseus, Hannibal and Scipio; Athanasius's preface to the psalms; Boccaccio's *De Praeclaris Mulieribus*; and Erasmus's paean to the Virgin, cf. Henry Parker Lord Morley, *The Triumphes of Petrarch*, Stafford Henry Earl of Iddesleigh (ed.) (Roxburghe Club, Nichols & Son, London, 1887), pp. xii–xiii; for Cromwell's reading to the new testament, cf. R. B. Merriman, *Life and Letters of Thomas Cromwell* (2 vols., Clarendon Press, Oxford, 1902), vol. 1, p. 23. Thomas Boleyn's copy of *Martial*, published in Paris, 1539, is at Hever Castle, Kent; his postscript to Erasmus is in Allen, *Erasmi Epistolae*, no. 2232. For George Boleyn's Latin, Edmond Bapst, *Deux Gentilshommes — Poetes de la Cour de Henry VIII* (E. Plon, Nourrit et Cie, Paris, 1891), p. 10; for Bryan's, British Library, Additional MS 25, 114, fo. 49 (*L&P*, vol. 5, no. 548), Henry VIII to Bryan, Tayler and Foxe.

37. Quoted in Edwin Casady, *Henry Howard Earl of Surrey* (Modern Language Association of America, New York, 1938), p. 31.

38. Ellis, *Original Letters*, series 3, vol. 1, p. 208.

39. British Library, Royal MS 20 B XXI, 'poems of Jean Le Fèvre'.

40. For Wyatt, Sidney Lee, *The French Renaissance in England* (Clarendon Press, Oxford, 1910), p. 118; Nicholas Bielby, *Three Early Tudor Poets* (Wheaton, Exeter, 1976), pp. 38–9; *Sir Thomas Wyatt, Collected Poems*, Joost Daalder (ed.) (Clarendon Press, Oxford, 1975), pp. 7 and *passim*. For Surrey, Emrys Jones, *Henry Howard, Earl of Surrey: Poems* (Clarendon Press, Oxford, 1972), pp. xii–xiv, xxi.

41. Sergio Baldi, 'The Secretary of the Duke of Norfolk and the First Italian Grammar in England', in Siegfried Korninger (ed.), *Studies in English Language and Literature presented to Karl Brunner* (Willhelm Baumuller, Vienna and Stuttgart, 1957). Baldi's aim is to distinguish this John Clerke from both the bishop of Bath and Wells and the vicar of Sele, and to show that he was not Surrey's tutor and mentor.

42. Ellis, *Original Letters*, series 3, vol. 2, p. 177, Bonner to Cromwell; ibid., series 3, vol. 3, pp. 64–7, Morley to Cromwell. Cf. R. B. Merriman, *Life and Letters of Thomas Cromwell* (Clarendon Press, Oxford, 1902), vol. 1, p. 86.

43. Cf. John Bourchier, *The Castle of Love*, W. G. Crane (ed.) (Scholars' Facsimiles and Reprints, Gainesville, Florida, 1950).

44. For the classics in England, Henrietta R. Palmer, *List of English Editions and Translations of Greek and Latin Classics Printed Before 1641* (Bibliographical

Society, Blades, East & Blades, London, 1911), and H. B. Lathrop, *Translations from the Classics into English, from Caxton to Chapman* (University of Wisconsin Press, Madison, 1933).

45. For Thomas Boleyn's motive in commissioning works from Erasmus, and Erasmus's awareness of this, Allen *Erasmi Epistolae*, no. 2315.

46. For Becon's dedications, *Early Works of Thomas Becon*, John Ayre (ed.) (Parker Society, Cambridge University Press, 1843).

47. For a list of printed dedications to English patrons during the reign, Maria Dowling, 'Scholarship, Politics and the Court of Henry VIII' (unpublished PhD dissertation, London, 1981), Appendix.

48. Quoted in Gerald Brenan and Edward Phillips Statham, *The House of Howard* (2 vols., Hutchinson & Co, London, 1907), vol. 1, p. 439.

49. 'The Guardrobe of the Manor of Bedington, in the charge of Sir Michael Stanhope, Keeper of the House', British Library, Harleian MS 1419, fos. 373ff.

50. Two recent and markedly different views of More are Alistair Fox, *Thomas More, History and Providence* (Basil Blackwell, Oxford, 1982), and Richard Marius, *Thomas More* (J. M. Dent & Son Ltd, London and Melbourne, 1985). I am unable to agree with either of these estimates of More's humanism.

51. Printed in Morley, *Triumphes of Petrarch*, pp. xiv–xvi.

52. For court albums, Bielby, *Three Tudor Poets*, p. 11; E. K. Chambers, *Sir Thomas Wyatt and some Collected Studies* (Sidgwick & Jackson, London, 1933), pp. 108–9; Daalder, *Wyatt's Poetry*, passim. There are three volumes of verses and lyrics — some by Henry VIII — in the British Library; Additional MSS 5465, 5665, 31, 992. For George Boleyn's reputation, Bapst, *Deux Gentilshommes — Poetes*, pp. 138ff. Wyatt's sonnet 'My lute awake' used to be ascribed to Boleyn, and William Tydeman believes the poem 'Death O death, rock me asleep' to be his work; *English Poetry, 1400–1580* (Heinemann, London, 1970), pp. 122–3, 238–9.

53. Antonio de Guevara, *A Looking-Glass for the Court*, Sir Francis Bryan (trans.) (for William Norton, London, 1575), prefatory verses. For *Songs and Sonnets, Tottel's Miscellany, 1557–1587*, Hyder Edward Rollins (ed.) (2 vols., Harvard University Press, Cambridge, Massachusetts, 1928, 1929).

54. Thomas Churchyard, *Churchyard's Charge* (John Kyngston, London, 1580), sig. aij. For Surrey as a poet, Emrys Jones, *Surrey's Poems*, pp. xxvii; xxx; Bielby, *Three Tudor Poets*, pp. 27, 42. For the French princes' praise, *State Papers Published Under the Authority of His Majesty's Commission* (HMSO, London, 1849), vol. 8, p. 500.

55. Emrys Jones, *Surrey's Poems*, p. 27.

56. J. G. Nichols, 'Memoir and Letters of the Duke of Richmond', *Camden Miscellany 3* (Camden Society, J. B. Nichols & Sons, London, 1857), pp. xlix–1, xiv; W. S. Childe-Pemberton, *Elizabeth Blount and Henry VIII* (Eveleigh Nash, London, 1913), p. 156.

57. *Correspondence of Sir Thomas More*, E. F. Rogers (ed.) (Princeton University Press, Princeton, 1947), pp. 403–5, Palsgrave to More; PRO SP1/55, fo. 13, Palsgrave to Henry VIII. Both letters calendared in *L&P*, vol. 4, nos. 5806 and 5806 (2), misdated 1529. Most of the educational works consulted by Palsgrave were not widely available in England, but Palsgrave had travelled widely, see Chapter 5 above.

58. More, *Correspondence*, loc. cit.

59. Ellis, *Original Letters*, series 3, vol. 1, p. 333 (*L&P*, vol. 4, no. 1948), Croke to Wolsey.

60. *Literary Remains of King Edward VI*, J. G. Nichols (ed.) (2 vols., Roxburghe Club, Burt Franklin, New York, 1857), vol. 2, p. 209. For the learning of Katherine Parr, see Chapter 7 below. For a more detailed discussion of the myth of the royal nursery, Dowling, *Scholarship*, pp. 247ff.

61. John Foxe, *Acts and Monuments*, S. R. Cattley (ed.) (8 vols., Seeley & Burnside, London, 1837), vol. 5, pp. 4–6. Foxe credits Goodrich — formerly a Cambridge client of Anne Boleyn — with introducing Coxe to the King.

62. Nichols, *Literary Remains*, vol. 1, p. lii. Cheke and Coxe assisted another Cambridge scholar, Walter Haddon, to gain Edward's favour, ibid., p. lxxvii. Sir Anthony Cooke is also claimed as Edward's tutor, but his appointment (if it took place) was probably post-accession.

63. Nichols, *Literary Remains*, vol. 1, pp. lvvii–lxviii.

64. J. G. Nichols and John Bruce (eds), *Wills from Doctors' Commons* (Camden Society, J. B. Nichols & Son, London, 1863), pp. 33–4; Walter Haddon, *Vita et Obitus Duoroum Fratrem Suffolcensium* (in aed. Ric. Grafton, London, 1551); Thomas Wilson, *The Art of Rhetoric*, G. H. Mair (ed.) (Clarendon Press, Oxford, 1909), passim.

65. Ascham, *Whole Works*, vol. 1, epistle 19 to Charles Lord Mountjoy, 20 to Redman, Lady Day 1544; ibid., epistle 38 to Barnaby Fitzpatrick (1545); PRO SP63/16, fo. 201, Cecil to Sidney, 31 March 1566 (I am grateful to Dr Simon Adams for this reference); PRO SP1/195, fos. 213–14 (*L&P*, vol. 19, ii, no. 726), Cox to Paget, 10 December 1544.

66. Nichols, *Literary Remains*, vol. 1, epistles 10 and 23 to Katherine Parr, 12 May and 12 August 1546 (*L&P*, vol. 21, i, nos. 802, 1446).

67. Ibid., vol. 1, p. 3, Cox to Cranmer (1546) (*L&P*, vol. 21, i, no. 61); ibid., epistle 40, Edward to Day, 25 January 1547 (*L&P*, vol. 21, ii, no. 745); PRO SP1/195, fo. 213 (*L&P*, vol. 21, ii, no. 726), Cox to Paget, 10 December 1544; T. W. Baldwin, *William Shakespere's Small Latine and Lesse Greeke* (2 vols., University of Illinois Press, Urbana, 1944), vol. 2, appendix 2.

68. Nichols, *Literary Remains*, vol. 1, epistle 31, Edward to Elizabeth, 18 December 1546 (*L&P*, vol. 21, ii, no. 571). The exact date of Edward's first French lesson is fixed by Coxe's letter to Paget.

7   Women and the New Learning

I

> For what is more fruitful than the good education and order of women, the one half of all mankind, and that half also whose good behaviour or evil tatches giveth or bereaveth the other half, almost all the whole pleasure and commodity of this present life, besides the furtherance or hindrance further growing thereupon, concerning the life to come?

Thus Richard Hyrde, dedicating his version of *The Instruction of a Christian Woman* to Katherine of Aragon, stated the revolutionary attitude of humanists to women's education.[1] Before the sixteenth century it had been thought that academic learning was not only useless but positively harmful to women, since knowledge prompted imagination and curiosity, which led to sin. The two chief objections to feminine education were summarised — and answered — by Hyrde in another work. Firstly, many men doubted whether women should learn Latin and Greek, some saying that it would be harmful because women were naturally frail and prone to vice, and therefore would be influenced by unwholesome literature. Secondly, some men were afraid that their wives would become too familiar with priests and friars if they knew the tongues.[2]

Humanists, on the other hand, appreciated that learning could be beneficial to women, albeit for the negative reason that, since they had fertile minds and were inclined to idleness, boredom and mischief, it was useful to keep them occupied with study. Thus Thomas More told William Gonnell, one of his children's tutors:

> I do not see why learning in like manner may not equally agree with both sexes; for by it, reason is cultivated, and (as a field) sowed with the wholesome seed of good precepts, it bringeth forth excellent fruit. But if the soil of woman's brain be of its own nature bad, and apter to bear fern than corn (by which saying many do terrify women from learning) I am of opinion, therefore, that a woman's wit is the more diligently by good instructions and

learning to be manured, to the end, the defect of nature may be redressed by industry.[3]

Similarly, Hyrde discussed the utility of learning in keeping women too busy to get into trouble:

reading and studying of books so occupieth the mind, that it can have no leisure to muse or delight in other fantasies, when in all handiworks that men say be more meet for a woman, the body may be busy in one place, and the mind walking in another: and while they sit sewing and spinning with their fingers, may cast and compass many peevish fantasies in their minds, which must needs be occupied either with good or bad, so long as they be waking.

According to Hyrde, humanist studies were eminently suitable for women:

And the Latin and the Greek tongue I see not but there is as little hurt in them as in books of English and French . . . And in them be many holy doctors' writings, so devout and effectuous, that whosoever readeth them must needs be either much better or less evil, which every good body, both man and woman, will read and follow.[4]

Before the reign of Henry VIII women did not receive anything approaching an academic education. In the fifteenth century some women were literate in English and French, but more advanced learning was denied them. In a memorial sermon for Margaret Beaufort John Fisher recalled:

she was of singular wisdom far passing the common rate of women, she was good in remembrance and of holding memory . . . right studious she was in books which she had in great number both in English and French, and for her exercise and for the profit of other she did translate divers matters of devotion out of French into English. Full often she complained that in her youth she had not given her to the understanding of Latin.[5]

Margaret, guided by Fisher, established preacherships, lectures and colleges at the universities and had boys educated in her household, but it is typical of the age that even this most 'learned' of women made no provision for the education of her own sex. She was content with the role of patron of university studies, and made no attempt to encourage female scholarship. Not until humanism was established in England under Henry VIII would academic studies become accessible to women.

Even for humanists, however, female education had only a limited purpose. With one sole exception — the King's daughter Mary — Henrician women were not trained for public office; their domain was the household, their cares were their own moral well-being and the upbringing of their children. At the same time, they were not to study for mere parlour accomplishments; the precepts of humanist educators show that women's learning was meant to cultivate their minds and souls, to guard and enhance those twin jewels, piety and chastity.[6]

It is well-known that the phenomenon of female erudition first appeared in England in More's household, where the tutors included Gonnell, Hyrde, John Clement and Nicholas Kratzer. Much is known of More's 'school' (as he called it) from the letters of More himself to his children and their tutors, and through the enthusiastic descriptions of Erasmus and other humanist visitors. More deliberately chose a young, unsophisticated wife whom he could form and educate according to his own tastes, and though thwarted by her early death and somewhat simple character he was more successful with his three daughters, son, daughter-in-law, foster-daughter and niece. It is clear that his children all received an identical education, and when More wrote to his 'school' that he preferred his son's letter to the others' he said, not that the boy's letter must be automatically better than the girls', but that John seemed to have taken more care with his effort than they had. More's daughters, most unusually, read pagan writers like Quintilian, made declamations and wrote dialogues in Latin, and even studied Greek. The humanist John Palsgrave referred to an occasion when they 'disputed in philosophy afore the King's grace'. They were praised to the reading public of Europe in Erasmus's colloquy *The Priest and the Learned Woman* and in Vives's treatise *The Instruction of a Christian Woman*, while Simon Grynaeus in a dedication to John More spoke of 'your sisters the Muses'.[7]

Margaret, More's eldest daughter, was particularly noted for her learning. She corresponded with Erasmus; received from him the dedication of a commentary on Prudentius; and at the age of 19 translated his *Devout Treatise upon the Pater Noster* into English.

This was published anonymously and dedicated by Hyrde to Margaret's cousin and fellow-student, Frances Yelverton. His preface, naturally enough, contained a panegyric on the translator:

> whose virtuous conversation, living, and sad [serious] demeanour may be proof evident enough what good learning doth, where it is surely rooted: of whom other women may take example of prudent, humble and wifely behaviour, charitable and very Christian virtue . . . with her virtuous, worshipful, wise and well learned husband, she hath by the occasion of her learning and his delight therein, such especial comfort, pleasure and pastime, as were not well possible for one unlearned couple, either to take together, or to conceive in their minds, what pleasure is therein.

Margaret also emended a corrupt passage in the Greek text of Cyprian, and at her father's bidding composed a treatise on the 'four last things' (no longer extant) which he considered superior to his own work on the subject. Ironically enough, Margaret was sent to her father in prison to use her humanist eloquence to persuade him to swear to the succession and supremacy. After his death she attempted to have his works printed, and was imprisoned for this as well as for keeping his head as a sacred relic. Margaret extended her educational experience to her own children, and some time before her death in December 1544 attempted to engage Roger Ascham as their tutor. Ascham declined the invitation, but later praised her daughter Mary Basset. This grand-daughter of More translated his *History of the Passion* from Latin to English, and was considered one of the learned lights of Queen Mary's court.[8]

Another notable female scholar was More's foster-daughter Margaret Gigs, who married the medical humanist John Clement in about 1530. Her speciality was probably algebra, since More sent back her algorism stone with his last letter from the Tower, though she was also noted as a student of medicine. Her learning was particularly praised in John Coke's *The Debate* of 1550.[9]

The More household, brilliant and admired though it was, does not seem to have induced any spirit of emulation; girls like Margaret à Barrow, future wife of Sir Thomas Elyot, were sent to More for their studies, but there is no record of any father following his example in the early years of Henry's reign. It was in fact political necessity, drawing on the 'school' of More for precedent and inspiration, which made female education more generally desirable.

The marriage of Henry VIII and Katherine of Aragon produced many children, but only Mary, born in 1516, survived infancy. Queens regnant were almost unheard of in England, and many, including the King, were apprehensive at the prospect of female succession. Katherine, however, had no qualms about either her daughter's right to succeed or the ability of women to rule. Her own mother Isabella had been Queen regnant of Castile, she herself had been Regent of England in 1513, and the times were rich in examples of women governing competently for absent or juvenile male relatives: Anne de Beaujeu and Louise of Savoy in France; Margaret of Austria and (later) Mary of Hungary in the Netherlands; and the Empress Isabella in Spain. Herself well-educated in the humanities under Isabella the Catholic's auspices and a fervent champion of the new learning in England, Katherine chose to prepare Mary for rule by a thorough programme of humanist instruction. As yet, however, there were no educational textbooks, and so the Queen began the search for a likely authority.

Before July 1521 she was supporting the studies of Juan Luis Vives, who came to England in 1523. (See Chapter Five, above.) In that year Katherine commissioned from him the first of several handbooks, which was published at Antwerp as *De Institutione Fœminae Christianae* and later translated by Hyrde as *The Instruction of a Christian Woman*. The book was a general treatise with little of direct relevance to Princess Mary, a fact which suggests that Katherine intended it for a wider audience. Certainly Vives in his preface to her spoke of 'the favour, love and zeal that your grace beareth toward holy study and learning'. Hyrde showed his translation to his master More, who thought that it would please Katherine because of 'the gracious zeal that ye bear to the virtuous education of the womankind of this realm, whereof Our Lord hath ordained you to be Queen'.[10] In championing women's studies for Mary's sake, Katherine became a pioneer of female education in England.

In his dedication to the Queen, Vives revealed his consciousness of innovation in writing on such a subject:

For Xenophon and Aristotle, giving rules of housekeeping, and Plato making precepts of ordering the common weal, spake many things appertaining to the woman's office and duty; and St Cyprian, St Hierome, St Ambrose and St Augustine have entreated of maids and widows, but in such wise, that they appear rather to exhort and counsel them unto some kind of living, than to instruct and teach them.

His own work, in keeping with the moral preoccupations of the age, is chiefly concerned with woman's piety, modesty and deportment as maiden, wife and widow, but he does lay down some important educational precepts. Women were not to read medieval romances, which were dangerous because of their emphasis on love and war. Love poetry — particularly Ovid's — was also proscribed, because it inclined women to silly fancies and to lust. They should read scripture, the fathers, certain 'acceptable' classics and the lives of good women, whether Christian saints or virtuous pagans. In keeping with the maiden's modesty and the concomitant avoidance of contaminating male company, she should not go outside the home for education but should be taught by her mother. Nor were women to keep schools; they lacked the intellectual ability of men, and the authority conferred by a teaching post might make them pass on shallow opinions by which they themselves had been deceived — as our mother Eve was deceived by the serpent. However, women should teach their children, and their own education should be a lifelong process.[11]

The *Christian Woman*, at first sight reactionary and restrictive, is actually revolutionary on several counts. Though shielding women from 'harmful' literature, Vives allowed them a wide choice of reading matter. In giving women the instruction of their children, he differed even from other humanists like Erasmus and Elyot, who recommended that boys be taken from their mothers and nurses at an early age and given over to male tutors. The book is also refreshing in its statement that education is a continuous process; Vives declared that the work was meant to be a word-portrait of Queen Katherine, who studied continually and as late as 1514 had tried to secure Erasmus as her tutor.

The *Christian Woman* was not specifically designed for Princess Mary, but Vives, knowing her mother's preoccupation, declared in the preface: 'your dearest daughter Mary shall read these instructions of mine, and follow in living. Which she must needs do, if she order herself after the example that she hath at home with her, of your virtue and wisdom.' Even so, more detailed instruction was required for a female ruler than a course of pious reading and exhortations to virtue, and consequently Katherine commissioned from

Vives a practical outline of studies for Mary, *De Ratione Studii Puerilis*.[12]

Since the Princess was to be a governor and not a private individual, Vives recommended that she read some of the dialogues of Plato which refer to government of the state, More's *Utopia* and Erasmus's *Institutio Christiani Principis*. Since she was to follow her father as defender of the faith, he advised that she be thoroughly grounded in scripture, the fathers and other edifying works. She was to study the new testament night and morning, some works of Ambrose and Augustine with the epistles of Jerome, Christian poets such as Prudentius, Juvencus, Sidonius, Paulinus, Aratus and Prosper, and Erasmus's *Enchiridion*. Nor was her classical education to be neglected: 'let her learn the Distichs of Cato, the *Mimi* of Publius Syrus, and the *Sentences* of the Seven Wise Men, all of which have been collected together in the same little book of Erasmus, and explained by him.' (For the use of this compilation in the education of men, see Chapter Six, above.) Justinus, Florus and Valerius Maximus were particularly recommended for history, as well as Plutarch. The more salutary (or less pernicious) heathen poets were to be studied, Lucian, Seneca and parts of Horace were suitable, and some of Erasmus's colloquies might be used at the discretion of her tutor, but, Vives advised:

> The authors in whom she should be versed are those who, at the same time, cultivate right language and right living: those who help to inculcate not only knowledge, but living well . . . Let her be given pleasure in stories which teach the art of life. Let these be such as she can tell to others — e.g., the life of the boy Papirius Praetextatus in Aulus Gellius, of Joseph in the holy books, of Lucretia in Livy, of Griselda and others, as found in Valerius, Sabellicus and other writers of the same kind — stories which tend to some commendation of virtue, and detestation of vice.

Besides Christian and classical literature Mary was to be instructed in Latin and Greek, which were to be absorbed through reading recommended authors and collecting witty *sententiae* rather than by the arid rehearsal of grammatical rules. The Princess should possess a good Latin-English dictionary, and should use modern grammatical works by Linacre, Melanchthon and Mancinellus.

Vives's plan of Mary's studies, refreshingly innovatory in its emphasis on the tongues and on humanist literature, was composed as a rough outline rather than a complete syllabus which, as Vives told the Queen, should be amplified once her abilities had shown themselves: 'Time will admonish her as to more exact details, and thy singular wisdom will discover for her what they should be.' Other books were produced for Mary's use and Katherine's guidance. Vives himself contributed the *Satellitium vel Symbola*, a collection of mottoes and devices in the style of Erasmus's *Adagia* which Mary was to take as a 'mystical guard' about her princely mind and person.[13] The proverbs and edifying stories used were taken from the classics and from Vives's own experience: one described a river journey to Syon during which he discussed good and ill-fortune with Katherine of Aragon; another referred to his former pupil the Cardinal de Croy. They were to have a double application to Mary as both private person and future ruler. (Cf., for example, no. 146, on waging war on vices.) Interestingly enough, the work was also used by the tutors of Prince Edward.

Other scholars, too, contributed textbooks for Mary. Linacre produced a simplified Latin grammar for her use, and Giles Duwes, her French tutor, prepared a similar work for that language. In addition, Katherine commissioned a work on marriage from Erasmus in 1524, which was published by Froben in 1526 as *Christiani matrimonii Institutio*. The choice of subject has led to speculation that the book was intended as ammunition in the coming royal divorce, but the early date of the Queen's request to Erasmus suggests that it was intended for her daughter's edification. Erasmus himself was not sure what Katherine wanted since she had already commissioned the *Christian Woman*, and indeed, this general treatise on the role, duties and occupations of women closely resembles Vives's slightly earlier work. The dedication to the Queen contains, besides the usual eulogy of Katherine as a model of feminine rectitude, an allusion to the Princess: 'We expect no less of your daughter Mary. For what cannot be hoped of a daughter born of such devout parents, and educated under such a mother?'[14]

Little detail survives of the actual instruction of Mary in her early years, but Katherine herself took more than a directing part in her daughter's upbringing. Although Erasmus's praise of the girl's 'education' under her mother could be dismissed as general and conventional, the Queen herself wrote to the Princess after her departure to Wales in 1525:

As for your writing in Latin, I am glad that ye shall change from

me to Master Federston, for that shall do you much good to learn
by him to write aright. But yet sometimes I would be glad when ye
do write to Master Federston of your own enditing, when he hath
read it that I might see it. For it shall be a great comfort to me to
see you keep your Latin and fair writing and all.[15]

Vives was retained to supervise Mary's education, though *De
Ratione Studii* reveals that he did not actually teach her: he told
Katherine, 'since thou hast chosen as her teacher a man above all
learned and honest, as was fit, I was content to point out details, as
with a finger. He will explain the rest of the matters.' This may refer
to Richard Fetherston, mentioned in the Queen's letter to her
daughter, whose promotion to the archdeaconry of Brecknock in
April 1523 possibly signals the beginning of his tuition of Mary.[16]
There is no allusion to Vives as the Princess's tutor until 1528, when
he was summoned to England ostensibly to give her Latin lessons
but in fact to advise the Queen over the conduct of the royal divorce.

Some light is thrown on the details of Mary's education by the
events of 1525. Henry VIII and Wolsey, facing the succession
problem, decided to despatch both the King's children to distant
parts of the realm, there to govern in their father's name and to be
displayed in public as potential rulers. While Henry Fitzroy, the
King's bastard son, departed for the nominal governorship of the
northern Marches, Mary and her household, with a council led by
Veysey, bishop of Exeter, moved to the Welsh borders. The
Princess set out in the charge of Margaret Pole, Countess of
Salisbury and her governess since at least 1520, and of her tutors
Fetherston and Giles Duwes.

Duwes has left in the French grammar prepared for Mary's use at
the King's command an interesting and at times amusing picture of
her life at this time. The work is filled with dialogues, letters and
verses designed not merely to teach her the language, but also to
prepare her for conduct at court and to teach her about philosophy
and religion. There are dialogues between the Princess and
messengers from her father and from a foreign ruler, and a 'confabu-
lation' between her and her French tutor on the peace made with
France. They also discuss the nature of the soul according to St
Isidore and the old and new testaments, and there is an exposition of
the mass by various members of the household and council. On the
lighter side, Mary and her treasurer of the household (her 'husband
adoptive' for the occasion) discourse on the different kinds of love,

and there is an epitaph on the death of French, which has pined away through the indifference of Mary's servants. Duwes's is not the first French grammar published in England, but its very feminine flavour must have made it particularly appealing to those who had care of the instruction of girls.[17]

A small relic survives of the Princess's own scholarly labours in her earlier years. In a later dedication to her, Henry Parker, Lord Morley, recalled:

> I do well remember that scant ye were come to twelve years of age but that ye were so ripe in the Latin tongue, that rare doth happen to the woman sex, that your grace not only could perfectly read, write and construe Latin, but furthermore translate any hard thing of the Latin into our English tongue. And among all other your most virtuous occupations, I have seen one prayer translated of your doing of Saint Thomas Alquyne [*sic*] that I do assure your grace is so well done, so near to the Latin, that when I look upon it . . . I have not only marvel at the doing of it, but further, for the well doing set it in my book or books, as also in my poor wife's . . . and my children.

There is in fact a lady's book of hours in the British Library which contains, besides the autographs of Henry VII and Elizabeth of York and of Henry VIII and Katherine, a copy of 'The Prayer of St Thomas of Aquine' translated by Mary in 1527, when she was aged twelve.[18]

Erasmus also professed admiration for Mary's erudition, singling out the Princess and her parents, with Mountjoy and the More family, as outstanding examples of learning in his 1528 edition of the *Adagia*, and telling John Vergara in 1529, 'We have in the Queen of England a woman distinguished by her learning, whose daughter Mary composes fine Latin epistles.'[19] Thus through the determination of her mother and the labours of scholars and tutors Mary, despite the handicap of her sex, was given all that the new learning could provide by way of training for a governor of the renaissance.

Mary's education as a humanist ruler continued during the troubled years of her parents' divorce. Katherine often wrote to her daughter in Spanish, which the Princess understood perfectly, and in a letter of 1533 primarily concerned with the girl's morale and moral welfare she promised to send her two Latin books: 'one shall be *De Vita Christi*, with the declaration of the gospels; and the other the epistles of Hierome, that he did write always to St Paula and Eustochium; and in them I trust you shall see good things.' A French verse-biography of Anne Boleyn by Launcelot de Carles, Bishop of Riez which was finished on 2 June 1536 pictures Mary as solacing herself by learning theology, philosophy, music, science, foreign languages and mathematics.[20]

Mary's education, like her mother's, continued to be admired in this period. The Vicomte de Turenne, sent from France to negotiate the betrothal of the Princess in 1527, deplored the fact that she was too small and thin to be married in the near future but found her admirable on account of her uncommon mental endowments. Another member of the embassy, Claude Dodieu, described Mary speaking to the Frenchmen in Latin, Italian and French, besides playing on the virginals for them.[21] Mary's education was of direct use to her in 1534. She was then living in the hostile atmosphere of the infant Princess Elizabeth's household, where she was visited by her old tutor Fetherston. On the pretext of exercising her rusty Latin she spoke to him in that language and managed to tell him that the King had threatened to behead her if she did not accept the Act of Succession. Fetherston replied that her Latin was indeed bad, and passed the information to the Emperor's ambassador.[22]

In the closing years of the reign Mary was persuaded by Katherine Parr to undertake the translation of Erasmus's paraphrase of the gospel of John, though she was forced to abandon the work because of ill health and it was completed by her chaplain Mallet. None the less she won praise from Udall, the general editor of the *Paraphrases*, who declared in the preface to John:

> O how greatly may we all glory in such a peerless flower of virginity as her grace is: who in the midst of courtly delights and amidst the enticements of worldly vanities hath by her own choice and election so virtuously and so fruitfully passed her tender youth, that to the public comfort and gladful rejoicing which at her birth she brought to all England she doth now also confer unto the same the inestimable benefit of furthering both us and our posterity in the knowledge of God's word, and to the more clear understanding of Christ's gospel.[23]

Mary's studies were thus a great consolation in her troubles. Katherine of Aragon, too, maintained her interest in and allegiance to the new learning throughout the vicissitudes of her last years. In the early stages of the divorce proceedings she commissioned from Sir Thomas Wyatt an English translation of Petrarch's work 'on the remedy of ill fortune'. The translator became bored with the repetitiveness of the tract, and substituted Plutarch's *Quiet of Mind* — an equally apt subject for Queen Katherine.[24]

Despite the fact that she had plainly fallen from favour the Queen won generous eulogies from several authors, humanist and otherwise. The evangelicals Barlowe and Roy praised her virtues in *The Burial of the Mass*. The anonymous play *Godly Queen Hester* is apparently an allegory of the initial stages of the divorce, with Wolsey cast as the villainous Haman and Katherine portrayed as Esther. Unlike the biblical prototype, Esther is described as

> In learning and literature profoundly seen,
> In wisdom eke semblant to Saba the Queen.[25]

Katherine was also praised by Vives in his *De Officio Mariti* of 1529, despite the fact that she had withdrawn her favour from him. (For Vives's part in the divorce, which lost him the favour and financial support of the Queen and King, see Chapter Five, above.) In true humanist fashion Vives looked to the classics for a woman comparable to the Queen:

> Nor Christ would not that even in our time we should be without an example . . . the which should flow and descend unto our posterity, left and exhibited unto us by Katherine the Spaniard, Queen of England . . . of whom that may be more truly spoken of than that, that Valerius writeth of Lucrece, that there was in her feminine body a man's heart by the error and fault of nature. I am ashamed of myself and of all those that have read so many things when I behold that woman so strongly to support and suffer so many and diverse adversities that there is not one, although he were well worthy to be remembered and spoken of among our elders, that with such constancy of mind hath suffered cruel fortune, or could so have ruled flattering felicity as she did. If such incredible virtue had fortuned then, when honour was the reward of virtue, this woman had dusked the brightness of the heroes, and as a divine thing and a godly sent down from heaven had been prayed to in temples.[26]

Erasmus, too, was lavish in his praise of the Queen. His own contribution to her cause extended no further than a cautious letter of consolation, but he mentioned her with honour in, among other works, his *Vidua Christiana* of 1529. Katherine herself continued to read his books, and was fortified on her deathbed by his *De Praeparatione ad mortem*, ironically commissioned by her rival's father, Sir Thomas Boleyn.[27]

II

A very different figure from Katherine of Aragon and Mary was their rival and supplanter, Anne Boleyn. Though her education was not as directly humanistic as theirs, she was equally interested in learning.

Her early life is obscure. According to the bishop of Riez she went to France in 1514 in the retinue of Henry's sister Mary, the French Queen, and her name in fact occurs in Mary's suite as 'Mademoiselle de Boulan'. When Mary returned to England Anne entered the household of Claude of France, remaining there until 1522 when she herself came back to England. She may have known Margaret de Valois, Francis I's learned and evangelical sister, though this seems unlikely; Sir Roger Twysden, writing in the seventeenth century, was the first to cite Margaret's influence as the cause of Anne's subsequent interest in reformed religion.[28]

Little is known of Anne's actual education. Like Margaret Beaufort before her she lamented her ignorance of Latin, though she may have had some basic knowledge; certainly a music book prepared for her contains complex Latin lyrics, and she received laudatory verses from the poet Nicholas Bourbon and the grammarian Robert Whittinton.[29] Possibly it was a lack of proficiency in Latin which turned her interest towards vernacular scripture and devotional works in both English and French.

Anne's personal piety was firmly based on scripture. At new year 1530 one Loys de Brun presented her with a treatise in French on letter-writing in which he praised her constant reading of pious and moral French books, including translations from the bible: 'And chiefly I have seen you this last Lent, when I was in this magnificent, excellent and triumphant court, reading the salutary epistles of St Paul, in which are contained the whole manner and rule of a good life.' As Marquess of Pembroke she commissioned from a kinsman a manuscript volume of the epistles and gospels for the Sundays in the year; the scriptural texts were in French, and each was accompanied by an 'exhortation' in English. She received from an unknown donor a manuscript version of the '*Sermon du bon pasteur et du mauvais*' by the evangelical French poet Clement Marot.[30]

Anne's chaplain and biographer William Latymer describes her as 'very expert in the French tongue, exercising herself continually in reading the French bible and other French books of like effect, and conceived great pleasure in the same', and says that she commanded her chaplains 'to be furnished of all kind of French books that reverently treated of the holy scriptures'. Latymer himself was sent abroad by Anne to buy books, and was dismayed on his return from one such journey in May 1536 to find that she had been arrested. In addition, Rose Hickman, the daughter of the evangelical mercer William Locke, remembered her father saying 'that when he was a young merchant and used to go beyond sea Queen Anne Boloin . . . caused him to get her the gospels and epistles written in parchment in French, together with the psalms'.[31]

Like Katherine before her, Anne was a generous patron of scholars. Also like Katherine, who had devotional works read to her ladies in her apartments, Anne tried to educate her waiting-women in scriptural piety. According to Latymer she kept an English bible in her chamber for all to consult, and this may well have been her copy of Tyndale's new testament of 1534 which is now in the British Library. Not content with having scripture read privately, she also arranged for its discussion at table, particularly when the King was present.[32]

Anne also gave her ladies books of devotions which they could hang from their girdles and carry about with them. Wyatt family legend has it that she gave one to a woman of the family on the scaffold, and two extant manuscript volumes are claimed for the honour. The first contains English metrical versions of thirteen psalms or parts of psalms translated by John Croke, a clerk in Chancery, and carries a miniature of Henry VIII. The second has a miniature of the holy trinity and contains twelve prayers and thanksgivings in English. Of particular interest is a prayer of thanks to God for having inspired the King to liberate the scriptures, 'this great while oppressed with tyranny of thy adversary of Rome and his faulters and kept close under his Latin letters'.[33] It is quite possible that each of these volumes belonged to one of Anne's ladies, since she would not necessarily have given them all identical manuscript books.

Latymer claims that Anne was immensely concerned about the reading matter of her household; hence the open bible in her chamber. He depicts her commanding her ladies that 'all trifles and wanton poesies should be eschewed upon her displeasure', and relates that one of her maids, her cousin Mary Shelton, received a strong reproof for having 'idle poesies' written in her prayer book.[34] Anne Boleyn in the role of puritanical censor may seem irreconcilable with the usual view of her as a court butterfly deeply — and in the event dangerously — interested in the attitudes and conventions of courtly love, but it is well to remember that even the saintly Isabella the Catholic expected and enjoyed the flattery and posturings of *amour courtois*. Latymer's pious portrait of his mistress may be exaggerated, but there is no reason to doubt its essential veracity. Anne Boleyn's court was certainly not a formal 'school' for ladies, but it is significant that she valued learning and piety in the women of her household and felt it important for them to have a sound education in scripture.

One of Anne's chief public concerns was with the production and circulation of the bible in English. Such was her reputation as a lover of scripture that in 1533 George Joye 'printed two leaves of Genesis in a great form, and sent one copy to the King, and another to the new Queen, with a letter to N. to deliver them; and to purchase licence, that he might so go through all the bible'. Henry, however, was not at this point amenable to a new bible in English, and Joye's application failed. Equally unsuccessful was Tristram Revell, a former scholar of Christ's, Cambridge who tried to present Anne with his translation of Lambertus's *Farrago Rerum Theologicarum* (*The sum of Christianity, gathered out almost of all places of scripture*) early in 1536. Not only was Anne herself in a precarious position because of the death of Katherine of Aragon, the rise of Jane Seymour and her own miscarriage of a son; the book itself was so extreme in doctrine that even Hugh Latimer found it unacceptable. More fortunate was Richard Herman who had been expelled from the English merchants' house at Antwerp in Wolsey's time, 'for nothing else', as Anne told Cromwell, 'but only for that, that he did both with his goods and policy, to his great hurt and hindrance in this world, help to the setting forth of the new testament in English'. Accordingly, she commanded Cromwell to effect his reinstatement.[35]

It might be expected that Anne would imitate Katherine of Aragon in having her daughter educated in humanist fashion, though Anne, unlike her predecessor, was in hope of a male heir until the last few months of her life. Certainly Latymer claims that she planned to have Elizabeth taught ancient and modern languages and other humanistic accomplishments. Anne, of course, died too soon for any concrete schemes to be made, but it is known that she entrusted Elizabeth to the care of her chaplain Matthew Parker. As Parker himself told Sir Nicholas Bacon in 1559, 'My heart would right fain serve my sovereign lady the Queen's majesty, in more respects than of mine allegiance, not forgetting what words her grace's mother said to me of her, not six days before her apprehension.' How far Parker oversaw Elizabeth's studies is uncertain, but in 1547 he composed an epigram praising her proficiency in Greek, Italian and French.[36]

Little mention is made of Elizabeth's studies until 1544, when William Grindal, a pupil of Ascham at St John's, came to court and was appointed her tutor. However, it seems that she was as thoroughly grounded in the humanities as her brother and sister, and it is reasonable to suppose that Mary's education was the model for Elizabeth's. This becomes significant in the history of women's studies when it is remembered that Elizabeth, unlike Mary, was declared a bastard in her infancy, and so was not educated for future rule.

In 1544 Grindal found the King's younger daughter, then aged ten, well advanced in learning. By July of that year she was capable of writing in Italian to Katherine Parr. Ascham praised her progress in study under Grindal and Lady Champernoun. The latter was Lady Denny's mother, and Elizabeth's governess, Katherine Astley, was a sister of Lady Denny who was married to a cousin of Anne Boleyn. Elizabeth's usual residence in the 1540s was a house at Cheshunt which belonged to Sir Anthony Denny, and it is perhaps not too much to suggest that Denny — *alumnus* of St John's and Cromwell's successor in the patronage of scholarship and reform — was the architect of her education.

Ascham told Cheke in 1548 that if Elizabeth continued to advance at her present rate the knowledge of Greek and Latin she would acquire would be unbelievable. Ascham himself was careful to maintain contact with Grindal, Elizabeth and the governess, and it is evident that he acted as writing master to the Princess. He mended pens for her and sent her an Italian book and a book of prayers, while he sent Katherine Astley a silver pen in thanks for her favour towards Grindal and himself, besides an interesting letter of advice on how Elizabeth should be taught:

I wish all increase of virtue and honour to that good lady whose wit, good Mistress Astley, I beseech you somewhat favour. The younger, the more tender; the quicker, the easier to break. Blunt edges be dull, and dure much pain to little profit; the free edge is soon turned if it be not handled thereafter. If you pour much drink at once into a goblet, the most part will dash out and run over; if you pour it softly you may fill it even to the top, and so her grace, I doubt not, by little and little, may be increased in learning, that at length greater cannot be required.[37]

Little concrete detail survives of Elizabeth's education during her father's lifetime, though she did own a copy of Tyndale's *Obedience of a Christian Man*, first brought to Henry's attention by her mother during the divorce. In addition, three of her own literary productions survive, and can be taken to indicate her studies. She made an English translation of Margaret de Valois's *Mirror or Glass of the Sinful Soul*, dedicated to Katherine Parr as a new year's gift for 1545, and a French translation of Erasmus's *Dialogus Fidei*, dedicated to her father. She also produced a version in Latin, French and Italian of Katherine Parr's *Prayers or Meditations*; this was also dedicated to the King, and probably intended as a new year's gift.[38]

The case of Henry VIII's sixth wife reveals the extent to which learning had become fashionable for court ladies. Katherine Parr's reputation for erudition and religious influence has been greatly exaggerated by modern commentators. Katherine was neither the head of reform at Henry's court nor the director of a 'royal nursery' for his children. (For Katherine Parr and the reform faction at court, see Chapter Two, above; for the education of Prince Edward, see Chapter Six.) Furthermore, her attitude to learning was not unequivocal, and she displayed at times a somewhat anti-intellectual streak. In 1546, for example, she warned the humanists of Cambridge:

forasmuch as I do well understand all kind of learning doth flourish amongst you in this age as it did among the Greeks at Athens long ago, I require and desire you all, not so to hunger for the exquisite knowledge of profane learning that it may be thought the Greeks' university was but transposed or now in England again revived, forgetting our Christianity . . . That it may not be laid against you in evidence at the tribunal seat of God, how ye were ashamed of Christ's doctrine.

This admonition is echoed in her book *The Lamentation of a Sinner*, where she condemned those who possessed a 'dead, humane, historical faith (which they have learned in their scholastical books)', and declared, 'I have certainly no curious learning . . . but a simple love and earnest zeal to the truth, inspired of God.'[39]

Thus Katherine Parr cannot be described as a humanist princess in the sense that Katherine of Aragon was. However, she is important in relation to feminine education because her adult interest in learning is an indication of a new awareness of the relevance of study to women.

Contrary to legend, Katherine was not well-educated as a young girl; it was only after her marriage to the King that she began to learn Latin and to practise the Roman handwriting so prized by humanists. In 1546 Prince Edward complimented her on her progress in Latin grammar and literature and praised her handwriting; evidently these were new pursuits and accomplishments. Moreover, though Edward wrote to her in Latin as to all his correspondents (the *epistola* being his main exercise in composition), the only reply of hers which survives, a corrected draft written on the cover of Edward's letter, is not in her hand.[40] It may also be noted that although she commissioned the translation of Erasmus's *Paraphrases* and even employed Princess Mary on the project, she undertook no part of the work herself. Indeed, her denial of proficiency in Latin in the letter to Cambridge should be taken at face value rather than as false modesty; though it is interesting that the university should assume that she would prefer to be addressed in Latin, when they had written to Anne Boleyn in English.

Notwithstanding all this, within her limitations Katherine Parr added considerably to the culture of the court. She produced two works herself: the *Prayers or Meditations, wherein the mind is stirred patiently to suffer all afflictions*, which is largely derived from Erasmus and Thomas à Kempis; and *The Lamentation of a Sinner*, which is quite explicitly Lutheran.[41] Her patronage of the translation of the *Paraphrases* was intended to encourage lay reading of the bible. Nicholas Udall in his preface to the gospel of Luke, which was dedicated to Katherine, hoped that the King

> will not suffer it to lie buried in silence, but will one day, when his godly wisdom shall so think expedient, cause the same paraphrase to be published and set abroad in print, to the same use that your highness hath meant it, that is to say, to the public

commodity and benefit of good English people now a long time sore thirsting and hungering the sincere and plain knowledge of God's word.[42]

Unfortunately neither Henry's inclination nor Katherine's influence with him were sufficient to ensure publication, and the entire project, like *The Lamentation of a Sinner*, remained in manuscript until the following reign. Similarly, Katherine argued theology with her didactic and sour-tempered husband, until she so annoyed him that he nearly allowed her to fall into the hands of her conservative enemies. (For Katherine's 'trouble on account of the gospel', see Chapter Two, above.)

Katherine Parr took reformers of the calibre of John Parkhurst and Anthony Cope into her service, and her chaplain Francis Goldsmith praised her piety by saying that she made every day like a Sunday. It is evident, too, that she prized learning and piety as qualities in her ladies, some of whom (including Lady Denny) were married to reform-minded gentlemen of the King's privy chamber. Her sister Anne, Lady Herbert was lauded by Ascham, and the early poems of her chaplain John Parkhurst, who joined her household in 1543 after attracting attention during a royal visit to Oxford, contain verses to Katherine herself, her maid Anne Carew, Katherine Brandon, Duchess of Suffolk and Lady Jane Grey. Katherine of Suffolk was a noted gospeller and later an exile under Queen Mary. Nothing is known of her own education, but she was sufficiently interested in humanism to send her two sons to St John's and to be a benefactor to the college.[43] Jane Grey entered Katherine Parr's household at the age of nine and remained with her until the Queen's death in 1548; it seems likely that Katherine was at least partly responsible for Jane's subsequent enthusiasm for the new learning.

III

How widespread was interest in the new learning among women? A consideration of the literary works dedicated to women during Henry's reign (omitting those already mentioned in this chapter) might provide some rough guidelines, but this source of information should be treated with caution. It must be stressed that many printed works and manuscript treatises have disappeared in the course of time and political vicissitude, and so it is impossible to compile a definitive list of dedications. One must also remember that works were usually dedicated in order to elicit patronage, and so women with genuine interest but little influence might be overlooked; thus Princess Elizabeth received no dedications during her father's lifetime because she was a person of minor importance.

Looking at dedications, then, is not a foolproof method of determining the extent of feminine interest in humanism. At the same time, however, the fact that authors presented particular women with books when they might easily have given a gift of food, wine, jewellery or dress trimmings can be taken to mean that they expected the potential patron to be sufficiently interested to reward them. For example, Princess Mary was notoriously fond of clothes and jewels, yet still Lord Morley dedicated a number of manuscript treatises to her when he could have given her a length of cloth or a trinket which would have cost him far less personal effort.

Which women received dedications, and what sort of books were offered to them? Of the King's six wives, Jane Seymour and Anne of Cleves received none (though Anne was later given a pietistic treatise by Thomas Becon), while Katherine Howard's sole dedication was to a work on gynaecology, *The Birth of Mankind* by one Richard Jonas. A modern commentator postulates that Jonas was a relative of Justus Jonas of Wittenberg and probably came to England in the train of Anne of Cleves; that the work was possibly originally intended for Anne; and that Jonas offered it in view of Jane Seymour's death soon after childbirth. Certainly Katherine Howard does not seem to have shown any interest in literature, and her education by all accounts was haphazard, to say the least. Indeed, she is popularly supposed to have been illiterate, though one letter survives which is mostly in her hand, and of very eccentric spelling and tortuous grammar.[44]

As might be expected, most of the recipients of dedications were either royal or noble ladies or (up until 1539) nuns, and most of the works they received were pietistic; though not all were humanistic. The nuns of Denny in Cambridgeshire received from Erasmus an *Epistola consolatoria in adversis* in 1528 on account of their connection with Thomas Grey, the scholar's friend and former pupil, and Elizabeth Gybbes, Abbess of Syon in 1537, received from Richard Whitford of the same house *A Daily Exercise and Experience of Death*. However an earlier Abbess, Agnes Jordan, received *The Mirror of Our Lady* — a work evidently not of a humanistic cast — in 1530. Similarly, Katherine of Aragon received a rather traditional *Life of St Katherine* in manuscript, while Morley dedicated to Princess Mary medieval as well as humanistic works.[45]

Margaret Pole's interest in humanist piety can be adduced from her commission of an English translation of Erasmus's *De Immensa Misericordia Dei* from the family protégé Gentian Hervet of Orleans. One would expect the mother of Reginald Pole and governess of Princess Mary to have commissioned or been offered a number of works, but possibly these were lost or destroyed after the wholesale attainder of her family. Lady Jane Denny, as befitted the wife of an eminent evangelical courtier, received a pietistic treatise from her servant William Hugh, *A sweet consolation, and the second book of the troubled man's medicine*. Thomas Paynell dedicated devotional works to Princess Mary and to her aunt, Mary the Dowager Queen of France, while Ladies Anne Grey and Jane Seymour received pietistic tracts from Thomas Becon.[46]

The non-pietistic works dedicated to female patrons generally reflect the circumstances or preoccupations of the recipient. In 1535 Anne Boleyn, who was deeply interested in poor relief, received from William Marshall *The form and manner of subvention or helping for poor people, devised and practised in the city of Ypres in Flanders*.[47] Marshall, a client of Cromwell, was engaged in helping to draft the poor law of 1536, and his preface reveals his reason for offering the work to Anne:

> my very mind, intent and meaning is (by putting of this honourable and charitable provision in mind) to occasion your grace (which at all times is ready to further all goodness) to be a mediatrix and mean unto our most dread sovereign lord . . . for the stablishing and practising of the same (if it shall seem so worthy) or of some other, as good or better, such as by his majesty or his most honourable council shall be devised.

In 1526 Princess Mary received a tract on *The Extirpation of Ignorancy*: a fit subject for a girl undergoing the rigours of a humanist education. Sir Thomas Elyot dedicated *The Education or bringing up of children, translated out of Plutarch* to his sister, Margery Puttenham. The book, though printed, was a personal gift to guide Margery in the upbringing and instruction of her sons. Elyot's preface to his sister is interesting in terms of educational theory because it gives an inkling of his view of what women were capable of understanding and what they ought to read:

I have not only used therein the office of a translator, but also
have declared at length divers historicans only touched by
Plutarch, to the intent that difficulty of understanding shall not
cause the matter to be to you fastidious [irksome], as it oftentimes
hath happened to other. Also of purpose I have omitted to
translate some part of this matter contained in the Greek as in the
Latin, partly for that it is strange from the experience or usage of
this present time, partly that some vices be in those tongues
reproved which ought rather to be unknown than in a vulgar
tongue to be expressed.

Elyot's censorship recalls Vives's strictures on what women —
including Princess Mary — should not read, and indeed it was rare
for humanists to advocate complete equality of education for the
sexes; Sir Thomas More and Sir Anthony Cooke are the only
examples that spring to mind. Elyot also echoes Vives, however, in
allowing that women should have a say in the education of their
children, though unlike Vives he ordains that they should be
instructed by men. As a matter of interest, Elyot's father
bequeathed his French books to his daughter Margery but his Latin
books to his son Thomas.

As with the devotional treatises, not all the secular works offered
to women were necessarily humanistic. Lady Margaret Douglas, the
King's niece, received a translation of Nova Villa's *Defence of Age
and Recovery of Youth* from her servant Jonas Drumunde, while
Lady Elizabeth Carew, wife of Sir Nicholas and sister of Sir Frances
Bryan, would seem to have had no interest in the new learning. Not
only did she own a copy of Lydgate's *Fall of Princes* in manuscript,
but she commissioned from her uncle Lord Berners a translation of
Diego de San Pedro's *Castle of Love*. This was a medieval romance,
and would have horrified humanist educators like Erasmus, Vives
and Ascham.

The dearth of information about the education of women in early
Tudor England makes it impossible to gauge the influence of
humanism in this sphere. Eileen Power has exploded the myth (born
of both Catholic and Protestant nostalgia) that before the reformation nunneries provided excellent schools for girls, and certainly
there was no provision for the public instruction of women.[48] Scant
detail has survived about the private education and attainments of
individuals, but some examples of learned ladies are known.

The six daughters of Edward Seymour, Earl of Hertford were

noted for their learned accomplishments. Thomas Becon, dedicating his *Governance of Virtue* to Lady Jane Seymour in 1543, praised her parents for bringing up both their sons and daughters in 'good literature and in the knowledge of God's most holy laws'. Jane and her two elder sisters, Margaret and Anne, were later famous for composing one hundred Latin verses on the death of that eminently learned French princess, Margaret of Valois, and were lauded by Ronsard.[49]

The four daughters of Sir Anthony Cooke, born between roughly 1526 and 1530, were collectively praised by Ascham some 20 years later as among those ladies who eclipsed even the daughters of Thomas More in learning. Mildred Cooke, later the wife of William Cecil, was particularly noted for her knowledge of Greek, and would be described by a Spanish ambassador in the reign of Elizabeth as a 'tiresome bluestocking'. Anne Cooke, who later married Sir Nicholas Bacon and was the mother of Francis and Anthony, was said to have been able to read French, Italian, Latin and Greek as well as she could read English. Tradition holds that she assisted her father in teaching Edward VI, though humanist educational theory and the evidence of Edward's own journal make this impossible. She and Jane Grey were praised by Ascham as the two most learned women in England. Katherine Cooke knew Hebrew as well as Greek and Latin, and Elizabeth, a scholar in her own right, later married Sir Thomas Hoby, the translator of Castiglione's *Il Cortegiano*.[50]

Occasional glimpses appear of the instruction and accomplishments of other women and girls. The heretic Anne Askew was the first woman to have her poetry published in English, albeit posthumously. Rose Hickman's mother read to her daughters from forbidden English religious books imported by her husband's agents, and Anne Locke, who married Rose's brother Henry, was in later life a translator of Calvin. Jane Wilkinson, like Anne Locke's mother a silkwoman of Anne Boleyn, was involved with William Latymer in importing scriptural works for their mistress; such a charge would have called, not merely for literacy, but for an understanding of the nature of the books she was required to handle. How far these women could be termed humanistic — if at all — is, of course, highly debatable, though it is possible to argue that the new learning gave an impetus to vernacular learning among women.[51]

Thus by the end of the reign study had become acceptable — and even fashionable — for women, as the adult education of Katherine

Parr testifies. It would be wrong, of course, to assume that interest in humanism was universal among women, just as it would be wrong to assume that all Henrician gentlemen were educated in the new learning. Anne Basset, daughter of Honor, Lady Lisle by her first marriage, was chiefly brought up in France and later sent to the English court. In March 1538 she wrote — or rather, dictated a letter — to her mother from London, confessing that 'where your ladyship doth think that I can write English, in very deed I cannot, but that little that I can write is French'. Mistress Basset, it seems, was quite unconcerned with her lack of literacy, since in February 1540 she nonchalantly told her mother:

> And whereas ye do write to me that I do not write with my own hand, the truth is, that I cannot write nothing myself but mine own name; and as for that, when I had haste to go up to the Queen's chamber, my man did write it which did write my letter.[52]

Anne Basset was apparently handsome and high-spirited, and seems not to have felt the need of learned accomplishments to win favour at Henry's court. Her mother Lady Lisle, wife of the Deputy of Calais, kept up a voluminous correspondence, but the new learning does not seem to have been a subject close to her heart. Even when considering the galaxy of learned ladies, it is well to remember that when Roger Ascham visited Bradgate in 1552 he found that Jane Grey was the only member of her family who preferred reading Plato at home to hunting in the park.[53] At the same time, it is surely significant that Jane's parents, conscious of her proximity to the throne, took care to give her a humanist education.

How great, then, was the impact of the new learning on the lives of women in the earlier sixteenth century? The available information is scarce and it is difficult to assess how many women had the benefit of humanist instruction. Probably there were not many, since learning was far from universal even among the most privileged class, the court ladies. Learned women were applauded as much for their rarity as for their personal excellence, and their education did not give them egress into public life. With the single exception of Princess Mary, they were not trained for office, nor — apart from the Queens Regent, Katherine of Aragon and Katherine Parr — were they allowed to fill positions of political responsibility.

In comparison with the theoretical literature which concerned the education of laymen, there were very few handbooks intended for the instruction of women — and all of these were specifically commissioned by Katherine of Aragon. Similarly, a mere handful of women — Margaret Roper, Margaret Beaufort and Katherine Parr — had their literary work published during the reign, and indeed, there is little extant evidence of the composition or translation of works by women under Henry VIII. Feminine signatures and messages are sometimes to be found in the court albums passed around and used by the gentlemen poets of the period, and possibly some of the verses in the albums are by women; but this will probably never be known positively. (For the difficulty in identifying the different authors of poems in court albums, see Chapter Six, above.)

Humanism, then, affected only a minority of women. However, the new learning by its recognition of the utility of education to women marked a fundamental change in the general attitude to women's studies; these were now a means of inculcating piety and morality rather than a hindrance to them. If the Henrician achievement in feminine learning seems relatively small, it compares well with the bleak situation of the late fifteenth century. The pioneering work of Thomas More, Katherine of Aragon and those who followed them was crucial in the development of English culture later in the sixteenth century, and in the general history of women's studies. Without Queen Katherine's education of Mary there would have been no model — and no textbooks — for those who supervised the instruction of Elizabeth, Jane Grey and their like; and without the foundations laid in the reign of Henry VIII the age of Elizabeth would have been far less remarkable for its erudite women.

Notes

1. Printed in Foster Watson (ed.), *Vives and the Renascence Education of Women* (Edward Arnold, London, 1912), p. 30.

2. Hyrde's preface to Margaret Roper's translation of Erasmus's *Precatio Dominica*, published by Berthelet in 1524. Reprinted in Watson, *Vives and Women*, pp. 162–73, though with some inaccuracies.

3. Watson, *Vives and Women*, p. 179. Cf. P. S. and H. M. Allen, H. W. Garrod (eds), *Opus Epistolarum Des. Erasmi Roterodami* (11 vols., Clarendon Press, Oxford, 1906–47), no. 1847 from Vives. Erasmus's *Vidua Christiana* (Gourmont, Paris, 1529) paints a more flattering picture.

4. Watson, *Vives and Women*, pp. 165, 166–7.

5. *The English Works of John Fisher*, John E. B. Mayor (ed.) (Early English Text Society, N. Trübner & Co., London, 1876), pp. 291–2.

6. Cf. Watson, *Vives and Women*, p. 34.

7. E, F. Rogers (ed.), *Correspondence of Sir Thomas More* (Princeton University Press, Princeton, 1947), p. 405 for Palsgrave's letter; Simon Grynaeus (ed.), *Platonis Opera Omnia* (apud. Ioan. Valderum, Basle, 1534), preface to John More. Thomas More's letters are printed in Watson, *Vives and Women*, pp. 175–94. Cf. Allen, *Erasmi Epistolae*, no. 1233 to Budé.

8. Allen, *Erasmi Epistolae*, no. 1404 to Margaret Roper; Roger Ascham, *Whole Works*, Rev. Dr Giles (ed.) (3 vols., J. R. Smith, London, 1865, 64), vol. 1, epistle 166, to Mary Basset.

9. More, *Correspondence*, pp. 563–5. For Margaret Gigs, William Roper and Nicholas Harpsfield, *Lives of St Thomas More*, E. E. Reynolds (ed.) (Everyman, London, 1963), pp. 103–4.

10. Watson, *Vives and Women*, p. 31–2.

11. Hyrde's translation of *De Institutione Foeminae Christianae* is reprinted in full in ibid., pp. 29–136; the quote is on pp. 32–3. The translation was published in England several times both before and after Katherine's repudiation.

12. Translation and printed in Watson, *Vives and Women*, pp. 137–50, whence the quotations come.

13. Vives, *Opera Omnia*, G. Majamsius (ed.) (8 vols., In Officina Benedicti Monfort, Valencia, 1782–90), vol. 4. Unlike Vives's two previous works on women's education, the *Symbola* was dedicated to Mary rather than Katherine.

14. Allen, *Erasmi Epistolae*, no. 1727.

15. Quoted in Garrett Mattingly, *Catherine of Aragon* (Jonathan Cape, London, 1944), p. 189.

16. J. S. Brewer, J. Gairdner, R. H. Brodie (eds), *Letters and Papers, Foreign and Domestic, of the Reign of Henry VIII*, (21 vols., HMSO, London, 1862–1932), vol. 3, no. 2992 (8), grants in April 1523 (hereafter cited as *L&P*). Foster Watson's hypothesis (*Vives and Women*, p. 14) that Vives and Linacre were given a joint educational and medical trust over Mary must be questioned, since Linacre died in 1524 after a long and painful illness, and declared in his *Rudimenta Grammatices* prepared for the Princess that he was sending her the work because he was too ill to attend her. The only evidence of collaboration is an undated letter in which Vives asks Linacre what he intends to do about his grammar and speaks of his illness; *Opera*, vol. 7, pp. 207–8.

17. Giles Duwes, *An Introductory to read, to pronounce and to speak French truly* (Bourman, London, 1534?), *passim*. The work was published at least twice during the Boleyn marriage and was altered to show Mary apparently acquiescing in the divorce and her own bastardisation; she was given her new title of 'the Lady Mary of England', and made to refer to Katherine simply as 'the good lady my mother'. These 'divorce' editions carried an address full of good wishes for the King, 'Queen' Anne and 'your right dear and well-beloved daughter Elizabeth, Princess of England and of Wales'. Not surprisingly, this was omitted from the edition printed after the fall of Anne Boleyn.

18. British Library, Royal MS 17 C XVI, Morley's translation of Aquinas on the angelic salutation and Anselm on the stature, form and life of the Virgin, preface; Additional MS 17,012, lady's book of hours. The prayer is written on a blank leaf at the end, and Mary's title of 'Princess' has been defaced.

19. Allen, *Erasmi Epistolae*, nos. 2023, 2133.

20. Lancelot de Carles, bishop of Riez, 'Traité pour feue dame Anne de Boulant, jadis Reine d'Angleterre', Bibliotheque Royale, Brussels, MS 19378. This treatise was published at Lyons in 1545. It was also printed by G. A. Crapelet, in *Lettres de Henry VIII à Anne Boleyn* (L'Imprimerie de Carpelet, Paris, 1835), pp. 167ff. Crapelet, however, was unaware of the Brussels MS and had not seen the printed edition; he took his version from two manuscripts in the French royal library.

21. British Library, Additional MS 12,192 fos. 42–89 (*L&P*, vol. 4, no. 3105), narrative of Claude Dodieu.

22. Cf. John E. Paul, *Catherine of Aragon and her Friends* (Burns & Oates, London, 1966), p. 228. The source of this story is the imperial ambassador Chapuys, who does not actually name the tutor as Fetherston; none the less, he seems the most likely candidate.

23. Nicholas Udall (ed.), *The first tome or volume of the Paraphrase of Erasmus upon the new testament* (Whitchurch, London, 1548), preface to John's gospel from Udall to Katherine Parr.

24. Thomas Wyatt, *Plutarch's Quyete of Mynde*, C. R. Baskervill (ed.) (Harvard University Press, Cambridge, Mass., 1931), sig. aij–aiij.

25. Modern editions of this play are by Alexander B. Grosart, *A newe enterlude . . . of godly queene Hester* (Miscellanies of the Fuller Worthies Library, 4 vols., privately printed, London, 1870–76), vol. 4, pp. 544–610; and W. W. Greg, *A New Enterlude of Godly Queene Hester* (Materialen zur Kunde des älteren Englischen Dramas, A. Uystpruyst, Louvain, 1904). For a fuller discussion of the play as an allegory of the divorce, Maria Dowling, 'Scholarship, Politics and the Court of Henry VIII' (unpublished PhD dissertation, University of London, 1981), pp. 176–7.

26. *The office and duty of an husband, made by the excellent philosopher Lodovicus Vives, and translated into English by Thomas Paynell* (Cawood, London, 1550?), sig. eiii[b]. The Latin original was published at Antwerp in 1529.

27. Erasmus, *Vidua Christiana*, pp. 6[b], 14[a]; Allen, *Erasmi Epistolae*, no. 3090 from Chapuys, 1 February 1536.

28. Launcelot de Carles, 'Traité pour Anne de Boulant', fo. 1[b]; Twysden's account is in George Wyatt, *Extracts from the Life of the Virtuous, Christian and Renowned Queen Anne Boleigne*, R. Triphook (ed.) (privately printed, London, 1817), p. 14.

29. Edward E. Lowinsky, 'A music book for Anne Boleyn', in J. G. Rowe and W. H. Stockdale (eds), *Florilegium Historiale, Essays Presented to Wallace K. Ferguson* (University of Toronto Press, Toronto and Buffalo, 1971); Bourbon, *Nugae* (Dolet, Lyons, 1538), passim; Whittinton's verses are described in *Historical Manuscripts Commission, Calendar of the Manuscripts of the Marquis of Salisbury* (18 vols, HMSO, London, 1883–1940), vol. 1, pp. 9–10.

30. British Library, Royal MS 20 B XVII, French treatise on letter-writing; Harleian MS 6561, epistles and gospels for the 52 Sundays in the year; Royal MS 16 E XIII, 'Le Pasteur Evangélique', identified as Marot's work by Lowinsky, 'Music book', pp. 189, 230.

31. William Latymer, 'A Brief Treatise or Chronicle of the most virtuous Lady Anne Boleyn', Bodleian Library, Oxford, MS C Don 42 fos. 20–33 (hereafter cited as *Brief Treatise*); PRO SP1/103, fos. 262–3 (*L&P*, vol. 10, no. 829), Mayor and Jurates of Sandwich to Henry VIII, 8 May 1536; British Library, Additional MS 43,827 fo. 2, narrative of Rose Hickman, edited by Joy Shakespeare and Maria Dowling as 'Religion and Politics in mid-Tudor England through the Eyes of an English Protestant Woman', *Bulletin of the Institute of Historical Research*, vol. 55, no. 131 (May 1982), pp. 94–102.

32. Latymer, *Brief Treatise*, fos. 31[b]–32.

33. The first prayer book is British Library, Stowe MS 956; the second is described by Robert Marsham in *Archaeologia*, vol. 44 (Society of Antiquaries of London, 1873), part 2, pp. 259ff.

34. Latymer, *Brief Treatise*, fo. 31[b].

35. John Foxe, *Acts and Monuments*, S. R. Cattley (ed.) (8 vols., Seeley & Burnside, London, 1837), vol. 5, p. 132, letter of Tyndale to Frith, 1533; PRO SP1/102, fo. 125 (*L&P*, vol. 10, no. 371), confession of Tristram Revel; Sir Henry Ellis (ed.), *Original Letters Illustrative of English History* (11 vols., 3 series, Harding,

Triphook & Lepard, London, 1824, 1827, 1846), series 1, vol. 2, p. 45, Anne Boleyn to Cromwell about Herman.

36. Latymer, *Brief Treatise*, fo. 32; John Bruce and Thomas Perowne (eds), *Correspondence of Matthew Parker* (Parker Society, Cambridge University Press, Cambridge, 1853), no. 46, to Sir Nicholas Bacon, 1 March 1559 (cf. ibid., no. 54, to Elizabeth; T. W. Baldwin, *William Shakespere's Small Latine and Lesse Greeke* (2 vols., University of Illinois Press, Urbana, 1944), vol. 1, p. 258.

37. Ascham, *Whole Works*, vol. 1, epistle, 39.

38. J. G. Nichols (ed.), *Narratives of the Days of the Reformation* (Camden Society, J. B. Nichols & Son, 1859), p. 52 for Elizabeth's copy of Tyndale's *Obedience*. Her version of Katherine Parr's *Prayers or Meditations* is British Library, Royal MS 7 D X.

39. Katherine Parr, *Lamentation of a Sinner* (Whitchurch, London, 1548), sig. bviii–ci; John Strype, *Ecclesiastical Memorials* (3 vols., Clarendon Press, Oxford, 1820–40), vol. 2, ii, p. 337, Katherine Parr to Cambridge.

40. J. G. Nichols (ed.), *Literary Remains of King Edward VI* (2 vols., Roxburghe Club, Burt Franklin, New York, 1857), vol. 1, letter no. 17 (*L&P*, vol. 21, i, no. 1036), Edward to Katherine Parr, 10 June 1546; British Library, Cotton MS Nero C X fo. 6 (*L&P*, vol. 21, ii, no. 686 (2)), Katherine to Edward (January 1547).

41. *Prayers or Meditations* was published in 1545 by the royal printer Berthelet, but the *Lamentations* were not published until 1548, after Katherine's death.

42. Udall, *Paraphrase*, preface to Luke.

43. British Library, Lansdowne MS 97, fo. 43 (*L&P*, vol. 18, ii, no. 331), Goldsmith to Katherine Parr; John Parkhurst, *Ludicra sive Epigrammata Juvenilia* (apud. J. Dayum, London, 1573), passim. For Katherine Brandon, *Calendar of State Papers, Spanish*, G. Bergenroth, P. Gayangos, M. A. S. Hume (eds) (8 vols., HMSO, London, 1862–1904), vol. 8, p. 555, Chapuys to Mary of Hungary; and *Notes from the Records of St John's College, Cambridge*, R. F. Scott (ed.) (3 series, privately printed, 1889–1913), series 2, pp. 1–27.

44. J. W. Ballantyne, 'The "Byrth of Mankynde": Its Author, Editions and Contents', *Journal of Obstetrics and Gynaecology of the British Empire, 1906–7*; reprinted by Sheratt & Hughes, no date. Katherine Howard's letter is calendared in *L&P*, vol. 16, no. 1134 and is displayed in the museum of the Public Record Office, London.

45. Allen, *Erasmi Epistolae*, no. 1925, to the nuns of Denny; British Library, Royal MS 12 B XIV, life of St Katherine. Morley's translations for Mary are Royal MS 17 A XXX, 17 A XLVI, 18 A XV, 17 C XVI.

46. Paynell's tracts are *A Treatise of Well Living* (Petyt, London, 1545?), dedicated to Princess Mary, and *The Assault and Conquest of Heaven* and a translation of Erasmus's *De Contemptu Mundi* (Berthelet, London, 1529 and 1532), dedicated to Mary of France. Becon's works are *The right pathway unto prayer* (Maylor for Grafton, London, 1543) for Lady Anne Grey, and *The governance of virtue* (Maylor for Gough, London, 1543) for Lady Jane Seymour.

47. Published in Godfray, London, 1535. For Marshall and the poor law, G. R. Elton, 'An Early Tudor Poor Law', *Economic History Review*, second series, vol. 6, no. 1 (1953). For Anne Boleyn's interest in poor relief, Latymer, *Brief Treatise*, fos. 25–7.

48. Eileen Power, *Medieval English Nunneries, c. 1275–1535* (Cambridge University Press, Cambridge, 1922), pp. 260–84.

49. Cf. Sidney Lee, *The French Renaissance in England* (Clarendon Press, Oxford, 1910), p. 45.

50. For references to the learning of the Cooke sisters in a later period, James Spedding, *Life and Times of Sir Francis Bacon* (2 vols., Houghton, Osgood & Co., Boston, 1878); Catherine Drinker Bowen, *Francis Bacon, the Temper of a Man*

(Hamish Hamilton, London, 1963); Patrick Collinson, 'A Mirror of Elizabethan Protestantism: The Life and Letters of "Godly Master Dering"', in *Godly People: Essays on English Protestantism and Puritanism* (Hambledon Press, London, 1983), pp. 289–323; Conyers Read, *Master Secretary Cecil and Queen Elizabeth* (Jonathan Cape, London, 1955) and *Lord Burleigh and Queen Elizabeth* (Jonathan Cape, London, 1960).

51. It is also true, however, that Lollard women were often literate, and sometimes acted as teachers to both adults and children. I am grateful for discussion on this subject to Andrew Hope and to Susan Wabuda, who also supplied the information about Anne Askew. For Lollard women, cf. John Davis, 'Joan of Kent, Lollardy and the English Reformation', *Journal of Ecclesiastical History*, vol. 33, no. 2 (April 1982), pp. 225–33.

52. Muriel St Clare Byrne (ed.), *The Lisle Letters* (6 vols., University of Chicago Press, London and Chicago, 1981), vol. 5, no. 1126, vol. 6, no. 1653.

53. For the anecdote in full, Ascham, *Whole Works*, vol. 3, pp. 117–19.

Bibliography

1. Manuscript sources

British Library, London

Additional Manuscripts 5815; 5842; 5853; 5873; 8715; 15,387; 17,012; 19,398; 21,982; 25,114; 26,837; 28,196; 28,587; 28,786; 29,431; 30,662; 43,827.

Arundel Manuscripts 8; 151; 152.

Cotton Manuscripts Caligula B VI, E I; Cleopatra E IV, E V, E VI; Faustina C II, C III, C VII; Galba B VI, B VIII, B IX; Nero B VI, B VII, C X; Otho C X; Titus B I, B VIII; Vespasianus C VI, C XIII, F III F XIII; Vitellius B III, B IV, B V, B XIII, B XIV, C I.

Egerton Manuscripts 97; 1,998.

Harleian Manuscripts 78; 283; 417; 423; 604; 4990; 5087; 6148; 6561; 6986; 6989; 7036; 7041; 7048.

Lansdowne Manuscripts 989; 1236.

Royal Manuscripts 7 C XVI; 12 A X; 12 A XVI; 12 A XXX; 13 A IX; 17 A XXX; 17 A XLVI; 18 A XV; 18 A XL; 18 A L; 18 A LXIV; 20 A IV; 8 B II; 12 B II; 12 B XIII; 12 B XIV; 12 B XV; 13 B XX; 17 B XXXV; 20 B VII; 20 B XII; 20 B XVII; 20 B XXI; 12 C VIII; 16 C IX; 17 C XII; 17 C XVI; 7 D X; 7 D XI; 7 D XIII; 17 D II; 17 D XI; 18 D VI; 13 E XIII; 16 E X; 16 E XI; 16 E XIV; 20 E IX; 7 F XIV; 12 F V; 17 F XIV; Appendix 80.

Sloane Manuscripts 1207; 2495; 4031.

Stowe Manuscript 956.

Public Record Office, London

State Papers of Henry VIII (SP1).
Lisle Papers (SP3).
Theological Tracts (SP6).
Wriothesley Letters (SP7).

Bodleian Library, Oxford

Bodleian MS C. Don. 42.

Bibliothèque Albert I, Brussels

Bibliothèque Royale MS 19,378.

2. Calendars and Catalogues of Primary Sources

Calendar of State Papers, Spanish, G. Bergenroth, P. Gayangos, M. A. S. Hume (eds) (8 vols., HMSO, London, 1862–1904).

Historical Manuscripts Commission: Calendar of the Manuscripts of the Marquess of Salisbury (18 vols., HMSO, London, 1883–1940), vol. 1.

Index of Dedications and Commendatory Verses in English Books Before 1641, Franklin B. Williams (ed.) (Bibliographical Society, Oxford University Press, London, 1962).

Letters and Papers, Foreign and Domestic, of the Reign of Henry VIII, J. S. Brewer, J. Gairdner, R. H. Brodie (eds) (21 vols., HMSO, London, 1862–1932).

Short-Title Catalogue of Books Printed in England, Scotland and Ireland, and of English Books Printed Abroad. 1475–1640, A. Pollard and G. R. Redgrave (eds) (Bibliographical Society, Oxford University Press, London, 1926); second edition of volume 2, W. A. Jackson, F. S. Ferguson, Katherine F. Pantzer (eds) (Bibliographical Society, Oxford University Press, London, 1976).

3. Printed Primary Sources

Allen, P. S. and H. M., H. W. Garrod (eds), *Opus Epistolarum Des. Erasmi Roterodami* (11 vols., Clarendon Press, Oxford, 1906–47).

Allen, P. S. and H. M. (eds), *Letters of Richard Fox* (Clarendon Press, Oxford, 1929).

Anstey, Henry (ed.), *Epistolae Academiae Oxon.* (2 vols., Clarendon Press, Oxford, 1898).

Batten, Edmund Chisholm (ed.), *The Register of Richard Fox while Bishop of Bath and Wells* (Harrison & Sons, London, 1889).

Boase, C. W. (ed.), *Registrum Collegii Exoniensis* (Clarendon Press, Oxford, 1894).

Bond, E. A. (ed.), *Statutes of the Colleges of Oxford* (3 vols., J. H. Parker and Longman, Brown, Green & Longmans, Oxford and London, 1853).

Brown, Rawdon (ed. and trans.), *Four Years at the Court of Henry VIII: Selection of Despatches Written by the Venetian Ambassador, Sebastian Giustinian* (2 vols., Smith, Elder & Co., London, 1854).

Bruce, John and Thomas Perowne (eds), *Correspondence of Matthew Parker* (Parker Society, Cambridge University Press, Cambridge, 1853).

Burrows, Montagu (ed.), 'Linacre's Catalogue of Grocyn's Books', *Oxford Historical Society Collectanea* (2nd series, Clarendon Press, Oxford, 1890), pp. 317–80.

Byrne, Muriel St Clare (ed.), *Letters of Henry VIII* (Cassell & Co., London, 1968).

——*The Lisle Letters* (6 vols., University of Chicago Press, London and Chicago, 1981).

Cooper, C. H. (ed.), *Annals of Cambridge* (5 vols., Warwick & Co., and Cambridge University Press, London and Cambridge, 1842–1908).

Corrie, G. E. (ed.), *Sermons and Remains of Hugh Latimer* (Parker Society, Cambridge University Press, Cambridge, 1845).

Cox, J. E. (ed.), *Miscellaneous Writings and Letters of Thomas Cranmer* (Parker Society, Cambridge University Press, Cambridge, 1846).

Crapelet, G. A. (ed.), *Lettres de Henry VIII à Anne Boleyn* (L'Imprimerie de Crapelet, Paris, 1835).

Ellis, Sir Henry (ed.), *Original Letters Illustrative of English History* (11 vols., 3 series, Harding, Triphook & Lepard, London, 1824, 1827, 1846).

Ferguson, Wallace K. (ed.), *The Epistles of Erasmus* (6 vols., University of Toronto Press, Toronto, Buffalo, London, 1974–82).

Fletcher, John M. (ed.), *Registrum Annalium Collegii Mertonensis*, vol. 2, *1521–1567* (Clarendon Press, Oxford, 1974).

Gardiner, R. B. (ed.), *Admission Registers of St Paul's School* (2 vols., George Bell & Sons, London, 1884, 1906).

Hughes, Paul L. and James F. Larkin (eds), *Tudor Royal Proclamations* (3 vols., Yale University Press, New Haven and London, 1964–9).

Madden, F. W. (ed.), *Privy Purse Expenses of the Princess Mary, December 1536 to December 1544* (William Pickering, London, 1831).

Marsham, Robert (ed.), 'On a Manuscript Book of Prayers . . . said to have been given by Queen Anne Boleyn to a Lady of the Wyatt Family', *Archaeologia*, vol. 44, part 2 (Society of Antiquaries, London, 1873, pp. 259ff.

Mayor J. E. B. (ed.), *Early Statutes of the College of St John the Evangelist* (Macmillan & Co., Cambridge, 1859).

Merriman, R. B. (ed.), *Life and Letters of Thomas Cromwell* (2 vols., Clarendon Press, Oxford, 1902).

Muller, J. A. (ed.), *Letters of Stephen Gardiner* (Cambridge University Press, Cambridge, 1933).

Nichols J. G. (ed.), *Literary Remains of King Edward VI* (2 vols., Roxburghe Club, Burt Franklin, New York, 1857).

——'Memoir and Letters of the Duke of Richmond', *Camden Miscellany 3* (Camden Society, J. B. Nichols & Sons, London, 1857).

——*Narratives of the Days of the Reformation* (Camden Society, J. B. Nichols & Sons, London, 1859).

——and John Bruce (eds), *Wills from Doctors' Commons* (Camden Society, J. B. Nichols & Sons, London, 1863).

Nicolas, Sir N. H. (ed.), *Privy Purse Expences of Henry VIII* (William Pickering, London, 1827).

Ogle, Octavius (ed.), *Royal Letters Addressed to Oxford* (James Parker & Co., Oxford and London, 1892).

Pearson, George (ed.), *Remains of Myles Coverdale* (Parker Society, Cambridge University Press, Cambridge, 1846).

Rackham, H. (ed.), *Early Statutes of Christ's College, Cambridge* (Fabb & Tyler, Cambridge, 1927).

Richards, G. C. and H. E. Salter (eds), *The Dean's Register of Oriel* (Clarendon Press, Oxford, 1926).

Robinson, Hastings (ed.), *Original Letters Relative to the English Reformation* (Parker Society, Cambridge University Press, Cambridge, 1846).

Rogers, E. F. (ed.), *Correspondence of Sir Thomas More* (Princeton University Press, Princeton, 1947).

——*St Thomas More: Selected Letters* (Yale University Press, New Haven and London, 1961).

Rouschausse, Jean (ed.), *Erasmus and Fisher: Their Correspondence* (J. Vrin, Paris, 1968).

Salter, H. E. (ed), *Registrum Annalium Collegii Mertonensis*, vol. 1, 1483–1521 (Clarendon Press, Oxford, 1923).

Schillings, A. (ed.), *Matricule de L'Université de Louvain* (10 vols., Palais des Academies, Brussels, 1952–67).

Scott, R. F. (ed.), *Notes from the Records of St John's College, Cambridge* (3 series, privately printed, 1889–1913).

Shadwell, C. L. (ed.), *Registrum Orielense, vol. 1, 1500–1700* (Henry Frowde, London, 1893).

Shadwell, L. L. (ed.), *Enactments in Parliament Concerning Oxford and Cambridge* (4 vols., Clarendon Press, Oxford, 1911).

Shakespeare, Joy and Maria Dowling, 'The Recollections of Rose Hickman', *Bulletin of the Institute of Historical Research*, vol. 55, no. 131 (May 1982), pp. 94–102.

Venn, John (ed.), John Caius, *Annals of Gonville and Caius College* (Cambridge Antiquarian Society, Cambridge, 1904).

Ward, G. R. M. (ed. and trans.), *Foundation Statutes of Bishop Fox for Corpus Christi College, with a Life of the Founder* (Longman, Brown, Green & Longmans, London, 1843).

Wood, M. A. E. (ed.), *Letters of Royal and Illustrious Ladies* (3 vols., Henry Colburn, London, 1846).

Epistolae Tigurinae, 1531–1558 (Parker Society, Cambridge University Press, Cambridge, 1848).

Hadrianus Junius Epistolae (Vincent Caimax, Dordrecht, 1602).

State Papers Published Under the Authority of His Majesty's Commission, Volume One, King Henry the Eighth (HMSO, London, 1830).

4. Contemporary and Early Modern Books

Abell, Thomas *Invicta Veritas* (Lüneberg, 1532).

Agrippa, Henry Cornelius von Nettesheim *The commendation of matrimony*, David Clapham (trans.) (in aed. Berthelet, London, 1540).

——*De nobilitate et praecellentia fœminei sexus* (I. Soter, Cologne, 1535).

Barclay, Alexander *The mirror of good manners* (Pynson, London, 1518?).

Barlow, William *A dialogue describing the original ground of these Lutheran factions* (W. Rastell, London, 1531).

Barnes, Robert *Supplication . . . unto the most excellent and redoubted prince King Henry the Eighth* (Byddell, London, 1534).

Bekinsaw, John *De supremo et absoluto regis imperio* (in aed. Berthelet, London, 1546).

Bishops, The *The institution of a Christian man* (in aed. Berthelet, London, 1537).

Bourbon, Nicholas *Nugae* (Dolet, Lyons, 1538).

Bourchier, John Lord Berners *Golden book of Marcus Aurelius* (in aed. Berthelet, London, 1535).

Bourchier, Thomas *Historia ecclesiastica de martyrio fratrum ordinis Divi Francisci, dictorum de Observantia, qui partim in Anglia sub Henrico Octavo Rege* (apud I. Poupy, Paris, 1582).

Burrant, Robert *Precepts of Cato the Sage, with annotations of D. Erasmus of Rotterdam* (Grafton, London, 1545).

Capito, Wolfgang *An epitome of the psalms*, Richard Taverner (trans.) (London, 1539).

Caxton, William *The book of Eneydos* (Caxton, London, 1489).

Chaloner, Thomas *Homily of St John Chrysostom* (in off. Berthelet, London, 1544).

Champaigne, Peter de *Salus corporis salus anime* (Faques, London, 1509).

Cheke, John *D. Ioannis Chrysostomi homiliae duae* (Reyner Wolfe, London, 1543).

——*D. Ioannis Chrysostomi de providentia Dei, ac fato, oratories sex* (Reyner Wolfe, London, 1545).

Churchyard, Thomas *Churchyard's charge* (John Kyngston, London, 1580).

Clerke, John *L'amant mal traité de sa mie* (Wyer, London, 1543).

——*Opusculum plane divinum de mortuorum resurrectione* (Hertford, London, 1545).

Cognatus, Gilbertus *Of the office of servants*, Thomas Chaloner (trans.) (in off. Berthelet, London, 1534).

Constable, John *Epigrammata* (Pynson, London, 1520).

Cope, Anthony *History of Hannibal and Scipio* (Berthelet, London, 1544).

——*A godly meditation upon twenty select and chosen psalms of the prophet David* (Daye, London, 1547).

Duwes, Giles *An introductory to read, to pronounce and to speak French truly* (Bourman, London, 1534?).

Edgar, David *De indiciis et praecognitionibus, opus utile medicis* (Redman, London, 1532).

Elyot, Sir Thomas *The banquet of sapience* (in aed. Berthelet, London, 1534).

——*The castle of health* (in aed. Berthelet, London, 1539).

——*Defence of good women* (Berthelet, London, 1545).

——*Dictionary* (in aed. Berthelet, London, 1538).

——*The doctrinal of princes* (in aed. Berthelet, London, 1538).

——*The image of governance* (Berthelet, London, 1544).
——Plutarch, *The education or bringing up of children* (Berthelet, London, 1535?).
——*A preservative against death* (Berthelet, London, 1545).
Erasmus, Desiderius *Apophthegmes, that is to say, prompt sayings*, Nicholas Udall (trans.) (ex typis R. Grafton, London, 1542).
——*Christiani matrimonii institutio* (Froben, Basle, 1526).
——*De conscribendis epistolis* (Siberch, Cambridge, 1521).
——*De contemptu mundi*, Thomas Paynell (trans.) (Berthelet, London, 1532).
——*De copia* (Bade, Paris, 1512).
——*Devout treatise upon the Pater Noster*, Margaret Roper (trans.) (Berthelet, London, 1524).
——*Dilucida et pia explanatio Symboli quod apostolorum dicitur* (Froben, Basle, 1533).
——*A plain or godly exposition of the common Creed* (Redman, London, 1533).
——*Ecclesiastae sive de ratione concionandi* (Froben, Basle, 1535).
——Enarratio triplex in Psalmum XXII (Froben, Basle, 1530).
——*A very pleasant and fruitful dialogue called the epicure*, Philip Gerard (trans.) (Grafton, London, 1545).
——*De immensa misericordia Dei*, Gentian Hervet (trans.) (Berthelet, London, 1526?).
——*A right fruitful epistle in laud and praise of matrimony*, Richard Taverner (trans.) (Redman, London, 1530?).
——*De praeparatione ad mortem* (Froben, Basle, 1534).
——*Preparation to death* (in aed. Berthelet, London, 1538).
——*The first tome or volume of the paraphrase of Erasmus upon the new testament*, Nicholas Udall (ed.) (Whitchurch, London, 1548).
——*Vidua Christiana* (Gourmont, Paris, 1529).
Fewterer, John *The mirror or glass of Christ's passion* (Redman, London, 1534).
Fish, Simon *Supplication for the beggars* (Antwerp, 1528).
Fisher, John *Sacri sacerdotii defensio contra Lutherum* (Quentell, Cologne, 1525).
——*Assertionis Lutheranae confutatio* (Quentell, Cologne, 1523).
——*Defensio Regie assertionis contra Babylonicam captivitatem* (Quentell, Cologne, 1525).
——*The sermon of John the Bishop of Rochester made against the*

pernicious doctrine of Martin Luther (Wynkyn de Worde, London, 1521).

——*A sermon . . . said by John the Bishop of Rochester . . . concerning certain heretics* (Berthelet, London, 1526).

——*De veritate corporis et sanguinis Christi in Eucharistia* (Quentell, Cologne, 1527).

Foxe, Edward *De vera differentia regiae potestatis et ecclesiasticae* (Berthelet, London, 1534).

Frontinus, Julius *The stratagems, sleights and policies of war*, Richard Morison (trans.) (in aed. Berthelet, London, 1539).

Gemini, Thomas *Compendiosa totius anatomie delineatio* (in off. Hertford, London, 1545).

Geraldini, Alessandro *Itinerarium ad regiones sub aequinoctiali plaga* (G. Facciotti, Rome, 1631).

Giovio, Paolo *A short treatise upon the Turks' chronicles*, Peter Assheton (trans.) (Whitchurch, London, 1546).

Grynaeus, Simon, (ed.) *Platonis Opera Omnia* (apud. Ioan. Valderum, Basle, (1534).

Guevara, Antonio de *Dispraise of the life of a courtier, and a commendation of the life of a labouring man*, Sir Francis Bryan (trans.) (in aed. Grafton, London, 1548).

——*A looking-glass for the court*, Sir Francis Bryan (trans.) (for William Norton, London, 1575).

Haddon, Walter *Vita et obitus duorum fratrem Suffolcensium* (in aed. Grafton, London, 1551).

Hales, John *The precepts of . . . Plutarch for the preservation of good health* (in off. Grafton, London, 1543).

Hervet, Gentian *Quaedam Opuscula* (Dolet, Lyons, 1541).

Hugh, William *A sweet consolation, and the second book of the troubled man's medicine* (Hertford, London, 1546).

Langley, Thomas *Abridgement of the notable work of Polydore Vergil* (Grafton, London, 1546).

Leland, John *Assertio inclytissimi Arthurii regis Britanniae* (Hertford, London, 1544).

——*Cygnea cantio* (Hertford, London, 1545).

——*Genethliacon illustrissimi Eäduerdi principis Cambriae* (Reyner Wolfe, London, 1543).

——*Naeniae in mortem T. Viati* (Reyner Wolfe, London, 1545).

Linacre, Thomas *Rudimenta grammatices* (in aed. Pynson, London, 1525?).

Marshall, William *The form and manner of subvention or helping for poor people, devised and practised in the city of Ypres in Flanders* (Godfray, London, 1535).

Morison, Richard *Apomaxis* (Berthelet, London, 1538).

——*The epistle that J. Sturmius . . . sent unto the cardinals and prelates . . . appointed by the Bishop of Rome to search out the abuses of the church* (Berthelet, London, 1538).

——*An exhortation to stir all Englishmen to the defence of their country* (Berthelet, London, 1539).

——*An invective against treason* (Berthelet, London, 1539).

——*A lamentation* (Berthelet, London, 1536).

——*A remedy for sedition* (Berthelet, London, 1536).

Nausea, Frederick *In divam Catharinam serenissimam nuper Angliae Reginam funebris oratio* (Ivo Scoeffer, Morguntiae, 1536).

——*Sermon of the sacrament of the altar*, John More (trans.) (Rastell, London, 1533).

Palsgrave, John *L'Eclairçissement de la langue Française* (Hawkins, London, 1530).

Parker, Henry Lord Morley *Exposition and declaration of the psalm: Deus ultionum dominus* (in aed. Berthelet, London, 1539).

Parkhurst, John *Ludicra sive epigrammata juvenilia* (Daye, London, 1573).

Parr, Katherine *Lamentation of a sinner* (Whitchurch, London, 1548).

——*Prayers or meditations, wherein the mind is stirred patiently to suffer all afflictions* (Berthelet, London, 1545).

Paynell, Thomas *The assault and conquest of heaven (Berthelet, London, 1529).*

——*Precepts teaching a prince or a noble estate his duty* (Berthelet, London, 1530–33).

——*Regimen sanitatis Salerni* (Berthelet, London, 1528).

——*Sermon of St Cyprian made on the Lord's prayer* (Berthelet, London, 1539).

——*A treatise of well living* (Petyt, London, 1545?).

Porcia, Jacopo di *Precepts of war*, Peter Betham (trans.) (Whitchurch, London, 1544).

Powell, Edward *Propugnaculum summi sacerdotii adver. M. Lutherum* (Pynson, London, 1523).

Revell, Tristram *The sum of Christianity, gathered out almost of all places of scripture by . . . Francis Lambert of Avignon* (Redman?, London, 1536).

Roy, William and Jerome Barlow *The Burial of the Mass* (Antwerp, 1528).

Sallust *Jugurthine War,* Alexander Barclay (trans.) (Pynson, London, 1520?).

Sampson, Richard *In priores quinquaginta psalmos Daviticos, familiaris explanatio* (in aed. Berthelet, London, 1539).

Sarcerius, Erasmus *Common places of scripture*, Richard Taverner (trans.) (Byddell, London, 1538).

Seton, John *Dialectica* (in aed. Berthelet, London, 1545).

Smith, Richard *The assertion and defence of the sacrament of the altar* (Hertford, at the charges of Robert Toye, London, 1546).

——*A defence of the sacrifice of the mass* (Hertford, London, 1546).

Starkey, Thomas *An exhortation to . . . unity and obedience* (in aed. Berthelet, London, 1536).

Stokesley, John, Thomas Cranmer and Edward Foxe (The determinations of the most famous and most excellent universities of Italy and of France (Berthelet, London, 1531).

Taverner, Richard *Confession of the faith of the Germans . . . at Augusta* (Redman, London, 1536).

Tracey, Richard *The proof and declaration of this proposition: faith only justifieth* (Whitchurch, London, 1543?).

——*A supplication to King Henry the Eighth* (Antwerp?, 1544).

Turner, William *The hunting of the romish fox* (Basle, 1543).

——*The rescuing of the romish fox* (Froschauer?, Zurich?, 1545).

Twine, John *De rebus Albionicis, Britannicis atque Anglicis, commentariorum* (Edm. Bollifantus pro Ric. Watkins, London, 1590).

Tyndale, William *The obedience of a Christian man* (J. Hoochstraten, Antwerp, 1528).

——*The practice of prelates* (Antwerp, 1530).

Udall, Nicholas *Flowers for Latin speaking, selected and gathered out of Terence* (Berthelet, London, 1534).

Vergil, Polydore *Adagiorum Liber* (Froben, Basle, 1521).

Villa Nova, Arnaldus de *The defence of age and recovery of youth*, Jonas Drumunde (trans.) (Wyer, London, 1540?).

Villa Sancta, Alphonso de *De libero arbitrio, adversus Melanchthonem* (Pynson, London, 1523).

——*Problema indulgentiarum* (in aed. Pynson, 1523).

Vives, Juan Luis *An introduction to wisdom*, Richard Morison (trans.) (in aed. Berthelet, London, 1540).

——*The office and duty of an husband*, Thomas Paynell (trans.) (Cawood, London, 1550?).

——*St Augustine of the city of God: with the learned comments of Io. Lud. Vives* (G. Eld and M. Flesher, 1620).

——(attr.) *Non esse neque divino, neque naturae iure prohibitum, quin summus pontifex dispensare possit . . .* (Lüneberg, 1532).

Wakefield, Robert *Kotser codicis* (Berthelet, London, c. 1534).

——*Oratio de laudibus et utilitate trium linguarum Arabicae, Chaldaicae et Hebraicae* (Wynkyn de Worde, London, 1524).

Walshe, Edward *The office and duty in fighting for our country* (Hertford for Toye, London, 1545).

Whitford, Richard *A daily exercise and experience of death* (Waylande, London, 1537).

——*Divers holy instructions and teachings very necessary for the health of man's soul* (Middleton, London, 1541).

——*Pipe or tun of the life of perfection* (Redman, London, 1542).

——*A work for householders* (Wynkyn de Worde, London, 1533).

Whittinton, Robert *Mirror or glass of manners and wisdom* (Middleton, London, 1547).

——*De nominum generibus* (Wynkyn de Worde, London, 1521).

——*Opusculum* (Wynkyn de Worde, London, 1519).

——*The three books of Tully's offices* (Wynkyn de Worde, London, 1534).

——*Tullius de senectute* (Byddell, London, 1535?).

Xenophon *Treatise of household*, Gentian Hervet (trans.) (Berthelet, London, 1532).

5. Modern Editions of Early Works

Ammonio, Andrea *Carmina Omnia*, Clemente Pizzi (ed.) (Leonis S. Olschki, Florence, 1958).

Ascham, Roger *English Works*, William Aldis Wright (ed.) (Cambridge University Press, Cambridge, 1904).

——*Whole Works*, Rev. Dr Giles (ed.) (3 vols., J. R. Smith, London, 1865, 1864).

Barclay, Alexander *Eclogues*, Beatrice White (ed.) (Early English Text Society, Oxford University Press, London, 1928).

Barker, William *The Nobility of Women*, R. Warwick Bond (ed.) (2 vols., Roxburghe Club, privately printed, London, 1904–5).

Beccatelli, Lodovico *Life of Cardinal Reginald Pole*, Benjamin Pye (ed.) (C. Bathurst, London, 1766).

Becon, Thomas *Early Works*, John Ayre (ed.) (Parker Society, Cambridge University Press, Cambridge, 1843).

Borde, Andrew *Introduction and Dietary*, F. J. Furnivall (ed.) (Early English Text Society, Kegan Paul, Trench, Trübner & Co., London, 1870).

Cavendish, George *Life and Death of Cardinal Wolsey*, J. Singer (ed.) (Early English Text Society, Oxford University Press, London, 1959).

Clifford, Henry *Life of Jane Dormer, Duchess of Feria*, Joseph Stevenson (ed.) (Burns & Oates, London, 1887).

Elyot, Sir Thomas *The Book Named the Governor*, H. H. S. Croft (ed.) (2 vols., Kegan Paul, Trench & Co., London, 1883).

Erasmus, Desiderius *The Comparition of a Virgin and a Martyr*, Thomas Paynell (trans.), W. J. Hirten (ed.) (Scholars' Facsimiles and Reprints, Gainesville, Florida, 1970).

——*Declamatio de Pueris statim ac Liberaliter Instituendis*, Jean-Claude Margolin (ed.) (Travaux d'Humanisme et Renaissance, no. 77, Geneva, 1966).

——*The Education of a Christian Prince*, Lester K. Born (ed. and trans.) (Columbia University Press, New York, 1936).

——*Lives of Jehan Vitrier and John Colet*, J. H. Lupton (ed. and trans.) (George Bell & Sons, London, 1883).

——*The Essential Erasmus*, John P. Dolan (ed. and trans.) (New American Library, New York, 1964). Volume of the *Enchiridion*, *Praise of Folly*, *Complaint of Peace* and other works.

Fisher, John *English Works*, J. E. B. Mayor (ed.) (Early English Text Society, N. Trübner & Co., London, 1876).

——*Funeral Sermon of Lady Margaret*, J. Hymers (ed.) (Cambridge University Press, Cambridge, 1840).

Foxe, John *Acts and Monuments*, S. R. Cattley (ed.) (8 vols., Seeley & Burnside, London, 1837).

Furnivall, F. J., (ed.) *Manners and Meals in the Olden Time*, (Early English Text Society, Oxford University Press, London, 1868).

Gardiner, Stephen *Obedience in Church and State*, Pierre Janelle (ed.) (Cambridge University Press, Cambridge, 1930).

Greg, W. W., (ed.) *A New Interlude of Godly Queen Hester* (Materialen zur Kunde des älteren Englischen Dramas, A. Uystpruyst, Louvain, 1904).

Grosart, Alexander B. (ed.) *A New Interlude . . . of Godly Queen Hester* (Miscellanies of the Fuller Worthies' Library, 4 vols., privately printed, London, 1870–6), vol. 4.

Guevara, Antonio de *The Castle of Love*, John Bourchier, Lord Berners (trans.), W. G. Crane (ed.) (Scholars' Facsimiles and Reprints, Gainesville, Florida, 1950).

Hall, Richard (attr.) *Life of Fisher*, Ronald Bayne (ed.) (Early English Text Society, Oxford University Press, London, 1921).

Henry VIII *Assertio Septem Sacramentorum*, Thomas Webster (ed. and trans.) (N. Thompson, London, 1687).

Henry Howard, Earl of Surrey *Poems*, Emrys Jones (ed.) (Clarendon Press, Oxford, 1972).

More, Sir Thomas *Apology*, J. B. Trapp (ed.) (Yale University Press, New Haven and London, 1979).

——*Latin Epigrams*, Leicester Bradner and Charles Arthur Lynch (eds and trans.) (University of Chicago Press, Chicago, 1953).

——*History of the Passion*, Mary Basset (trans.), P. E. Hallett (ed.) (Burns, Oates & Washbourne Ltd, London, 1941).

——*Responsio ad Lutherum*, John M. Headley (ed.) (Yale University Press, New Haven and London, 1969).

Pace, Richard *De Fructu Qui Ex Doctrina Percipitur*, F. Manley and R. S. Sylvester (eds and trans.) (Ungar, New York, 1967).

Palsgrave, John *Comedy of Acolastus*, P. L. Carver (ed.) (Early English Text Society, Oxford University Press, London, 1937).

Parker, Henry Lord Morley *The Triumphes of Petrarch*, Stafford Henry, Earl of Iddlesleigh (ed.) (Roxburghe Club, Nichols & Son, London, 1887).

Rollins, Hyder Edward (ed.) *Tottel's Miscellany* (2 vols., Harvard University Press, Cambridge, Mass., 1928, 1929).

Roper, William and Nicholas Harpsfield *Lives of St Thomas More*, E. E. Reynolds (ed.) (Everyman, London, 1963).

Skelton, John *Speculum Principis*, F. M. Salter (ed.) (*Speculum*, vol. 9, no. 1 (January 1934), pp. 25–37).

——*Magnificence*, Robert Lee Ramsay (ed.) (Early English Text Society, Kegan Paul, Trench, Trübner & Co. Ltd, 1908).

——*Complete Poems*, Philip Henderson (ed.) (J. M. Dent & Sons, London and Toronto, 1948).

Stanbridge, John and Robert Whittinton, *Vulgaria*, Beatrice White (ed.) (Early English Text Society, Oxford University Press, London, 1932).

Stapleton, Thomas, *Histoire de Thomas More*, A. Martin and M.

Audin (eds and trans.) (L. Maison, Paris, 1849).

Starkey, Thomas *A Dialogue Between Reginald Pole and Thomas Lupset*, Kathleen M. Burton (ed.) (Chatto & Windus, London, 1948).

Tydeman, William (ed.) *English Poetry, 1400–1580* (Heinemann, London, 1970).

Udall, Nicholas *Dramatic Writings*, John S. Farmer (ed.) (privately printed, London, 1906).

Vergil, Polydore *Anglica Historia*, Denys Hay (ed.) (Camden Society, Offices of the Royal Historical Society, London, 1950).

Vives, Juan Luis *Opera Omnia*, G. Majansius (ed.) (8 vols., in off. Benedicti Monfort, Valencia, 1782–90).

Vowell, John alias Hooker, *Life and Times of Sir Peter Carew*, John MacLean (ed.) (Bell & Daldy, London, 1857).

Watson, Foster (ed.) *Vives and the Renascence Education of Women* (Edward Arnold, London, 1912). Volume containing *The Instruction of a Christian Woman*, *De Ratione Studii Puerilis* and other words.

Wilson, Thomas *The Art of Rhetoric*, G. H. Mair (ed.) (Clarendon Press, Oxford, 1909).

Wyatt, George *Extracts from the Life of the Virtuous, Christian and Renowned Queen Anne Boleigne*, R. Triphook (ed.) (privately printed, London 1817).

Wyatt, Sir Thomas *Poems*, A. K. Foxwell (ed.) (2 vols., University of London Press, London, 1913).

——*Collected Poems*, Joost Daalder (ed.) (Clarendon Press, Oxford, 1975).

——Plutarch's *Quiet of Mind*, C. R. Baskervill (ed.) (Harvard University Press, Cambridge, Mass., 1931).

6. Secondary Works

Adams, Robert P. *The Better Part of Valor* (University of Washington Press, Seattle, 1962).

Aston, T. H., G. D. Duncan, T. A. R. Evans 'The Medieval Alumni of Cambridge', *Past & Present*, no. 86 (February 1980), pp. 9–86.

Aungier, G. J. *History and Antiquities of Syon Monastery* (J. B. Nichols & Sons, London, 1840).

Baker, Thomas *History of the College of St John the Evangelist,*

Cambridge, J. E. B. Mayor (ed.) (2 vols., Cambridge University Press, 1869).

Baldi, Sergio 'The Secretary of the Duke of Norfolk and the First Italian Grammar in England', *Studies in English Language and Literature presented to Karl Brunner*, Siegfried Korninger (ed.) (Wilhelm Braumüller, Vienna and Stuttgart, 1957).

Baldwin, T. W. *William Shakespere's Small Latine and Lesse Greeke* (2 vols., University of Illinois Press, Urbana, 1944).

Ball, W. W. Rouse and Venn, J. A. *Admissions to Trinity College, Cambridge. Vol. 1, 1546–1700* (Macmillan & Co., London, 1913).

Ballantyne, J. W. 'The "Byrth of Mankynde": Its Author, Editions and Contents', *Journal of Obstetrics and Gynaecology of the British Empire*, 1906–7; reprinted by Sheratt & Hughes, London, without date.

Bapst, Edmond *Deux Gentilshommes-Poètes de la Court de Henry VIII* (E. Plon, Nourrit et Cie, Paris, 1891).

Benians, E. A. *John Fisher* (Cambridge University Press, Cambridge, 1935).

Bielby, Nicholas *Three Tudor Poets* (Wheaton, Exeter, 1976).

Brenan, Gerald and Edward Phillips Statham *The House of Howard* (2 vols., Hutchinson & Co., London, 1907).

Bridgett, T. E. *Life of Blessed John Fisher* (Burns & Oates, London, 1890).

——*Life and Writings of Blessed Thomas More* (Burns & Oates, London, 1891).

Bruce, Marie Louise *Anne Boleyn* (Collins, London, 1972).

Burnet, Gilbert *History of the Reformation of the Church of England*, Nicholas Pocock (ed.) (7 vols., Clarendon Press, Oxford, 1865).

Burton, Edward (attr.) *Life of John Leland* (Alfred Cooper, London, 1896).

Campbell, W. E. *Erasmus, Tyndale and More* (Eyre & Spottiswoode, London, 1949).

Casady, Edwin *Henry Howard, Earl of Surrey* (Modern Language Association of America, New York, 1938).

Caspari, Fritz *Humanism and the Social Order in Tudor England* (University of Chicago Press, Chicago, 1954).

Chambers, E. K. *Sir Thomas Wyatt and some Collected Studies* (Sidgwick & Jackson, London, 1933).

Chester, Allan G. *Hugh Latimer, Apostle to the English* (University of Pennsylvania Press, Philadelphia, 1954).

Clark, Andrew *The Colleges of Oxford* (Methuen & Co., London, 1891).

Clebsch, William A. *England's Earliest Protestants, 1520–1535* (Yale University Press, New Haven and London, 1964).

Collinson, Patrick *Godly People: Essays on English Protestantism and Puritanism* (Hambledon Press, London, 1983).

Conley, C. H. *The First English Translators of the Classics* (Yale University Press, New Haven, 1927).

Cooper, C. H. *Memoir of Margaret, Countess of Richmond and Derby*, J. E. B. Mayor (ed.) (Deighton, Bell & Co., Cambridge, 1874).

——and Thomas Cooper (Athenae Cantabrigienses (2 vols., Deighton, Bell & Co., Cambridge, 1858, 1861).

Dawson, Jane E. A. 'The Foundation of Christ Church, Oxford and Trinity College, Cambridge in 1546', *Bulletin of the Institute of Historical Research*, vol. 57, no. 136 (November 1984).

Demaus, Robert *William Tyndale, A Biography*, Richard Lovett (ed.) (Religious Tract Society, London, 1886).

Dewar, Mary *Sir Thomas Smith, a Tudor Intellectual in Office* (Athlone Press, London, 1964).

Dickens, A. G. *The English Reformation* (Fontana, London, 1973).

Doernberg, Erwin *Henry VIII and Luther, An Account of their Personal Relations* (Barrie & Rockliff, London, 1961).

Dowling, Maria 'Anne Boleyn and Reform', *Journal of Ecclesiastical History*, vol. 35, no. 1 (January 1984).

——'Humanist Support for Katherine of Aragon', *Bulletin of the Institute of Historical Research*, vol. 57, no. 135 (May 1984).

——'Scholarship, Politics and the Court of Henry VIII', unpublished PhD thesis, London University, 1981.

Dresden, Samuel *Humanism in the Renaissance*, Margaret King (trans.) (Weidenfeld & Nicholson, London, 1968).

Du Boys, Albert *Catharine of Aragon and the Sources of the English Reformation*, C. M. Yonge (trans.) (2 vols., Hurst and Blackett, London, 1881).

Edwards, H. L. R. *Skelton: The Life and Times of an early Tudor Poet* (Jonathan Cape, London, 1949).

Elton, G. R. 'An Early Tudor Poor Law', *Economic History Review*, 2 series, vol. 6, no. 1 (1953).

——*Policy and Police* (Cambridge University Press, London, 1972).

——*Reform and Reformation* (Edward Arnold, London, 1979).

——*Reform and Renewal* (Cambridge University Press, Cambridge, 1973).

——'Sir Thomas More and the Opposition to Henry VIII', *Bulletin of the Institute of Historical Research*, vol. 41, no. 103 (May 1968).

——'Tudor Government: The Points of Contact. III, The Court', *Transactions of the Royal Historical Society*, 5 series, vol. 26 (1976).

Emden, A. B. *A Biographical Register of the University of Oxford, 1501–1540* (Clarendon Press, Oxford, 1974).

Ferguson, C. W. *Naked to Mine Enemies: The Life of Cardinal Wolsey* (Longmans, Green & Co., London, 1958).

Fiddes, Richard *Life of Cardinal Wolsey* (J. Knapton, London, 1726).

Foster, Joseph *Alumni Oxonienses, 1500–1714* (4 vols., Parker & Co., Oxford and London, 1888).

Fowler, Thomas *History of Corpus Christ College* (Clarendon Press, Oxford, 1893).

Fox, Alistair *Thomas More, History and Providence* (Basil Blackwell, Oxford, 1982).

Friedmann, Paul *Anne Boleyn, A Chapter of English History* (2 vols., Macmillan & Co., London, 1884).

Froude, J. A. *Life and Letters of Erasmus* (Longmans & Co., London, 1894–5).

Gasquet, F. A. *Cardinal Pole and his Early Friends* (G. Bell & Sons, London, 1927).

Gee, J. A. *Life and Works of Thomas Lupset* (Yale University Press, New Haven 1928).

Gilpin, William *Lives of Hugh Latimer and Bernard Gilpin* (R. Blamire, London, 1780).

Goff, Cecilie *A Woman of the Tudor Age* (John Murray, London, 1930).

Goldschmidt, E. P. *The First Cambridge Press in its European Setting* (Cambridge University Press, Cambridge, 1955).

Gordon, Ian A. *John Skelton, Poet Laureate* (Melbourne University Press, Melbourne and London, 1943).

Gordon, M. A. *Life of Queen Katharine Parr* (Titus Wilson & Sons, Kendal, 1951).

Graves, James *A Brief Memoir of the Lady Elizabeth Fitzgerald* (privately printed, Dublin, 1874).

Gray, J. H. *The Queens' College* (F. E. Robinson & Co., London, 1899).

Guy, J. A. 'The Tudor Commonwealth: Revising Thomas Cromwell', *Historical Journal*, vol. 23, no. 3 (September 1980).

Haas, Steven 'Henry VIII's *Glasse of Truthe*', *History*, vol. 64, no. 212 (October 1979).

Haile, Martin *Life of Reginald Pole* (Sir Isaac Pitman & Sons, London, 1910).

Hay, Denys *Polydore Vergil, Renaissance Historian and Man of Letters* (Clarendon Press, Oxford, 1952).

Herbert of Cherbury, Edward Lord *Life and Reign of King Henry VIII* (J. Martyn, London, 1672).

Hexter, J. H. 'The education of the aristocracy in the renaissance', *Journal of Modern History*, vol. 22, no. 1 (March 1950).

Hogrefe, Pearl *Life and Times of Sir Thomas Elyot, Englishman* (Iowa State University Press, Iowa, 1967).

Holbein and the Court of Henry VIII (catalogue of an exhbition at the Queen's Gallery, Buckingham Palace, 1978–9) (Lund Humphries, London and Bradford, 1978).

Howard, Charles, *Historical Anecdotes of Some of the Howard Family* (W. Clarke, London, 1817).

Hudson, Hoyt Hopewell *The Epigram in the English Renaissance* (Princeton University Press, Princeton, 1947).

Hudson, Winthrop S. *The Cambridge Connection and the Elizabethan Settlement* (Duke University Press, Durham, North Carolina, 1980).

Ives, E. W. 'Faction at the Court of Henry VIII: the Fall of Anne Boleyn', *History*, vol. 57, no. 190 (June 1972).

Jamieson, T. H. *Notice of the Life and Writings of Alexander Barclay* (privately printed, Edinburgh, 1874).

Jaquot, J.-A. *Notice Historique sur Nicolas Bourbon de Vandoeuvre* (Bouquot, Troyes, 1857).

Johnson, John Noble *Life of Thomas Linacre*, Robert Graves (ed.) (Edward Lumley, London, 1835).

Kearney, Hugh *Scholars and Gentlemen: Universities and Society in Pre-Industrial Britain, 1500–1700* (Faber, London, 1970).

Kelso, Ruth *Doctrine of the English Gentleman in the Sixteenth Century* (University of Illinois Press, Urbana, 1929).

King, John N. *English Reformation Literature* (Princeton University Press, Princeton, 1982).

Knight, Samuel *Life of Dean Colet* (J. Downing, London, 1724).

——*Life of Erasmus* (C. Crownfield, Cambridge, 1726).

Kristeller, Paul Oskar *Renaissance Concepts of Man and Other Essays* (Harper & Row, New York, 1972).

Lathrop, H. B. *Translations from the Classics into English, from Caxton to Chapman* (University of Wisconsin Press, Madison, 1933).

Lee, Sidney *The French Renaissance in England* (Clarendon Press, Oxford, 1910).

Lehmberg, Stanford E. *The Reformation Parliament, 1529–36* (Cambridge University Press, Cambridge, 1970).

——*Sir Thomas Elyot, Tudor Humanist* (University of Texas Press, Austin, 1960).

Lloyd, A. H. *Early History of Christ's, Cambridge* (Cambridge University Press, Cambridge, 1934).

Lloyd, David *State Worthies*, Charles Whitworth (ed.) (J. Robson, London, 1766).

Loades, D. M. *Reign of Mary Tudor* (Benn, London, 1979).

Lowinsky, Edward E. 'A music book for Anne Boleyn', *Florilegium Historiale, Essays Presented to Wallace K. Ferguson*, J. G. Rowe and W. H. Stockdale (eds) (University of Toronto Press, Toronto and Buffalo, 1971).

Lupton, J. H. *A Life of Dean Colet* (George Bell & Sons, London, 1909).

Lyte, H. C. Maxwell *A History of the University of Oxford* (Macmillan, London, 1886).

McConica, J. K. *English Humanists and Reformation Politics Under Henry VIII and Edward VI* (Clarendon Press, Oxford, 1968).

——*Thomas More* (HMSO, London, 1977).

McDonnell, M. F. J. *A History of St Paul's School* (Chapman & Hall, London, 1909).

McLean, Andrew '"A noughty and a false lyeng boke": William Barlow and the Lutheran Factions', *Renaissance Quarterly*, vol. 31, part 2 (summer 1978).

McNalty, A. S. *Henry VIII, A Difficult Patient* (Christopher Johnson, London, 1952).

Malden, Henry Elliott *Trinity Hall* (F. E. Robinson & Co., London, 1902).

Mallet, Charles Edward *A History of the University of Oxford* (3 vols., Methuen & Co., London, 1924, 1927).

Marius, Richard *Thomas More* (J. M. Dent & Son, London and Melbourne, 1985).

Martienssen, Anthony, *Queen Katherine Parr* (Secker & Warburg, London, 1973).

Mattingly, Garrett *Catherine of Aragon* (Johnathan Cape, London, 1944).

——'A Humanist Ambassador', *Journal of Modern History*, vol. 4, no. 2 (June 1932).

Meads, Dorothy M. 'The Education of Women and Girls in England in the Time of the Tudors', unpublished MA thesis, London University, 1928.

More, Cresacre *Life of Sir Thomas More*, Joseph Hunter (ed.) (W. Pickering, London, 1828).

Morley, Henry *Life of Henry Cornelius Agrippa von Nettesheim* (2 vols., Chapman & Hall, London, 1856).

Muir, Kenneth *Life and Letters of Sir Thomas Wyatt* (Liverpool University Press, Liverpool, 1963).

Mullinger, J. B. *St John's College* (F. E. Robinson & Co., London, 1901).

Mumford, A. A. *Hugh Oldham* (Faber & Faber, London, 1936).

Nelson, William *John Skelton, Laureate* (Columbia University Press, New York, 1939).

Nichols, F. M. *The Hall of Lawford Hall* (privately printed, London, 1891).

Nicholson, G. D. 'The Nature and Function of Historical Argument in the Henrician Reformation', unpublished PhD thesis, Cambridge University, 1977.

O'Malley, C. D. *English Medical Humanists* (University of Kansas Press, Lawrence, 1965).

Orme, Nicholas *Education in the West of England, 1066–1548* (Exeter University Press, Exeter, 1976).

Palmer, Henrietta R. *List of English Editions of Greek and Latin Classics Printed Before 1641* (Bibliographical Society, Blades, East & Blades, London, 1911).

Paul, John E. *Catherine of Aragon and Her Friends* (Burns & Oates, London, 1966).

Peile, John *Biographical Register of Christ's College* (2 vols., Cambridge University Press, Cambridge, 1910, 1913).

——*Christ's College* (F. E. Robinson & Co., London, 1900).

Childe-Pemberton, W. S. *Elizabeth Blount and Henry VIII* (Eveleigh Nash, London, 1913).

Peters, A. M. 'Richard Whitford and St Ignatius' Visit to England', *Archivum Historicum Societatis Jesu*, vol. 25 (1956).

Power, Eileen *Medieval English Nunneries, c. 1275–1535* (Cambridge University Press, Cambridge, 1922).

Prescott, H. F. M. *Mary Tudor* (Eyre & Spottiswoode, London, 1952).

Prescott, W. H. *History of the Reign of Ferdinand and Isabella* (3 vols., Richard Bentley, London, 1838).

Reed, A. W. *Early Tudor Drama* (Methuen & Co., London, 1926).

Reid, Rachel, *The King's Council in the North* (Longmans, Green & Co., London, 1921).

Richardson, W. C. *Stephen Vaughan, Financial Agent of Henry VIII* (Louisiana State University Press, Baton Rouge, 1953).

Rieger, J. H. 'Erasmus, Colet and the Schoolboy Jesus', *Studies in the Renaissance*, vol. 9 (1962).

Ritz, J. G. 'Un ambassadeur de Charles-Quint a la cour d'Henry VIII: Le Savoyard Eustace Chapuys', *Cahiers d'Histoire*, vol. 11, part 2 (1966).

Ryan, Lawrence V. *Roger Ascham* (Oxford University Press, London, 1963).

Scarisbrick, J. J. *Henry VIII* (Pelican, London, 1974).

Schenk, W. *Reginald Pole, Cardinal of England* (Longmans, Green & Co., London, 1950).

Searle, W. G. *History of the Queens' College* (2 vols., Cambridge University Press, Cambridge, 1867, 1871).

Seebohm, Frederick *The Oxford Reformers*, 3rd edition (Longmans, Green & Co., London, 1887).

Sheppard, J. T. *Richard Croke, a Sixteenth Century Don* (W. Heffer & Sons, Cambridge, 1919).

Shirley, T. F. *Thomas Thirlby, Tudor Bishop* (SPCK, London, 1964).

Simon, Joan *Education and Society in Tudor England* (Cambridge University Press, Cambridge, 1966).

Smith, Lacey Baldwin *Henry VIII, the Mask of Royalty* (Panther, St Albans, 1973).

Smith, Preserved *Erasmus* (Harper & Bros., New York and London, 1923).

——'Luther and Henry VIII', *English Historical Review*, vol. 25, no. 100 (October 1910).

Sowards, J. K. 'The Two Lost Years of Erasmus: Summary, Review and Speculation', *Studies in the Renaissance*, vol. 9 (1962).

Stanier, R. S. *Magdalen School* (Basil Blackwell, Oxford, 1940).

Starkey, D. R. 'The King's Privy Chamber, 1485–1547', unpublished PhD Thesis, Cambridge University, 1973.

Stephen, Leslie and Sidney Lee *Dictionary of National Biography* (21 vols., Smith, Elder & Co., London, 1908–9)

Strickland, Agnes and Elizabeth *Lives of the Queens of England* (6 vols., G. Bell & Sons, London, 1889).

Strype, John *Ecclesiastical Memorials* (3 vols., Clarendon Press, Oxford, 1820–1840).

——*Life and Acts of John Aylmer* (Clarendon Press, Oxford, 1821).

——*Life of the Learned Sir John Cheke* (Clarendon Press, Oxford, 1821).

——*Life and Acts of Matthew Parker* (3 vols., Clarendon Press, Oxford, 1821).

——*Life of the Learned Sir Thomas Smith* (Clarendon Press, Oxford, 1820).

——*Memorials of Thomas Cranmer* (2 vols., Oxford University Press, Oxford, 1840).

Sturge, Charles *Cuthbert Tunstal* (Longmans, Green & Co., London, 1938).

Surtz, E. L. *Works and Days of John Fisher* (Harvard University Press, Cambridge, Mass., 1967).

Thompson, Henry L. *Christ Church* (F. E. Robinson & Co., London, 1900).

Thomson, Patricia *Sir Thomas Wyatt and His Background* (Routledge & Kegan Paul, London, 1964).

Venn, John *Biographical History of Gonville and Caius College, 1349–1713* (7 vols., Cambridge University Press, Cambridge, 1897).

——*Caius College* (F. E. Robinson & Co., London, 1901).

Venn, John and J. A. *Alumni Cantabrigienses, Part One, from the Earliest Times to 1751* (4 vols., Cambridge University Press, Cambridge, 1922–7).

Vocht, Henry de *Monumenta Humanistica Lovaniensa* (2 vols., Louvain University Press, Louvain, 1928, 1934).

Watson, Foster *Luis Vives* (Oxford University Press, London, 1922).

——*English Writers on Education: A Source Book* (Scholars' Facsimiles and Reprints, Gainesville, Florida, 1967).

Wegg, Jervis *Richard Pace, A Tudor Diplomatist* (Methuen & Co., London, 1932).

Weiss, Roberto *Humanism in England During the Fifteenth Century*, 3rd edition (Basil Blackwell, Oxford, 1967).

Whatton, W. R. *History of Manchester School* (William Pickering, London, 1834).

White, Beatrice *Mary Tudor* (Macmillan & Co., London, 1935).

Wilson, H. A. *Magdalen College* (F. E. Robinson & Co., London, 1899).

Zeeveld, W. Gordon *Foundations of Tudor Policy* (Harvard University Press, Cambridge, Mass. 1948).

Index